South Vietnam

U.S.-Communist
Confrontation in
Southeast Asia

Volume 5

1970

South Vietnam

U.S.-Communist Confrontation in Southeast Asia

Volume 5

1970

Edited by Lester A. Sobel
Contributing editor: Hal Kosut

FACTS ON FILE, INC.   NEW YORK, N.Y.

South Vietnam

U.S.-Communist Confrontation in Southeast Asia

Volume 5

1970

Library of Congress Card Catalog No. 66-23943
ISBN 0-87196-237-3

9 8 7 6 5 4 3 2 1
PRINTED IN
THE UNITED STATES OF AMERICA

Contents

	Page
Foreword	1
U.S. Policy: Firmness & Vietnamization	3
International Peace Efforts	11
The Fighting	15
Laotian Involvement	21
Cambodian Involvement, Sihanouk Overthrown	31
U.S.-South Vietnamese Offensive in Cambodia	45
Fighting in Vietnam & Laos	87
Cambodia After U.S. Exit	111
Peace Efforts	121
U.S. Dissent	135
Prisoners & Atrocities	163
Other South Vietnam Developments	177
Index	185

Foreword

THIS FIFTH VOLUME IN THE FACTS ON FILE record of the
U.S. involvement in Vietnam covers the year 1970.

This was a period when President Richard M. Nixon's
policy of Vietnamization—of withdrawing U.S. ground
forces from Vietnam and turning over responsibility for the
fighting to the South Vietnamese—was in full swing. But
Nixon warned that increases in enemy attacks could persuade him to slow the withdrawal.

Under the Vietnamization policy, the number of U.S.
troops in Vietnam declined from the peak of about
543,000 (in April 1969) to a figure given as approximately
280,000 at the end of December 1970. A major result of
Vietnamization was a dramatic decline in the rate of U.S.
combat deaths in Indochina. The number of Americans
killed in 1970 was reported as 4,204, the lowest total since
1965. This compared, for example, with 14,314 in 1968, the
year before Nixon became President. But the total number
of Americans killed in the decade of U.S. military involvement in Indochina rose to more than 44,200 by the end
of 1970. South Vietnam lost 20,914 servicemen and at least
25,000 civilians killed in hostilities during 1970. And
5,951 Saigon government officials, their supporters and
innocent bystanders were reported killed in terrorist attacks
during 1970.

1

Peace talks continued in Paris with little observable progress, and the fighting actually expanded: North Vietnamese troops moved into Laos in increasing numbers in early 1970 and won complete control of the Plaine des Jarres. A coup in Cambodia deposed Prince Norodom Sihanouk as chief of state. U.S. and South Vietnamese forces made a thrust into Cambodia to eliminate Communist "sanctuaries" from which Viet Cong and North Vietnamese troops, it was charged, attacked targets in South Vietnam and to which they allegedly could withdraw later with relative safety. The incursion into Cambodia provoked wide, angry denunciations of the Nixon Administration both in the U.S. and abroad. All U.S. troops were withdrawn from Cambodia in two months as promised. A U.S. task force landed near Hanoi in an unsuccessful attempt to free U.S. POWs, U.S. planes made heavy attacks on North Vietnam, and Lt. William Calley went on trial for his role in the Mylai massacre.

The material that follows consists almost entirely of the printed record that appeared in the weekly issues of FACTS ON FILE. The editorial changes that were made were generally minor, their purpose usually being to eliminate repetition, correct errors or add facts that might not have been available when the original record was being compiled. As in all FACTS ON FILE books, great pains were taken to make this volume a balanced and accurate reference work and to keep it free of bias.

U.S. Policy: Firmness & Vietnamization

President Richard M. Nixon continued to emphasize during the early months of 1970 that the U.S. would respond firmly to any North Vietnamese escalation of fighting but otherwise would continue the policy of Vietnamization—the withdrawal of U.S. troops from South Vietnam and the turning over of the fighting to the South Vietnamese.

Warning against infiltration. In his first televised news conference of 1970, Nixon warned Jan. 30 that he was watching the rate of enemy infiltration into South Vietnam and was prepared to take strong steps should an increase in enemy troops lead to an escalation in the level of fighting. He warned that if North Vietnam sought to step up its activities in the South during U.S. troop withdrawals so as to jeopardize the remaining U.S. combat units, he was prepared to deal with that situation "more strongly than we have dealt with it in the past."

The President said future U.S. troop withdrawals would depend on the level of enemy activity, the progress of the Paris peace talks and other criteria. He said, however, that despite any changes in his time-table for a total pullout, "the policy of Vietnamization is irreversible." He pointed out that this pullout would include only combat units and not necessarily U.S. support troops. He said his plan to end the war "envisages support for the South Vietnamese logistically." "And until they are ready to take over,

support in the sea and support in the air . . . will stay there for a longer time than support in terms of ground forces."

Nixon said he had not given up hope for a negotiated settlement. He said the recent moratorium on criticism of the war at home should be "an incentive for them [the North Vietnamese] to negotiate" because the moratorium represented U.S. determination to block a North Vietnamese military victory.

(There appeared to have been a drop in infiltration from the North. The U.S. State Department had reported Jan. 7 that North Vietnamese infiltration into South Vietnam in 1969 had totaled 100,000—250,000 men, compared with 250,000 in 1968. The department said North Vietnamese troops and Hanoi's political functionaries in or near South Vietnam totaled 240,000 men, a drop of 50,000 from 1968.)

Democrats urge Vietnam pullout. The Democratic Policy Council adopted a resolution Feb. 9 advocating "a firm and unequivocal commitment to the American people that all U.S. forces be withdrawn from Vietnam." "We see no reason," the resolution said, "why this withdrawal should not be completed within 18 months."

The resolution, drafted by a panel headed by W. Averell Harriman, former U.S. delegate to the Paris peace talks, said the withdrawal "can be accelerated by efforts to create the conditions neces-

3

sary for a peaceful political settlement."
But withdrawal decisions, it said, should
be based "primarily" on "the interest
and policy" of the U.S. and should
not be dependent on North or South Vietnamese action, progress of the Paris
talks, the level of violence or "the progress of so-called Vietnamization."

The Democrats urged the immediate
appointment of a "high-level" negotiator
to head the Paris delegation and reduction of the level of violence as a subject
to be pressed in the negotiations. It questioned the Administration's rejection of
a letter concerning the negotiations from
North Vietnamese leader Ho Chi
Minh shortly before his death.

The policy statement also questioned
U.S. support of the South Vietnamese
government of President Nguyen Van
Thieu. "Our continued unconditional
support of the Thieu government as now
constituted is not only unjustifiable but
delusive," it said. The U.S. should insist
that the Saigon government include persons "who represent wider public opinion
desiring a peaceful solution and who are
prepared to negotiate such a settlement."

Foreign affairs message. President
Nixon submitted to Congress Feb. 18
a foreign policy message outlining, and
entitled, "United States Foreign Policy
for the 1970's: A New Strategy for
Peace." The President referred to it as
the first "annual report" by an American
president on the state of the world.

Based on the same principles under-
lying the "Nixon Doctrine" enunciated
at Guam in July 1969, the message stressed
these themes: the U.S. would maintain its
global treaty commitments, but would
also bring into its commitment appraisals
a firm assessment of the U.S. interests
involved. It emphasized (a) the partnership relationship as opposed to one of
domination, (b) negotiation and multina-
tional cooperation as opposed to great-
power rivalry or ideological contention.

The President spoke of his statement
as "a new approach to foreign policy."
He said the modern challenge was "to
get at the causes of crises, to take a
longer view and to help build the international relationships that will provide
the framework of a durable peace." He
favored a foreign policy guided by three

basic principles: (1) partnership; (2)
strength, with high priority on cooperative arms control; and (3) "a willingness
to negotiate."

"The peace we seek," he declared,
"must be the work of all nations. For
peace will endure only when every nation has a greater stake in preserving
than in breaking it."

In fleshing out these general themes,
Nixon referred to his Guam doctrine
with its central thesis that the U.S.
would "participate in the defense and
development" of its allies but would not
"conceive all the plans, design all the
programs, execute all the decisions and
undertake all the defense of the free
nations of the world. We will help where
it makes a real difference and is considered in our interest." "Others now
have," he said, "the ability and responsibility to deal with local disputes which
once might have required our intervention."

While "America cannot live in iso-
lation," he said, and peace required
the U.S. "to maintain our commitments," a "more balanced and realistic
American role in the world is essential if
American commitments are to be sustained over the long pull. . . . We are not
involved in the world because we have
commitments; we have commitments
because we are involved. Our interests
must shape our commitments, rather
than the other way around. We will view
new commitments in the light of a careful assessment of our own national interests and those of other countries, of the
specific threats to those interests and of
our capacity to counter those threats at
an acceptable risk and cost."

The President explained how his policy
would apply in various situations, including relations with Asia, Vietnam and the
Soviet Union:

Asia—The Nixon Doctrine would apply: Treaty commitments would be kept
and a shield would be provided "if a nuclear power threatened the freedom of
a nation allied with us, or of a nation
whose survival we consider vital to our
security and the security of the region
as a whole"; but, "in cases involving
other types of aggression we shall furnish military and economic assistance
when requested and as appropriate, but

we shall look to the nation directly threatened to assume the primary responsibility of providing the manpower for its defense."

The "fostering of self-reliance" was stressed. The U.S. had "no desire to impose its own prescriptions for relationships in Asia." It did have an interest "in averting great-power dominance over Asia." The President stated that world peace "would be endangered by great-power conflict" there.

Vietnam—Regarding the two major parts of the Vietnamization program—strengthening the South Vietnamese armed forces and the pacification program—there had been "tangible progress" in the first. The latter was "succeeding." The South Vietnamese forces had increased in number and improved in most areas in effectiveness. Enemy main-force units had more and more been forced back into remote areas. Since 1967, the percentage of the rural population living in areas with adequate defense and a functioning local government had more than doubled. Viet Cong control over the rural population had dropped to less than 10%. The enemy was having recruitment and supply difficulties: North Vietnamese fillers were being used in Viet Cong main force and local force units.

U.S. forces would continue to be withdrawn "in accordance with an orderly schedule" based on the level of enemy activity, progress in negotiations and the ability of the South Vietnamese to defend themselves.

Although U.S. military spending in Vietnam was expected to decrease with the reduced U.S. presence there, the requirement for economic aid was expected to go up.

However, Vietnamization was "still a developing process and enemy intentions on the battlefield are unclear." Also, the enemy "still refuses to negotiate seriously." "The key to peace lies in Hanoi—in its decision to end the bloodshed and to negotiate in the true sense of the word." The U.S. would be "flexible and generous when serious negotiations start at last." In the meantime, the enemy "could make no greater mistake than to assume that an increase in violence would be to its advantage." The

U.S. would "not hesitate to take strong and effective measures to deal with that situation."

The Soviet Union—U.S. policy was "not to employ negotiations as a forum for cold-war invective or ideological debate" but to "regard our Communist adversaries first and foremost as nations pursuing their own interests as they perceive these interests." Negotiations should consist of "authentic give-and-take" on the issues, and there should be an appreciation of the "interrelationship of international events."

Among the lessons of the past two decades for the Soviet Union and the U.S. were the limitations of great power and "the worldwide decline in the appeal of ideology."

The overall relationship with the U.S.S.R. "remains far from satisfactory." Soviet leaders had failed to exert a helpful influence on the North Vietnamese in Paris and continued to supply North Vietnam with war material.

Democrats attack Nixon message. The Democrats March 14 issued a critical review of President Nixon's Feb. 18 "state of the world" message. Leaders said it was marked by "singularly empty phrases" and "simplistic sermonizing." In a statement released by W. Averell Harriman, head of a Democratic Policy Council panel, the Democrats said the Administration "has confused system with substance . . . [and] substituted institutionalized mechanics for creative action." "What is missing," they said, "is an understanding that far more important than the procedures of decision-making are the decisions themselves and people who make them. A few good appointments are worth a score of committees. One wise decision is worth a stack of studies."

In addition to criticism of the Administration's "leisurely approach" to nuclear arms control, and the absence from the Nixon message of any mention of Laos, the Democrats attacked the Administration's Vietnam policy. The Nixon message revealed "nothing new" on Vietnam, the paper said, and Vietnamization "at best" was only a perpetuation of the fighting with continued U.S.

involvement. As for the Paris peace talks, it said the Administration "continues to give a veto over U.S. efforts for a negotiated settlement to the repressive minority government" in Saigon.

Other Democratic criticism—Sen. Edmund S. Muskie (D, Me.) also viewed Vietnamization as "a policy for the perpetuation of the war." Muskie March 5 called for a "new national debate" on Vietnam and spoke of the "mystery" of Administration policy that was "virtually blotting out domestic criticism of the war." "Without information and without alternatives," he said, "it is no wonder that a majority of the American people are now silent."

Sen. Walter F. Mondale (D, Minn.) called Feb. 2 for a "political Vietnamization" of policy to broaden the base of the South Vietnamese government.

Another policy critic, Sen. Eugene J. McCarthy (D, Minn.), told the Senate Foreign Relations Committee Feb. 19 the Administration was misleading the nation "over the issues at stake" in the war. McCarthy, who had conferred in Paris Jan. 12–13 with North Vietnamese and Viet Cong delegates to the peace talks and in Moscow Jan. 11 with Soviet Premier Aleksei Kosygin, considered a negotiated political settlement of the war a "real possibility" if the U.S. agreed to withdraw its forces and a coalition regime was formed in Saigon. "Serious negotiations cannot proceed unless we are willing to support a coalition government to control the process of transition," he said.

Agnew visits Vietnam, claims success. Vice President Spiro T. Agnew visited South Vietnam Jan. 1–2 while on a ten-nation Asian tour begun in December 1969. Later, after returning to the U.S., he claimed success for U.S. policies in Vietnam. Agnew met Jan. 20 with President Nixon, who called the trip "enormously effective." "What is called the Nixon Doctrine is now far better understood by our allies than it was before this trip," Nixon said.

In Saigon, Agnew conferred Jan. 1 with South Vietnamese President Nguyen Van Thieu and U.S. Ambassador Ellsworth Bunker, then visited two combat artillery bases north of Saigon. He visited wounded GIs at the 24th Evacuation Hospital in Longbinh Jan. 2. His official talks, he said, covered the "strengths and weaknesses" of the U.S. position there in Vietnam. His message to the troops was that "the people back home are pretty darn proud of you and what you're doing over here." "Don't be misled," he said, "by what you may see and read in certain publications. This doesn't reflect the feeling of the American people about the job that's being done by American fighting men in Vietnam."

In his remarks at his departure from Bienhoa Jan. 2, Agnew spoke of his visit as having "confirmed to me the wisdom of our policies." "We are following the right path," he said, in seeking a negotiated settlement while giving the South Vietnamese time to gain strength and "demonstrate to the Communists that they have nothing to gain by prolonging the fighting." He felt, he said, that the new year would "bring us closer to our common goal."

In Kuala Lumpur Jan. 8, Agnew met with Malaysian Prime Minister Tunku Abdul Rahman and his deputy, Tun Abdul Razak. Rahman said afterwards he had gained the impression that the U.S. "will not leave us defenseless against aggression from without."

In Canberra, Australia Jan. 13–14, the Agnew entourage was beset by antiwar demonstrators. But in a major statement of his tour, Agnew told the Australians Jan. 13 that the U.S. was "proud to be your partner" and was "not withdrawing from Asia and the Pacific" but was "one anchor of a vast Pacific community." "Both our interest and our ideals propel us eastward across the Pacific, not as conquerors but as partners," he said.

In Auckland Jan. 16, Agnew conferred with New Zealand Prime Minister Keith Holyoake, his cabinet and opposition leader Norman Kirk. At a state dinner—with antiwar demonstrators chanting outside—Agnew said the allied forces in Vietnam should not "cut and run because a small corps of malcontents" advocated immediate troop pullout.

In Honolulu Jan. 17, where he spent the weekend before returning to the mainland U.S., Agnew said he was encouraged by the generally sympathetic attitude toward the U.S. he had encountered on his tour. He said the Asian leaders wanted a continuing U.S. presence in the Pacific and had themselves been "encouraged about our decision to do everything to stimulate regional cooperation, not only of a military or defense security nature but of what you might call an economic nature, too." The purpose of his trip, he said, had been "to define what we are talking about" concerning the Nixon Doctrine.

Agnew addressed 2,000 Republicans at a fund-raising dinner in Columbia April 24. After describing what he saw as indications of success in Nixon's Vietnamization policy, Agnew said the policy was "a tribute to the calm, determined leadership of the President, who refused to be pushed into a precipitate withdrawal of our troops by the barrage of criticism from Senate liberals and the roaring and cavorting in the streets last fall by peaceniks."

Laird visits Vietnam. U.S. Defense Secretary Melvin R. Laird visited South Vietnam Feb. 10–13 to study the progress of the Vietnamization program and to discuss further U.S. troop withdrawals with American commanders.

Laird, accompanied by Gen. Earle G. Wheeler, chairman of the Joint Chiefs of Staff, affirmed President Nixon's decision to continue the withdrawals at a meeting with President Nguyen Van Thieu in Saigon Feb. 12. He conferred later with Vice President Nguyen Cao Ky.

(Thieu had said Jan. 9 that it would be "impossible and impractical" to withdraw U.S. combat troops from South Vietnam in 1970 because the logistical and support forces "left behind would then be unprotected and would run the risk of Communist attacks." Thieu predicted that it would be "many years" before all U.S. troops could be removed.)

Before departing Feb. 13, Laird said the U.S. pullout would continue despite the deadlocked Paris peace talks and the possible threat of a Communist military offensive. Although Communist forces had not compensated for their heavy combat losses through infiltration, the likelihood of a major drive remained "a significant threat and I don't want to un-derstate it," Laird said. Laird noted progress in the Vietnamization program, but cautioned that "we must anticipate some temporary setbacks. The road to sucessful completion of Vietnamization is not going to be free of some hard knocks."

At a news conference in Saigon Feb. 11, Laird had reiterated Nixon's decision not to make any public announcement of any specific timetable for withdrawal. Laird said the troop removal would continue until Phase III was reached, when the only American presence would be a military assistance group composed largely of advisers. He explained that Phase I would be completed when the South Vietnamese assumed full battle responsibility and Phase II would involve turning over planes, artillery and other support equipment to Saigon's forces.

Laird upheld the right to take whatever steps were necessary to protect American reconnaissance flights over North Vietnam against Communist gunfire and to carry out ground actions against Communist forces which strike at U.S. troops in South Vietnam from Laos or Cambodia.

Laird had recalled at the start of his visit Feb. 10 that in his previous visit to South Vietnam in March 1969, American troop strength in the country was authorized at 549,000 men. "That ceiling will be down to 434,000 by mid-April," he said.

U.S. pullout to continue. President Nixon told the nation April 20 he planned to have 150,000 more U.S. troops withdrawn from Vietnam by the spring of 1971. The reduction would lower the authorized force ceiling from 434,000 to 284,000, a continuation of the current pullout rate of about 12,000 men a month. Actual troop strength was somewhat below the authorized level, totaling 425,000 men the week before the President's speech.

In an address televised from the Western White House in San Clemente, Calif., the President said his decision on continued withdrawal meant "that we finally have in sight the just peace we are seeking."

"We can now say with confidence," he declared, that "pacification is succeeding," that "the South Vietnamese can develop the capability for their own defense" and that "all American combat forces can and will be withdrawn."

The decision was "based entirely on the progress" of the Administration's Vietnamization program, one of three criteria, cited again by Nixon, used to determine the withdrawal policy. Progress in training and equipping South Vietnamese forces "has substantially exceeded our original expectations," he said. "Very significant advances have also been made in pacification. Although we recognize that problems remain, these are encouraging trends."

"No progress has taken place on the negotiation front" (the second criteria), Nixon said, although more than 150,000 troops could be withdrawn in a year if progress were made there. In fact, negotiation could be "a better, shorter path to peace," the President said, and he called upon "our adversaries to join us in working at the conference table."

As for the third criteria (the level of enemy activity), the President said the level "has substantially increased" in several areas since December 1969— new offensives had been launched in Laos, 40,000 Communist troops were conducting "overt aggression" against Cambodia and in the past two weeks the Communists had "stepped up their attacks upon allied forces in South Vietnam."

However, the President said, despite this activity, there had been an overall decline in enemy force levels in South Vietnam since December and a decline in U.S. casualties.

The timing and pace of the new withdrawals were to be determined "by our best judgment of the current military and diplomatic situation." In view of the enemy escalation in Laos and Cambodia and "the stepped-up attacks this month in South Vietnam, this decision clearly involves risks," the President said. But he reminded the leaders of North Vietnam that "they will be taking grave risks should they attempt to use the occasion to jeopardize the security of our remaining forces in Vietnam by increased military action in Vietnam, in Cambodia or in Laos." He would not hesitate "to take strong and effective measures to deal with that situation," he said.

The President "noted with interest the recent statement by Soviet Deputy Foreign Minister [Yakov A.] Malik concerning a possible new Geneva conference on Indochina and said the U.S. would explore its "full implication."

The U.S. was "ready for a settlement fair to everyone," Nixon stated, and its "overriding objective is a political solution that reflects the will of the South Vietnamese people and allows them to determine their future without outside interference."

He reaffirmed U.S. acceptance "of eventual total withdrawal of American troops" in return for "the permanent withdrawal of all North Vietnamese troops" and "reasonable assurances that they will not return."

He said "a fair political solution should reflect the existing relationship of political forces within South Vietnam." Although the U.S. recognized "the complexity of shaping machinery that would fairly apportion political power in South Vietnam," Nixon said, "we're flexible. We have offered nothing on a take-it-or-leave-it basis."

Nixon further affirmed that the U.S. would "abide by the outcome of the political process agreed upon. [South Vietnamese] President Thieu and I repeatedly stated our willingness to accept the free decision of the South Vietnamese people. But we will not agree to the arrogant demand that the elected leaders of the government of Vietnam be overthrown before real negotiations begin."

"It is Hanoi and Hanoi alone," Nixon asserted, "that stands today blocking the path to a just peace for all the peoples of Southeast Asia."

The President also appended to his speech "an expression of . . . concern for the fate of the American prisoners of war," accusing Hanoi of "an unforgivable breach of the elementary rules of conduct between civilized peoples" in regard to their handling of them.

Some senators April 21 lauded Nixon's plan for Vietnam withdrawals. Senate Democratic Leader Mike Mansfield (Mont.) said the President was "continuing in the right direction—out." Griffin said the President had "put to an end the doubts, the criticism and the quibbling over the Administration's earnest desire to end the war." Sen. Edward W. Brooke (R, Mass.) said he had made "a historic and far-reaching commitment for peace."

The view that the U.S. should "begin militarily to get out of Southeast Asia lock, stock and barrel" had been expressed by Sen. Edward M. Kennedy (D, Mass.) in a speech in Peabody, Mass. April 3. He called the Administration's Vietnamization policy "misguided and inhuman" and "a policy of continued war with a lessening of tensions here in the United States. It is based on the hope of military success in a struggle that knows no such solution."

Australian troop cutback. Prime Minister John Gorton announced plans April 22 to withdraw one of Australia's three battalions with some support troops from South Vietnam. The 750-man unit had been scheduled to end its tour of duty in November, but Gorton said the timing of its removal would depend on developments.

Gorton also announced that Australia would provide a number of small mobile army teams totaling about 130 men to carry out liaison and training duties with South Vietnam's regional and popular forces.

Australia's army, navy and air force contingents in Vietnam numbered about 8,000 men, including more than 6,000 soldiers.

International Peace Efforts

France urges international conference. The French government April 1 proposed a general international conference on Vietnam, Laos and Cambodia to create "a zone of neutrality and peace."

Asserting that the Vietnam war was spreading to Cambodia and Laos, the statement said "the extension of a war that tends to become indivisible can be avoided only by negotiation between all interested parties with a view to seeking and guaranteeing the bases for peace, itself indivisible."

A French government spokesman said one approach could be the reconvening of the 1954 Geneva Conference, which had ended the French-Indochinese war. The Paris statement implied that such a parley could replace the Paris peace talks on Vietnam.

France had proposed March 11 that U.S. and North Vietnamese troops be withdrawn from Laos to help end the fighting in that country. "Any international solution must result in a return to the Geneva accords, their current application, a complete termination of foreign interference and the respect for Laotian neutrality," Foreign Minister Maurice Schumann was quoted.

France renewed its appeal March 19 for the preservation of Laos and Cambodia as neutral states, urging "all interested parties" to prevent the Vietnam war from spreading to all of Indochina.

"The remaining chances of re-establishing peace in Vietnam itself can only be compromised by such a development while international tension would dangerously increase in that part of the world," the statement said.

U.S. backs French pleas—France's call for an international conference for a political settlement covering Vietnam, Laos and Cambodia gained support in the U.S. Senate April 2. A resolution advocating such a conference was introduced by Sens. Fred R. Harris (D, Okla.) and James B. Pearson (R, Kan.).

The "indivisibility of the conflicts" in Laos, Cambodia and Vietnam, and the need for an overall "political settlement" were cited by Chairman J. W. Fulbright (D, Ark.) of the Senate Foreign Relations Committee in a Senate speech April 2. Fulbright endorsed the French proposal for negotiations to make all Indochina into a "zone of neutrality and peace."

The French initiative also received favorable comment April 2 from Secretary of State William P. Rogers, who said the French "proposals talk about negotiations" and "we are interested in any kind of negotiations that would lead to peace." He made the comment to newsmen after testifying before the Fulbright committee on the Administration's effort to maintain the neutrality of Cambodia and to avoid entanglement in an all-Indochina war.

Senate Democratic Leader Mike Mansfield (Mont.) said afterwards "the attitude of the Administration [toward Cambodia] is a correct one." "All the Administration wants—and all I want," he said, "is maintenance of neutrality and no involvement in what could become an Indochina war."

In his speech April 2, Fulbright attacked the Administration's "Vietnamization" program and warned that tensions in the U.S. "will be aggravated if Vietnamization is allowed to continue until a major military disaster occurs in Indochina."

Vietnamization was "not working" and was "not likely to," Fulbright said, pointing out that if the U.S. could not beat the Communists with half a million "well-led, well-trained and superbly equipped" men, "we can hardly expect" the South Vietnamese army to do the job on its own.

Fulbright said a political settlement was possible "if we can bring ourselves to give up the untenable dream of an anti-Communist government in Saigon" and the Communists gave up the hope of a complete takeover. He advocated a settlement that comprised a "transitional coalition government for what would become a neutralist, independent South Vietnam and a commitment to a definite schedule for the ultimate total withdrawal of American forces."

The State Department March 12 endorsed France's March 11 appeal for the withdrawal of all U.S. and North Vietnamese from Laos. The department also called on the 14 nations which had signed the 1962 Geneva accords neutralizing Laos to "live up to their responsibilities."

Viet Cong bar parley—The Viet Cong April 20 rejected France's call for talks on Indochina. Mrs. Nguyen Thi Binh, foreign minister of the Viet Cong's Provisional Revolutionary Government, said in Paris that the French plan "could not contribute to solving the problems" of Vietnam, Laos and Cambodia. She noted that an international conference on South Vietnam already was in progress in Paris, that there had been an agreement on Laos and that deposed

Cambodian Chief of State Prince Norodom Sihanouk had called for the withdrawal of U.S. forces. "Thus to settle these problems only requires that the United States end its policy of aggression and let the people of each of these three countries settle their own affairs."

The French peace proposal had evoked differing reactions April 4 from two high-ranking South Vietnamese government officials—Vice President Nguyen Cao Ky and Foreign Minister Tran Van Lam. Ky expressed approval of the proposal, but Lam dismissed it as "unrealistic and inapplicable to the present situation."

Moscow reverses parley stand. A Soviet suggestion April 16 that a new Geneva conference be convened to solve the crisis in Southeast Asia was apparently reversed the following day.

The original statement and follow-up remark were delivered by Yakov A. Malik, the Soviet Union's chief delegate to the U.N. Malik told a news conference April 16 that the situation in Southeast Asia "is not a matter for the United Nations." He said that since the 1954 and 1962 Geneva agreements on Laos, Cambodia and Vietnam had not been carried out, "only a new Geneva conference could bring a new solution and relax tensions." "If this was the point of the French proposal [for the reconvening of an international parley on Indochina, announced April 1] then it is deserving of attention," Malik said.

In an apparent retraction of this statement, Malik said in an ABC radio interview April 17 that the reconvening of a Geneva conference "is unrealistic because the source of conflicts and tensions in Indochina is rooted in the overt armed intervention of the United States and its allies in Vietnam and other countries in the area." Malik said lasting peace could only be achieved by "the withdrawal of American and allied troops from Indochina."

A "clarification" circulated by the Soviet delegation at the U.N. April 20 reiterated Malik's view that a new conference on Indochina was "unrealistic at this time."

The Soviet press agency Tass reported neither of Malik's statements.

Malik's original remarks had aroused U.S. interest as reflected in statements issued by the White House April 17 and by Secretary of State William P. Rogers April 18. Rogers said he had instructed Charles Yost, U.S. ambassador to the U.N., to ask Malik for further clarification. Rogers said the U.S. "welcomes initiatives by countries in or outside the area which might lead to progress toward restoration of peace in Southeast Asia."

The Soviet Union April 27 formally expressed opposition to the holding of an international conference to take up the crisis in Cambodia.

Moscow's objections, expressed in Pravda, the Communist Party newspaper, and in Izvestia, the government journal, centered on a plan by Indonesian Foreign Minister Adam Malik to have the five-member Association of Southeast Asian Nations (ASEAN) organize a regional conference to discuss the situation in Cambodia. Pravda said the ASEAN nations (Indonesia, Malaysia, the Philippines, Thailand and Singapore) and the other countries that would attend such a parley were "linked to the imperialist powers. They are either directly responsible for the dirty war in Vietnam or to one or another degree support the Saigon regime." "Such a conference would merely be a verbal screen hiding foreign intervention in Cambodian affairs," Pravda said.

Malik had announced plans for the meeting April 23 after conferring in Jakarta with diplomats of the other four ASEAN nations. He said the projected conference would "not provide Cambodia with any form of military aid because we would like to solve the Cambodian crisis in a peaceful way." Malik said Australia, Japan and New Zealand had agreed to attend and that invitations had been extended to North Vietnam, Pakistan, India and Ceylon.

Secretary of State Rogers had criticized the Soviet Union April 25 for failing to take steps to reconvene the Geneva conference to help restore peace in Indochina. Speaking in New York at a dinner of the American Society of International Law, Rogers said such a meeting was warranted by North Vietnamese military activity in Laos and Cambodia, which he asserted was in violation of the 1954 and 1962 Geneva agreements. The

failure of the Soviet Union, as co-chairman of the Geneva conference, to reconvene the international meeting, he said, represented a "flouting" of its "international responsibilities." Rogers noted that Yakov A. Malik, the Soviet ambassador to the U.N., had first proposed reconvening the Geneva conference but that Moscow "has been backpedaling ever since."

No progress in talks. The U.S. delegation at the Paris peace talks Jan. 8 had renewed its proposal for private sessions and the Communists again rejected the idea.

Calling his plan "a way of ending sterile debate" and of getting down "to serious discussions," acting chief U.S. delegate Philip Habib suggested a restricted meeting Jan. 15. He would alternate formal plenary sessions with the restricted ones. "We would propose to do away with lengthy prepared statements [to the press] and, instead, to engage in open discussion of concrete proposals" at the private meetings, Habib said.

The North Vietnamese delegation rejected the proposal as a "perfidious maneuver" to downgrade and sabotage the conference. The North Vietnamese countered with Hanoi's previous demand for private talks between the U.S. and the Viet Cong's Provisional Revolutionary Government delegations.

North Vietnamese delegate Ha Van Lau asserted at the Jan. 15 session that the U.S. "always links the withdrawal of U.S. troops with what it calls the three criteria, which in fact can never be met." President Nixon's "real policy," therefore, "is to promote indefinitely the U.S. military occupation of South Vietnam," Lau said. The American criteria referred to by Lau were the progress at the peace talks, a reduction of the fighting and Vietnamization of the conflict.

Habib denounced the Communist position as one-sided, distorted and illogical.

Xuan Thuy, chief of the North Vietnamese delegation to the Paris talks, confirmed Feb. 11 that there would be no secret discussions with the U.S. as long as Habib headed the American delegation. The Communists had hinted at this at the Feb. 5 session. They based their stand on the fact that Habib, a replacement for Henry Cabot Lodge, who had resigned as chief of the U.S. delegation, was a person of "unelevated rank", and that his appointment, therefore, was an American attempt to downgrade the talks. Thuy had given this as his reason for boycotting the sessions since Dec. 11, 1969.

Following one of the briefest sessions of the peace negotiations Feb. 12, Habib attempted a new approach to break the deadlock at the Feb. 19 meeting. He arrived without a prepared text in an effort to engage the other side in informal discussions. The Communists, however, did not reply directly, and instead reiterated their position that the U.S. first had to agree to withdraw its forces unconditionally and abandon the present South Vietnamese government. Habib had opened the debate by saying that the U.S. was prepared to withdraw, but asked what the other side was ready to do in return.

The discussions were further downgraded when Mrs. Nguyen Thi Binh, head of the Viet Cong's Provisional Revolutionary Government (PRG) delegation, boycotted the Feb. 26 session. Habib again attempted to engage the Communists in informal debate but failed to get a response.

North Vietnamese delegate Nguyen Minh Vy charged at the March 12 meeting that there had been 130 American air raids on North Vietnam in February, three times as many as in January. U.S. press spokesman Stephen Ledogar denied the accusation.

Vy raised the issue of the ouster of Cambodian Chief of State Prince Norodom Sihanouk at the March 19 session, hinting at American involvement in the March 18 coup. He charged that the U.S. had "maneuvered to change the present policy of Cambodia, . . . of peace and neutrality. . . ." U.S. delegate Philip Habib ignored the accusation and again sought to elicit information from the Communists on American prisoners of war.

The Viet Cong and North Vietnamese delegation again brought up alleged American involvement in the Cambodian coup at the March 26 session. The U.S. delegation dismissed the charge as erroneous.

The South Vietnamese delegation offered to repatriate 343 sick and wounded North Vietnamese prisoners at the March 26 meeting. Hanoi's representative rejected the offer in line with North Vietnam's policy of refusing to publicly acknowledge the presence of its troops in South Vietnam.

At the April 2 session, the South Vietnamese and Communist delegations reacted coolly to France's appeal for an international parley on Indochina. A Viet Cong statement said the only solution was for an end to American military involvement in Vietnam, Laos and Cambodia. North Vietnamese spokesman Le Quang Hiep called on France to recognize Prince Sihanouk as the legitimate ruler of Cambodia. South Vietnamese spokesman Nguyen Trieu Dan expressed reservations about the French assertion that South Vietnam's neutrality should be the goal of its proposed parley on Indochina. Saigon had called in foreign assistance because it was a victim of Communist aggression, Dan said.

The North Vietnamese announced at the April 9 session that Le Duc Tho, chief adviser to its delegation, would return to Hanoi the next day. Tho, a member of the North Vietnamese Communist Party Politburo, had come to Paris Jan. 30, ostensibly to attend the congress of the French Communist Party. His presence in the French capital was regarded as a possible indication that Hanoi was ready to get the talks moving, but Tho made no contacts with the American delegation during his stay. U.S. press spokesman Stephen Ledogar said after the April 9 session that "All the time he [Tho] was here, he knew that Habib was empowered to deal with a serious proposal, if indeed he had one."

Before leaving Paris April 10, Tho warned France that its recognition of the anti-Sihanouk government "would accentuate and increase the gravity of the situation in Cambodia."

The Fighting

New Year truces end. The fighting had resumed in South Vietnam Jan. 2 on the expiration of two separate New Year's cease-fires observed by allied and Communist forces. The 24-hour allied truce ended at 6 p.m. Jan. 1, while the three-day standdown proclaimed by the Viet Cong concluded at 1 a.m. Jan. 2.

The U.S. command charged Jan. 2 that Communist forces had committed 111 cease-fire violations, 58 of them serious, during the allied truce. The fatalities in that 24-hour period numbered 167 Communists, six Americans and more than 20 South Vietnamese soldiers and civilians. U.S. deaths in the post-Christmas truce period and early hours of the New Year's cease-fire brought the number of Americans killed in Vietnam by the end of 1969 to more than 40,000.

In the post-New Year's truce fighting, North Vietnamese troops Jan. 2 assaulted a U.S. night camp near Ducpho, south of Quangngai, killing seven Americans and wounding 12. The U.S. command said the defending forces repelled the enemy with a loss of 29 killed.

Another U.S. night camp, 26 miles south of Danang, came under North Vietnamese attack Jan. 6 and 13 Marines were killed and 63 wounded. The enemy penetrated the 7th Regiment's defense perimeter and lost five men of its own in the three-hour battle.

In another clash Jan. 6 south of Danang, U.S. tanks, supported by South Vietnamese militiamen, killed 45 Viet Cong without suffering any fatalities. Three U.S. helicopters were downed by Viet Cong gunners during the six-hour clash, bringing to 1,446 the number of U.S. 'copters shot down since 1961. The fighting took place four miles west of Tamky, 40 miles southeast of Danang.

1969 civilian death toll. A South Vietnamese protest filed with the International Control Commission Jan. 24 charged that Communist terror attacks in 1969 had killed 4,619 civilians and injured 14,412. The statement said 1,879 civilians had been kidnaped in that period. The protest accused North Vietnam of violating the 1954 Geneva agreements on Vietnam by showing "no disposition to scale down the fighting and to seriously negotiate at the Paris peace talks."

The Viet Cong's Liberation Radio Jan. 17 had called for an increase in guerrilla and terror attacks on major population areas to frustrate the American plan to Vietnamize the war. It also urged hit-and-run attacks against U.S. units training South Vietnamese soldiers. These attacks, the broadcast said, would "disrupt, foil and crush the aggressors' plan for using Vietnamese to kill Vietnamese."

In the latest Viet Cong attack on civilians, a Communist force Jan. 16 moved into the Batangan Peninsula refugee village of Chauthuan and hurled dynamite charges into houses, killing 16 persons and wounding 21.

Other military developments. Allied forces reported inflicting heavy casualties on Communist troops in scattered battles throughout South Vietnam Jan. 7–26. Enemy action was marked by widespread rocket and mortar shelling and ground attacks against allied bases. U.S. B-52s struck enemy targets in areas where fighting had increased, dropping bombs on troop concentrations and supplies in the Mekong Delta, the Saigon area and the Ho Chi Minh Trail in Laos.

U.S. troops killed 109 North Vietnamese and Viet Cong in fighting Jan. 8–9 on the slopes of Nuibaden mountain overlooking the U.S. base at Tayninh, 55 miles northeast of Saigon. The Americans had been in possession of the top of the mountain, while the enemy had been dug in for months in caves below, shelling the Tayninh base periodically.

Four Americans were killed and 79 wounded in the North Vietnamese shelling Jan. 9 of a U.S. artillery base near Bongson in the coastal province of Binhdinh. The U.S. force, a battalion of the 173rd Airborne Brigade, was largely assigned to pacification of the rice bowl in the province and three North Vietnamese army divisions were said to have moved into the area to disrupt the operations.

U.S. soldiers Jan. 13 captured a freshly-abandoned North Vietnamese camp in the foothills west of Tamky, about 30 miles south of Danang.

A high-ranking North Vietnamese officer defected to the South Vietnamese side Jan. 13. The defector, who identified himself as Col. Dang Ngoc Toa, chief of staff of the Second Army Division, surrendered in Quangnam Province, about 17 miles southwest of Danang.

The stepped-up fighting resulted in a rise in American combat fatalities for the Jan. 4–17 period. Ninety-eight men were reported killed Jan. 4–10, the highest weekly toll in six weeks, and 84 were listed as slain the following week.

Three U.S. helicopters were shot down Jan. 17–18,

Viet Cong-planted mines Jan. 18 blasted the Thuduc Officers Training School 12 miles northeast of Saigon, killing 18

persons, including 16 government officer cadets and their instructor. Thirty-three cadets and an instructor were wounded.

U.S. forces Jan. 20 killed 54 North Vietnamese troops in three sharp clashes north and northwest of Saigon. The heaviest fighting centered near the U.S. Budop Special Forces camp, 88 miles north of Saigon and about two miles from Cambodia. American casualties were listed as light.

In the most extensive shelling in seven weeks, Communist gunners fired rockets and mortars into 55 military and civilian targets Jan. 20. Eighteen of the targets included U.S. installations, in which two Americans were killed and 23 were wounded.

A combined North Vietnamese-Viet Cong mortar and ground assault Jan. 22 on a South Vietnamese Marine brigade command post in the Mekong Delta resulted in fatalities to 15 government troops and 72 Communists. The 600-man defending force threw back the attackers, said to number about 400.

The first convoy of North Vietnamese supply trucks sighted in the Ashau Valley since the summer of 1969 came under U.S. air attack Jan. 25.

The U.S. command reported Jan. 26 that 175 North Vietnamese and Viet Cong had been killed Jan. 25–26 in a dozen engagements ranging from the Mekong Delta to coastal lowlands below Danang.

Viet Cong and North Vietnamese forces carried out more than 100 rocket, mortar and ground attacks Jan. 31–Feb. 1 against allied bases and towns from the demilitarized zone to the Mekong Delta. The U.S. command, describing the attacks as the heaviest in six months, reported Feb. 2 that more than 400 enemy soldiers were killed, while American casualties totaled 11 killed and 119 wounded. Government losses were put at 11 killed and 86 wounded in 20 clashes between allied and enemy forces. More than 250 rockets and mortar rounds struck 48 allied bases and towns, including four major U.S. strongpoints.

In the wake of the Communist onslaught, U.S. B-52 bombers Feb. 2 carried out widespread raids on enemy infiltration routes, supply depots and staging areas in a move to interdict the flow of men and material into South Vietnam. As many as 30 B-52s were reported to have dropped up to 900 tons of bombs in the Ashau Valley along the Laotian border, on the central coastal plains and in Tayninh Province bordering Cambodia.

Thirteen U.S. Marines were killed and 12 were wounded when their patrol was ambushed by North Vietnamese troops Feb. 13 in the Queson Valley south of Danang. Six of the enemy were reported killed.

A Communist demolition battalion was reported to have been wiped out Feb. 15 by South Vietnamese rangers and an armored brigade (accompanied by U.S. advisers) in a clash 18 miles south of Danang. The enemy force, made up largely of North Vietnamese and numbering about 200 men, lost 145 killed and 12 captured. Four miles away, South Vietnamese militiamen reported killing 37 more enemy soldiers, possibly stragglers from the earlier battle.

Hanoi sees long war. North Vietnam warned Feb. 1 that its people "must be prepared to fight many years more" until the American "enemy gives up his aggressive design, brings home all his troops and respects the sovereignty of our people and the territorial integrity of our country."

The statement was made by Le Duan, first secretary of the Vietnamese Workers (Communist) party at the opening of celebrations in Hanoi to mark the 40th anniversary of the party. Duan coupled his warning with an appeal for greater domestic economic productivity. Although claiming progress in this field, Duan said "the material life of our people at present is still low, still meeting many difficulties." "Labor productivity is still low . . . , and many potential capabilities, including technical capabilities, have not yet turned to full account" and "we are still wasting manpower and material resources," he said.

Duan's speech coincided with an editorial appearing in Nhan Dan, the North Vietnamese Communist Party newspaper, denouncing President Nixon's Jan. 30 statement warning that the U.S. would use military means to counter any Communist attempt to re-escalate the war. "This constitutes an insolent threat," and "once again bared the stubborn and warlike policy" of the U.S. the newspaper said.

Tet truces. Scattered clashes continued throughout South Vietnam despite separate allied and Communist truces Feb. 5-9, honoring Tet, the Buddhist Lunar New Year. Allied forces observed a 24-hour truce, starting at 6 p.m. Feb. 5, but did not recognize the Viet Cong's announced standdown, which went into effect 7 a.m. Feb. 5 and ended at 7 a.m. Feb. 9.

The U.S. command reported Feb. 7 that Communist troops had committed 113 violations during the allied truce, resulting in fatalities to 133 enemy soldiers, three Americans and five South Vietnamese. A Viet Cong broadcast Feb. 7 accused allied forces of violating the Communist four-day cease-fire by bombing and shelling "liberated areas" and "illegally arresting our people."

Despite the cease-fires, U.S. combat deaths increased to 95 Feb. 1-7. compared with 70 the previous week.

113 GIs die in week. The U.S. command reported March 5 that 113 Americans had been slain Feb. 22-28, the highest weekly death toll in 3½ months and the first time American battle deaths had risen past 100 since Jan. 1.

The command attributed the increased casualties to helicopter losses in which 17 men had been killed and to "an unusually high number of U.S. soldiers killed in indirect fire attacks" in one day. Seven of the Americans had died and six were wounded in the downing of three helicopters by enemy gunners Feb. 25. Two other helicopters had been lost Feb. 17, taking the lives of 19 men. One was downed by Communist groundfire; the other was said to have crashed as a result of mechanical failure.

The high one-day death toll reported by the command was in reference to widespread Communist rocket and mortar barrages directed at bases and camps. No date for the attacks and no exact losses were given.

U.S. troops had suffered their highest casualties in any single previous battle since Jan. 1 when 14 were killed and 29 were wounded in a five-hour engagement with North Vietnamese forces in the

Queson Valley south of Danang Feb. 20. The fighting erupted when an armored unit of the 196th Infantry Brigade of the Americal Division was ambushed. As the fighting continued, American reinforcements were flown in. A groundsweep of the area Feb. 21 turned up four North Vietnamese bodies.

South Vietnamese headquarters disclosed March 3 that 323 Communist soldiers had been killed in a three-week government sweep of the Mekong Delta that ended Feb. 28. Ten government battalions fighting in the Vinhbinh Province operation also sustained losses, 31 killed and 401 wounded.

U.S. combat deaths totaled 101 in the week March 8–14 and 100 March 15–21. The high American death toll for the two-week period reflected a slight increase in fighting, U.S. command spokesmen said.

In the heaviest fighting in the area since January, U.S. troops and planes March 10 killed 130 enemy soldiers near the Cambodian border northwest of Saigon. U.S. deaths in the clashes totaled eight.

U.S. forces suffered a heavy loss of helicopters March 6–16. Two were downed by enemy groundfire March 6 and 7. A Marine 'copter crashed and burned on takeoff at Danang March 10, killing five and injuring five others. Three helicopters were riddled by enemy groundfire March 11 as they were trying to evacuate wounded from fighting near Quangngai City. Eleven Americans were killed in the crash of two helicopters March 12. Ten of them died in the crash of one of the aircraft near Baria, 40 miles northeast of Saigon. Six 'copters were struck by enemy fire along the Cambodian border March 15. One of them was shot down but its four crewmen escaped injury. One helicopter was shot down March 16 about 20 miles north of the provincial capital of Songbe.

U.S. artillery fired at North Vietnamese troops in the demilitarized zone March 14 in the first significant incident in the DMZ in more than two months.

Fourteen women and children were killed and 20 others were wounded March 22 by a bomb hurled at a Buddhist religious gathering at Hocmon, seven miles northwest of Saigon. The blast was attributed to a Viet Cong.

South Vietnamese rangers and armored units were shifted from the Cambodian border to the Mekong Delta March 30. The move was aimed at reinforcing a government training camp near the town of Triton that had been under heavy North Vietnamese attack March 28–29. About 30–40 persons, including soldiers and civilians, had been killed and 200 wounded in the assaults.

Reds launch major drive. A general lull that had prevailed over the South Vietnam battlefield since September 1969 was shattered by a major assault launched by Communist forces throughout the country April 1. The Communists bombed and shelled major cities and carried out fierce ground assaults against major allied bases.

Unusually high allied and Communist combat deaths for the March 29–April 4 period reflected the upsurge in the fighting. According to figures released by allied authorities April 9, U.S. fatalities totaled 138, the highest weekly figure since September 1969. South Vietnamese deaths totaled 754, highest toll since May 1968, and 3,336 Viet Cong and North Vietnamese troops were reported killed, the highest weekly Communist total since August 1969.

More than 100 Vietnamese civilians were killed, many of them victims of Communist terror attacks.

The heaviest fighting raged around a Special Forces Camp at Dakseang in the Central Highlands, along the demilitarized zone and at U.S. Artillery Base Illingworth in northern Tayninh Province.

Enemy fire on the opening day of the offensive April 1 killed a U.S. general, the fifth to die in the war. He was Brig. Gen. William R. Bond, 51, commander of the 199th Light Infantry Brigade. Bond was struck by a bullet shortly after he had landed by helicopter to inspect a patrol along the southeastern edge of War Zone D, about 70 miles northeast of Saigon.

The Dakseang base first came under siege by about 2,000 North Vietnamese troops April 1. Later reinforcements raised the total to more than 3,000. A similar number of South Vietnamese troops was committed to the battle. The strong-point was located in northern Kontum Province, near the Laotian and Cambodian borders, 277 miles north of Saigon. The base was defended by about 400 Montagnard irregular troops and a small team of U.S. Special Forces. American involvement in the fighting was confined largely to aerial defense. Seven American aircraft were downed through April 12. Three of them were lost during airlift operations; nine crewmen were killed.

A government relief battalion fought its way into Dakseang April 10. Although the reinforcements did not lift the siege, a government officer said "the situation was substantially eased up" as a result. The South Vietnamese unit, with the aid of Australian advisers, then moved out of the base to the south to drive off the Communists, but encountered heavy resistance.

Fatalities in the fight for Dakseang as of April 12 were listed at more than 100 government soldiers, 11 Americans and 1,400 North Vietnamese.

Another U.S. Special Forces base, at Dakpek, 17 miles north of Dakseang, was reported April 12 to have come under North Vietnamese siege. Rocket and mortar barrages that preceded the Communist ground attack were said to have destroyed bunkers and buildings at the base. Initial reports said at least 60 North Vietnamese and six defenders were slain. The Communist forces also moved into villages north of the camp. U.S. fighter-bombers dropped napalm bombs in an attempt to drive back the attackers.

The fighting along the DMZ occurred April 4–5 and was centered four miles southwest of Conthien and a mile south of the 17th parallel, which divided North and South Vietnam. Six Americans were killed and 40 wounded in an eight-hour battle the first day, the heaviest fighting in the area since Nov. 14, 1969. Two more Americans and 24 government troops were slain in a three-hour fight near the DMZ April 5.

Twenty-five Americans were killed and 54 were wounded in three separate actions April 15. Fourteen of the casualties were caused by the explosion of a

U.S. artillery shell rigged as a Viet Cong booby trap near Ducpho, 105 miles south of Danang. Thirty-two Americans were wounded.

Ten government troops were killed and 20 wounded April 28 in an accidental American air attack. Two U.S. Marine Skyhawks bombed a South Vietnamese outpost during a battle in Quangngai Province.

The South Vietnamese military command suspended operations April 29 around the U.S. Special Forces Camp at Dakseang, under Communist siege since the start of the Communist offensive April 1. The action was in response to a Viet Cong proposal for an eight-hour cease-fire that day to permit the release of wounded South Vietnamese prisoners. The Communists, however, did not free the captives but Saigon military authorities said the 800 government troops protecting the camp would observe the cease-fire indefinitely.

Another U.S. Special Forces Camp at Dakpek, 17 miles south of Dakseang, had been recaptured by government irregulars April 14. The bodies of 25 North Vietnamese were found in the camp. In other action that day, Saigon military officials reported 110 North Vietnamese troops were killed in a Communist attempt to push into South Vietnam from across the Cambodian border. Seventy-five enemy prisoners were captured. A force of about 1,000 North Vietnamese were said to have launched the attack on a government regional force at Anthanh, within 1,000 yards of the Cambodian frontier.

Allied military authorities reported April 25 that 9,848 North Vietnamese and Viet Cong troops had been killed since the start of the Communist offensive April 1. Allied fatalities during that period were 380 Americans and 2,036 South Vietnamese. An American death toll of 141 for the April 5–11 period was the highest in seven months. The number of U.S. fatalities dropped to 101 in action April 12–18, bringing to 41,516 the number of Americans killed since 1961.

In the air war at least 17 U.S. planes and helicopters were downed by enemy fire over South Vietnam between April 22 and 30.

Black battle deaths decrease. The Defense Department reported Aug. 1 that the percentage of black servicemen killed in Vietnam combat had declined substantially the first three months in 1970. The Pentagon said that for the first time, the percentage of Negro soldiers killed in action in Southeast Asia had fallen below the percentage of blacks among U.S. forces there.

The Pentagon data showed that as of March 31, Negroes serving in Indochina represented about 10% of the total American military presence in the area. During the same months, black battle fatalities accounted for 8.5% of the combat deaths in Southeast Asia. In 1969, blacks represented 9.7% of the total American force in the area and accounted for 10.8% of the combat fatalities. From 1961-1968, Negroes represented 10.6% of the GIs serving in Southeast Asia and accounted for 13.5% of the battle deaths. Defense officials said there had been no specific effort to decrease the casualty rates among black servicemen in Indochina.

U.S. bombs the North. U.S. jets had bombed an antiaircraft missile site 90 miles inside North Vietnam Jan. 28 after an unarmed RF-4C reconnaissance plane was fired on by North Vietnamese surface-to-air missiles, the U.S. command announced Jan. 30.

Communist ground fire brought down one of the recon plane's several jet escorts, an F-105 Thunderchief. A rescue helicopter sent to search for the jet's two missing pilots was destroyed by a MiG-21 in the vicinity of the North Veitnamese-Laotian border. The downed 'copter's six-man crew also was listed as missing.

The RF-4C had been on a routine surveillance flight over North Vietnam—which had been conducted daily since the bombing halt of Nov. 1, 1968—when it came under fire along with the accompanying jets 19 miles north of the Mugia Pass.

The U.S. command acknowledged that there had been clashes "from time to time" between U.S. planes and North Vietnamese ground fire since the bombing halt but they had not been made public because they were considered to be "insignificant." A command spokesman said all the U.S. air strikes had been in response to North Vietnamese antiaircraft fire or to missiles.

A White House statement said the incident did not signify a resumption of U.S. air attacks on the North, and added that there was "absolutely no change" in the bombing suspension policy.

A Defense Department official said U.S. retaliatory air strikes against North Vietnamese missile sites "are not a daily occurrence by any means, but it has happened before."

The North Vietnamese delegate at the Jan. 29 session of the Paris peace talks charged that "several formations of U.S. planes bombed and strafed a number of populated areas in Quangbinh and Hatinh Provinces" the previous day and that three of the planes were shot down. Philip C. Habib, acting head of the U.S. delegation, acknowledged that U.S. reconnaissance planes flew over North Vietnam with fighter escorts, but insisted that this was not in violation of the 1968 understanding that stopped the bombing raids.

The U.S. command disclosed Feb. 5 that American fighter-bombers had attacked and silenced two Communist missile and gun positions in North Vietnam Feb. 2 for the second time in a week. The command said the raid was in retaliation for an antiaircraft attack on a U.S. reconnaissance plane in the area of Bankarai Pass, and infiltration route leading into Laos through North Vietnamese mountains 20 miles north of the DMZ.

A U.S. Navy F-4 Phantom jet shot down a North Vietnamese MiG-21 in a clash over North Vietnam March 28, the U.S. military command in Saigon reported April 1. It was the first downing of an enemy plane over the North since the halt in American bombing of North Vietnam Nov. 1, 1968. The MiG was shot down near Thanhhoa, about 85 miles south of Hanoi and 210 miles north of the demilitarized zone. The Phantom had been flying with an unarmed reconnaissance aircraft.

U.S. jets bombed antiaircraft sites in North Vietnam May 25. The target, 90 miles north of the demilitarized zone near Donghoi, was attacked after a reconnaissance plane, accompanied by the U.S. aircraft, was fired on, the Defense Department reported May 27. It said none of the planes were damaged.

Laotian Involvement

Laos was deeply involved in the conflict in neighboring Vietnam. Eastern Laos was the unwilling host to Hanoi's Ho Chi Minh Trail, the network of roads and footpaths used by the Communist forces to infiltrate men and materiel from North Vietnam into South Vietnam. And North Vietnam provided both troops and military supplies to aid the pro-Communist Pathet Lao in their struggle to overthrow the Laotian government.

Laotian fighting increases. The U.S. State Department Jan. 20 expressed concern about the recent increase of fighting in Laos and the infiltration of more North Vietnamese troops into the country. A department statement Jan. 23 said 15,000 North Vietnamese troops had massed near the Plaine des Jarres, poised for an attack on the U.S.-supported Meo tribesman army of Maj. Gen. Vang Pao in an effort to retrieve the area they had lost in 1969. Hanoi's buildup had started in the fall of 1969, bringing the current North Vietnamese force in Laos to 50,000 men, an increase of 10,000, the department said.

Three North Vietnamese battalions were reported to have seized a hill position six miles from Ban Ban at a vital road junction east of the Plaines des Jarres in fighting Jan. 10–11. The attackers were said to have suffered 270 dead and wounded, while government troop losses were reported as "serious."

In a previous action, Pathet Lao and North Vietnamese forces Jan. 9 had fired 15 rockets into Pakse, Laos' second largest city, killing a civilian. One of the targets struck was the U.S. Agency for International Development compound.

President Nixon, at a televised news conference Jan. 30, was asked about Sen. Mike Mansfield's (D, Mont.) request for information regarding U.S. troop deployment in Laos. The President repeated a statement he had made during his Dec. 8, 1969 news conference, explaining "that our activities there are solely for the purpose of seeing . . . that they are not overwhelmed by the North Vietnamese and other Communist forces."

Reds seize Plaine des Jarres. North Vietnamese troops Feb. 21 captured the last Laotian government military stronghold in the strategic Plaine des Jarres following a major offensive launched in northeastern Laos Feb. 12.

Although it was not officially confirmed, U.S. B-52 bombers were reported to have attempted to stem the Communist advance with widespread bombing attacks. It was the first apparent intervention of American air power in the Laotian fighting, apart from the U.S. bombing of the Ho Chi Minh Trail in eastern Laos. The B-52s were said to have twice suspended their strikes in Vietnam recently to concentrate on the latest fighting in Laos.

The last government position on the plain captured by 3,000 North Vietnamese troops was the airfield at Xiengkhouang, 100 miles northeast of the capital of Vientiane. Government officials said more than 500 of the 1,500 garrison defenders were killed or missing. A Defense Ministry official reported that in fighting at the airfield Feb. 20, 70 North Vietnamese had been killed, bringing to about 500 the number of North Vietnamese and Pathet Lao slain since the start of their drive. The remaining airfield garrison troops fled to join a larger government force preparing to defend the headquarters of Gen. Vang Pao, the Laotian commander, at Long Cheng, 30 miles southwest of the plain.

A report in the Los Angeles Times Feb. 25 said that Asian pilots were flying American planes out of Long Cheng in support of government forces fighting near the plain. The report also told of many "armed Americans in civilian clothes" supporting the Laotian command.

The U.S. State Department said Feb. 24 that the North Vietnamese army was using more men and equipment "than ever before" in the latest fighting in Laos.

In a parallel action, it was reported Feb. 24 that North Vietnam had launched the biggest supply operation down the Ho Chi Minh Trail. The report said U.S. B-52s had mounted a massive aerial drive to halt the movement of the Communist troops and supplies into Laos and South Vietnam. More than 500 B-52 sorties were said to have been flown along the trail since Feb. 1.

In anticipation of the major Communist thrust into the Plaine des Jarres, U.S. Air Force planes had evacuated 23,000 civilians from the area Feb. 5-9. The Laotian government had decided on the airlift after the Pathet Lao and North Vietnamese had rejected a Vientiane proposal to neutralize the plain. Under the plan advanced Feb. 4 by Premier Souvanna Phouma, North Vietnamese troops would withdraw from the plain and the region would then be occupied by neutralist forces loyal to Souvanna and to Col. Deuane, a former Souvanna backer who had defected to the Pathet Lao in 1963.

The Pathet Lao spurned Souvanna's proposal Feb. 5, charging that it was part of deceitful psychological warfare. The rebels said they were determined to capture the entire plain. Hanoi turned down the proposal Feb. 6, describing it as "a new campaign of slanders against North Vietnam," which did not acknowledge the presence of its troops in Laos.

Reds capture Muong Soui. North Vietnamese-Pathet Lao forces followed up their seizure of the Plaine des Jarres with the capture Feb. 24 of Muong Soui and the nearby Laotian-U.S. air base. Muong Soui, 25 miles west of the plain, was on one of the roads leading across eastern Laos to Luang Prabang.

U.S. B-52s Feb. 25 carried out heavy raids in northeast Laos, and especially around Muong Soui, in a mission aimed at destroying abandoned government ammunition and other supplies before they could be used by the advancing Communist forces.

A North Vietnamese battalion was reported Feb. 26 to have been sighted about 12 miles northeast of Long Cheng, the operational headquarters of the U.S.-backed Meo tribal army led by Gen. Vang Pao.

Another North Vietnamese force was reported Feb. 25 to have approached the Mekong River town of Paksane bordering Thailand. As a result, Thai border troops were placed on the alert. Navy units were sent along the Mekong River and about 50 special mobile squads were sent out to protect roads and bridges in strategic areas.

The commander of the northernmost military region of Laos disclosed March 2 that the U.S. had rejected his repeated requests for aerial bombing support in the region because of the existence of a line beyond which the U.S. did not bomb in Laos. According to Maj. Gen. Tiao Sayavong, the restricted area was in the northwestern corner of Laos that was bordered by a road the Chinese Communists were building from Botene to Moung Houne and beyond toward the Thai border.

Reds warn U.S. on raids. The Soviet Union Feb. 28 assailed the American air raids in Laos, saying that they only make "it more difficult to find the ways for the solution of the problems of Indo-China and lead to further heightening of tensions in Southeast Asia."

The statement, issued by Tass, asserted that American planes based in Thailand and on aircraft carriers "daily fly more than 400 bombing missions to Laos, and mostly the Plaine des Jarres." These air strikes, the statement said, were in "disrespect for Laos neutrality" and added, the Soviet Union "supports the just demands of the Patriotic Front of Laos [Pathet Lao] for the immediate end to the United States armed interference in the internal affairs of the Laotian people."

A Hanoi broadcast Feb. 26 had called on the U.S. to halt the bombing and to permit Laos to settle its affairs on the basis of the 1962 Geneva agreements. The North Vietnamese statement said the American raids had caused many civilian casualties.

A communique issued by the North Vietnamese embassy in Vientiane Feb. 24 had warned that the U.S. and Laos "must be held responsible for all consequences arising from the intensification of the war."

The Pathet Lao reported Feb. 23 that they had filed a protest with Britain and the Soviet Union charging that U.S. B–52 raids on the Plaine des Jarres and the Xieng Khouang area posed "a new, serious adventurous escalation" of the Laotian war by the U.S. The Pathet Lao claimed that B–52 attacks Feb. 17–18 had destroyed many villages in a six-mile area between Bansone and Khang Khay.

Laos files protest. Premier Souvanna Phouma protested North Vietnamese military activity in Laos in a letter sent to Britain and the Soviet Union, co-chairmen of the 1962 Geneva conference on Laos, it was reported March 1.

The contents of Souvanna's note were not disclosed. But in announcing his intention to file the protest, the premier had said Feb. 26 that he would ask Britain and the Soviet Union to apply Clause IV of the 1962 agreements, which called for the 14 signatory nations to consult one another in the event of a threat against the independence, territorial integrity and neutrality of Laos.

Souvanna had conferred in Vientiane Feb. 25 with U.S. Ambassador George Godley about the deteriorating military situation. The discussions followed a Laotian cabinet meeting which reportedly had said "the situation in northern Laos is more serious than last week."

U.S. senators decry U.S. role. Alarm was expressed in the U.S. Senate Feb. 25 over the reported growth of U.S. military involvement in Laos. The criticism continued despite assurances by Defense Secretary Melvin R. Laird Feb. 26 that U.S. policy had not changed and that Congressional approval would be sought concerning any use of U.S. ground combat forces in Laos. Laird would not confirm or deny reports that U.S. planes were being employed in support of Laotian forces in northern Laos.

In the Senate Feb. 25, Sen. Charles McC. Mathias Jr. (R, Md.) said U.S. military activity in Laos violated a 1969 Senate resolution calling for Congressional approval of any new commitment of U.S. troops abroad. He said it also conflicted with a specific Congressional prohibition against the use of U.S. ground combat troops in Laos or Thailand.

Mathias warned that the Laos situation was being turned into "an arena for the repetition of the mistakes of our Vietnamese involvement." He said if the success of the Administration's Vietnamization program in South Vietnam "depends on escalation" of the U.S. role in Laos, then U.S. policy "should be fully reappraised."

Similar alarm was expressed by other senators Feb. 25. Democratic Leader Mike Mansfield (Mont.) said if the Laotian war continued to expand, "all the plans for Vietnamization and all else will go down the drain and we will find ourselves in a most difficult and dangerous situation." Sen. John Sherman Cooper (R, Ky.) said he did not see "how we are going to get out of . . . [Vietnam] by getting involved in another war." Sen. Stuart Symington (D, Mo.) spoke of "a heavy escalation" of U.S. military activity in Laos and said it was not confined only to the Plaine des Jarres area. Sen. Albert Gore (D, Tenn.) accused the Administration of "misleading" the public about the situation and suggested that the Administration's refusal to permit release of previous Congressional testimony on Laos was because the testimony would reveal that the U.S. activity was in violation of the 1962 Geneva Accord on Laos. (Gore told the Senate Feb. 9 that the testimony, before a Senate foreign relations subcommittee headed by Symington, contained evidence that U.S. participation in the Laotian war had been "secretly but greatly escalated." "We have increased our involvement and our presence in Laos, and the government refuses publicly to admit it," he declared. "What goes on here?")

Laird's rebuttal was made at a news conference Feb. 26. He said "the President has made it very clear that should any decision be made, or a recommendation on his part be made, as far as the use of American military ground combat forces in Laos, that he would come to the Congress of the United States for such approval."

Laird said no U.S. ground troops, including Special Forces, were engaged in Laos and U.S. air power was being employed in Laos only to interdict North Vietnamese supply lines through eastern Laos to South Vietnam.

The criticism continued. In a nationally televised interview March 1, Mathias said: "I think we're reaching the point now that we might be close to the commitment that we inched into in Vietnam, where if something goes wrong we find ourselves committed far beyond the intention" of Congress or the American people.

In a Senate speech March 2, Mansfield said: Despite the Geneva Accord, North Vietnam and the U.S. both were "deeply involved" in the Laotian war and "press reports indicate that the Thais may also be engaged"; "the presence of American military 'advisers' and others in Laos cannot be camouflaged any longer"; there were indications that U.S. bombing in Laos was heavier than it was in North Vietnam.

The speech followed a closed session of the Senate Foreign Relations Committee for testimony by Central Intelligence Agency Director Richard Helms. After the hearing, Gore said he was "more concerned" than before about the Laotian situation. Chairman J. William Fulbright (D, Ark.) said he was "very

afraid we are gradually being sucked into a new Vietnam-type war."

Fulbright introduced a resolution in the Senate March 11 stating that it was the "sense of the Senate" that the President could not commit U.S. armed forces "in combat in or over Laos" without "affirmative action" by Congress. He told the Senate the President did not have authority nor had Congress given him authority to wage combat in Laos "whether on the land, in the air or from the sea" and "the Senate must not remain silent now" while U.S. armed forces were being used "to fight an undeclared and undisclosed war in Laos." He also said "efforts have been made to distinguish between combat action in the air and combat action on the ground" in Laos and "such a distinction is specious."

Laird asserted categorically March 3, after testifying at a closed session of the House Armed Services Committee, that "there has been no buildup of [U.S.] individuals, whether civilians or military, on the ground in Laos or within the country."

Secretary of State William P. Rogers, in a private meeting March 3 with the Senate Foreign Relations Committee (disclosed March 4 by the State Department), gave assurance that no American ground forces would be sent to Laos but conceded that U.S. air activity over Laos had increased.

Vice President Spiro T. Agnew also discounted the likelihood of U.S. ground forces going into Laos. He told an interviewer March 9 that the U.S. was forced to get involved "in a small way" in Laos because it was "inextricably linked" to the security of U.S. forces in South Vietnam. In a reference to U.S. policy critics, Agnew wondered why so much attention was paid "to the very calculated and limited responses we've made to requests of the Laotian government." He had not seen published in U.S. media, he said, criticism of the North Vietnamese aggression in Laos.

Nixon asks U.S.S.R., British aid. President Nixon reported to the American public March 6 on the U.S. military role in the Laotian war and appealed to the

Soviet Union and Britain to help restore the 1962 Geneva agreements for Laos.

The President said he had written letters that day to the Soviet Union and Britain, as co-chairmen of the 1962 conference, to initiate efforts with other signatories of the Geneva accords to restore the agreements. He said his letters noted "the persistent North Vietnamese violations of the accords and their current offensives." Full U.S. cooperation was pledged.

The U.S. statement was issued in response to "intense public speculation" in the U.S. about the Laotian involvement, the President said. He reported that "the levels" of U.S. assistance—equipment, training and logistics—to the Royal Laotian forces and the level of U.S. combat air operations had risen at the request of the Royal Laotian government and in reaction to a rise in the level of aggression in Laos by North Vietnamese forces. The latter, he said, had reached a level of 67,000 men, and 13,000 combat ground troops had been added in the past few months.

But, Nixon said: there were no U.S. ground combat troops in Laos, he had no plans for introducing such forces, no American stationed in Laos had ever been killed in ground combat operations and the number of U.S. personnel in Laos had not increased during the past year.

The President said there were 616 Americans directly employed by the U.S. government in Laos, an additional 424 Americans employed on contract or subcontract to the government and of these, 320 (including 92 civilians) were engaged as military advisers and 323 in logistics.

Further details were given by White House sources March 6: U.S. casualties in Laos in six years totaled about 300, including 193 presumed captured or missing; U.S. plane losses in Laos in six years totaled about 400; only one raid had been conducted by B-52 bombers on a single day in Northern Laos, that one on Presidential authority.

The U.S. goal in Laos, Nixon said, was "to see a return to the Geneva agreements and the withdrawal of North Vietnamese troops, leaving the Lao people to settle their own differences in a peaceful manner." The U.S. effort in Laos also was related by the President to the Viet-

nam war effort as an effort to counter the "continual" enemy infiltration of troops and supplies along the Ho Chi Minh trail.

Senate criticism continues. Committee Chairman J. W. Fulbright (D, Ark.) reported March 3 that a high Administration official (the State Department asserted that the official was not State Secretary William Rogers) had told his Foreign Relations Committee that Laos was "even more important than Vietnam." That kind of thinking "scares me to death," Fulbright said. The same day Sen. George S. McGovern (D, S.D.) said "in spite of the painful lessons of Vietnam, we are going down the same road in Laos and we are doing it in secret." McGovern protested March 5 that the Administration was "covering up the facts of a bloody military operation in Laos that has secretly cost the lives of scores of American bombing crews and American aircraft."

In a televised broadcast March 8, Fulbright advocated withdrawal of U.S. personnel from Laos and said he did not believe the Administration's Vietnamization policy was "a policy to bring the war to an end." (Rogers had declared Jan. 18 that while the level of enemy activity in Vietnam might affect the U.S. troop withdrawal timetable, the withdrawal policy was "irreversible.")

Both Fulbright and Sen. Mike Mansfield (D, Mont.) criticized Nixon's March 6 statement on Laos as not having gone far enough and called for an end to the U.S. involvement there.

The President's statement also was attacked by Sen. Stuart Symington (D, Mo.), who said March 6 the Administration made "a big point" of publicizing the "relatively few casualties on the ground" but did not mention the "much greater casualties in the air." The latter, he suggested, were listed by the Administration in the "noncombatant" category because "we constantly say our forces are not engaged in combat in Laos."

Sen. Alan Cranston (D, Calif.), accusing the Administration of using "quibbles" to hide combat missions in Laos, March 9 requested release of information concerning armed U.S. troop missions into Laos from South Vietnam. Casualties from such missions normally were included in the Vietnam war statistics.

U.S. casualties to be listed. As a further response to the public pressure, especially from Senatorial critics about the growing U.S. involvement in Laos, the Nixon Administration announced March 9 a new policy of listing U.S. casualties and aircraft losses in Laos. Previously, such statistics had been included among those for the Vietnam war. The announcement said six civilians and an Army captain had been killed in Laos since 1969 when the Nixon Administration took office.

The U.S. casualty total for the past six years—those killed by Communist troops or listed as missing as a result of enemy action—was 26 civilians, who had been stationed there on government business, and the Army captain, Joseph K. Bush, Jr. This was announced by the Administration March 8 after Bush's death had been reported in The Los Angeles Times earlier that day as having occurred Feb. 10, 1969 near Muong Soui as a result of "ground combat"—coordinating ground action involving Thai artillery, U.S. air power and Meo infantrymen against a Communist force.

The White House spokesman said Bush had not been engaged in combat operations but died as a result of "hostile action." He also said the President had not been aware of Bush's death when the Laos statement was issued March 6.

(The U.S. State Department had said Feb. 5 that about 150 Americans, nearly all pilots, were missing or had been captured in Laos. A U.S. embassy report in Vientiane Feb. 25 said this number had risen to 184. The embassy said 36 Americans had been killed in connection with the ground fighting in Laos since 1962.)

U.S. hostile-fire pay. The U.S. State Department disclosed March 10 American military men serving in Laos had been receiving "hostile-fire pay" since Jan. 1, 1966. Officers and enlisted men assisting to train and advise Laotian soldiers received an additional $65 a month, the same amount received by American troops fighting in South Vietnam. However, since Laos had not been designated a "combat zone," enlisted men serving there were not entitled to the same special tax benefits received by Americans fighting in South Vietnam, which was labeled a combat zone, the department said.

Pathet Lao peace plan. A five-point proposal aimed at ending the conflict in Laos was announced March 6 by the Neo Lao Hak Xat, the political arm of the pro-Communist Pathet Lao rebels.

The proposal: (1) The U.S. must "stop escalating the war, . . . withdraw from Laos all U.S. advisers and military personnel as well as United States weapons and material, stop using military bases in Thailand and Thailand mercenaries for purposes of aggression against Laos and stop using Laotian territory for intervention and aggression against other countries"; (2) a standfast cease-fire to end the fighting between the Pathet Lao and Laotian government troops; (3) a conference of all political parties on establishment of a provisional coalition government. Elections to form a national assembly; (4) a demilitarized zone where the political conference and the coalition government would function; and (5) in accord with the 1962 Geneva agreements, Laos must not form military alliances with other countries. Laos must also respect the independence, sovereignty, unity and territorial integrity of Vietnam and Cambodia.

The Pathet Lao program was made public in Hanoi by Phau Phimpachman, a member of the central committee of the Neo Lao Hak Xat. It was broadcast March 7 by Hanoi radio.

The Laotian government announced March 9 that Premier Souvanna Phouma had agreed to an exchange of views on the peace plan with Pathet Lao leader Prince Souphanouvong, his half-brother.

Souvanna March 6 had reiterated his previous offer to permit North Vietnam use of the Ho Chi Minh Trail in eastern Laos in exchange for withdrawal of North Vietnamese forces from the rest of the country. Hanoi had rejected the offer on the ground that Souvanna refused to get the Americans to stop the bombing of those supply routes. Souvanna denied that the American air strikes in Laos were in violation of the 1962 Geneva accords. "You must distinguish between two things—cause and effect. The cause is North Vietnamese interference in Laos."

Souvanna had said March 3 that the Communist drive was a normal dry-season offensive and "one should not give too much importance to it." He said American air support of his forces was preventing all of Laos from falling into the hands of the Communists.

Vientiane sources reported March 4 that the Communists had virtually abandoned the Plaine des Jarres because of continuing U.S. and government air attacks on the recently captured region.

Lt. Col. Khouang Sounthavong, commander of the Royal Laotian Air Force, disclosed March 7 that a Combined Operations Center had been established in Vietiane to coordinate U.S. and Laotian aerial missions against Communist forces in Laos. Khouang said the joint missions were led by Col. Robert L. F. Tyrell, the U.S. Air Force attache at the American embassy in Vientiane, and Col. Oudone Maniboth of the Laotian general staff.

Senate Democratic Leader Mike Mansfield (Mont.) said March 14 he had received "good enough assurance to suit me" that the Administration did not plan to repeat the use of B-52 bombing strikes in northern Laos as distinct from the regular bombing strikes against the Ho Chi Minh trail in southern Laos. He said the use of small fighter aircraft in Laos was continuing.

Vice President Agnew, appearing on the "Today" program March 16, indicated that a cessation of U.S. bombing in Laos was contingent upon withdrawal of North Vietnamese troops from that country. It was the North Vietnamese who had upset the 1962 Geneva accords by refusing to pull out all their troops, he said, and "now, to go back and continue to prostrate ourselves on the altar of sacrifice to satisfy the critics, whose opinions seem to concur with the opinions of the enemy, seems to me to be self-defeating."

U.S.-Soviet peace exchange. Soviet Premier Aleksei N. Kosygin called on President Nixon to halt American "escalation of the war" in Laos and to "stop fully and unconditionally the bombings of Laotian territory." Tass reported

March 16 that Kosygin called Nixon's March 6 call for cooperation "unrealistic" because the U.S. "continues the war in Vietnam, expands interference in Laos, and the coalition government created in Vientiane is paralyzed by the actions of rightwing forces." Kosygin said the "restoration of peace should be started with consultations between political forces of the country." He praised the five-point peace plan advanced by the Pathet Lao March 6 as a "concrete and quite realistic" proposal.

In a reply sent to Kosygin March 23, Nixon again called on the Soviet Union to initiate international consultations to help end the fighting in Laos. Nixon was said to have pointed out that Kosygin's rejҽction of his March 6 appeal had failed to mention the presence of an estimated 67,000 North Vietnamese troops in Laos. Secretary of State William P. Rogers, who disclosed Nixon's message earlier March 23, said "it is quite clear now, from the facts that have developed in receнt months, where the trouble lies."

Rogers expressed hope that the Soviet Union would "respond affirmatively" to the President's suggestion that Moscow "seek consultations among the signatories" of the Geneva accord, which guaranteed Laos' neutrality.

Laos gets Pathet Lao plan. The Pathet Lao's five-point plan aimed at ending the fighting in Laos was formally submitted to the Vientiane government in a message sent to Laotian Premier Souvanna Phouma March 22. The note was written by Pathet Lao leader Prince Souphanouvong.

Although the exact contents of the message was not disclosed, its tone was indicated in a follow-up statement broadcast by Souphanouvong March 23. Addressing himself to Souvanna from the Pathet Lao headquarters at Samneua, Souphanouvong asserted that the premier "must bear full responsibility for the dangerous situation" in Laos. He demanded that Souvanna agree to "an immediate, complete and unconditional halt to the U.S. bombing raids against Laos to create conditions for all parties concerned in Laos to negotiate and solve Laotian internal affairs." This was one of the Pathet Lao's five points. The message accused the U.S. of escalating the fighting in Laos by the introduction of its military personnel into combat with "a large number of U.S. weapons and other war materials and Thai infantry and artillery."

Souvanna said in a speech March 23 that his government was giving careful study to the five-point plan as a "basis for discussion" with the Pathet Lao. He charged that the North Vietnamese capture of the Plaine des Jarres in February had led to "very dangerous tension." North Vietnam's offensive on the plain, he said, was "perhaps only a step in the more ambitious strategy of certain powers."

In response to Souphanouvong's broadcast message, Souvanna March 26 reiterated his proposal for reactivation of the International Control Commission to check on the presence of foreign troops in Laos. The only foreign troops in Laos, he insisted, were North Vietnamese.

In an interview March 28, Souvanna rejected Pathet Lao demands for a halt to American air strikes against Communist forces in Laos. "We cannot stop the bombing and leave Laotian troops at the mercy of the North Vietnamese," Souvanna said.

Fulbright probes involvement. Sen. J. W. Fulbright (D, Ark.) continued to press his inquiry into the U.S. military and paramilitary role in the Laotian fighting. He made public March 16 a statement by Secretary of State William P. Rogers that the Nixon Administration had "no present plans" to commit ground combat troops to Laos even "if it is overrun" by Communist forces. Rogers also pledged to seek the "advance approval" of Congress if the Administration decided to commit ground troops. Rogers' statements had been made in a closed sesion of Fulbright's Foreign Relations Committee March 3.

Fulbright revealed the testimony March 16 during a public committee hearing after Undersecretary of State Elliot L. Richardson told the committee that no ground troops would be sent to Laos without Congressional approval but indicated that such approval might be in the form of consultation with Congressional leaders. Richardson said that

Congressional approval or authority was not needed for engagement in air combat over Laos since this had been initiated under the Johnson Administration. Richardson further declared that the Administration was not dependent upon the 1964 Tonkin Gulf Resolution or any other resolutions as the legal basis of its foreign policy. The neutral position on the Tonkin Resolution contrasted to the frequent citation of the Resolution by the Johnson Administration as the basic Congressional authority for the U.S. military commitment in Vietnam.

Rogers, appearing on the NBC "Today" broadcast March 17, stressed that his March 3 testimony to the Fulbright panel had been set in the context of "no present plans." He had told the committee, he said, that he "was not in a position to foreclose the President in making any decision which might be required in the future." "If a situation should arise that would require consideration of combat forces in Laos," he said, "I told the Senate . . . that we would consult with them to the fullest extent possible."

After a closed committee session March 13 with Richard Helms, director of the Central Intelligence Agency (CIA), Fulbright told newsmen that reports of CIA paramilitary activity in Laos under cover of the Agency for International Development (AID) had been generally confirmed. He said such activity had not been initiated by the CIA itself but under policy established by the National Security Council. During a public confirmation hearing March 11, Robert H. Nooter, designated to be an assistant administrator of AID in charge of the Vietnam program, refused to discuss a report by Jack Foisie of the Los Angeles Times that about half of the AID staff in Laos were actually CIA men. "We prefer that these matters should not be discussed—either confirmed or denied in public session," Nooter said. Fulbright saw this as confirmation that "a relationship exists."

Sen. Stephen M. Young (D, Ohio) also commented March 14 that such disclosures of the activities "of our CIA in Laos and of our air and ground forces" were "shocking."

The same day, Senate Democratic Whip Edward M. Kennedy (Mass.) said the escalation of U.S. military involvement in Laos was "following the pattern of Vietnam in the destruction of the countryside, the generation of refugees and the occurrence of civilian war casualties."

Kennedy sent a letter to Rogers March 13 requesting information about reports indicating that "the number of refugees in Laos has escalated to at least one-quarter of the country's population."

Government bases threatened. North Vietnamese and Pathet Lao troops continued their advance in Laos, threatening the capture of the key government bases of Sam Thong and Long Tieng, south of the Communist-occupied Plaine des Jarres. American air losses in the fighting mounted as U.S. air assistance to the embattled government troops increased. Meanwhile, the scope of the fighting in Laos appeared to be widening with a report March 20 that Thai troops had been flown to Long Tieng to reinforce the strongpoint.

Two Thai battalions were reported March 20 to have been flown into Long Tieng in planes of Air America, a Thailand-based civilian airline under charter to the U.S. Central Intelligence Agency. The report, denied by the Laotian and Thai governments, was confirmed by the U.S. March 20 and 21. White House spokesman Ronald Ziegler said March 20 that Thai involvement was "very limited." He said accounts of two Thai battalions (about 500 men) airlifted into the Laotian base was "grossly exaggerated." President Nixon March 21 defended the use of Thai troops reinforcements as a legitimate response to an appeal for assistance from the Laotian government under the 1962 Geneva accords.

In the air war, 10 U.S. planes were downed since March 10, the U.S. command in Saigon reported March 23. Washington had ordered the U.S. command to disclose information about American air operations in Laos March 10.

Cambodian Involvement, Sihanouk Overthrown

Both sides in the Vietnam conflict have violated Cambodia's borders with increasing frequency. In a development at least partly stemming from this involvement in the Vietnam war, Prince Norodom Sihanouk was overthrown as chief of state. This took place while he was on a trip to Moscow and Peking seeking help to rid Cambodia of the North Vietnamese and Viet Cong. His downfall came some six weeks before U.S. and South Vietnamese forces launched a massive drive into Cambodia in an effort to wipe out the North Vietnamese and Viet Cong sanctuaries there.

Prince Sihanouk deposed. Prince Norodom Sihanouk was ousted as Cambodian chief of state in a bloodless coup carried out in Pnompenh March 18 by Lt. Gen. Lon Nol, premier and defense minister, and First Deputy Premier Prince Sisowath Sirik Matak, a cousin of Sihanouk. Sihanouk, out of the country at the time, declared in Peking March 23 that he would form a "national union government" in exile and a "national liberation army" to restore his authority.

News of Sihanouk's overthrow was contained in a communique issued by the coup leaders and broadcast March 18 by Pnompenh radio. It said: "Following the political crisis provoked by Prince Norodom Sihanouk in the past few days, the National Assembly and the Royal Council in joint session, in accordance with the constitution of the kingdom, withdrew their confidence from Sihanouk." The statement said Sihanouk would be replaced by National Assembly President Cheng Heng, who would serve until the election of a permanent chief of state. (Cheng was officially sworn in March 21.) The "political crisis" referred to were the recent public demonstrations in Pnompenh against the presence of Viet Cong and North Vietnamese troops in Cambodia.

The National Assembly March 19 granted what it called "full power" to Premier Lon Nol, declared a state of emergency and suspended four articles of the constitution, permitting arbitrary arrest and banning public assembly.

The new government March 23 officially exiled Sihanouk, his family and other prominent figures connected with his rule. They included Penn Nouth, his former premier and now his personal aide, Gen. Nhiek Tioulong, a former head of the army, and Pomme Peang, mother of Princess Monique, Sihanouk's wife.

Background to coup—Sihanouk, who had been king of Cambodia, abdicated the throne in 1955 because he said he could rule more effectively without being bound by the rigidity of the monarchy. He became chief of state and turned over his throne to his father, King Norodom Suramarit. After the king's death in

1960, Sihanouk's mother, Queen Kossamak Nearireath, represented the monarchy.

Sihanouk's attempt to steer Cambodia on a neutral course and his alleged personal excesses brought him into conflict with his opponents. He ran afoul of the military as a result of his efforts to maintain the country's neutrality in the face of use of Cambodian territory by Viet Cong and North Vietnamese forces seeking to escape U.S. fire power in the fighting in neighboring South Vietnam. Cambodian military authorities had charged that although he made speeches condemning the Vietnamese Communists, he had pressured the military to release all Viet Cong captured by Cambodian soldiers. Lon Nol was said to have insisted on a tougher stand against the Viet Cong. In National Assembly speeches March 18, several legislators accused Sihanouk of supplying arms to the Viet Cong.

The strategic base of Sam Thong, 10 miles north of Long Tieng, was captured by the North Vietnamese March 18 but retaken by Laotian government forces March 30. All 200 Americans at Sam Thong and more than 2,000 Meo tribesmen and Laotian peasants had been flown out March 17 before the North Vietnamese launched their assault in the area.

After the recapture of Sam Thong, the counterattacking Laotian force continued to strike at North Vietnamese troops April 1 with aircraft and artillery beyond a ridge of hills north of Sam Thong. An estimated 20–30 of the enemy were reported killed. Returning troops found Sam Thong virtually destroyed by the fighting that had raged around it for two weeks.

The recapture of Sam Thong and the pounding of Communist forces around Long Tieng followed a general offensive launched by Laotian forces. Assisted by U.S. bombers, the government troops were reported March 27 to have captured Phou Pa Sai, 10 miles northeast of Long Tieng, clearing North Vietnamese from a ridge they had used for probing attacks against the base.

Sihanouk attributed the "turbulence" in his country to the coup leaders and the U.S. Central Intelligence Agency.

Sihanouk said March 22 that the Soviet Union and Communist China had granted his request to live in exile alternately in Moscow and Peking.

Neutralist policy pledged. Premier Lon Nol and Deputy Premier Sirik Matak assured foreign governments March 19 that Sihanouk's ouster would bring no change in Cambodia's policy of "independence, sovereignty, peace, strict neutrality and territorial integrity."

Further stressing their desire to maintain Cambodia's neutrality, the new leaders March 22 urged Britain and the Soviet Union, co-chairmen of the 1954 Geneva conference, to reactivate the International Control Commission (ICC) in Cambodia to "help put a stop in a peaceful way to the occupation of its national territories" by Viet Cong and North Vietnamese forces. (Sihanouk had ordered the removal of the ICC in 1969 on the ground that Cambodia could not afford the cost of its operations.)

A government communique March 22 said Pnompenh would resume talks with Viet Cong and North Vietnamese representatives in an effort to seek withdrawal of their troops from Cambodia. The discussions, begun March 16, were broken off the same day when the Communist delegations reportedly refused to discuss anything until Cambodia assured compensation for damage committed to their embassies in Pnompenh by anti-Communist demonstrators March 11.

Lon Nol declared in an interview March 23 that his government was determined to recover the nation's "active neutrality" through the peaceful removal of the Viet Cong and North Vietnamese troops. Lon Nol denied charges that the U.S. Central Intelligence Agency had been behind Sihanouk's ouster. "We have never had any contacts with any foreigners, not only the CIA, but with no other foreigners either," he said. Cambodia, Lon Nol insisted, adhered to the Geneva agreement, which "specifies we are simply neutral." Sihanouk's "tendency not to respect" this neutrality was the root cause of his ouster, the premier asserted.

Cambodia's new chief of state, Cheng Heng, accused Sihanouk March 24 of "absolute despotism." At the same time, he vowed that his government would "accomplish the total evacuation of our territory of Viet Cong and North Vietnamese" troops. Cheng Heng spoke at the 15th anniversary meeting of Sangkum, the political movement founded by Sihanouk. The meeting elected a new central committee, which in turn chose National Assembly President In Tam as president of the Sangkum. In Tam had been instrumental March 18 in pushing through a resolution in a joint session of the National Assembly ousting Sihanouk.

North Vietnam and the Viet Cong informed the new government March 25 of their decision to withdraw all their diplomats from Cambodia. The step, just short of a break in diplomatic relations, was disclosed by Cambodian First Deputy Premier Sisowath Sirik Matek. The Communist aides left the country and returned to Hanoi March 28.

Foreign reaction. North Vietnam and the Viet Cong accused the U.S. of instigating the coup against Prince Sihanouk and pledged support to the deposed Cambodian chief of state.

A statement broadcast by Radio Hanoi March 21 said the uprising was "the end result of a process of sabotage, subversion and aggressive activities carried out by the U.S imperialists against the independence and the policy of peace and neutrality" in Cambodia.

North Vietnam's backing of Sihanouk was broadcast March 22. The statement said "we are determined to support the just struggle that Sihanouk and the Cambodian people are waging" against the new government in Pnompenh.

The Soviet Communist Party newspaper Pravda March 22 attributed the crisis in Cambodia to "military fever born of American aggression."

Prince Souphanouvong, leader of the pro-Communist Pathet Lao rebels in Laos, expressed support for Sihanouk March 24.

South Vietnamese support of the new government of Cambodia was expressed March 24 by Vice President Nguyen Cao Ky in a note to Cheng Heng, interim chief of state. Ky said he hoped the two countries would cooperate closely in their struggle against the Communists.

The U.S. continued to recognize Cambodia despite Sihanouk's ouster, the State Department said March 19. "Our position is that the question of recognition does not arise" department spokesman Carl A. Bartch said.

Pre-coup developments. U.S. fighter-bombers had attacked Communist gun positions inside Cambodia Feb. 11 after an American observation helicopter, flying over South Vietnamese territory, was downed by groundfire from inside Cambodia. Two crewmen were missing after their craft apparently fell inside Cambodia. In reporting the incident, the U.S. command reiterated American policy, which stated that "when fired upon from enemy positions outside" South Vietnam, "U.S. forces are authorized to return fire. This is an inherent right of self-defense."

The State Department reported Feb. 20 that the U.S. had formally apologized to Cambodia and had paid $11,400 in compensation for the 35 Cambodians killed or wounded in a U.S. air attack on Viet Cong artillery positions in Cambodia Nov. 16–17, 1969. The targets were near a Cambodian army post. In a note delivered to the Cambodian government, U.S. Charge d'Affaires Lloyd M. Rives also appealed to Cambodia to prevent the use of its territory by Viet Cong and North Vietnamese forces.

Cambodia Feb. 28 released five U.S. Navy men who had been captured Feb. 5 when their gunboat strayed into Cambodian territory while on a Mekong River patrol. The men were turned over to the U.S. embassy at Pnompenh and then flown to Bangkok, Thailand. Their release had been negotiated by U.S. and Cambodian officials since their seizure.

The U.S. command reported March 5 that American planes had bombed Communist gun positions in Cambodia March 3 following the shelling of the South Vietnamese district town of Hatien, 150 miles west of Saigon. The command communique said "the enemy fire was suppressed."

(A Cambodian army spokesman said March 13 that there had been 164 skirmishes between Cambodian border forces and the Viet Cong since Jan. 1. The latest incident was said to have occurred March 13 when Cambodian troops fought briefly with 300 Viet Cong in Soarieng Province, forcing the infiltrators back into South Vietnam. No casualties were reported.)

U.S arms ship seized. A 7,500-ton U.S. freighter (Columbia Eagle) bound for Sattahip, Thailand with munitions for the U.S. Air Force was seized by two armed crewmen March 14 in the Gulf of Siam and was forced to sail to Cambodian waters. The mutiny was described as a protest against the U.S. war effort in Vietnam.

Twenty-four of the ship's 39 crewmen, set adrift in two lifeboats, were picked up by another American munitions ship enroute to Sattahip. The Columbia Eagle anchored near a small island five miles from the Cambodian port of Sihanoukville. The Cambodian government advised the U.S. March 16 that it planned to grant political asylum to the two mutineers, identified as Clyde W. McKay Jr., 25, of Escondido, Calif. and Alvin Glatkowski, 20, of Long Beach, Calif. The U.S. requested Cambodia to return the ship, its cargo and 13 crewmen to American jurisdiction, including the captain, Donald A. Swann, 51, of Portland, Ore.

As the Columbia Eagle sailed into Cambodian waters, the U.S. Coast Guard cutter Mellon followed it after receiving a message from the radio officer that armed men were seizing the ship. The Mellon was ordered March 15 to bring the freighter out by force. The order, issued by Adm. John Hyland, commander of the Pacific Fleet, was rescinded within minutes, however, by Adm. John S. McCain, Commander in Chief, Pacific. The U.S. State Department disclosed March 17 that the recapture of the vessel was a "contingency" plan "among a number of other options." Five U.S. ships were off Sihanoukville in international waters and were to remain there to offer "contingency assistance," the State Department said.

In a radio message sent from his ship March 16, Capt. Swann said he had been warned by McKay and Glatkowski that "this was the first in a series of such mutinies" aimed to "impede the war effort in Vietnam."

Sen. Mark O. Hatfield (R, Ore.) said Defense Department officials had told him that Navy authorities concluded that the capture of the Columbia Eagle was an antiwar protest.

According to government officials, the Defense Department had failed to inform the White House and the State Department of the incident for nearly 24 hours. Although U.S. authorities had not issued an official report of the ship's seizure, crewmen aboard the freighter that picked up the 24 Columbia Eagle crewmen provided this account:

While steaming up the Gulf of Siam, 100 miles off Cambodia, Capt. Swann, under threat by a gunman, ordered the ship abandoned because of an impending bomb explosion. The gunman told Swann that he was taking the ship to neutralist Cambodia to ask for political asylum and would blow up the vessel if the asylum request were refused. The 24 crewmen, some thinking that a boat drill was in progress, were hustled into two lifeboats, which were ordered cast off after they were lowered. The Columbia Eagle was then diverted and headed for Cambodia with the remaining crewmen aboard.

Premier Lon Nol said in a March 23 interview that Cambodia would not return the Columbia Eagle. There would be "a risk of misunderstanding" in releasing the vessel, so "we are just going to leave it here," he said.

But Cambodia released the ship April 8. It arrived in Subic Bay, the Philippines April 13 with the remaining crew of 13 and a cargo of aerial bombs and napalm that originally had been destined for U.S. Air Force units in Thailand. (The London Times reported the ship was loaded with 10,000 tons of napalm; the New York Times placed the figure at 1,750 tons.) U.S.-Cambodian agreement on release of the vessel had been announced by the State Department March 31.

McKay had said in an interview March 25 that he and his companion were supporters of the militant Students for a Democratic Society in the U.S. and that their seizure of the ship was "an SDS plot more than anything else." McKay, who was opposed to the Vietnam war, said he and Glatkowski were not SDS members, but "we support the groups we believe in if we hold similar ideas and have common enemies."

Cambodia demands Red withdrawal. Cambodia opened talks March 16 with Viet Cong and North Vietnamese representatives to press its demands for the removal of an estimated 40,000–60,000 Communist troops using Cambodian border areas for operations against U.S. and South Vietnamese forces in neighboring South Vietnam. The Communist delegates in turn demanded compensation for the damage done to their embassies in Pnompenh March 11 by 20,000 Cambodians demonstrating against the presence of North Vietnamese and Viet Cong troops in their country.

The meeting, held at an undisclosed location in Cambodia, had been proposed by Hanoi March 14 following the March 11 demonstrations and similar outbursts in Pnompenh March 12–13. The Viet Cong and North Vietnamese embassies were sacked and burned by the rioters. The demonstrators rampaged through Pnompenh's streets the following two days, attacking Vietnamese shops and homes. (An estimated 500,000 Vietnamese lived in Cambodia.) The violent disturbances had been preceded by an anti-Communist demonstration March 7 in Svyarieng Province bordering South Vietnam.

The attack on the embassies was followed by Cambodian notes of apology March 12 and a demand that the Viet Cong and North Vietnamese troops be withdrawn from the country by March 15. The notes, issued by Premier Lon Nol, asserted that the presence of these forces and their continued infiltration into the country were "contrary to the vital interests of the Cambodian people." The notes fell short of an ultimatum since Cambodia did not back up its demands with a threat of force. The March 15 deadline passed with no apparent exodus of the Communist troops.

Allies aid Cambodia vs. Reds. Two days after Sihanouk's ouster, Cambodian troops March 20 battled Viet Cong soldiers for two hours inside Cambodia with the aid of an American spotter plane and South Vietnamese artillery inside South Vietnam. The action marked the first coordinated allied-Cambodian effort against Communist forces and represented the most determined Cambodian drive to clear the border areas of Viet Cong.

The fighting erupted when a 150-man Viet Cong company attacked a Cambodian outpost about 10 miles north of the South Vietnamese district capital of Anphu in Chaudoc Province. South Vietnamese howitzers at Anphu fired on the Communist attackers after receiving a radioed request for aid from the Cambodian commander. The shelling forced the Viet Cong to withdraw. The Cambodian commander later requested allied aerial observation as his troops were about to make a sweep of the area in search of the enemy force. A U.S. spotter plane sighted enemy movement and the Anphu howitzers shelled the area again at the Cambodians' request.

Allied involvement in the fighting with the Cambodians followed reports that South Vietnamese district officials in Chaudoc Province had been instructed March 18 by Col. Tran Van Hue, province chief, to provide all possible aid to the Cambodians short of troops in operations against Communist forces. The U.S. command in Saigon March 19 directed its military advisers in the border districts to attempt to establish radio communications with Cambodian commanders on the opposite side of the frontier. Maj. Gen. Nguyen Viet Thanh, commander of the IV Corps, which took in Chaudoc Province, had authorized his commanders earlier March 20 to provide forward artillery spotters for the Cambodians if they requested it.

War involvement increases. Cambodia became increasingly involved in the Vietnam war as South Vietnamese troops and U.S. planes, with Pnompenh's acquiescence, stepped up their ground and air attacks on Viet Cong and North Vietnamese forces operating in Cambodia border areas March 20–28. Saigon and Washington officially denied involvement of their forces inside Cambodia. Cambodia's shaky neutrality was seen further imperiled by a Pnompenh government report March 29 that the Vietnamese Communists were pressing their military activity against Cambodian troops and moving deeper into its territory. In view of this, Cambodia called on U.N. Secretary General U Thant March 30 to use his influence to have the Communist troops withdrawn from the country.

Among the major developments in the Cambodian crisis:

Allied attacks in Cambodia—South Vietnamese fighter-bombers March 20 and 23 attacked Communist positions a few miles inside Cambodia across from Anphu district in Chaudoc Province, Saigon sources reported March 25. Both air strikes were said to have been requested by the Cambodian area commander in meetings with the Anphu district chief, Lt. Col. Truong Dinh Chat. South Vietnamese howitzers in Anphu were reported to have provided close combat support for Cambodian units on at least four occasions since March 16.

U.S. fighter-bombers attacked North Vietnamese gun positions in Cambodia March 24 after they had fired on South Vietnamese rangers operating in the northern part of South Vietnam's Plain of Reeds, about 65 miles west of Saigon. A U.S. command spokesman said the attack was the fifth air strike in Cambodia since Jan. 1 by American forces in exercise of their "inherent right of self-defense." The government operation in the Plain of Reeds March 19-25 had resulted in the deaths of 152 enemy and 30 South Vietnamese troops.

South Vietnamese troops carried out their first major ground operation in Cambodia March 27-28. A ranger battalion, supported by artillery and advance air strikes, penetrated two miles into Kandal Province in a sweep of a known Viet Cong sanctuary March 27. U.S. helicopter gunships supported the assault, attacking targets inside Cambodia. One U.S. observer 'copter was hit by antiaircraft but landed safely in South Vietnam. The South Vietnamese killed 53 of a force of 300 enemy troops. Three rangers were reported killed. The engagement was fought 10 miles northeast of Anphu. The battle strategy was said to have been planned in meetings March 23 between Col. Chat and Cambodian military commanders.

Government rangers crossed into Cambodia again March 28 in an attempt to trap two Viet Cong battalions on the edge of Paknam Forest in Kandal Province. American helicopters supported the

operation but remained over South Vietnam. Two battalions of Cambodian troops were said to have served as a blocking force to prevent the Viet Cong from escaping north, but did not actually engage in the fighting.

U.S. authorities in Washington said March 27 that American air support of the South Vietnamese operation in Cambodia that day had occurred without their prior knowledge or consent. The officials reaffirmed the U.S. policy of not widening the war in Vietnam and said that incursions or firing into Cambodia would continue to be carried out for self-defense purposes. These rules had been reiterated to South Vietnamese authorities, the officials said.

South Vietnamese and U.S. military authorities in Saigon March 28 flatly denied participation of their forces in Cambodia the previous day. An unnamed ranking South Vietnamese officer, however, confirmed the operation. "This involves delicate diplomatic matters between our country and Cambodia, so officially, we cannot admit it," he said.

U.S. sources in Saigon said March 28 that American advisers and commanders had been given a classified directive the previous week, telling them not to participate in any ground crossings into Cambodia planned by South Vietnam. But the directive did not prohibit the Americans from taking part in actually planning such operations.

Col. Ernest Terrell Jr., the senior American adviser in Kintuong Province, accompanying South Vietnamese officers, met inside Cambodia March 28 with a Cambodian commander. The meeting took place a few miles from the South Vietnamese frontier, six miles north of the provincial capital of Moc Hoa. Terrell said he was under orders "to encourage meetings between Vietnamese and Cambodians."

A White House statement March 28 said the U.S. government was "not aware" of American ground incursions into Cambodia and could not confirm whether U.S. helicopter gunships had flown into that country. American forces were permitted to cross into Cambodia in response to enemy threats, at the discretion of field commanders, the statement said. Press Secretary Ronald

Ziegler said this policy was only a restatement of previous Defense Department rulings already in force along the border.

Cambodian Premier Lon Nol denied March 30 that South Vietnamese, U.S. and Cambodian officers had been consulting each other on action against Vietnamese Communist forces in Cambodia.

Cambodia charges Red attacks—A Pnompenh communiqué March 29 charged the Viet Cong with "flagrant violations of Cambodian territory" and listed a series of incidents to support its allegations. The statement said Viet Cong troops had been sighted March 28 near the vital road center of Neak Luong, 40 miles southeast of the capital.

According to the communiqué:

Viet Cong forces March 27 seized two members of the national police force, a paramilitary organization, 12 miles inside Cambodia at Peamchor in Preyveng Province. One man had been released. A "sizable" Communist force the same day attacked a government unit two miles inside the frontier near Prekchrieu in Kratie Province, killing two Cambodians and wounding eight. Six were missing. A 3,000-man Communist force occupied Svayandong, five miles from the border in Preyveng Province, posing a threat to the military post at Preah Shach in the same area. The government post of Ankgen, five miles from the border, was assaulted by a Communist unit which surrounded a government platoon garrisoned there. Other Communist troops were sighted near Tukmeas in the southernmost border province of Kampot, 12 miles inside Cambodia and near Po Tassuy in Takeo Province, about six miles from the frontier.

An accompanying statement issued by Premier Lon Nol appealed to the "Socialist Vietnamese leaders" to halt their attacks. It said: "Why do you want to invade our country? Why are you helping the same Sihanouk whom in your subversive propaganda you used to accuse as a tyrant, a reactionary and a lackey of the imperialists?"

A government statement March 27 charged that the Viet Cong had "implanted their troops on Cambodian soil, that they had indoctrinated, trained

and armed" Cambodian rebels fighting the government, and that at Prince Sihanouk's behest they were increasing their attacks on Cambodian territory.

Lon Nol disclosed March 30 that he had instructed the Cambodian mission to the U.N. to ask the Security Council to send observers to verify Pnompenh's charges of Communist troop incursions into Cambodia. U Thant said after meeting with Or Kosalak, the acting head of the Cambodian delegation, that he would "look into the matter" of the presence of Viet Cong and North Vietnamese troops in Cambodia.

The government disclosed March 31 that it had renewed its appeal to Britain and the Soviet Union, co-chairmen of the 1954 Geneva Conference, to return the International Control Commission (ICC) to Cambodia to investigate Pnompenh's charges of North Vietnamese and Viet Cong military intervention. The appeal had been filed with the British and Soviet embassies March 22. It charged that the Communist troops "not only refused to withdraw from Cambodian territory but now attacked openly Cambodian posts and defense forces inside Cambodia." Britain responded favorably to the Cambodian request and called on the Soviet Union March 26 to cooperate in recalling the ICC to Cambodia.

Meanwhile, Cambodia took mobilization measures to cope with the growing Communist military threat. Reservists and veterans were recalled to military service and all other men between the ages of 18 and 45 were to be called on to volunteer for military duty.

Foreign diplomats in Pnompenh had reported March 25 that the government had closed the port of Sihanoukville to ships carrying arms for the Viet Cong. The port was a vital supply funnel for the Communists in their operations against South Vietnam.

Pro-Sihanouk demonstrations—Violent demonstrations demanding the return of Prince Norodom Sihanouk, allegedly instigated by the Viet Cong, were staged March 26–29 in Cambodian provinces along the South Vietnamese frontier. The most violent of the demonstrations occurred March 26 at **Kompong**

Cham, 35 miles northeast of Pnompenh. Up to 10,000 persons rioted, sacking an official building and destroying documents. Dozens of persons were killed or wounded. Among those slain were two National Assembly deputies. More than a thousand demonstrators were held. After the rioting, the demonstrators commandeered trucks and cars in an attempt to drive on Pnompenh. A 15-vehicle convoy from Kampong Cham was stopped by police on a bridge leading into the capital. Shots were exchanged but no casualties were reported. Another protest column from Siaorieng Province also was halted about 20 miles from Pnompenh.

Many of those arrested in Kompong Cham were Vietnamese. A North Vietnamese protest March 29 charged their seizure was illegal.

Hin Nil, brother of Premier Lon Nol, was stabbed to death March 28 by Vietnamese rubber plantation workers, it was reported March 31. The incident occurred at Hin Nil's home at Chup, near Kompong Cham, scene of violent clashes between Cambodian security forces and pro-Sihanouk demonstrators.

Foreign incursions scored. The Cambodian government April 1 denounced all foreign incursions into its territory—Communist or U.S. and South Vietnamese. The statement, made amid reports of fresh Viet Cong attacks on Cambodian troops, was followed by the third major South Vietnamese ground strike against Communist sanctuaries in Cambodia April 5.

The Pnompenh regime's communique assailed the American policy of "hot pursuit," which permitted U.S. and South Vietnamese forces to cross into Cambodia to attack Communist soldiers. "Faithful to its policy of strict neutrality, Cambodia will not in fact accept the right of pursuit to be exercised on its territory," the communique said. The statement added that the government "intends also to protest against all violations of Cambodian territory by foreign forces, whatever camp they come from."

The U.S. government responded to the Pnompenh communique by stating April 1 that "all governments ought to respect Cambodia's desire for neutrality."

The Pnompenh communique further reported that "several thousand Viet Cong and North Vietnamese" had entered Cambodia March 31 in the Snuol region in Kratie Province and attacked a detachment of Cambodian soldiers, inflicting heavy casualties. Pnompenh filed a complaint with the U.N. Security Council April 1.

Another government communique April 2 told of a "massive attack" the previous night by about 100 Viet Cong soldiers against a civil defense post at Phum Kampo, five miles from the Vietnamese border and 12 miles from the provincial capital of Svayrieng.

The South Vietnamese raid April 5 took place 10 miles inside Cambodia, in an area that jutted into South Vietnam's Tayninh Province, about 40 miles northwest of Saigon. Government troops were airlifted by helicopter and attacked a Communist sanctuary with the support of tanks and planes. The action, involving two battalions of South Vietnamese soldiers, lasted two hours.

South Vietnamese action. The South Vietnamese government continued to deny ground strikes by its forces into Cambodia despite persistent reports to the contrary. Among the major actions reportedly taken by Saigon's troops:

Government troops, supported by armored vehicles and artillery, conducted a sweep against Communist forces inside Cambodia opposite Chaudoc Province in South Vietnam April 9–10. U.S. military advisers were said to have witnessed the operation and participated in its planning from a command post atop a mountain overlooking Cambodia. Allied artillery and helicopter gunships struck suspected Viet Cong and North Vietnamese positions, setting fields afire.

South Vietnamese troops, accompanied by a token force of 100 Cambodians, reportedly pushed at least a mile into Cambodia April 14, destroying a North Vietnamese base and killing 179 of the enemy. The battle, involving 2,000 government troops, was said to have erupted five hours after the North Vietnamese had attacked a nearby South Vietnamese border post and were repulsed. This would be the first instance of Cambodians joining South Vietnamese in a large operation. Heretofore, the Cambodians were reported to have served only as a blocking force in South Vietnamese actions against Communist troops in Cambodia.

Saigon insisted that the battle took place a half mile inside South Vietnam. Government losses were listed as seven killed.

Another South Vietnamese incursion into Cambodia was observed April 16 by CBS correspondent Gary Sheppard. He said he had filmed a line of trucks crossing on the highway connecting Pnompenh and Saigon.

Saigon sources reported April 18 that government troops fighting two operations in Cambodia earlier in the week had smashed two Communist bases, killing 450 enemy soldiers and seizing huge munitions stockpiles. South Vietnamese losses were put at 13 killed and 104 wounded. A government communiqué issued April 18 repeated the assertion that they had taken place in South Vietnam.

Further South Vietnamese ground strikes into Cambodia were said to have occurred April 18 and 20. In the latter incident, 2,000 government soldiers attacked across the border from the western Mekong Delta, about 55 miles west of Saigon, killing 144 North Vietnamese and Viet Cong. Twenty government troops were reported killed. The attackers, supported by bombers and artillery, were said to have driven at least two miles into Svayrieng Province. A Saigon communique April 20 mentioned the action but placed it just inside South Vietnam.

Lon Nol appeals for arms. Premier Lon Nol issued a world appeal for arms April 14 to help government forces combat "an escalation of systematic acts of aggression" launched by Viet Cong and North Vietnamese troops against eastern Cambodia the previous week.

In a broadcast statement, the premier said the Pnompenh government "has the duty to inform the nation that in view of the gravity of the present situation, it finds it necessary to accept all unconditional foreign aid, wherever it may come from, for the salvation of the nation."

The Communist drive was concentrated in Svayrieng Province located in the Parrot's Beak, the southeastern area which jutted into Viet Cong-controlled areas of South Vietnam. The Communists had intensified their activity there since March 18 when Prince Norodom Sihanouk was deposed. Lon Nol's arms plea was spurred by the opening of a new Communist offensive north of the Parrot's Beak. In fighting in that sector April 14, the Viet Cong captured the village of Krek, 10 miles from the Vietnamese border, cutting Highway 7, the main road between Pnompenh and Cambodia's rich plantation area.

Saigon sources had reported April 8 that South Vietnamese forces were cooperating with the Cambodians in the fighting in Svayrieng Province. South Vietnamese helicopter gunships were said to have flown five miles inside Cambodia in the previous 24 hours and killed an estimated 150 Communist troops.

Cambodian forces were reported April 9 to have evacuated the Parrot's Beak following Communist attacks April 6–7 on Chiphou, near the eastern end of Svayrieng Province. About 30,000 civilians also were removed from the area. Most of those remaining were Vietnamese who were not permitted to flee westward. Cambodian government losses in the Chiphou battle were placed at 20 killed, 30 wounded and 30 missing. Communist casualties were listed at 40 dead.

Cambodian troops abandoned Chiphou and the border post of Brevet April 9, withdrawing to Svayrieng town and Prasot to the west. Fighting broke out between Svayrieng and Prasot April 9. It was reported that a government ambush killed 300 Viet Cong soldiers April 10.

The Viet Cong were reported to have seized eight foreign newsmen April 5, 6 and 8 near a Communist roadblock near Chiphou. The correspondents included two Americans, two Japanese and two Frenchmen. The Americans were identified as Sean Flynn, 29, son of the late actor Errol Flynn, and Dana Stone, a free-lance photographer for CBS. U.S. Secretary of State William

P. Rogers called on the Viet Cong April 13 to release all the newsmen.

U.S. weighs arms request. No immediate U.S. reply to Cambodia's request for military aid was forthcoming, but the appeal was given a firm rebuff by the Senate Foreign Relations Committee April 27. After hearing testimony on the Cambodian request in closed session from Secretary of State William P. Rogers, Chairman J. W. Fulbright (D, Ark.) told newsmen that the panel's members were "virtually unanimous" and "very firmly" against "sending any military assistance under the present circumstances alluded to by the secretary." Republican member George D. Aiken (Vt.) expressed hope that the President would give "earnest consideration" to the committee's view.

Rogers reportedly informed the committee that no decision had been made by the Administration concerning the request, which Fulbright said totaled "hundreds of millions of dollars." Rogers also reportedly indicated that the executive branch had the authority to fulfill the request without Congressional assent but, encountering some opposition by the committee to this view, he suggested that the question depended on the amount of aid given.

The argument that the Cambodian situation offered the U.S. an opportunity to shorten the Vietnam war was expressed April 26 by Senate Republican Whip Robert P. Griffin (Mich.). Speaking on the CBS "Face the Nation" broadcast, he said the U.S. would lose the opportunity if it "didn't move at this time" by helping the Cambodians fight "the same enemy that we're fighting in South Vietnam." While he would be "very leery" about sending advisers along with weapons, he said, he did favor "some flexibility" in regard to air strikes. He would back the President 100% if he made "the tough decision to provide limited military assistance to Cambodia," he declared.

Other Senators spoke out against sending Cambodia aid. Sen. Edmund S. Muskie (D, Me.), appearing on NBC's "Issues and Answers" program April 26, called the prospect of further involvement in Cambodia "disquieting." He said the arguments advocating it were

similar to the "measured response" approach that had escalated U.S. involvement in Vietnam under the Johnson Administration.

Plans to introduce legislation to bar the use of U.S. combat forces in Cambodia were announced April 11 by Sens. Frank Church (D, Idaho) and John Sherman Cooper (R, Ky.) and April 23 by Sen. Charles E. Goodell (R, N.Y.).

Premier Lon Nol sent President Nixon a personal appeal April 20 for extensive military equipment. The premier also was said to have urged that Cambodian mercenaries now assisting U.S. Army Special Forces in South Vietnam be sent back to Cambodia to help fight the Communist invaders.

Pnompenh government sources reported April 22 that Indonesia had agreed in principle to provide Cambodia with military aid and that the assistance would be arriving soon. Lon Nol was said to be negotiating the matter with Indonesian representatives.

A Cambodian letter of complaint filed with the U.N. Security Council April 22 contained a renewed appeal "to all countries which love peace and justice" to aid Cambodia in stemming the Communist invasion. The letter charged that Communist forces in Cambodia "were supported by local Vietnamese inhabitants."

Pnompenh gets 'Saigon' arms. A shipment of several thousand rifles and ammunition captured from Communist forces in South Vietnam were flown to Cambodia April 23. The weapons, AK-47 automatic rifles of Soviet design and Chinese manufacture, were sent in response to an urgent Cambodian appeal to the U.S. and other countries for arms assistance against the invading Communist forces. The equipment reportedly arrived in three cargo planes at Pnompenh.

The U.S. and the Pnompenh regime of Premier Lon Nol confirmed the arms shipment April 23 and 24. A White House statement said the weapons were being supplied to Cambodia by South Vietnam "with our knowledge and approval." The American decision to send the guns had been transmitted by Washington April 17 to Lloyd M. Rives, the U.S. charge d'affaires in Pnompenh. But Rives had been instructed to warm Pnompenh officials against "inflated expectation" of further military assistance. Washington's message was said to have expressed American readiness to ship 1,500 AK-47 rifles immediately and 4,000 to 5,000 more within two or three weeks.

Communists advance on Pnompenh. Vietnamese Communist forces continued to press their advance into Cambodia and by April 20 reached within 15 miles of the capital of Pnompenh. Meanwhile, South Vietnamese troops carried out major thrusts into Cambodia April 9–20 to strike at Viet Cong and North Vietnamese forces along the Vietnamese frontier. One of the operations was conducted jointly with Cambodian troops. Success of the Communist drive was evidenced by a Cambodian military spokesman's admission April 17 that the Viet Cong were in virtual control of three Cambodian provinces.

The Communist threat to Pnompenh was heightened with the capture April 19 of Saang, 15 miles south of the capital. The village was occupied after Cambodian troops had abandoned it. Cambodian reinforcements established a defensive line just north of Saang. The Communists' action directly south of Pnompenh represented a shift from their previous area of major operations in the southeast sector in the Parrot's Beak.

In other military action, a Pnompenh official reported April 19 that the Communists had blown up railroad tracks south of Takeo, about 50 miles south of the capital. Communist troops had raided Takeo April 15 but were repulsed with a loss of six killed, a military spokesman reported the following day. Enemy soldiers also were said to have raided the town of Mareng, south of Pnompenh, and kidnaped a district chief, his deputy and eight militiamen.

The Cambodian areas reported April 17 to be under Viet Cong control were the provinces of Ratankiri and Mondulkiri in the northeast and Svayrieng in the Parrot's Beak to the south. The Pnompenh spokesman said five more of the country's 17 provinces were half occupied by the Communist forces— Kompot, Kandal, Preyveng, Takeo and Kompong Cham.

Vietnamese civilians massacred. The bodies of hundreds of Vietnamese civilian residents of Cambodia, suspected victims of a mass killing, floated down the Mekong River in the southeastern part of the country April 11–17. Another 100 Vietnamese civilians were reported slain in a Cambodian government compound in Takeo April 16.

The first bodies were sighted on the Mekong April 11 at a ferry landing at Neak Leung, 36 miles southeast of Pnompenh. A police official at Neak Leung reported counting 400 bodies April 15. Other sources said as many as 1,000 bodies had been seen in the river. Most of the victims were men. Many had their hands tied behind their backs.

A Reuters dispatch April 17 quoted witnesses as saying that the Vietnamese had been shot to death on Tachhor, a small island in the Mekong four miles upstream from Neak Leung. According to the witnesses, farmers and fishermen nearby, the shootings had started on the island April 10 after the arrival from the direction of Pnompenh of a passenger boat containing about 100 Cambodians and Vietnamese escorted by Cambodian soldiers. The disembarkation from boats followed by the shooting of the civilians continued for five successive nights, the reports said.

The Cambodian Information Ministry said April 14 that the killings were "not the result of collective assassination perpetrated by Cambodian armed forces." The ministry said the civilians had been caught inside their detention camp "between the firing of the Viet Cong invaders and the Cambodian forces defending" the village of Prasot. The statement noted that the Viet Cong had frequently "used Vietnamese residents of Cambodia as auxiliaries of their aggression."

The incident described apparently had taken place April 10 when Prasot came under Communist attack. Cambodian sources said 89 Vietnamese civilians caught in the crossfire of battle were killed. Other sources placed the death toll between 90 and 100. The victims, including women and children, were in a barbed-wire compound where they had been placed by Cambodian authorities April 8 as suspected Viet Cong sympathizers. ABC correspondent Steve Bell quoted refugees as saying that the Cambodian soldiers had told the

Vietnamese to run when the Viet Cong approached, then opened fire. Cambodian artillery in Svayrieng pounded the Viet Cong and prevented them from overrunning Prasot.

The Associated Press reported April 15 that according to available evidence, the Prasot killings had been perpetrated by Cambodian troops. At least seven more Vietnamese were shot to death by Cambodian troops April 11 just south of Kompong Trabek, near the border west of Prasot.

In the incident at Takeo, about 150 Vietnamese civilians, herded under detention in a school building April 13, came under fire by Cambodian soldiers April 16. About 100, including perhaps 30 children, were killed. The account of the slaughter was related to foreign newsmen who visited the scene April 17 by some of the 50 survivors. The survivors said they had given no provocation and did not know why the shootings took place. Soldiers on guard at the school, who did not contradict the account of the slayings, indicated that the killings were in reprisal for a Viet Cong attack on Takeo April 15.

Information Minister Trinh Heanh reiterated April 16 that the corpses sighted in the Mekong River "were victims of a battle" between the Viet Cong and Cambodian troops. He said the dead included Cambodians and Vietnamese civilians who had been thrown into the river by the Viet Cong after the fighting.

An apparent contradiction of the government's version of the incident was contained in a statement issued April 16 by Lt. Col. Kim Eng Kouroudeth, chief of army intelligence. He assumed that the victims might have been slain by Cambodian civilians aroused by the alleged collusion between Vietnamese residents of Cambodia and the Viet Cong and North Vietnamese forces that invaded the country. Kim said he had ordered an investigation.

A U.S. government statement April 17 said "we consider the massacre of innocent civilians to be abhorrent and to be actions that warrant condemnation."

The South Vietnamese government had said April 15 that it was asking the Pnompenh government to permit a "people's delegation" from charitable agencies to enter Cambodia to investigate the alleged massacre of Vietnamese civilians.

South Vietnamese Foreign Minister Tran Van Lam told a news conference April 17 that his government was asking Pnompenh to receive an official mission to arrange for the repatriation of 50,000 Vietnamese. Lam said 1,467 Vietnamese refugees had been registered by South Vietnamese border officials since March 18. He said several times that number had probably crossed into South Vietnam without authorization. Cambodian authorities April 10 had cut off the flow of Vietnamese refugees into South Vietnam. A 6 p.m.-to-6 a.m. curfew was imposed on Pnompenh's 120,000 Vietnamese residents April 11. The action was taken to curb an increase in "subversive activities," government authorities said.

In fighting for the village of Saang, which the Viet Cong had seized, Cambodian troops April 21 had forced Vietnamese civilians to march through the village and thus to draw gunfire from the entrenched Viet Cong. At least two of the Vietnamese were reported wounded and 10 were missing. The commander in the area, Gen. Sosthene Fernandez, told newsmen the move "was a good way to discover where the Viets have their automatic weapons. This exercise now gave us a good reading for our 105-mm. cannon." Sosthene Fernandez said April 22 that the plan was conceived by Premier Lon Nol.

Cambodian officers said the Vietnamese had volunteered for the mission. But a member of the march said the civilians had been rounded up in four villages and were brought to Saang by truck.

The Pnopmpenh government reportedly had been fomenting a campaign against both the Vietnamese residents of Cambodia and the Vietnamese Communist invaders since the ouster of Prince Norodom Sihanouk March 18. The Cambodians and the Annamese of Vietnam had been traditional enemies. Government planes April 11 had dropped leaflets on Pnompenh recalling a historic massacre "when the Khmers [Cambodians] once rose up and killed all Annamites on Cambodian territory in one night."

A Cambodian government statement April 19 denied a campaign was in progress against Vietnamese civilians in the country. It said the drive was directed only at Viet Cong and North Vietnamese invaders and not "against the peaceful Vietnamese . . . as long as they do not seek to trouble public order."

Vietnamese safety pledged. Cambodia assured Saigon April 27 that it would take all measures necessary to protect the lives of Vietnamese civilians residing in the country. The pledge followed widespread reports of a Cambodian massacre of hundreds of Vietnamese civilians. The assurances of safety were given to South Vietnamese Foreign Ministry official Pham Huy Ty in talks with Cambodian Foreign Minister Yem Sambaur in Pnompenh.

Yem Sambaur attributed these "horrible crimes" to Viet Cong forces and said that Cambodian officials were victims of the atrocities as well. Ty said the foreign minister also had responded favorably to Saigon's proposal to repatriate to South Vietnam any of the Vietnamese who wished to leave. More than 200 refugees arrived in Saigon April 27 at the start of an organized airlift. Another group of refugees had flown to Saigon April 26 aboard a plane carrying a five-man South Vietnamese delegation that had discussed the repatriation plan that day with Cambodian officials in Pnompenh.

Cambodia had agreed April 23 to receive the delegation following two weeks of discussion with the South Vietnamese government. The negotiations had been assisted by Australians and Japanese.

Saigon's evacuation plan had been disclosed April 17 by Foreign Minister Tran Van Lam. Lam said the proposal had been prompted by "a situation of panic" among the Vietnamese in Cambodia.

Commenting on the alleged massacre, Premier Lon Nol had expressed regret April 20, but he said it was difficult to distinguish between Vietnamese citizens who were Viet Cong and those who were peaceful. Lon Nol charged April 23 that Vietnamese civilians had fired on Cambodian troops. "So it is quite normal that the reaction of Cambodian troops, who feel themselves betrayed, is difficult to control," he said.

The South Vietnamese House of Representatives April 20 appealed to "all nations in the world and all international organizations" to intervene to protect the lives of Vietnamese resident in Cambodia. The French government was specifically urged to have Cambodia "prevent renewed massacres of Vietnamese" in a plea made by Pham Dang Lam, head of the Saigon delegation to the Paris peace talks.

Saang recaptured. Cambodian soldiers recaptured Saang April 23. The village, 15 miles south of Phompenh, had been abandoned by the Viet Cong.

In the counterattack aimed at recapturing Saang, Cambodian forces April 20 had strafed enemy troops along the Bassac River with U.S.-made T-28 aircraft.

Major action shifted to Angtassom, 35 miles south of Pnompenh, where Vietnamese Communist forces fought their way into the center of the town April 24 after two days of heavy clashes. Cambodia claimed April 26 that its forces had counterattacked and recaptured the village following fierce hand-to-hand fighting. Four government battalions were said to have pushed the Viet Cong about a half a mile to the south. Newsmen, however, reported that Viet Cong still occupied the roads leading into Angtassom. A Communist roadblock had been set up April 24 about 500 yards north of the village, cutting off Pnompenh from Kampot, a port on the south coast. The government reversed itself April 27, admitting that its forces had not cleared Communist troops from Angtassom.

In other military activity south of Pnompenh, the Viet Cong reportedly occupied the district capital of Tani, several miles south of Angtassom April 26 and set up an administration there. The provincial capital of Takeo, six miles south of Angtassom, continued to come under Communist harassment and was struck by recoilless rifle fire April 25. Communist forces April 24 staged a terrorist raid on Kep, a coastal resort town, setting several buildings afire and killing three civilians. The raid was carried out from Communist-held offshore-islands.

About 5,000 South Vietnamese troops were reported to have crossed back into South Vietnam April 24 following a four-day operation against Communist forces about two miles inside Cambodia. The drive, which had been launched from the Mekong Delta west of Saigon, was reported to have resulted in the killing of 245 North Vietnamese and Viet Cong. Saigon's losses were said to have totaled 28 dead and 127 wounded.

The Pnompenh government was reported April 24 to have requested U.S. military commanders to send B-52 bombers to attack a Viet Cong headquarters at Mimot, about 100 miles northeast of Pnompenh. State Department officials in Washington said April 25 no such request had been received.

Brig. Gen. Srey Saman, Cambodian army chief of staff, said April 24 that "about 3,500" Cambodians had been killed, wounded or had "disappeared" in a month of fighting the Vietnamese Communists. Srey issued the statement in Paris where he had completed two days of talks with Cambodian ambassadors from Europe, Africa and the Americas.

(A White House statement April 24 had labeled the presence of Viet Cong and North Vietnamese troops in Cambodia "a foreign invasion of a neutral country.")

Sihanouk initiates talks. A high-level meeting of Communist leaders from North and South Vietnam and Laos was held at a secret site April 24–25 on the initiative of Prince Norodom Sihanouk, deposed Cambodian chief of state. The conferees pledged cooperation in their' struggle against U.S. and other forces that opposed them in Indochina.

The meeting was disclosed by Hanoi radio April 27. It said it was held "in a locality of the Lao-Vietnam-China area." Sihanouk headed a delegation of seven. The other delegations were led by Premier Pham Van Dong of North Vietnam, Prince Souphanouvong, head of the pro-Communist Pathet Lao of Laos, and Nguyen Huu Tho, president of the Presidium of the Central Committee of the South Vietnamese National Liberation Front.

A declaration adopted by the parley assailed the U.S. as an "imperialist aggressor" determined to prolong and widen the war in Indochina. It called on the people of Vietnam, Cambodia and Laos to "step up the fight against the common enemy—American imperialism and its lackeys in the three countries—until total victory." The text of the declaration, released by Hsinhua, the Chinese Communist News agency, "condemned all attempts by the United States, its agents and other Asian reactionaries to misuse the name of the United Nations or any organization or any international or Asian conference to legitimize the illegal power of the Lon Nol-Sirik Matek reactionaries and interfere in Combodia." (Sirik Matek was Combodian first deputy premier.)

Communist China played a major role in the meeting, according to official reports from Peking and Hanoi April 30. Premier Chou En-lai flew from Peking to the conference site April 25 to give a banquet for the delegates. In a speech at the dinner, Chou had assailed the "U.S. imperialists" for believing that the Cambodian rightists who had deposed Prince Norodom Sihanouk could "place Cambodia under their sway and thwart the resistance of the Vietnamese people and thereby materialize their foolish ambition of occupying Indochina as a whole." Chou pledged that China would "fight shoulder to shoulder" with "the three fraternal Indochinese people" and "win victory together."

Soviet Premier Aleksei N. Kosygin endorsed the aims of the conference in a message sent to the participants April 29. Kosygin expressed confidence that the parley would bring about "a further strengthening of the united anti-imperialist front of the peoples of Indochina. . . ."

U.S.-South Vietnamese Offensive in Cambodia

American and South Vietnamese forces began a powerful drive April 29–May 1 against what were described as North Vietnamese and Viet Cong sanctuaries in Cambodia. The operation provoked wide international criticism and a massive outpouring of dissent in the U.S. After two months of fighting in Cambodia, the U.S. ground troops were all withdrawn as promised, but some South Vietnamese ground forces continued operations in Cambodia, and U.S. combat air assistance to Cambodian forces was also reported.

Nixon announces U.S. move. President Nixon April 30 announced a major U.S. troop offensive into Cambodia to clear out sanctuaries utilized by North Vietnamese and Viet Cong forces in waging the war in South Vietnam. The thrust, which was under way as the President addressed the nation on television, involved several thousand American soldiers in the Fishhook area of Cambodia 50 miles northwest of Saigon. Nixon called the area a "key control center" for the enemy and its "headquarters for the entire Communist military operation in South Vietnam."

(White House sources said April 30 they expected the operation to be concluded in six to eight weeks.)

The U.S. attack, he said, was "not an invasion of Cambodia" since the areas were "completely occupied and controlled by North Vietnamese forces."

The U.S. purpose, he continued, was not to occupy the areas. Once the enemy was driven out and his military supplies destroyed, Nixon said, "we will withdraw." "We take this action not for the purpose of expanding the war into Cambodia, but for the purpose of ending the war in Vietnam."

Nixon said the move was taken "to protect our men who are in Vietnam and to guarantee the continued success of our withdrawal and Vietnamization program." Within the last 10 days, Nixon said, the enemy had taken actions that "clearly endanger the lives of Americans who are in Vietnam now and would constitute an unacceptable risk to those who will be there after withdrawal of another 150,000." "I shall meet my responsibility as commander in chief of our armed forces to take the action I consider necessary to defend the security of our American men," he declared.

Because of the increased enemy activity in Cambodia, Nixon said, Cambodia could "become a vast enemy staging area and a springboard for attacks on South Vietnam."

Faced with this, he said, the U.S. had three options: It could "do nothing," which would "gravely" threaten the lives of U.S. forces remaining in Vietnam after withdrawal of the 150,000 and possibly confront the U.S. and South Vietnam in the area with "an untenable military position." Or it could provide massive military assistance to Cambodia. But this "could not be rapidly and effectively utilized" by the small Cambodian Army. The President said the U.S. would "do our best to provide the small arms and other equipment" needed by Cambodia for its defense, but the aid "will be limited for the purpose of enabling Cambodia to defend its neutrality and not for the purpose of making it an active belligerent on one side or the other."

Nixon rejected these two options. The third, he said, "is to go to the heart of the trouble" and "means cleaning out major North Vietnamese- and Viet Cong-occupied territories" serving as bases for enemy attacks on Cambodia and South Vietnam.

Nixon spoke of two allied thrusts into Cambodia. One was an "exclusively South Vietnamese ground" operation into the Parrot's Beak area only 33 miles from Saigon, with the U.S. providing air

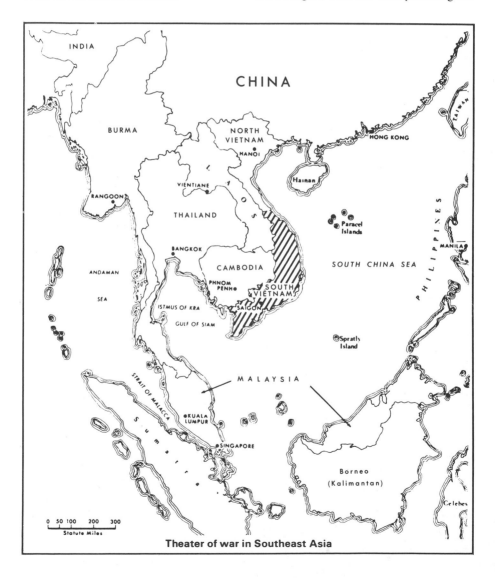

Theater of war in Southeast Asia

and logistical support. The second was the Fishhook operation assisted by South Vietnamese units.

(The Parrot's Beak operation had been announced April 29 by the South Vietnam Defense Ministry in Saigon and confirmed by U.S. Assistant Defense Secretary Daniel Z. Henkin, and then by a White House press spokesman.)

Citing past U.S. efforts to end the war through negotiation, Nixon said "the answer of the enemy has been intransigence at the conference table, belligerence at Hanoi, massive military aggression in Laos and Cambodia and stepped-up attacks in South Vietnam designed to increase American casualties. . . . We will not react to this threat to American lives merely by plaintive diplomatic protests. If we did, credibility of the United States would be destroyed in every area of the world where only the power of the United States deters aggression."

The U.S. would be "patient in working for peace" and "conciliatory at the conference table," he said, "but we will not be humiliated. We will not be defeated. We will not allow American men by the thousands to be killed by an enemy from privileged sanctuary."

The President observed: "We live in an age of anarchy, both abroad and at home. We see mindless attacks on all the great institutions which have been created by free civilizations in the last 500 years. Even here in the United States, great universities are being systematically destroyed.

"Small nations all over the world find themselves under attack from within and from without. If when the chips are down, the world's most powerful nation . . . [the U.S.] acts like a pitiful, helpless giant, the forces of totalitarianism and anarchy will threaten free nations and free institutions throughout the world. . . . If we fail to meet this challenge all other nations will be on notice that despite its overwhelming power the United States when a real crisis comes will be found wanting."

Nixon also mentioned the "political consequences" of his decision, noting a Republican senator's [George D. Aiken of Vermont] comment that it meant "that my party has lost all chance

of winning the November elections" and comments by "others" that the action would "make me a one-term President." But he "rejected all political considerations in making this decision," Nixon said. Whether he was a one-term president was "insignificant." "I would rather be a one-term president and do what I believe was right than to be a two-term president at the cost of seeing America become a second-rate power and to see this nation accept the first defeat in its proud 190-year history."

Lon Nol on U.S. moves. Cambodian Premier Lon Nol said May 1 that the U.S. and South Vietnam had not given him prior notice of their plans to invade his country to attack Communist sanctuaries. He was first informed of the attack by U.S. Charge d'Affaires Lloyd M. Rives, who brought him the text of the President Nixon's speech announcing the incursion. Lon Nol called the operation a violation of Cambodia's territorial integrity. He said he would have preferred that "our friends give us the arms to do the operation ourselves."

Lon Nol eased his position on the allied attack May 2, saying that the operations represented a positive response to Cambodia's request for military aid. Visiting Philippines Sen. Benigno Aquino Jr., who interviewed Lon Nol, said that although the premier did not approve the American intervention, he did not criticize the action. Lon Nol said the number of Communist forces in Cambodia now totaled 150,000 compared with 50,000 previously cited.

Allied troops begin drive. The offensive in Cambodia began April 28 and May 1 with a two-pronged drive by more than 20,000 U.S. and South Vietnamese troops.

The drive against North Vietnamese and Viet Cong bases in the eastern border regions of Cambodia concentrated in the Parrot's Beak that jutted into South Vietnam, about 33 miles from Saigon, and the Fishhook area, about 70 miles north of the South Vietnamese capital along Binhlong Province. By May 4 neither force was reported to have made any substantial contact with the enemy. Cambodian residents in both areas reported that thousands of Communist soldiers had fled to the west before the invasion began. Allied forces in both missions uncovered large caches of small arms, food and medical supplies.

The Fishhook operation, launched May 1, involved about 8,000 Americans and more than 2,000 South Vietnamese soldiers and penetrated 20 miles into Cambodia. About 1,500 U.S. reinforcements were brought into the area May 4. Hundreds of helicopters, tanks and armored cars took part in what was described as the largest allied war effort in two years.

The attack in the Parrot's Beak started initially April 29 with 6,000 government soldiers supported by U.S. warplanes and artillery and accompanied by American advisers. The force penetrated 24 miles to the vicinity of Prasaut.

Military spokesmen in Saigon reported May 4 that 641 enemy soldiers had been killed in the Fishhook operation and 118 persons were detained, mostly women, children and old men. Most of the enemy fatalities had been inflicted by aerial and artillery strikes. American casualties were listed as 10 killed and 35 wounded. South Vietnamese losses in both operations were put at 95 killed and 400 wounded.

The principal target of the Fishhook drive was the Communist base known as the Central Office for South Vietnam (COSVN), described as the control center for all Communist military and political operations in South Vietnam. It was believed to be a mobile headquarters, including hospital, sleeping and working quarters for top commanders and an advance communications network. Allied troops May 4 reached the site of what was believed to be the largest North Vietnamese base area discovered thus far. The stronghold was identified on tactical maps as "The City," and was located near the northwestern tip of South Vietnam's Binhlong Province.

An allied reconnaissance force May 3 had penetrated to the north and west about 30 miles inside Cambodia. In one of the few direct actions that day, U.S. helicopter gunships and bombers destroyed part of the rubber plantation town of Memot after enemy gunners reportedly shot at American helicopters from the village. Memot had been cap-

tured by Communist troops April 28 after three days of encirclement.

While allied soldiers pressed their drive along the eastern border region, Communist forces launched heavy attacks in the area around Pnompenh. Viet Cong and North Vietnamese units May 4 cut the Pnompenh-Saigon highway at a point 29 miles from the capital. Communist troops the previous day had attacked and partly occupied Neak Luong, a key Mekong River crossing point 35 miles southeast of Pnompenh.

Beleaguered Cambodian troops were reinforced by the arrival of 2,000 Cambodian mercenaries who had been flown to Pnompenh from South Vietnam May 2–3. The men had served with U.S. Special Forces and had been requested by Premier Lon Nol in a message to President Nixon April 20.

A statement issued April 29 by the South Vietnamese Defense Ministry on the Parrot's Beak operation said it represented "an indispensable and efficient measure to save the lives" of the South Vietnamese people, its soldiers and allies. The operation also was "a necessary measure in the framework of the policy" of giving the South Vietnamese forces greater responsibility in waging the war, the ministry said.

(Saigon military spokesmen May 14 confirmed that South Vietnamese forces had carried out four "unannounced operations" into Cambodia prior to the massive thrust into the Parrot's Beak April 29. The spokesmen said government troops, accompanied by American advisers, had pushed into the beak March 20, April 13, 20 and 29. Some of these operations previously had been reported in the Western press but they had been denied at the time by Saigon.)

Opposition rises in U.S. Senate. The U.S. military drive into Cambodia evoked surprise and considerable criticism in the Senate. Opposition to the action, while centered in the Senate Foreign Relations Committee headed by Sen. J. W. Fulbright (D, Ark.), extended beyond the regular dove ranks. The conflict was aggravated by the Adminstration's failure to consult Congressional leaders. There was also growing concern about a Constitutional conflict between the President and Congress over whether the chief executive had the authority to engage in such a military venture without the consent of Congress.

The first announcement of U.S. involvement in the Cambodia incursions, supporting the South Vietnamese thrust into the Parrot's Beak sector April 29, drew angry Senate responses, some from those who generally supported the Administration's Vietnam policy. Sen. George D. Aiken (R, Vt.) said April 29 he "did not think the President would do what he reportedly has done." Sen. John Sherman Cooper (R, Ky.) called the action a "U-turn" in the Administration's Southeast Asia policy. Sen. Norris Cotton (R, N.H.) expressed shock and dismay and anticipated early Senate action "to register its disapproval." Senate Democratic Leader Mike Mansfield (Mont.) announced his backing of a move to bar Congressionally appropriated funds for military operations in Cambodia.

Other criticism came from New York GOP Senators Jacob K. Javits, who said it meant "the President's decision to expand the war," and Charles E. Goodell, who said it "demonstrates how the strategy of Vietnamization has failed and how it pulls us inexorably into a wider war."

The Parrot's Peak action was backed April 29 by Sen. John Stennis (D, Miss.), chairman of the Armed Services Committee, Assistant Senate Republican Leader Robert P. Griffin (Mich.), John G. Tower (R, Tex.) and Peter H. Dominick (R, Colo.). Stennis said it "could be a turning point in the war for us for the good." It was not in itself, he said, "an escalation—not yet, not yet." Griffin said the President's national security adviser, Henry A. Kissinger, had advised him the operation was "a limited action" undertaken to protect U.S. troops in Vietnam and in no way related to the Cambodian request for U.S. military assistance.

Fulbright, whose committee had met two days earlier with Secretary of State William P. Rogers, said the action was "directly contrary to what we had been led to believe." He warned it might lead to a North Vietnamese "move on Pnompenh and then one thing leads to another."

His committee approved a statement expressing "deep concern" over the possibility of further U.S. involvement in Cambodia.

After the U.S. drive into the Fishhook area of Cambodia, there were more comments (April 30): Cooper thought that "the risks of escalation and prolongation of our presence in South Vietnam are much greater than the possible benefits." Aiken said "the President is taking a long chance." Sen. Lee Metcalf (D, Mont.) said Nixon "has definitely made it his war. The risks are considerable." Sen. Edmund S. Muskie (D, Me.) said the President was either "wrong 10 days ago" when he announced plans to withdraw 150,000 troops "or he is wrong now." Sen. Fred R. Harris (D, Okla.) said the President had indicated he "might hold off the troop withdrawals and might in some way escalate the war depending on Hanoi's reactions." Sen. Edward W. Brooke (R, Mass.) said the President had "undertaken an extremely hazardous policy."

In contrast, Sen. Marlow W. Cook (R, Ky.) thought the President had "shown more honesty than anyone involved in this thing." Sen. John Stennis (D, Miss.) said "it was time to do it if we are going to continue Vietnamization." Sen. John G. Tower (R, Tex.) said the logic of the action was "unassailable" in that it was not a new war nor another Vietnam but "it is Vietnam."

Fulbright, while stressing the Foreign Relations Committee's attempt to exercise its responsibility in a "restrained" way to persuade the President to its way of thinking, made clear May 1 it was the nearly unanimous view of the panel to oppose the dispatch of U.S. troops into Cambodia, which he said could result in "a major enlargement" of the war. He also brought up, as did Sen. Albert Gore (D, Tenn.), the issue of Constitutional authority.

On the Senate floor May 1, Mansfield, with rising anger, said the "vital" concern of the nation "must be to end our involvement in the war in Vietnam. It is not to become bogged down in another war in all of Indochina." Senate Republican Leader Hugh Scott (Pa.) defended the President's action as a "courageous" decision that could shorten the war.

Conference with Nixon requested—The Fulbright committee had requested May 1 a meeting with President Nixon to discuss the Cambodian developments. The White House assented but broadened the proposed session to a joint meeting with the House Foreign Affairs Committee. In addition, it invited the Senate and House Armed Services Committees to a separate joint session.

While accepting the offer May 4, the Fulbright panel indicated it would still seek a separate Presidential consultation. The chairman of the House counterpart committee, Rep. Thomas E. Morgan (D, Pa.) commented May 4 that "the House and Senate share an equal responsibility in this vital matter."

The meetings, attended by 28 senators and 72 representatives, were held May 5. Afterwards, several reported that Nixon had expressed "a firm commitment" that U.S. troops would be withdrawn from Cambodia in three to seven weeks and would not penetrate deeper than 30–35 kilometers (18.6-21.7 miles) into Cambodia without Congressional approval being sought. The Cambodian operation was reported to be proceeding successfully.

Afterwards, Sen. Stuart Symington (D, Mo.), a member of both the Armed Services and Foreign Relations Committees, reported on the Senate floor that the White House session did "little to lessen my apprehension."

Aiken, ranking Republican on the Fulbright committee, said "not a wealth of new information was presented . . . nor would I say that many minds were changed." Fulbright also said he had heard "nothing new" and objected to the format of the meeting, which Nixon conducted like a news conference with, Fulbright said, no chance for informative discussion.

International reaction. The U.S. offensive in Cambodia was sharply assailed by the Soviet Union and Communist China May 4. The move, however, had drawn praise May 1 from Washington's Asian allies—Thailand, South Korea and Nationalist China. Indonesian Foreign Minister Adam

Malik expressed regret over the move. Japanese Foreign Minister Kiichi Aichi called the intervention an "unavoidable step" under present circumstances.

The French government commented May 1 that it "can only deplore anything that aggravates, prolongs and extends the conflict." Most other European governments did not react immediately to the new situation in Indochina.

The invasion of Cambodia drew sharp denunciations May 1 from the North Vietnamese and Viet Cong delegations to the Paris peace talks. They described Nixon's actions as "warlike and perfidious."

The most virulent Communist reaction came from the North Vietnamese government newspaper Nhan Dan May 3. The Communist Party journal said Nixon had been attempting to justify the "U.S. aggression in Cambodia," but his April 30 speech was "even more absurd, unwittingly proving his dirty trickery."

Speaking at a rare news conference in Moscow, Soviet Premier Aleksei N. Kosygin charged that in ordering the invasion of Cambodia and the resumption of air raids on North Vietnam, President Nixon was "in effect also tearing up the decision of his predecessor, President Johnson, to end . . . all aerial bombing and other action involving the use of force" against North Vietnam. Kosygin said "the real meaning" of Nixon's April 30 speech announcing the invasion and U.S. policy in general in Southeast Asia "is to eliminate progressive regimes in the countries of the region, [and] to stifle the liberation movement" there.

(The Soviet Union April 30 had condemned the U.S.-supported South Vietnamese thrust into Cambodia the previous day as "a direct aggression against a member of the United Nations." The statement called the action "the grossest violation of Cambodia's neutrality.")

Peking's May 4 statement denouncing the U.S. pledged Chinese support for "the three Indochinese people" (Cambodia, Laos and Vietnam) in their "patriotic struggle" against American forces. Peking expressed backing of a statement issued by Prince Norodom Sihanouk May 2 urging international condemnation of the U.S. "armed intervention" in Cambodia.

British Prime Minister Harold Wilson, refraining from direct criticism of the American action, expressed fear May 5 that U.S. forces might penetrate further into Cambodia than the limits set by President Nixon, causing a change in Washington's policy of withdrawal of troops from Vietnam. Speaking in House of Commons debate, Wilson voiced "apprehension and anxiety" that the new American military moves would "add a new dimension to the area and scale of the fighting."

French Foreign Minister Maurice Schumann warned May 5 that any escalation of the war in Indochina would only solidify the Communists. Schumann said that a speech made by former President Charles de Gaulle in 1966 calling for the withdrawal of American troops from Vietnam "contained something of an advance reply" to Nixon's April 30 address announcing the American move into Cambodia.

U.N. Secretary General U Thant issued an appeal May 5 for an international conference to seek a peaceful settlement of the Indochinese war. He expressed fear that if the parties to the conflict "do not take urgent, . . . measures toward peace, it will become increasingly difficult to end a war" that threatened not only Indochina but "the whole of mankind."

Thant's statement followed a U.S. note to the president of the Security Council earlier May 5 informing him of the American action in Cambodia and the reasons for it. U.S. Ambassador Charles W. Yost had advised Thant of the contents of the letter May 4. It accused North Vietnam of aggression and described the dispatch of allied troops into Cambodia as "appropriate measures of collective self-defense by the armed forces" of the U.S. and South Vietnam.

The U.S. and Britain supported Thant's call for an international conference in statements issued by Secretary of State William P. Rogers May 6 and by Lord Caradon, London's ambassador to the U.N., May 7.

Indian Prime Minister Indira Gandhi May 6 called the invasion of Cambodia a "dangerous step" and urged President Nixon to reconsider his move.

Laotian Premier Souvanna Phouma said in an interview published May 8 that further U.S. and South Vietnamese penetration of Cambodia would imperil his country because it would force the North Vietnamese and Viet Cong to pull back into Laos. The North Vietnamese, anticipating a possible widening of the fronts in Cambodia, apparently had ordered the Pathet Lao in Laos to capture Attopeu April 29–30, Souvanna told a correspondent of the French newspaper France Soir. Souvanna said he supported France's proposal for an international conference on Indochina.

Allied coast & river operations—Allied operations in Cambodia were further widened May 9 by a U.S. and South Vietnamese naval blockade of a 100-mile stretch of the Cambodian coast, it was disclosed May 12 by Vice President Nguyen Cao Ky. The American command in Saigon confirmed that its naval forces were participating in the action aimed at preventing North Vietnamese and Viet Cong boats from landing any supplies on the Cambodian beaches, stretching from the principal port of Kompong Som (formerly Sihanoukville) to the South Vietnamese border.

The ships involved included heavily armed U.S. coastal patrol boats and South Vietnamese junks equipped with heavy machine guns.

Ky said the blockade had been discussed in advance by senior South Vietnamese and Cambodian military officers and the two governments. Citing previous joint military cooperation, Ky disclosed that his government had been providing air support for the Cambodians fighting on the western side of the Mekong River in the previous two days. He said this aerial assistance had enabled the Cambodians to recapture Takeo, which had been taken by the Communists two weeks before.

Anti-U.S. demonstrations—Worldwide demonstrations were held May 6–10 to protest the American advance into Cambodia. Among the major incidents:

Five thousand persons marched on the U.S. embassy in London May 9. Police blocked attempts by the marchers to force their way to the entrance of the building. Sixty demonstrators who fought past police lines were arrested. Nineteen demonstrators and 60 police were injured.

Thousands of antiwar demonstrators, hurling stones and gasoline bombs, fought police in front of the U.S. cultural center in West Berlin May 9. Three persons were wounded by police bullets.

Demonstrations were held May 6 in Montreal, Canada, Calcutta, India, where the library of the American University Center was sacked, Caracas, Venezuela, Canberra, Australia and Auckland, New Zealand. Two high school pupils were shot to death by sniper fire during continued protest rallies in Caracas May 7.

About 200,000 persons took to the streets in Melbourne, Sydney and other Australian cities May 8 to begin three days of organized protest against Australian and U.S. involvement in the Vietnam war. (Australian Prime Minister John Gorton had announced May 5 that his government supported American military moves in Cambodia.) Police used tear gas to disperse an anti-American demonstration by 300 Filipino youths in front of the U.S. embassy in Manila. About 3,500 students and workers marched in Tokyo to protest American action in Cambodia and the Asian conference in Cambodia, opening in Jakarta May 16.

An anti-American protest in Paris May 10 was attended by French Socialists and Viet Cong and Cambodian supporters of Prince Norodom Sihanouk and by Xuan Thuy, head of the North Vietnamese delegation to the Paris peace talks.

Allied operations expanded. U.S. and South Vietnamese troops extended their military operations against Communist sanctuaries in Cambodia by opening six new fronts May 5–9, bringing to eight the number of separate attacks launched since the initial allied thrusts across the border April 29–May 1. Allied operations were also widened May 9 by a naval blockade of a 100-mile stretch of the Cambodian coast. In another action, a flotilla of 140 U.S. and South Vietnamese craft pushed into Cambodia on the Mekong River May 9 in a move to secure the banks of the stream from

Communist forces and to aid in the repatriation of Vietnamese civilians. The South Vietnamese section of the fleet arrived in Pnompenh May 11, while U.S. ships and advisers halted their advance 40 miles downriver.

A White House report May 9 called the allied military sweep a success, announcing that U.S. and South Vietnamese forces had captured more Communist ammunition than the North Vietnamese and Viet Cong had fired in the January–April period. A White House list of casualties after nine days of operations said 60 Americans and 184 South Vietnamese had been killed. Communist fatalities were put at 3,740; 1,041 of the enemy were said to have been captured.

Allied command headquarters in Saigon reported May 9 that captured Communist equipment and supplies thus far totaled 6,757 rifles, 1,232 heavy machine guns, rocket launchers and other weapons, 865 tons of ammunition, 1,653 tons of rice, 12 tons of medical supplies and 130 trucks.

The third major allied incursion into Cambodia was carried out May 5 in the Sesan area of Ratanakiri Province, about 200 miles north of the Fishhook area, where other allied forces had been fighting since May 1. U.S. and South Vietnamese troops were airlifted into the area 50 miles south of Laos. Originally a force of 6,000 men was prepared for this invasion, but bad weather and heavy enemy fire limited the landing to 500 men. The scope of the operation was expanded May 6 with the airlifting of 2,000 more American troops into the sector. Heavy enemy fire was encountered as three U.S. battalions penetrated 3–10 miles inside Cambodia. The target of this drive was described as a Communist supply center and headquarters for the North Vietnamese troops operating against U.S. Special Forces camps in South Vietnam.

In the Fishhook area to the south, U.S. forces May 5 captured Snoul after a squadron of nearly 100 tanks of the 11th Armored Cavalry Regiment and jet planes virtually leveled the village that had been held by the North Vietnamese. The town was about 20 miles from the tip of the Fishhook.

Three new fronts were opened May 6 as American troops pushed into Cambodia northeast of the Fishhook and between the Fishhook and the Parrot's Beak, where South Vietnamese troops had been operating since April 29. One American spearhead, involving soldiers of the 25th Infantry Division, moved across the border from Tayninh Province, 60 miles north of Saigon. Another force, troops of the First Cavalry Division (Airmobile), were airlifted into jungles 23 miles north of Phocbinh.

South Vietnam May 7 announced the withdrawal of 10,000 government troops from the Parrot's Beak after successfully completing its mission there. The action reduced the number of troops in Cambodia to 40,000 men, including 20,-000–25,000 Americans. The first U.S. troops, totaling 800 men, moved into the Parrot's Beak May 8. Their mission was to watch for a possible renewal of Communist activity there. Previously, the only U.S. forces in the Parrot's Beak were 40 advisers who had accompanied the original South Vietnamese thrust into the area.

The opening of a new American front in the Parrot's Beak was followed by another U.S. operation into Cambodia, announced by the American high command May 9. Elements of the 25th Division pushed into an area west of the Fishhook to join the search for enemy supplies and bases.

The White House announced May 7 the American capture that day of an abandoned major Communist base in the Fishhook. A Defense Department statement, however, said "there is no verification from the field that this is part of COSVN," the Central Office for South Vietnam, described as the control center for all Communist military operations in South Vietnam. The latest stronghold, described as "the most sophisticated base complex" yet uncovered in Cambodia, was said to have consisted of 400–500 huts, a large bunker and a "huge cache" of equipment.

The U.S. command in Saigon reported May 10 that 21 helicopters had been lost in the Indochina war the previous week, nine of them downed in Cambodia. Seven were shot down by enemy fire and two others crashed. The plane losses resulted in the death of 33 Americans and caused injury to 30 others.

In fighting between Cambodian and Communist forces, about 2,000 government troops May 7 recaptured Kokithom and advanced to within four miles of the Neak Luong ferry crossing seized by the Viet Cong May 2. Kokithom, about 25 miles south of Pnompenh, had been occupied by the Viet Cong May 4. A government spokesman reported Viet Cong capture of Senomorom and Kratie, 170 and 100 miles northeast of the Cambodian capital.

The stepped-up fighting in Cambodia was reflected in the casualty report for the May 3–9 period, issued by allied military officials in Saigon May 14. It was announced that 863 South Vietnamese and 168 Americans had been killed that week in Cambodia as well as in South Vietnam. It was the second highest weekly death toll for government forces and the highest total for U.S. troops in eight months. North Vietnamese and Viet Cong fatalities May 3–9 totaled 5,898, the highest since the last week in February 1969.

Most of the ships used by the allies in the operation into Cambodia up the Mekong River assembled May 9 at the Neak Luong ferry crossing, recaptured from Communist forces by South Vietnamese troops earlier in the day. The fleet consisted of 30 U.S. river gunboats and 110 South Vietnamese craft. The South Vietnamese vessels carried 1,400 government sailors and 1,800 marines, about 600 of whom had landed outside Neak Luong to clear suspected enemy positions. This phase of the operation was assisted by U.S. jet fighters and helicopter gunships. The American vessels moved no further north than Neak Luong in compliance with the U.S. policy of limiting the American penetration of Cambodia to 21.7 miles. Forty-seven South Vietnamese vessels arrived in the heart of Pnompenh May 11. The remaining fleet had returned to South Vietnam with several thousand Vietnamese refugees picked up along the banks of the Mekong since the convoy had started upstream earlier in the week.

The military and humanitarian aspects of the Mekong operation had been hastily combined after South Vietnamese Foreign Minister Tran Van Lam had inadvertently announced publicly May 7 that a fleet would be sailing up the river to rescue Vietnamese refugees. Lam was said to have been unaware that a military operation also was planned for this area. A U.S. official remarked that "suddenly our entire attack was being broadcast days before it was set to start." The two plans were then merged and the fleet set sail May 9 from the South Vietnamese towns of Chaudoc and Tanchau on the Cambodian border.

U.S. dissent. U.S. antiwar forces re-acted to President Nixon's decision to use U.S. troops in Cambodia with calls for a nationwide student strike, demands for impeachment proceedings against the President and plans for massive demonstrations. There was also rising opposition in Congress. On many campuses, administrations sanctioned student strikes and demonstrations were peaceful; but elsewhere violence erupted. The worst outbreak occurred at Kent State University in Ohio were four students were killed by National Guard troops May 4.

The New Mobilization Committee to End the War in Vietnam (New Mobe) announced plans May 1 for a massive demonstration in Washington May 9 to protest the use of U.S. troops in Cambodia.

At a news conference called by the committee May 5, Dr. Benjamin Spock said: "The government is committing titanic violence in Vietnam and Cambodia . . . We must stand up in opposition to the government's illegal, immoral and brutal war." Rabbi Balfour Brickner, a member of the steering committee of Clergy and Laymen Concerned about Vietnam, said in reference to the Kent State shootings: "The shots that were fired were the first shots fired in a new and terrifying civil war in America."

Spock had been one of 75 persons arrested May 3 during a peaceful rally across from the White House called by the clergy and laymen group and the Fellowship of Reconciliation to protest Nixon's decision to send troops into Cambodia. The protesters, charged with disorderly conduct, had been arrested because they failed to give the police 15 days' notice of their demonstration, as required by law. Others arrested

included Sam Brown, David Hawk and David Mixner of the disbanded Vietnam Moratorium Committee; the Rev. Dr. John C. Bennett, retiring president of the Union Theological Seminary; the Rev. David R. Hunter, deputy general secretary of the National Council of Churches; and the Rev. Richard Fernandez, executive secretary of Clergy and Laymen Concerned About the War in Vietnam.

■Four Protestant church leaders assailed President Nixon at a Washington news conference May 6 for sending U.S. troops into Cambodia. In a joint statement, the churchmen said "We have heard a pledge to bring us together, and see action which is at this moment further tearing our already weakened social fabric." They estimated that more than 500 church leaders and representatives were in Washington that day lobbying against expansion of the war. The statement was issued by Bishop John Wesley Lord of Washington, president of the Council of Bishops of the United Methodist Church; Cynthia Wedel of Alexandria, Va., president of the National Council of Churches; William P. Thompson, chief executive of the United Presbyterian Church; and the Rev. Robert V. Moss of New York, president of the United Church of Christ.

■A group of 12 Harvard academics, each of whom had served as presidential advisers, met with Nixon aide Henry A. Kissinger May 8 to announce their public break with Nixon Administration domestic policies and policies in Southeast Asia. Among the group were Edwin Reischauer, former ambassador to Japan; George Kistiakowsky, chief science adviser to former President Eisenhower; Richard Neustadt, formerly on President Truman's White House staff; Ernest May, a former Army historian; Thomas Schelling, consultant to the Defense Department; Francis Bator, special assistant to President Johnson; Adam Yarmolinsky, former special assistant to the secretary of defense; and William Capron, former assistant director of the budget.

■John T. Connor, chairman of the board of Allied Chemical Corp. and President Johnson's secretary of commerce, said May 8 that President Nixon's decision to send U.S. troops into Cambodia "shakes the confidence of many Americans in his judgment and intentions." Addressing the Business Council, meeting in Hot Springs, Va., Connor said the President's action "will result in more widespread dissension in this country involving many other loyal citizens besides most of the young, the intellectuals and the blacks."

Congressional action. The issue of supporting the U.S. military incursion into Cambodia became an immediate subject of Congressional debate.

In the House, which was considering a $20.2 billion defense authorization bill, Rep. Ogden R. Reid (R, N.Y.) introduced an amendment April 30 to bar funds for support of U.S. ground troops in Cambodia, Laos or Thailand. But a vote, taken May 6 before galleries filled with student critics of the war, came on an amendment, offered by Rep. Paul Findley (R, Ill.) as a substitute for the Reid proposal. The Findley amendment, endorsed May 5 by President Nixon as "splendid," would have barred funds in the bill for introduction of ground troops into those areas without the consent of Congress unless the President deemed the action necessary to protect the lives of U.S. forces in Vietnam. The Findley amendment was tentatively approved May 6 by a 171–144 vote but rejected by a 221–32 final vote. The seeming reversal was interpreted as a way of both approving the President's action and skirting the Constitutional issue involved in the President's acting without specific sanction from Congress.

With student lobbyists again milling through Capitol halls May 7, the House rejected 220–134 a proposal by Rep. Edward P. Boland (D, Mass.) to set a July 1 cutoff for funds used to maintain ground combat troops in Cambodia.

In the Senate, war critics worked on a three-fold strategy to bar funds for use of combat troops in Cambodia, to repeal the Tonkin Gulf Resolution and to require, or request, a total troop withdrawal from Vietnam by mid-1971. A Committee to End the War to gain public support for the effort was announced May 8 by Sen. George McGovern (D, S.D.). The committee comprised a bipartisan group of 16 senators and 18 House members.

Legislative curbs prepared—In the Senate May 2, four Senators—Mark O. Hatfield (R, Ore.), George S. McGovern (D, S.D.), Harold E. Hughes (D, Iowa) and Charles E. Goodell (R, N.Y.)—prepared a proposal to end funds for military activities in Vietnam, Laos and Cambodia unless there was a declaration of war by Congress. In a statement, they said five successive presidents had "usurped" Congress' Constitutional responsibility "to decide the question of war or peace and to provide or refuse funds to wage war."

The Fulbright committee charged May 4 that the executive branch over the years had been "conducting a Constitutionally unauthorized, presidential war in Indochina." It said the Nixon Administration, by sending U.S. troops into Cambodia "without the consent or knowledge of Congress," was usurping Congress' war-making powers. The White House, in a statement by Press Secretary Ronald L. Ziegler, rejected the charge and said the President's action had been taken as commander in chief to protect the security of U.S. forces in Vietnam.

The committee's charges were made in a report urging repeal of the 1964 Tonkin Gulf Resolution, often cited by the Johnson Administration as the legal basis for the U.S. military buildup in Vietnam. (The report was withdrawn May 5 and returned to committee for deletion of the Cambodia references after two members, Cooper and Sen. John J. Williams [R, Del.] objected and pointed out the report had not been approved by the full panel.)

Nixon defends offensive. President Nixon May 8 held his first televised news conference in more than three months. He used the meeting to defend his deployment of U.S. troops in Cambodia as a necessary step to shorten the length of U.S. involvement in the war in Indochina. The President said preliminary briefings from U.S field officers indicated that the joint operations of South Vietnamese regulars and U.S. troops were so successful that some American units could be shifted out of Cambodia by May 16. He said all U.S.

ground forces would be redeployed outside Cambodia by the end of June.

The President, taking note that his decision had triggered a wave of protests on college campuses across the country, said he shared the goals and objectives of his critics but added that time and history would prove his decision "served the cause of a just peace in Vietnam."

The issues of U.S. involvement in Cambodia and the domestic reaction to the President's decisions, including the shooting of four Kent State University students by Ohio National Guardsmen, dominated the newsmen's questions. Other issues discussed by the President included his reaction to a letter in which Secretary of the Interior Walter J. Hickel had expressed his view that the Nixon Administration was insensitive to student concerns and a news dispatch that reported Secretary of State William P. Rogers opposed the move into Cambodia.

Among Nixon's comments:

On the progress of the war—President Nixon said U.S. operations in Cambodia would win six to eight months of time for the further training of South Vietnamese regulars and thus shorten the time of U.S. involvement. He said most American troops would be out of Cambodia by the middle of June and that some combat units would be withdrawn during the week ending May 16. The President emphasized that the move into Cambodia would not necessarily jeopardize his avowed withdrawal plans of 150,000 men from Vietnam by the spring of 1971.

Nixon explained that his decision to move troops into Cambodia was precipitated by reports of increased enemy action in Cambodia and that those moves could "leave the 240,000 Americans who would be there [South Vietnam] a year from now without many combat troops to help defend them . . . in an untenable position."

The President said despite the new moves into Cambodia, the U.S. would continue to seek an accord at the peace talks in Paris.

The President disclosed that the units of the South Vietnamese Army that had been participating in the Cambodian operations with U.S. troops would not necessarily be bound by the June dead-line that he had set for the withdrawal of American forces. Nixon said, however, that he expected the pullback of South Vietnamese forces to come "approximately at the same time that we do, because when we come out our logistical support and air support will also come out with them."

The President said he was planning a televised speech to the nation in June to explain the outcome of the U.S. operation in Cambodia. Nixon said he would respond in full at that time to questions about the success of the mission. He said, however, that all preliminary reports indicated the operation was a success. "We have also saved, I think, hundreds if not thousands of Americans. Rockets by the thousands and small arms by the millions have already been captured and those rockets and small arms will not be killing Americans in these next few months."

On new U.S. bombing strikes against North Vietnam, Nixon said "if the North Vietnamese did what some have suggested they might do—move a massive force of 250,000–300,000 across the DMZ [Demilitarized Zone] against our Marine Corps people who are there— I would certainly not allow those men to be massacred without using force and more effective force against North Vietnam."

The President said the U.S. would continue to explore all diplomatic channels in an attempt to secure Cambodia's neutrality once U.S. troops were withdrawn. He said that the U.S. would seek continued sessions with the Soviet Union, Great Britain, and other Asian nations "to see that neutrality is guaranteed without having the intervention of foreign forces." He reiterated that the U.S. does not intend to send American troops to protect Cambodia itself, in line with the Nixon Doctrine that he revealed in 1969 at Guam.

The President disclaimed responsibility for the war in Vietnam and stressed that the move into Cambodia did not represent an expansion of the war. He said that when he became President (and commander in chief) "I found 525,-000 Americans and my responsibility is to do everything that I could to protect their lives and to get them home as quickly as I can." The President said now that the U.S. was involved in the war, "if we do what many of our sincere critics think we should do—withdraw from Vietnam and allow the enemy to come into Vietnam and massacre the civilians there by the millions, as they would—if we do that, let me say that America is finished insofar as a peacekeeper in the Asian world is concerned."

On domestic reaction—The President denied reports that the intensity of the protests against his decision took him by surprise. He said that he shared the goals and concerns of student protestors and "I know that what I have done will accomplish the goals they want." He said that he was concerned about the protesters "because I know how deeply they feel."

Nixon said he would like to try and open up meaningful communications with the nation's youths. To achieve that end, Alexander Heard, chancellor of Vanderbilt University, had agreed to take a two-month leave from his post to seek to establish more open dialogue between the youths and their government, Nixon announced.

Nixon also said he would make no effort to restrain his secretary of interior, Walter J. Hickel, who had accused the Administration in a letter to the President of being insensitive to the concerns of students. The President said he would, "of course, be interested in his [Hickel's] advice."

Other Administration dissent. Other dissent within the Administration over the Cambodian military involvement was reported although the Cabinet members involved later affirmed their support of the President in his action.

In the New York Times May 6 and elsewhere there were reports that Defense Secretary Melvin R. Laird and Secretary of State William P. Rogers had serious reservations about the use of U.S. troops in Cambodia, largely because of concern about domestic political repercussions. Laird was said to have held out for no more involvement than use of advisers and air support for South Vietnamese troops. Rogers was quoted, in excerpts released May 5 from secret Congressional testimony given April 23, four days before the final decision on Cambodian troop use, as saying the Administration had "no incentive to escalate" since "we recognize that if we escalate and we get involved in Cambodia with our ground troops that our whole program [presumably Vietnamization] is defeated." "Our whole incentive is to de-escalate," he told a House appropriations subcommittee. The "one lesson" that the Vietnam war "has taught us," he said, "is that if you are going to fight a war of this kind satisfactorily you need public support and congressional support."

Neither Rogers nor his spokesmen would comment on the reports of apparent White House divergence from his advice except to affirm the secretary's support of the President's Cambodian decision.

Laird announced May 6 that he had "supported fully" the President's decision. He further stressed May 11 that the U.S. operation in Cambodia "was to last from three to six weeks and the timetable will be met." The U.S. troops had to be withdrawn from Cambodia before the monsoons began, he said. He specifically noted that the timetable would be met despite reports from field commanders in Cambodia that the timetable would not allow enough time to search all the occupied territory and remove or destroy all the enemy supplies found.

(South Vietnamese President Nguyen Van Thieu indicated in Tayninh May 11 that neither the timetable nor penetration limit would apply to the South Vietnamese troops. If the Cambodian government requested it, he said, the South Vietnamese forces "can go farther into Cambodia and there is no deadline yet for getting out.")

Nixon, asked at his news conference if Rogers had opposed the Cambodian decision, said May 8 "every one of my advisers" had "raised questions about the decision and, believe me, I raised the most questions because I knew the stakes that were involved," "the division that would be caused in this country," "the problems internationally" and "the military risks." "I made this decision," the President said, "I take the responsibility for it. I believe it was the right decision. I believe it will work out. If it doesn't, then I am to blame."

In related developments:

■Robert H. Finch, secretary of health, education and welfare, said, after a series of meetings with young war protesters May 9, that the President would have a "very serious case of credibility" if the U.S. troops were not withdrawn from Cambodia by the July 1 target date.

Finch had told reporters May 7 the campus turmoil had reached the proportions of a "national crisis" and that the Cambodian venture was "the straw that broke the camel's back."

■There was a report May 8 that more than 250 State Department and foreign aid employes signed and sent a letter to Rogers criticizing the U.S. military move into Cambodia.

■George Romney, secretary of housing and urban development, in a New York speech May 11, called the Vietnam war "the most tragic foreign policy mistake in the nation's history" and said he did not believe a democracy could "successfully engage in foreign military operations, except when responding to attack, without following constitutional processes." However, he defended the U.S. move into Cambodia as a "tactical" operation. Romney commented on the Hickel letter at a news conference May 11, that Hickel "rendered a real service" and he was pleased the President "recognized that he had made a sound suggestion and acted promptly."

Thousands protest in capital. A crowd estimated at 60,000–100,000 demonstrated in Washington, D.C. May 9 in a protest hastily organized after President Nixon announced U.S. troop movements into Cambodia April 30 and planned on a more massive scale after the May 4 deaths of four students at Kent State University in Ohio. Although more than 5,000 troops had been placed on alert, the mass protest was peaceful. However, after the rally organized by the New Mobilization Committee to End the War in Vietnam (New Mobe), police used tear gas to disperse small bands of demonstrators who roamed through the streets causing disruptions and throwing rocks.

The White House approached the demonstration in a more conciliatory manner than the last mass protest in No-

vember 1969. Troops remained out of sight, President Nixon voiced his belief that the demonstrators had peaceful intentions and made a surprise dawn appearance at the Lincoln Memorial, and Administration aides mingled with the crowd. A requirement of 15 days advance notice for demonstrations in the capital was waived at the government's request, and protesters were allowed to rally at the Ellipse, south of the White House.

The rally began at noon and stretched through several hours of speeches and songs while the temperature climbed to 90 degrees. Fifty persons were treated for heat prostration. The crowd was overwhelmingly young and white; mainly college students. Speakers denounced the President and his policy in Vietnam and Cambodia. Stewart Meacham of the American Friends Service Committee urged the group to "shut down the production of weapons . . . not just the universities." David Livingston of the Wholesale, Retail and Office Workers Union called for the impeachment of Nixon and a nationwide general strike against the war. Although congressmen were not among the speakers, nine members of the House appeared on the speaker's stand and Republican Sens. Jacob K. Javits and Charles E. Goodell of New York and Edward W. Brooke of Massachusetts mingled with the crowd.

As the rally began to break up at about 3 p.m., some 700 persons bearing coffins draped in black marched to Arlington Cemetery. Other more militant protesters, some carrying rocks and sticks, moved towards the Justice and Labor Department buildings. Thirty persons tried to turn over one of a string of buses blocking off the White House area. After 5 p.m. police began to use tear gas to disperse the young demonstrators. At the end of the day, police said 14 persons had been arrested, five of them counter-protesters identified as members of the American Nazi party and two others who undressed to splash in a fountain.

More serious disturbances occurred early the next morning. Protesters set fire to a car and truck and stoned police and firemen on the George Washington University campus. After leaving the campus, students caused disruptions at the Washington Monument, and a bomb exploded at the headquarters of the U.S. National Guard Association. Police arrested about 375 persons, mostly at the university, and damage was estimated at $1,000.

Democrats assail Administration. Lawrence F. O'Brien, Democratic National chairman, charged May 9 that the Nixon Administration had attempted to "divide us as a nation, to polarize us, and to create anarchy." In a speech prepared for delivery at a Jefferson-Jackson Day dinner in Milwaukee, O'Brien accused Nixon, Vice President Agnew and Attorney General John N. Mitchell of using "inflammatory rhetoric—the rhetoric that appeals to the fears and prejudice and darker impulses that lurk within mankind."

In reference to the Kent State tragedy, O'Brien said: "I can only wonder with all of you whether those triggers would have been pulled if the elected leaders in this country had acted differently."

He said that President Nixon, at his news conference May 8, had been unable to supply any good reasons as to why U.S. troops moved into Cambodia and instead chose "to fall back on lame military arguments and political rationalizations." He said Nixon's policy was "an open-ended U.S. commitment to sustain the existing South Vietnamese government by military force."

Democrats in Washington, where a copy of O'Brien's speech was released, saw the address as both a direct answer to President Nixon's May 8 news conference and as a major element in a Democratic offensive against the Nixon Administration Indochina policy.

In an earlier attack, W. Averell Harriman, chief negotiator at the Paris peace talks under the Johnson Administration, and Paul C. Warnke, Johnson's assistant secretary of defense for international affairs, said May 7 said the Cambodian action was an unwarranted expansion of the war. Both men were speaking at a Washington news conference on behalf of the Democratic Policy Council's International Affairs Committee. Harriman, chairman of the committee, said the intervention into Cambodia and renewed bombing of North Vietnam were "seri-

ous mistakes of judgment . . . There is no conceivable military success in Cambodia worth the awful price we are paying at home and abroad." He said the Cambodian action was "demonstrable proof that the President does not have and never has had an effective plan for peace in Vietnam. . . . The simple truth is that there is no way of achieving a political victory in Vietnam through military actions."

(At a dinner attended by Democratic party members in Chicago May 1, former President Lyndon B. Johnson said President Nixon should have the support of all "who want freedom" while he deliberated policy in Southeast Asia. "I hope," continued Johnson, "our President's voice is not drowned out by those other voices which are without knowledge and the responsibility to make this agonizing decision," apparently a reference to use of U.S. troops in Cambodia.)

(Fifty-seven per cent of Americans polled immediately after President Nixon's April 30 speech announcing troop movements into Cambodia said they approved of the way Nixon was handling his job as president. In the Gallup Poll survey results announced May 9, 31% disapproved of Nixon's handling of his job, and 12% offered no opinion.)

Offensive called 'success.' In an unscheduled talk to labor leaders, President Nixon said May 12 that the Cambodia attacks were a great "success"; 5,000 of the enemy had been killed in action and more ammunition captured than the enemy had expended in South Vietnam in the last five or six months. AFL-CIO President George Meany reported the President said "they're knocking out the sanctuaries ahead of schedule." (Nixon made the remarks during a surprise visit to AFL-CIO headquarters, where its executive council was beginning a two-day meeting. The council May 13, with only three dissents and one abstention, endorsed Meany's May 1 statement in support of Nixon's Cambodia operation.)

At a Medal of Honor ceremony May 14—the medal awarded to each of five soldiers, three Navy men, two Marines and two Air Force men—Nixon said the war in Southeast Asia was often "not understood and not supported in this country" but "as time goes on, millions more of your countrymen will look back and they will reach the conclusion that you served the cause of the land of the free by being brave—brave beyond the call of duty."

The President conferred May 14 with Raymond Gallagher, national commander of the Veterans of Foreign Wars, who expressed support for the Nixon policies in Southeast Asia.

(Gallagher and American Legion National Commander J. Milton Patrick were taken by Senate Republican Leader Hugh Scott (Pa.) to the Senate press gallery May 13 where they released a joint statement condemning the actions of senators "who would tie the President's hands" with proposals that amounted to a "a declaration of surrender to Communist forces" and constituted "a stab in the back for our boys in combat." Scott sent a letter of apology May 15 to Fulbright and others sponsoring such proposals. Dissociating himself from their statement, he said the veterans' leaders had been taken to the gallery at the request of the White House and he had not known beforehand what they were going to say.)

Secretary of State William P. Rogers put in a surprise appearance at a routine State Department briefing May 13 to affirm that the U.S. would not become "militarily involved" with troop or air support to defend the Cambodian government. He said South Vietnam and Thailand would be encouraged to cooperate with Cambodia in repulsing the Communist threat and that this policy was in line with the Nixon doctrine of fostering cooperation among the Asians to handle their own problems. Rogers stressed that the Cambodian incursion was "not an escalation" nor "an attempt to win a military victory" and said Nixon had "committed himself to limitations of time and distance and events will answer these anxieties." These limits, Rogers said, would also mellow the foreign reaction to the move, which initially had been "reserved or negative."

Referring to his April 23 Congressional testimony against involvement in ground fighting in Cambodia, Rogers said

that he was talking about sending troops to support the Lon Nol government and not "to the possibility of incursions, of temporary activities."

Rogers reaffirmed a pledge made by Defense Secretary Melvin R. Laird May 12 that U.S. troops "will be out of combat in South Vietnam by the middle of 1971."

Laird made the pledge before the Senate Armed Services Committee. Laird also told the committee that several thousand U.S. troops had already been withdrawn from Cambodia, that by June 15 "the major portion of our forces" would be withdrawn and that all would leave Cambodia by the end of June.

Other points made by Laird: (a) the Cambodian government "was informed and it had no objections" to the operation prior to its initiation; (b) he would "not permit South Vietnamese forces to be tied down [in Cambodia] to such an extent that it in any way slows down the withdrawal of American forces"; (c) he would not rule out the possibility that South Vietnamese forces might return to Cambodia on their own in the future if Communist forces moved back into the sanctuary areas; and (d) "the important thing that had an effect" on the President's decision to strike into Cambodia was information that the North Vietnamese "would in the coming months be using sanctuaries at an increasing rate to increase American casualties and this would have a decided effect on public opinion in the United States."

Laird told reporters May 14 the Communists had begun moving in mid-April out of their Cambodian sanctuaries westward toward Phnompenh and "this was the time to hit" the sanctuaries because of the reduced risk to U.S. forces. The reduction in risk, he said, "changes my mind" concerning sending U.S. troops into Cambodia since "at the start" of the planning for incursion the Fishhook area "looked like a very tough area."

Laird was one of three top Administration officials—along with Undersecretary of State Elliot L. Richardson and Henry A. Kissinger, the President's national security adviser—sent by the President May 14 to meet with Republican senators to discuss strategy to oppose proposed legislation cutting off funds for future military involvement in Cambodia without Congressional approval. Their argument was that passage of such an amendment would imply a lack of confidence in the President and, in light of Nixon's pledge to withdraw U.S. troops from Cambodia by the end of June, could impair the President's "credibility" abroad.

Senators adopt Cooper-Church plan. The amendment to cut off funds for future U.S. military operations in Cambodia was approved May 11 by the Senate Foreign Relations Committee. Sponsored by Sens. John Sherman Cooper (R, Ky.) and Frank Church (D, Idaho), it was attached to a foreign military sales bill. The approval, by a 9–4 vote, came after receipt of a State Department letter opposing it on Constitutional grounds that Presidential power should not be restricted in protecting U.S. armed forces.

Prior to the beginning of debate on the amendment May 13, Chairman John Stennis (D, Miss.) of the Armed Services Committee, a foe of the proposal, said he viewed the enemy sanctuaries in Cambodia as "part of the South Vietnamese battlefield" and said a curb on Presidential powers while the battle "is still going on" would be a "grave mistake." Warning that it might be necessary to send U.S. forces back in four or five months if the sanctuaries were rebuilt, he asked what would the President "have to do" then? "Get a law passed?"

Senate Republican Leader Hugh Scott (Pa.) had proposed a substitute amendment May 12 containing the Cooper-Church language but adding an exception that funds could be spent by the President for military action in Cambodia if "required to protect" U.S. troops.

In the Senate May 13, Church said the use of U.S. troops in Cambodia, "though presently limited in scope, could easily become the first step toward committing the United States to the defense of still another government in Southeast Asia." The Vietnam war, he said, "has already stretched the generation gap so wide that it threatens to pull the country apart." The Foreign Relations Committee report on the amend-

ment said it was time for Congress "to assert its Constitutional powers in order to prevent a widening of the war."

Committee Chairman J. W. Fulbright (D, Ark.) and Stennis clashed sharply May 15. Fulbright said since the President had pledged the pullout by June 30, there was nothing wrong with legislation to hold him to it. Stennis asked him if he believed the pledge. "No, I don't believe him," Fulbright answered. "I don't think he knows what's going to happen. No government is run just on people's words. It's run on laws."

"If he wants to go into another sanctuary," Fulbright said, "let him come to the Senate. One of those sanctuaries may be in China, another in Laos, why shouldn't he come ask the sanction of the Senate?"

The Senate, by 82–11 vote May 26, approved a preamble to the Cooper-Church amendment. The preamble declared that the proposed shutoff of funds for U.S. troops in Cambodia after July 1 was "in concert with the declared objectives" of the President to avoid U.S. involvement in Cambodia after June 30 and to expedite withdrawal of U.S. forces from Cambodia.

The preamble was considered a concession by the amendment's backers to the Administration because it indicated the amendment was not a repudiation of the President. Administration forces, however, remained aligned against the substance of the amendment on the ground it did not specify Presidential power to take any action necessary to protect American troops. An attempt to reach a compromise on the issue had been made by Cooper in discussions with Presidential Counselor Bryce N. Harlow.

On the floor May 20, Senate GOP Whip Robert P. Griffin (Mich.) said he knew it was not the intention of the amendment's sponsors "to aid the enemy" but "it does aid the enemy when we tie the hands of the commander in chief." Democratic Leader Mansfield insisted the amendment was not "an affront to the President as commander in chief" but "consistent with the President's pledge on Cambodia." When Griffin objected May 26 to the amendment as still "a slap in the face of the President" even with the preamble, which he described as "cosmetics," Cooper replied if the implication was that he was trying to "undermine" the President, "I challenge you from the very bottom of my soul." "All we are saying," Cooper said, "is that before the operation is extended and leads us into a war in Cambodia, under the Constitution, the President must come to Congress and get its approval."

Debate over policy increased. The domestic debate over the Administration's Southeast Asia policy intensified during the Cambodia operations.

In broadcast interviews May 17, Senate Democratic Leader Mike Mansfield (Mont.) and Sen. J. W. Fulbright (D, Ark.) denounced the Cambodian thrusts and Vice President Spiro T. Agnew denounced Congressional proposals to cut off funds for such future operations.

Agnew said the Congressional move "to jerk the rug out from under the commander in chief and the troops" was tainted with political motivation and a "reprehensible attitude on the part of the Congress and those that support those resolutions."

Agnew made these other comments: Some speakers at the antiwar rallies May 9 were "the same old tired radicals that everybody in the country's sick of listening to"; "I certainly don't agree that the demonstrations are really indicative of deep-seated student hostility to the Cambodian decision"; "the best place and the first place" to begin cooling the rhetoric "is on the editorial pages of some of the Eastern newspapers."

Mansfield, on the CBS "Face the Nation" program, viewed the Senate proposal to cut off funds for future Cambodia-like operations as "a protective device which will give . . . [the President] support and strength when he needs it because there will be other voices, undoubtedly, at that time trying to bring about a change in the situation."

Fulbright, on the ABC "Issues and Answers" broadcast, called the Cambodian thrust "a serious international disaster" that would prolong the war and had already "clearly weakened our power to influence the situation in the Middle East or nearly anywhere else." He ac-

cused Nixon of having "subverted the Constitution in invading another country without authorization of Congress."

The Cambodia action was endorsed May 18 by Robert H. Finch, secretary of health, education and welfare, who said he supported the President because "his goal in Vietnam is to end the fighting and the killing" and "every decision he has made has been consistent with that goal." Finch stressed the June 30 withdrawal deadline for the U.S. troops from Cambodia.

The political basis of the Cambodia decision was stressed May 15 by Deputy Defense Secretary David Packard in a speech at Fort Worth, Tex. "Our failure to disrupt Cambodia bases earlier," he said, "was dictated by political considerations which, as long as Prince Sihanouk remained in power, it was felt overrode military considerations. With the downfall of Sihanouk, there was no longer any reason to believe that action by South Vietnam or the United States in the occupied border areas would be objectionable to the government of Cambodia." "Our failure to strike these base areas earlier was an act of self-denial on our part which we would not have indulged in if we had been guided solely by military considerations."

Gov. Nelson A. Rockefeller (R, N.Y.), however, added his voice to those in dissent. In an Ithaca, N.Y. speech May 16, he said the U.S. should "get out of Cambodia as rapidly as possible" and "achieve a negotiated peace" for Vietnam.

Other antiwar statements:

Former Defense Secretary Clark M. Clifford (May 22 Life magazine, published May 16) said the Cambodia incursion was "reckless" and "foolhardy," Vietnamization "a formula for perpetual war." The U.S. should "get out of Vietnam on a scheduled and orderly basis no later than the end of 1971" and inform the Vietnamese a more rapid withdrawal could come if the safety of U.S. troops were assured by a ceasefire and cessation of military pressures in Laos and Cambodia. Clifford said the combat role of GIs in Southeast Asia should be ended no later than Dec. 31, 1970.

Ford Foundation President McGeorge Bundy, an adviser to Presidents Kennedy and Johnson, said May 15 another action like the Cambodian intervention "would tear the country and the Administration to pieces." It was imperative now to "call in the Congress as a required partner in any such decision" and "a track that would have Congressional support" would be withdrawal of U.S. troops from South Vietnam "at a rate which will be increased—and never decreased—until only volunteer supporting forces remain." "The maintenance of our own society is now more important by far than the precise rate of our disengagement in Vietnam."

In other developments:

■Senate Foreign Relations Committee Chairman J. W. Fulbright (D, Ark.) said May 21 a committee staff report indicated "no evidence there was about to be an invasion of South Vietnam from the sanctuaries" in Cambodia and "no evidence of a massive buildup" there by the enemy in the weeks and months prior to the Presidential decision to attack.

■Sen. Albert Gore (D, Tenn) objected May 21 to reports Nixon had told W. R. Smedberg III, president of the Reserve Officers Association, two days before his April 30 address to the nation of the attack he was ordering. Gore said Congress was not informed in advance.

■Retired Lt. Gen. James M. Gavin warned the Fulbright committee May 11 the U.S. might be headed for a "catastrophic confrontation" with Communist China and proposed that a Cabinet-level official be assigned to draft a plan to "extricate" the U.S. from Vietnam as soon as possible.

■Former Undersecretary of State George W. Ball told the House Foreign Affairs Committee May 26 there was little to gain and much to lose from "our Cambodian adventure" because the Indochina involvement was permitting the Soviet Union to threaten Israel and thus impair U.S. interests in an area of the world far more important to the U.S. than Southeast Asia.

Some U.S. troops withdrawn. These were the military developments as U.S. and South Vietnamese troops continued to scour Cambodian sanctuaries in search of Communist troops and supplies:

■The first withdrawal of U.S. troops was reported May 12–16. The capture of part of COSVN was reported.

■There were two new allied thrusts across the Cambodian border, reported May 14 and 16.

■Sharp fighting was reported between Cambodian and Communist troops for the major stronghold of Kompong Cham.

■High weekly death tolls were suffered by U.S. and South Vietnamese troops battling in both Cambodia and South Vietnam (reported May 14).

The areas vacated by the American troops were the Bathu sector of the Parrot's Beak and the Sesan region to the north, 40 miles west of Pleiku. More than 1,000 soldiers were withdrawn May 12–13. The U.S. high command announced May 16 that a total of 5,500 men had been removed from the Sesan front, reducing the remaining American force in Cambodia to at least 18,000 men, mostly in the area north of Tayninh Province. Up to 1,500 South Vietnamese rangers who had joined the American drive in the Sesan area May 5 were to remain there, assisted by American air cover and logistical support. According to preliminary statistics, the Sesan operation resulted in capture of 803 Communist weapons and 599 tons of rice. Thirty Americans and 184 Communists were killed.

U.S. Ambassador Ellsworth Bunker, who had returned from Saigon to Washington the previous week for consultations, said May 10 that he doubted that American troops would have to make repeated forays into Cambodia to prevent the rebuilding of North Vietnamese bases destroyed by allied forces. He predicted that the Communist sanctuaries would require 10 months of rebuilding "to get them functioning in the same magnitude." "This operation," Bunker said, "gives more time to develop the South Vietnamese forces."

Casualty figures for the entire Cambodian operation as of May 18, according to the allied command, were 7,843 Viet Cong and North Vietnamese killed; 150 Americans killed and 598 wounded; and 700 South Vietnamese soldiers slain and 1,878 wounded. In the first 17 days of the campaign, allied forces had captured 8,611 Communist weapons, 1,095 crew-served weapons, 1,551 tons of ammunition, and 3,223 tons of rice, the U.S. command reported.

(Newsweek magazine reported May 17 that Defense Secretary Melvin R. Laird, in a top-secret message sent to Gen. Creighton W. Abrams, commander of U.S. forces in Vietnam, said: "In light of the controversy over the U.S. move into Cambodia, the American public would be impressed" by evidence of the capture of: "1, high-ranking enemy prisoners; 2, major enemy headquarters; 3, large enemy caches." Laird May 18 denied the report and said Newsweek had apologized to him for its publication. Lester Bernstein, Newsweek managing editor, denied the magazine had apologized to Laird. Newsweek also reported that few Communists had been captured in the allied drive into Cambodia because they had started a major withdrawal from their border sanctuaries along with 20–50% of their supplies April 20, 10 days before the allied attacks began.)

In the opening of the new fronts in Cambodia, the burden of the fighting was carried by South Vietnamese forces assisted by American advisers and U.S. supportive fire. In the first operation, announced May 14, an undetermined number of government troops struck from South Vietnam's Central Highlands, 22 miles south of the Sesan region. The U.S. command reported May 15 that the drive was supported by American advisers, artillery, helicopter gunships and medical evacuation facilities. The South Vietnamese army newspaper reported May 15 that the purpose of the offensive was to relieve Cambodian troops defending the town of Bo Keo, 22 miles inside Cambodia.

The second new thrust into Cambodia, reported May 17, was centered in the Mekong Delta region between South Vietnam's Chaudoc Province and the Cambodian province of Takeo. The strike force, including 10,000 South Vietnamese troops supported by 200 American advisers, aircraft and logistical elements, reached Takeo May 17, killing 211 enemy soldiers in the 20-mile thrust.

In the fighting for Kompong Cham, North Vietnamese and Viet Cong forces penetrated the city in force May 16 but Cambodian troops regained it the following day. Earlier in the week, the Communists had overrun Tonle Bet, the town directly opposite Kompong Cham on the eastern bank of the Mekong River. Kompong Cham, a provincial capital 74 miles north of Pnompenh, was the Cambodian military headquarters for three surrounding provinces. U.S.-made T-28 bombers flown by Cambodian pilots had pounded Communist positions surrounding the city and Cambodian reinforcements were brought in. The government counterattacks had forced the Communists to withdraw and Cambodian soldiers were in complete control of Kompong Cham May 17.

Capture of part of COSVN, the Communists' Central Office for South Vietnam was reported May 17 by Lt. Gen. Michael S. Davison, commander of American forces in Cambodia. He said sections of the North Vietnamese and Viet Cong base headquarters had been uncovered between May 11 and 13, four to five miles north of Memot, about 10 miles inside Cambodia. Davison said the find included parts of the COSVN "post office" and of the base's finance, economy, education and training sections.

Sihanouk forms regime in exile. Prince Norodom Sihanouk, deposed Cambodian chief of state, announced the formation of a government in exile in Peking May 5. The regime was promptly recognized by Communist China as the "sole legal" government of Cambodia. As a consequence of its action, China May 6 severed diplomatic relations with the Cambodian government of Premier Lon Nol, as did North Vietnam and North Korea.

(Soviet Premier Aleksei N. Kosygin expressed support for the Sihanouk government in a telegram sent to the prince May 10, but avoided the subject of recognition of his regime. Moscow continued to maintain diplomatic relations with the Pnompenh government of Premier Lon Nol.)

In a proclamation announcing his new government, Sihanouk declared it was prepared "to make all sacrifices for achieving final victory over the American imperialists and their [Cambodian] lackeys," Lon Nol and First Deputy Premier Prince Sisowath Sirik Matak. The government's foreign policy would be one of "national independence, peace, neutrality and non-alignment," the proclamation said. The new government, according to the statement, would combat "the American imperialists" and overthrow "the dictatorship of their valets headed by Lon Nol-Sirik Matak."

The government was proclaimed under the leadership of the National United Front of Kampuchea, a recently formed group headed by Sihanouk. He said the front included Communists. The principal members of Sihanouk's cabinet were Penn Nouth, premier, and Sarim Chhak, foreign minister.

Diplomatic recognition of the Sihanouk government was reported May 6 to have been extended by North Vietnam, North Korea, Rumania, Yugoslavia, Cuba, Syria, Iraq, Albania, the Pathet Lao and the Viet Cong.

While the Communist countries ended ties with the Lon Nol government, South Vietnam took the first step to reestablish the diplomatic relations with Cambodia that had been severed by Sihanouk in 1963. A South Vietnamese Permanent Liaison Mission in the Cambodian capital that would function like an embassy had been agreed to by Pnompenh and Saigon May 5.

Rallies were reported May 8 to have been held throughout China hailing Sihanouk's government and pledging full support to him and all the Indochinese people in their struggle against the U.S. The Chinese news agency Hsinhua reported that Premier Penn Nouth had sent a message May 6 to U.S. Sen. Mike Mansfield, (D, Mont.) urging him to use his influence as majority leader to make "the great American people understand that they are being dangerously dragged by their President into a war spreading to the whole of Indochina." Penn Nouth was said to have expressed thanks to Mansfield and other U.S. senators for opposing President Nixon's move into Cambodia.

Sihanouk and members of his government-in-exile conferred with North Vietnamese officials in Hanoi May 25–27. A Hanoi broadcast May 27 said the conferees had reached agreement on "the struggle of the North Vietnamese and Cambodian people against the U.S. aggressors" but gave no further details. Sihanouk met with President Ton Duc Thang, Premier Pham Van Dong, Defense Minister Vo Nguyen Giap and other North Vietnamese leaders.

A Hanoi broadcast said Sihanouk and North Vietnamese Premier Pham Van Dong had signed a joint statement June 7, but gave no further details. Speaking at a banquet that night, Sihanouk pledged that the Cambodian people would fight alongside the Vietnamese Communists to defeat "United States imperialism." He rejected peace talks or negotiations as a means of achieving peace in Indochina.

In a statement before leaving Hanoi, Sihanouk lauded American critics of the Nixon Administration's Indochina policy. He urged Americans "to do their best to compel President Nixon to order the total and immediate withdrawal of United States and satellite troops" from Cambodia.

A Hanoi broadcast May 28 disclosed that members and supporters of Sihanouk's government had met in a "liberated area" of Cambodia May 7–8. The conference was described as a congress of the Cambodian People's Movement of United Resistance, a subordinate organization under Sihanouk's ruling National United Front of Kampuchea.

U.S. weighed Chinese move. U.S. Undersecretary of State Elliot Richardson said May 10 that the U.S. had decided to send troops into Cambodia despite the risk of Communist Chinese military intervention in Indochina.

Speaking on ABC's "Issues and Answers," Richardson said that prior to ordering American forces into Cambodia, President Nixon had received intelligence reports of veiled threats that Chinese "volunteers" might join North Vietnamese and Viet Cong forces fighting in Cambodia and Laos. "I don't think I could exclude it as a possibility, but nonetheless it was sufficiently remote, that looking at the situation on balance, it was concluded that this was an acceptable risk,"

Richardson said. He acknowledged that he and other Presidential advisers had voiced "misgivings with respect to possible wider repercussions" from the Cambodian move, but he emphasized that he had not opposed the decisions that were taken.

Saigon bars troop withdrawal. South Vietnamese President Nguyen Van Thieu said May 8 that his country's forces would not be bound by the June 30 time limit President Nixon had set for American troops operating in Cambodia. Thieu said: "We have no deadline, no limits. . . . When there is a target, we will strike it."

Thieu's statement was coupled with a disclosure that he and Cambodian Premier Lon Nol had reached "agreements in principle" for the continuing operation of Saigon's forces against the Communist sanctuaries in eastern Cambodia. Thieu said the understanding had been agreed to two or three days before President Nixon had announced his decision April 30 to send U.S. forces into Cambodia. Thieu said he already had provided the Pnompenh forces with 4,000 ethnic Cambodian mercenaries who had been fighting with Saigon's soldiers in South Vietnam.

The State Department said May 14 that there had been "no understanding or agreement" between Washington and Saigon on how long South Vietnamese forces would remain in Cambodia.

U.S. Ambassador to Saigon Ellsworth Bunker told the Senate Foreign Relations Committee May 14 that he did not know whether ARVN (Army of South Vietnam) units would be withdrawn from Cambodia according to the U.S. pullout schedule. The problem of U.S. support for such troops was "a problem we have to meet if they are there," he warned.

At Key Biscayne May 16, White House officials held a briefing for reporters (no direct quotes stipulated) to convey the impression that the White House had every reason to believe that South Vietnam would withdraw its combat forces from Cambodia near the U.S. deadline. The officials also indicated the Cambodian operation had deprived the enemy of the ability to mount major offensives for six to 10 months.

They denied speculation that the operation had been undertaken in part to demonstrate to the Soviet Union U.S. firmness at a time the Soviet influence in the Middle East was being reasserted. Hope was expressed that the Cambodian move would illustrate to the enemy the wisdom of bargaining seriously at the Paris peace talks.

Former U.S. chief negotiator at the talks, W. Averell Harriman, told the Joint Economic Committee of Congress May 14 the only way to force the Saigon government to undertake serious negotiations was to set a "fixed schedule" for withdrawal of all U.S. troops from Vietnam.

Vice President Nguyen Cao Ky May 21 reaffirmed previous Saigon government statements that South Vietnamese forces were determined to stay in Cambodia after June 30. "I wish to make clear that we will not let our hands be bound by anyone any more," Ky said. He called the "hypothesis" of a Saigon troop withdrawal along with an American pullout "a silly argument of silly people." Ky said South Vietnamese forces were capable of operating independently in Cambodia and would stay there "not only to destroy the Communists but also to provide protection for the lives and property of 600,000 resident Vietnamese."

South Vietnamese Foreign Minister Tran Van Lam said May 21 that "we have no timetable for the withdrawal of our troops from Cambodia."

The U.S. May 20 had publicly acknowledged for the first time the possibility of South Vietnamese troops remaining in Cambodia beyond June 30. "Determinations have not finally been made" whether Saigon's forces would follow the American departure, a State Department spokesman said. Heretofore, Nixon Administration officials had insisted they did not know about South Vietnam's intentions in Cambodia.

Defense Secretary Melvin R. Laird said May 22 that it would "be a mistake . . . to make a firm timetable and establish it here for South Vietnamese forces to withdraw." This was in contrast to President Nixon's May 8 press conference statement that "I would expect that the South Vietnamese would come out approximately at the same time we do." Laird, in a TV interview, warned that announcing the withdrawal of Saigon's forces in advance would "destroy the military or tactical advantage that might be established by keeping . . . the North Vietnamese off guard." Laird stressed, however, that there would be "no American advisers in Cambodia after June 30."

White House Press Secretary Ronald L. Ziegler, said May 21 "it would not be appropriate to put a timetable on South Vietnamese forces."

State Department press officer Carl Bartch said May 25 that American tactical air support for the South Vietnamese after June 30 was a possibility that was being left open. He said: "I think it's fair to say that when the United States withdraws its forces from Cambodia June 30, that air and logistic support might also be withdrawn. I am distinguishing between that and what might arise in the future after June 30." While U.S. logistic and air support would be withdrawn June 30, they could be restored July 1, he said.

Secretary of State William P. Rogers said May 24 that the U.S. was "not concerned at all" at reports that South Vietnamese forces would not be removed from Cambodia June 30. The continued presence of those troops in Cambodia, he said, fitted in with President Nixon's doctrine that "Asians work together to solve Asian problems." Rogers affirmed that American troops would be out of Cambodia by July 1. "But insofar as other aspects of the war are concerned, there is no point in signaling the enemy in advance," he said.

Cambodian Foreign Minister Yem Sambaur said May 25 that his government would ask the U.S. to keep its forces in Cambodia until the end of the war. He said the Pnompenh government might ask Thailand for soldiers. Thailand, the Philippines and South Korea had announced May 22 they would provide Cambodia with supplies but not weapons. Manila and Seoul said they would confine their assistance to humanitarian aid. Thailand said it would provide Cambodia with military equipment.

Saigon troops open new front. A force of 2,500 South Vietnamese troops opened a new front in Cambodia May 20. Supported by U.S. air power and advisers, the government soldiers pushed across the border west of the U.S. Special Forces Camp at Duclap, South Vietnam, 125 miles north of Saigon. The first Communist resistance was encountered May 23. Reports said 20 North Vietnamese and seven South Vietnamese were killed in the clash, about six miles inside Cambodia.

The new thrust brought to 40,000 the number of South Vietnamese troops operating in Cambodia, about twice the previous week's total. Official sources May 22 placed U.S. troop strength in the country at about 12,000, up 2,000 over the previous weekend. The additional troops were said to have been sent in to reinforce other ground troops operating to secure and evacuate captured Communist supplies.

Among other major military developments in Cambodia:

About 10,000 South Vietnamese troops May 24 captured Cambodia's largest rubber plantation at Chup, about 50 miles northeast of Pnompenh. A regiment of North Vietnamese and Viet Cong troops reportedly retreated within the 70-square mile plantation and were said to be surrounded by South Vietnamese troops. The attack was led by the Khmer Krom, ethnic Cambodian mercenaries assigned to the Cambodian army. They had previously fought with U.S. Special Forces in South Vietnam. South Vietnamese air assaults on the plantation May 23 left it a flaming ruin. The attacks killed 15 civilian workers and injured 80.

In the ground fighting at Chup, 12 Khmer Rouge, a Cambodian Communist guerrilla group, were killed and 15 were reported captured. Twenty-five more of the enemy were said to have been slain east of the plantation. Two South Vietnamese soldiers were killed.

The South Vietnamese force that occupied the plantation were said to have confiscated all its movable assets and ordered the French managers to leave in three days. Lt. Gen. Do Cao Tri, South Vietnamese commander of the operation, was said to have told the managers that his troops could not occupy the region and, therefore, had to remove all the material to prevent its capture by the Communists who might return. The plantation at Chup accounted for 50% of Cambodia's rubber production.

In another action May 24, Khmer Krom troops recaptured Tonle Bet, held by the North Vietnamese since May 11. The town, on the east bank of the Mekong River opposite Kompong Cham and less than 10 miles from Chup, had been abandoned by North Vietnamese troops a few hours earlier. Tonle Bet had been pounded by Cambodian artillery and mortars for a week.

In fighting to the south, Saigon troops linked up with Cambodian soldiers May 20 in a town 25 miles north of Takeo, following a drive launched May 17 from South Vietnam's Chaudoc Province. Saigon forces reported killing more than 400 Viet Cong during the operation. The link-up secured Route 2, a key road running between Pnompenh and Takeo, 54 miles south.

The U.S. Defense Department disclosed May 21 that preliminary intelligence reports indicated that COSVN, the Communists' Central Office for South Vietnam, had been shifted beyond the 21-mile limit set by President Nixon for U.S. ground operations in Cambodia. Deputy Assistant Secretary Jerry Friedheim said it appeared that COSVN, a mobile base headquarters, had been reestablished north of Mimot, a town in the Fishhook area where allied troops struck April 30.

The Cambodian government May 21 reported acts of sabotage in two regions previously believed to be secure. An explosion May 19 damaged a bridge on the road to Pnompenh and Angkor, about 75 miles north of the capital near the town of Kompong Thmar. The rail line linking Pnompenh and Thailand was put out of operation May 18 when a rail was removed near Muong, about 140 miles north of Pnompenh. Train traffic was resumed May 21.

Official sources in Saigon reported May 25 that the capture of large caches of Communist weapons and ammunition in Cambodia had resulted in a reduction of enemy firepower in South Vietnam. (As of May 25, more than 14,000 enemy weapons were said to have been seized.) The average enemy shelling attacks dropped to five or six mortar or artillery shells from the previous rate of 10–12.

Among other military developments:

■North Vietnamese forces May 28 pushed into the provincial capital of Preyveng, 30 miles east of Pnompenh, and engaged the Cambodian garrison in street fighting. A relief force of government soldiers and more than 1,000 South Vietnamese marines fought their way toward the city May 29 to relieve the beleaguered defenders. South Vietnamese marines were reported to have killed 19 North Vietnamese in an encounter near Banam, 10 miles southwest of Preyveng. The attack on Preyveng was described by official sources as part of the Communists' plan to strengthen their positions east of the Mekong River to obtain a new supply route beyond their invaded sanctuaries along the South Vietnamese border.

■The district capital of Tang Krasang, 45 miles northwest of Kompong Cham, was captured by Communist forces May 28. Its fall cut the road from Kompong Thom to Pnompenh. South Vietnamese troops were reported to have killed 72 Communists in a clash 10 miles east of Kompong Cham. South Vietnamese losses were put at 19 wounded.

■A force of about 1,000 Viet Cong June 3 captured Set Bo, 11 miles south of Pnompenh. Government troops, assisted by a series of air strikes, recaptured the Bassac River village June 5.

■The allies reduced the number of their forces in Cambodia. Saigon announced May 26 the withdrawal of 16,000 government troops, reducing the number of South Vietnamese forces in the country to 30,000 men. It was reported June 8 that 18,400 American troops had been withdrawn from Cambodia, leaving 12,600 that remained to be pulled out by the June 30 deadline.

Casualty totals—The U.S. command in Saigon reported May 25 that 201 Americans had been killed and 756 wounded since the start of operations in Cambodia April 30. Casualties of other forces during that period—South Vietnamese, more than 600 killed and more than 2,000 wounded; Communists, more than 9,000 killed.

The American command had reported May 21 that 217 Americans had been killed in Southeast Asia May 10–16. the highest weekly toll since August 1969.

Seventy-seven had been killed in Cambodia and 140 in South Vietnam.

Martial law in Cambodia. Martial law went into effect throughout Cambodia June 1. The emergency rule was coupled with a general one-hour alert in Pnompenh. The streets of the capital were cleared and stores and houses were locked and shuttered. Tanks, aircraft and troops patrolled the area.

The martial law decree provided death by firing squad for such crimes as revolt, aiding and abetting the enemy, desertion, political assassination and looting. Persons found listening to Hanoi, Peking or Viet Cong broadcasts were subject to prison terms of 5–10 years.

Premier Lon Nol had announced May 22 that martial law was necessary to cope with profiteers, persons who did not participate in "salvation activities" and military deserters.

Asians urge Indochina parley. The convening of a new international conference to end the conflict in Indochina and the reactivation of the International Control Commission in Cambodia were recommended at the conclusion of a two-day meeting of foreign ministers of 12 Asian nations in Jakarta, Indonesia May 17.

Participating states in the parley, convened specifically to consider the crisis in Cambodia, were Indonesia, Australia, New Zealand, Japan, South Korea, South Vietnam, Laos, Thailand, Malaysia, Singapore and the Philippines. Cambodia attended as a "special invitee."

A final communique urged "respect for the sovereignty, independence, neutrality and territorial integrity of Cambodia." It called for the immediate end of the fighting there and the withdrawal of all foreign troops. The statement urged the participants of the 1954 Geneva Conference on Indochina to cooperate in achieving those ends. The foreign ministers of Japan, Malaysia and Indonesia were appointed as a "task force" to start immediate talks with Britain and the Soviet Union, co-chairmen of the Geneva conference, to reactivate the ICC and to promote the new international peace conference. The task force also was authorized to meet with U.N. Secretary General U Thant to encourage U.N. intercession to help restore peace.

Indonesian Foreign Minister Adam Malik, chairman and organizer of the meeting, was instructed to continue consultations with the Jakarta conference participants and other interested nations on "further possible steps toward a peaceful solution in Cambodia."

The Jakarta communique made no mention of a reported Pnompenh government message sent to the opening meeting May 16 requesting Asian and Pacific nations to send troops to Cambodia to help fight the Communist invaders. The message was sent by the ruling National Committee of Salvation over the signature of Premier Lon Nol.

Cambodian Foreign Minister Yem Sambaur had said in Jakarta May 17 that he was not disappointed by the conference's refusal to provide his country with military aid. He said he came to the parley anticipating only "moral support and sympathy and understanding for the current situation in Cambodia."

Traditional animosities stirred. The increasing presence of South Vietnamese troops in Cambodia began to stir up the traditional animosities that existed between the two countries. Resentment was expressed by two Pnompenh officials.

Maj. Am Rong, a spokesman for the Cambodian military command, said in Pnompenh May 21 that Cambodians would rather die than "live under Vietnamese domination." Asked whether this applied to South Vietnamese as well as Viet Cong and North Vietnamese, Amrong replied he meant all Vietnamese. A Cambodian government broadcast May 24 denied that Amrong meant to be critical of Saigon. The statement said: "South Vietnamese forces are in Cambodia to help us liquidate the Viet Cong and North Vietnamese aggressors. The Saigon troops were consequently not aimed at in the spokesman's declaration, which had been exploited out of all proportion."

Posters demanding the withdrawal of South Vietnamese troops from Cambodia were pasted on the walls of the briefing room in which Am Rong made his statement to foreign newsmen. The placards accused Saigon's soldiers of "looting, raping our women, burning and massacring women and children."

The chief of the Cambodian information service asserted May 22 that "We now have two invasions being conducted in Cambodia, the North Vietnamese and the South Vietnamese. . . . The Vietnamese are expansionists and we fear that if this continues Cambodia will disappear, though we would die before this happens."

A statement criticizing the behavior of South Vietnamese troops had been made available at the Cambodian army information center in Pnompenh May 21, but was quickly withdrawn without explanation. It said: "Americans, withdraw quickly the South Vietnamese army from Cambodian territory. These Vietnamese soldiers have committed inhuman acts against the Cambodian population. . . . Americans bring out Vietnamese Cambodian compatriots in South Vietnam to help us kick out the Viet Cong and South Vietnamese who have always wanted to extinguish the Cambodian race from the world." The statement held the U.S. "responsible for these barbarous acts of the South Vietnamese army." The Cambodian government May 22 disclaimed any knowledge of the origins of the statement.

Refugee pullout halted. South Vietnam May 22 announced a halt in the repatriation of Vietnamese refugees in Cambodia. About 50,000–80,000 already had been removed to South Vietnam since the start of evacuation efforts May 10. About 70,000 remained stranded in assembly camps in Cambodia.

Saigon halted the refugee withdrawal because measures adopted by the Pnompenh government provided greater security for the Vietnamese residents in Cambodia, according to Pham Huy Ty, the head of South Vietnam's permanent liaison mission in Pnompenh. The second phase of the program, to be tested for 10 days, would remove Vietnamese from refugee camps to their homes in Cambodia where they would try to resume their normal routine, Ty said.

Lt. Gen. Do Cao Tri, commander of South Vietnamese troops in Cambodia, warned May 22 that "if the Cambodians should continue to mistreat our compatriots, then our army will have an ap-

propriate action." South Vietnamese State Minister Pham Quang Dan, chairman of a committee to aid Vietnamese repatriates, said Saigon's policy "is to transfer Vietnamese from dangerous to safe areas in Cambodia. Repatriation to Vietnam will be the exception from now on."

Ky visits Pnompenh. South Vietnamese Vice President Nguyen Cao Ky conferred with Cambodian officials in Pnompenh June 4–6 to resolve the questions of Saigon's military role in Cambodia and Vietnamese refugees in that country.

In an address to an extraordinary session of the Cambodian parliament June 6, Ky hailed the current allied operations in Cambodia as "a great victory." Lauding the military cooperation between his country and Cambodia, Ky said that Saigon's "fire power and combat units will be ready to intervene wherever you want us to be, as soon as you ask us." Speaking later at a news conference, Ky pledged Cambodia "whatever [arms] you need." "If we have it, we will give it to you for your fight against the Communist North Vietnamese enemy."

Returning to Saigon later June 6, Ky disclosed in an interview aboard his plane that the South Vietnamese air force had begun to support Cambodian troops in operations in central and western Cambodia. He said South Vietnamese planes had been involved in action in the battle for Kompong Thom June 5–6 [see below]. Ky said he had discussed with Pnompenh's leaders the possibility of establishing a joint Cambodian-Thai-South Vietnamese front that would stretch across Cambodia diagonally from the Thai border in the northwest to the tip of the Parrot's Beak in the southeast. He stressed the need to keep pressure on the Communist forces after June 30, when U.S. forces were scheduled to withdraw from the country. "If we stop, in the next two or three weeks they [the Communists] will mount a big attack," Ky said.

Ky said under an agreement reached with Cambodia, Saigon would accept those Vietnamese refugees who wished to return to South Vietnam. Those who decided to remain, would receive "all kinds of assurances and protection" from the Cambodian government, Ky said.

U.S. sent arms to Cambodia. The State Department disclosed May 16 that the U.S. had secretly begun to ship small arms to Cambodia April 25 while the Nixon Administration publicly announced it was still considering a request by Premier Lon Nol for the weapons.

The department explained that it was required by law to inform Congress within 30 days when arms were supplied from U.S. defense stocks. The department said it had 10 days remaining to comply with the notification requirement because M-2 carbines and other small weapons had been airlifted to Pnompenh April 25. The department officials disclosed that Cambodia already had received nearly 10,000 M-2s and that more were on the way. Other weapons to be sent to Pnompenh were to include mortars and recoilless rifles.

The State Department informed Chairman J. W. Fulbright of the Senate Foreign Relations Committee May 22 that the Administration had agreed to Cambodia's request for $7-1/2 million worth of arms. The department's letter to Fulbright was accompanied by a signed Presidential statement declaring the aid important to U.S. security, a declaration required under the 1969 foreign aid act since it did not specifically allocate military aid for Cambodia.

Cambodia gets Asian military aid. South Vietnam and Thailand decided to provide direct military assistance to Cambodia in its struggle against the Vietnamese Communists under separate agreements reached in Saigon May 27 and in Pnompenh May 27–28. The Saigon agreement gave South Vietnam a broad mandate to pursue its military operations in Cambodia. Thailand said it would send a volunteer force to Cambodia that was to be armed and equipped by the U.S.

The tripartite military efforts followed appeals by the U.S. to have South Vietnam, Thailand and Cambodia undertake joint defense plans.

The South Vietnamese-Cambodian agreement was contained in a 17-point communique signed May 27 following three days of talks in Saigon. The statement, signed by Cambodian and South Vietnamese Foreign Ministers Yem Sambaur and Tran Van Lam, said Saigon's military forces had entered Cambodia to "help Cambodian troops to drive out the Viet Cong and North Vietnamese forces, [and] will withdraw when their task is completed." The two ministers also signed three other documents reestablishing diplomatic relations, broken since 1963, providing for economic cooperation and dealing with the treatment of Vietnamese residents in Cambodia.

The agreement on sending the Thai volunteer force to Cambodia was announced by the Bangkok government June 1. A follow-up announcement June 2 said the troops would take up defense duties in Pnompenh and other Cambodian cities, releasing regular Cambodian troops for combat. The force would be composed of Thais of Cambodian descent and would be drawn mainly from an estimated half-million ethnic Cambodians residing in the eight Thai provinces along the Cambodian border.

The U.S. government expressed support for the agreement on the Thai expeditionary force June 1 and announced June 2 that it would provide the arms and equipment. State Department officials had said May 27 that the South Vietnamese and Thai governments were authorized to provide the Cambodian army with military equipment that had been supplied to them under terms of the U.S.' defense treaties with the Saigon and Bangkok regimes.

Nixon report on Cambodia. President Nixon June 3 called the U.S. and South Vietnamese military probes into Cambodia "the most successful operation of this long and very difficult war." Reporting to the nation in a televised address from the White House, Nixon said the successful operation "insured the continuance and success of our troop withdrawal program." He said 50,000 of the 150,000 U.S. troops whose withdrawal from Vietnam he had announced April 20 "will now be out on Oct. 15."

Nixon said the Cambodia operations also "guaranteed that the June 30 deadline I set for withdrawal of all American forces from Cambodia will be met" and that "this includes all American air support, logistics and military adviser personnel." "The only remaining American activity in Cambodia after July 1," he added, "will be air missions to interdict the movement of enemy troops and material where I find that is necessary to protect the lives and security of our men in South Vietnam."

As for the South Vietnamese activity in Cambodia, Nixon said "our discussions with the South Vietnamese government indicate that their primary objective remains the security of South Vietnam" and their activity in Cambodia "after their withdrawal from the sanctuaries will be determined by the actions of the enemy in Cambodia."

The President said "the door to a negotiated peace remains wide open. Every offer we have made at the conference table, publicly or privately, I herewith reaffirm. We are ready to negotiate whenever they are ready to negotiate."

If the enemy increased its attacks "in a way that jeopardizes the safety of the remaining forces in Vietnam," he said, "I shall, as my action five weeks ago clearly demonstrated, take strong and effective measures to deal with that situation."

The President reiterated his commitment to attain "a just peace in Vietnam." He called it "essential if there is to be a lasting peace in other parts of the world." "I pledged to end this war," he said. "And I shall keep that promise. But I am determined to end the war in a way that will promote peace rather than conflict throughout the world. I am determined to end it in a way that will bring an era of reconciliation to our people—and not an era of furious recrimination. . . . We

have a program for peace—and the greater the support the Administration receives in its efforts, the greater the opportunity to win that just peace we all desire."

The President took note of the "unprecedented barrage of criticism in this country" directed against his Cambodia decision. He expressed his "deep appreciation to the millions of Americans who supported me" and his understanding of "the deep divisions in this country over the war." He realized that many Americans were "deeply troubled" and wanted peace and "to bring the boys home." But, he said, "no group has a monopoly on those concerns. Every American shares those desires. I share them very deeply. Our differences are over the best means to achieve a just peace."

His responsibility as president was to listen to those "who disagree with my policies" but also to make the "hard decisions" necessary to protect the lives of the U.S. troops in Vietnam. If he had failed to meet the "clear threat" to these troops that "was emerging" in Cambodia a month ago, he asked, "would those nations and peoples who rely on America's power and treaty commitments for their security—in Latin America, Europe, the Mideast, other parts in Asia—retain any confidence in the United States?"

Between April 20 and 30, he said, the Communists had attacked "a number of key cities" in Cambodia to link their bases together. "This posed an unacceptable threat" since the entire 600-mile Cambodia-South Vietnam border would then "become one continuous hostile territory from which to launch assaults upon American and allied

---

Supplies Seized by U.S. Forces in Cambodia

The White House June 3 released this list of enemy equipment reported as captured or destroyed in Cambodia since April 30, when U.S. and South Vietnamese forces began their strikes against the sanctuary areas:

Individual weapons—15,251; crew-served weapons—2,114; bunkers and structures destroyed—8,296; machine-gun rounds—3,267,952; rifle rounds—6,910,972; grenades—34,813; mines—3,961; miscellaneous explosives, pounds

(includes 1,000 satchel charges)—76,600.

Antiaircraft rounds—132,694; mortar rounds—48,320; large rocket rounds—1,587; smaller rocket rounds—26,191; recoilless rifle rounds—22,202; rice, pounds—11,080,000; man-months (of rice)—243,760.

Vehicles—359; boats—40; generators—36; radios—186; medical supplies, pounds—50,800; enemy killed in action—9,145; POWs (includes detainees)—1,916.

forces." And, the enemy acted despite "an explicit warning from this government," Nixon said. Therefore, "failure to deal with the enemy action would have eroded the credibility of the United States before the entire world."

The Cambodia thrust had been ordered, he said, to destroy the major enemy bases along the Cambodian frontier, and he reported "that all of our major military objectives have been achieved."

The 43,000 South Vietnamese and 31,-000 U.S. troops that took part in the operations, he said, "moved with greater speed and success than we had planned" and "captured and destroyed far more in war material than we anticipated." In addition, casualties were "far lower than we expected." "In the month of May, in Cambodia alone," he continued, "we captured a total amount of enemy arms, equipment, ammunition and food nearly equal to what we captured in all of Vietnam in all of last year." The rice captured amounted to "more than enough rice to feed all the enemy's combat battalions in Vietnam for over three months." It would take the enemy months "to rebuild his shattered installations" and replace the captured and destroyed equipment, he said.

In assessing the long-range effects, Nixon said, in addition to insuring the success of the U.S. withdrawal, the Cambodia thrust had eliminated an immediate security threat to the troops in Vietnam and gained "precious time" for the South Vietnamese to prepare themselves to carry the burden of the war and release the U.S. troops. He said the splendid performance of the South Vietnamese Army was "one of the most dramatic and heartening developments of the operation." Their "effectiveness, the skill, the valor with which they fought far exceeded our expectations" and the operation "clearly demonstrated that our Vietnamization program is succeeding."

Rogers would retain Cambodia option —Secretary of State William P. Rogers reaffirmed June 7 that U.S. forces would be "out of Cambodia by June 30th" and asserted that U.S. troops would not be used to bolster the current Cambodian government. While a Communist take-over would be "an unfavorable development," he said, it was not so unacceptable that "we would use American forces." Rogers made the statements on the CBS "Face the Nation" broadcast program.

Rogers further stated the Administration's intention not to return U.S. forces to Cambodia but termed the decision not "irrevocable," indicating that U.S. forces could be returned into Cambodia "if it is necessary to protect the lives of American forces right on the border."

Rogers conceded that the U.S. would probably bear "a substantial part of the cost" of the war if it evolved into "South Vietnamese forces and Cambodian forces and even possibly Thai forces, fighting a common enemy."

Nixon sends group to war zone. A delegation of congressmen, senators, governors and White House aides left Washington June 3 at President Nixon's behest to inspect the war theater in South Vietnam and Cambodia.

All but one of the members were considered supporters of the President's Vietnam and Cambodia policies. The lone dissenter making the trip was Sen. Thomas J. McIntyre (D, N.H.). The others included Govs. Raymond P. Shafer (R, Pa.), John A. Love (R, Colo.) and Robert E. McNair (D, S.C.); Sens. John Tower (R, Tex.), George Murphy (R, Calif.) and Howard Cannon (D, Nev.); Reps. Melvin Price (D, Ill.), William G. Bray (R, Ind.), G. William Whitehurst (R, Va.) and O. C. Fisher (D, Tex.); Bryce N. Harlow, counselor to the president, and Herbert G. Klein, director of communications.

The group arrived in Saigon June 4, where they were met by Gen. Creighton W. Abrams, U.S. military commander in Vietnam, and U.S. Ambassador Ellsworth Bunker. After attending briefings, they visited pacified hamlets in the Mekong Delta and a district town in Southeast Cambodia June 6 and visited GIs in Cambodia and South Vietnam June 7. Shafer and Klein flew to Pnompenh June 8 for a meeting with Cambodian Premier Lon Nol. The group left on the return trip to Hawaii later June 8.

Nixon June 10 received an optimistic report from the 11-man delegation.

The group, with one dissenter—Sen. Thomas J. McIntyre (D, N.H.)—reported that the Cambodia operation had been "militarily successful, certainly for the short term" and that, "due at least in some measure to the Cambodian operation," the scheduled U.S. troop withdrawals "can safely and surely proceed." "We conceive and hope," their report said, "that in the coming months an acceleration of withdrawals may even become possible."

The White House made the report public after the group met with President Nixon. It did not distribute the dissent by McIntyre, who presented his views at a news conference. Agreeing that the Cambodia operation had been "a short-term military success," he expressed concern that it had "widened the war" and would not speed the troop withdrawal plan.

The majority report cautioned against excluding "the possibility of significant setbacks in the progress we have noted in Vietnam."

War foes win 2 Senate tests. Critics of Nixon Administration policy in Vietnam won two major Congressional tests June 3 and 11 as the Senate continued its debate on the Cooper-Church amendment to bar funds to "retain" U.S. troops in Cambodia after July 1 or to supply military advisers, mercenaries or combat air support to the Cambodian government without Congressional consent.

In the first of the tests, the Senate rejected by a 54–36 vote June 3 a proposal by Sen. Robert J. Dole (R, Kan.) to bar legislative curbs on the President's war-making authority in Cambodia so long as Americans were held prisoner in Cambodia. A White House spokesman May 27 raised the possibility of a Presidential veto of any measure restricting his powers as commander in chief.

Another move to head off or nullify adoption of this amendment was made June 3 by Sen. Robert C. Byrd (D, W. Va.), who offered to add words that the prohibition would not "preclude the president from taking such action as may be necessary to protect the lives" of U.S. forces in South Vietnam "or to hasten the withdrawal" of U.S. forces from South Vietnam.

Sen. Robert P. Griffin (Mich.), assistant Senate Republican leader, joined in co-sponsoring the Byrd proposal and Nixon informed Senate GOP Leader Hugh Scott (Pa.) by letter June 4 of his endorsement of the Byrd effort. Up to then, the Administration had officially opposed any amendment on Cambodia.

By 52–47 vote June 11, the Senate rejected a proposal by Byrd to affirm the President's authority as commander in chief to retain troops in Cambodia if he considered it necessary to protect U.S. forces in Vietnam.

In asking for defeat of the Byrd proposal June 11, Sen. Frank Church (D., Ida.), the amendment's co-author, said, "the real issue is to preserve the dignity and integrity of the constitutional role of Congress." Senate Democratic Leader Mike Mansfield had led the argument against the Byrd amendment June 9 by branding it "another Tonkin Gulf resolution" granting advance approval to Presidential war-making actions. If the Byrd modification were adopted, he said, "we will have cleared the way for another Vietnam in Cambodia and, perhaps, for still others elsewhere."

Administration supporters of the Byrd statement contended that the Cooper-Church amendment, without recognition of the powers of the President as commander in chief, would tie the President's hands.

After its defeat June 11, White House Press Secretary Ronald L. Ziegler denied Presidential endorsement of the Byrd amendment. The President, he said, had expressed his view only that the Byrd proposal "goes a long way toward eliminating my more serious objections to the Cooper-Church amendment."

In the vote June 11, 39 Democrats and 13 Republicans opposed the Byrd amendment and 29 Republicans and 18 Democrats backed it.

One senator counted on the Administration side of the issue—Sen. B. Everett Jordan (D, N.C.)—voted against the Byrd amendment and afterward referred to consultation with antiwar college students and his decision that the war in Southeast Asia "ought to be broadened only with the consent of Congress."

In an effort to clarify the constitutional issue involved in the debate, the Cooper-Church supporters offered to add language specifying that nothing in their amendment "shall be deemed to impugn" the constitutional powers of the President as commander in chief. This reflected their contention throughout the debate that their amendment did not and could not add to or detract from such Presidential authority. However, Administration supporters evidently considered the new language a potential escape clause permitting presidential action regardless of the Cooper-Church curbs, and the addition was approved 91–0.

The latter provision was further modified June 22 by a 79–5 vote adding this additional language as proposed by Byrd: "including the exercise of that constitutional power which may be necessary to protect the lives of United States armed forces wherever deployed."

The Cooper-Church forces had rejected a similar proposal by Byrd previously on the ground it was specific and, attached as it was to an operative clause, could turn the clause into an escape from the amendment's curbs. The second Byrd proposal was held acceptable on the ground it was a statement of principle.

After the vote June 22, Sen. Robert J. Dole offered an amendment to repeal the 1964 Gulf of Tonkin resolution used by the Johnson Administration as authorization for the U.S. military escalation in Vietnam.

Sen J. W. Fulbright (D, Ark.) deplored the trend in the debate June 23. He said the second Byrd proposal, which he had voted against, could be cited by the President "for starting a shooting war whenever he finds the lives of American forces threatened, wherever they are—indeed, wherever the President as commander in chief may have ordered them to be." By modifying the Cooper-Church amendment to reaffirm the President's power as commander in chief, and by proposing to repeal the Tonkin resolution as "meaningless," he said, the Senate was surrendering its war-making powers to the President. "We still have not made clear that the war power—the creation of situations making war inevitable—is a

power to be exercised by Congress alone," he said.

On the 35th day of debate on Cambodia since its vehicle—the Foreign Military Sales Act—reached the floor, Sen. Norris Cotton (R, N.H.) protested June 16 that the "needs of this country are suffering" and "the Administration would be far better off if we voted on this Church-Cooper amendment." Administration forces were being accused of trying to stall a vote on the Cooper-Church amendment until after the scheduled withdrawal of U.S. troops from Cambodia by the end of June. Democratic leaders were attempting to force a vote by keeping the amendment before the Senate as the backlog of other legislation mounted.

Cooper-Church plan dropped. The Cooper-Church amendment to limit U.S. military involvement in Cambodia was adopted by 58–37 Senate vote June 30. The House, however, rejected the amendment July 9, and it was ultimately dropped from the Foreign Military Sales Act in the year-end effort to get vital legislation passed. A watered-down version of Cooper-Church was finally passed Dec. 29 as part of the defense appropriation bill for fiscal 1971, but the measure barred the introduction of U.S. ground troops only into Thailand or Laos; efforts to retain Cambodia in the ban were defeated.

The Senate's adoption of Cooper-Church represented the first limitation ever voted on the president's powers as commander-in-chief during a war situation. The Foreign Military Sales Act, to which the amendment had been attached, was approved by 75–20 Senate vote later June 30 and sent to the House.

The bill carried another important amendment—repeal of the 1964 Gulf of Tonkin resolution utilized by President Johnson as authorization to escalate the war in Vietnam. The motion expressed Congressional approval of any "necessary measures" by the President to bar aggression in Southeast Asia. The repeal motion, approved June 24 by 81–10 vote, had been brought before the Senate in a controversial manner. The motion was offered by Sen. Robert J. Dole (R, Kan.) despite the fact that another repeal motion, originating in the Senate Foreign Relations Committee, was on the Senate calendar for later debate. Committee Chairman J. W. Fulbright (D, Ark.), a leading war critic, voted against the Dole proposal "to preserve the integrity of the procedures of the Senate." Other doves accused the Republicans—Dole was a key Administration supporter during the Cooper-Church debate—of cynical partisanship in the maneuver. The Nixon Administration had denied that the Tonkin resolution was the basis for its war-making authority in Southeast Asia. It asserted that it drew on the constitutional authority of the president as commander in chief to protect the lives of U.S. military forces.

In a similar move by Administration supporters to blunt the effect of the Cooper-Church amendment, Sen. Gordon P. Allott (Colo.), chairman of the Senate Republican Policy Committee, introduced June 25 a "stop the war amendment" drafted by Senate doves. Sponsored by Sens. George McGovern (D, S.D.) and Mark O. Hatfield (R, Ore.), it would cut off funds for combat activities in Vietnam after Dec. 31 and require the withdrawal of all U.S. forces from Vietnam by mid-1971. The dove fac-

tion planned to bring up the amendment for debate later in the summer after an advertising campaign to gain public support. Allott's commandeering of their proposal, with the express intent of engineering its defeat, was rebuffed. After objections were voiced to the violation of Senate protocol—proposals ordinarily were called up by their own sponsors— the Senate voted 62–29 June 29 to reject Allott's maneuver.

The final day of debate on the Cooper-Church amendment was the day of the announcement of the completed withdrawal of U.S. forces from Cambodia. A GOP effort to delay a vote on the amendment until the withdrawal was complete was climaxed by Senate GOP Whip Robert P. Griffin's (Mich.) declaration June 30 that the amendment was now legally meaningless because U.S. troops had left Cambodia. But the amendment's supporters, who had maintained that the proposal was intended to prevent future Cambodia incursions, persisted and, prior to the final vote, rebuffed a last Administration attempt to dilute the original amendment. With White House instigation, Griffin proposed a revision to authorize additional

---

Text of Cooper-Church Amendment

Limitations on United States involvement in Cambodia.

In concert with the declared objectives of the President of the United States to avoid the involvement of the United States in Cambodia after July 1, 1970, and to expedite the withdrawal of American forces from Cambodia, it is hereby provided that unless specifically authorized by law hereafter enacted, no funds authorized or appropriated pursuant to this act or any other law may be expended after July 1, 1970, for the purposes of—

(1) Retaining United States forces in Cambodia;

(2) Paying the compensation or allowances of, or otherwise supporting, directly or indirectly, any United States personnel in Cambodia who furnish military instruction to Cambodian forces or engage in any combat activity in support of Cambodian forces;

(3) Entering into or carrying out any contract or agreement to provide any contract or agreement to provide military instruction in Cambodia, or to provide persons to engage in any combat activity in support of Cambodian forces; or

(4) Conducting any combat activity in the air above Cambodia in direct support of Cambodian forces.

Nothing contained in this section shall be deemed to impugn the constitutional power of the President as Commander in Chief, including the exercise of that constitutional power which may be necessary to protect the lives of United States armed forces wherever deployed. Nothing contained in this section shall be deemed to impugn the constitutional powers of Congress including the power to declare war and to make rules for the Government and regulation of the armed forces of the United States.

pay for foreign troops going to the military assistance of Cambodia. It was offered on the ground that the amendment as worded would interfere with the Nixon Doctrine pledging the U.S. to help Asians defend themselves. The Cooper-Church forces contended that their amendment was designed only to bar the "hiring" of troops, or mercenaries, to fight in Cambodia and that it would not bar supplying military assistance to other countries helping Cambodia. On the fourth vote, after some switching, the Griffin revision was rejected 50–45.

In the final 58–37 vote approving the Cooper-Church amendment, 42 Democrats and 16 Republicans were aligned against 26 Republicans and 11 Democrats. How the Senate voted:

Democrats (42) for the amendment—Anderson (N.M.), Bayh (Ind.), Bible (Nev.), Burdick (N.D.), Byrd (W. Va.), Cannon (Nev.), Church (Idaho), Cranston (Calif.), Eagleton (Mo.), Fulbright (Ark.), Gore (Tenn.), Gravel (Alaska), Harris (Okla.), Hart (Mich.), Hartke (Ind.), Hollings (S.C.), Hughes (Iowa), Inouye (Hawaii), Jackson (Wash.), Jordan (N.C.), Kennedy (Mass.), Magnuson (Wash.), Mansfield (Mont.), McCarthy (Minn.), McGovern (S.D.), McIntyre (N.H.), Metcalf (Mont.), Mondale (Minn.), Montoya (N.M.), Moss (Utah), Muskie (Me.), Pastore (R.I.), Pell (R.I.), Proxmire (Wis.), Randolph (W. Va.), Ribicoff (Conn.), Spong (Va.), Symington (Mo.), Tydings (Md.), Williams (N.J.), Yarborough (Tex.), Young (Ohio).

Republicans (16) for the amendment—Aiken (Vt.), Brooke (Mass.), Case (N.J.), Cooper (Ky.), Dole (Kan.), Goodell (N.Y.), Hatfield (Ore.), Javits (N.Y.), Mathias (Md.), Packwood (Ore.), Pearson (Kan.), Percy (Ill.), Saxbe (Ohio), Schweiker (Pa.), Smith (Ill.), Stevens (Alaska).

Democrats (11) against the amendment—Allen (Ala.), Byrd (Va.), Eastland (Miss.), Ellender (La.), Ervin (N.C.), Holland (Fla.), McClellan (Ark.), McGee (Wyo.), Sparkman (Ala.), Stennis (Miss.), Talmadge (Ga.).

Republicans (26) against the amendment—Allott (Colo.), Baker (Tenn.), Bellmon (Okla.), Bennett (Utah), Boggs (Del.), Cook (Ky.), Cotton (N.H.), Curtis (Neb.), Dominick (Colo.), Fannin (Ariz.), Fong (Hawaii), Goldwater (Ariz.), Griffin (Mich.), Gurney (Fla.), Hanson (Wyo.), Hruska (Neb.), Jordan (Ohio), Miller (Iowa), Murphy (Calif.), Prouty (Vt.), Scott (Pa.), Smith (Me.), Thurmond (S.C.), Tower (Tex.), Williams (Del.), Young (N.D.).

Not voting but announced as paired (used to denote opposing positions of senators when one or both are absent)—Nelson (D, Wis.), for; Long (D, La.), against.

Senate reaffirms Tonkin repeal. For the second time in 16 days, the Senate voted July 10 to repeal the 1964 Gulf of Tonkin Resolution cited by the Johnson Administration as authorization for expansion of the Vietnam war. The latest repeal measure, approved by a 57–5 vote, was, like the original Tonkin Resolution, a concurrent resolution which did not require presidential action.

Sen. Charles McC. Mathias (R, Md.), original sponsor of the repeal resolution, noted July 10 that the Nixon Administration had "moved away" from the policies embodied in the 1964 resolution and urged the Senate to come up with its own "plan for withdrawal and peace in Asia" in order to avoid a "legislative void" concerning conduct of the war. The Administration relied on the president's power as commander in chief to continue the Indochina military action.

The opposition votes July 10 were cast by Sens. Sam J. Ervin Jr. (D, N.C.), Russell B. Long (D, La.), John L. McClellan (D, Ark.), Spessard Holland (D, Fla.) and James B. Allen (D, Ala.).

Communist forces, captured caches assessed. U.S. intelligence sources revised upwards the number of Communist troops believed operating in Cambodia and in the South Vietnam sector immediately north of Saigon, the New York Times reported June 8. The report also said American officials estimated that only about 30–40% of the Communists' materiel had been found in the Cambodian sanctuaries.

According to newly-discovered enemy documents, the number of Communist troops operating in the III Corps tactical zone, which included Saigon and the Cambodian territory adjacent to it, were placed at 91,000 men. Their strength previously had been estimated at 55,000. In the section of Cambodia opposite the III Corps, Communist forces were said to total 63,000, about 38,000 more than originally had been estimated by American commanders before U.S. troops moved into Cambodia May 1.

The new assessment of enemy strength was based on the discovery of documents indicating the existence of three recovery regiments and the upward revisions in the estimated number of troops in known units. The recovery regiments, totaling 17,700 men, were assigned to the task of rounding up defectors and wounded soldiers for reindoctrination or return to North Vietnam.

The Times report on captured enemy supplies said U.S. military commanders and intelligence analysts believed that allied forces had seized only 30–40% of Communist arms and supply stockpiles and that the figure would probably not exceed 60% when the U.S. operation in Cambodia ended July 1. Three factors were said to preclude the possibility of finding more caches: 1. The North Vietnamese had been extremely careful in concealing large quantities of supplies in heavily jungled areas. In some cases, American troops had found the hidden stores by stumbling over them; 2. The Communist supplies were placed in areas that were so dense that ground troops could miss large cache sites; 3. Since American troops had to be out of Cambodia by July 1, there was not enough time for a thorough search of the area, which some U.S. commanders believed would require several months.

Communists extend attacks. The war in Cambodia was further extended as North Vietnamese and Viet Cong forces launched attacks across the northern part of the country June 3. Cambodian troops engaged in heavy fighting with the Communists at Kompong Thom, 87 miles northeast of Pnompenh, and at Siemreap, 80 miles to the northwest. Siemreap, situated near the historic ruins of Angkor Wat, was only 65 miles from the Thai border. As a result of the fighting there, Thai forces were reported June 5 to have been placed on the alert along the border with Cambodia. The action was taken after North Vietnamese and Viet Cong units were sighted near the Thai provinces of Sisaket and Surin, 250 miles northeast of Bangkok.

In the fighting for Kompong Thom, Communist troops captured the city and the nearby town of Am Leang June 7. They were driven out of the center of Kompong Thom by Cambodian troops June 8, but sporadic fighting continued near the city. Pnompenh communiques reported that 128 Communists had been killed in and around both centers June 3–7. Government losses were listed at nine killed and 23 wounded.

■Communist troops were reported June 11 to have seized the ancient temple ruins of Angkor Wat and opened a new attack June 12 on Siemreap, four miles from the edge of the huge temple complex. Cambodian troops had fought heavy clashes with the Communists at Siemreap June 3–7. In their latest attacks, the Communists captured the Siemreap airport June 13 and moved into parts of the town the following day. Pnompenh reported June 14 that its troops regained control of both the airport and the town. Cambodia charged June 15 that the North Vietnamese had established a command post outside Angkor Wat, laid mines and built emplacements at the entrance of the shrine. A Hanoi broadcast June 12 had denied that North Vietnamese and Viet Cong troops had occupied Angkor Wat. Prince Norodom Sihanouk's government-in-exile June 15 denied that its forces had occupied the temple.

■U.S. troops engaged in heavy clashes with Communist soldiers June 8–13 within an 11-mile radius of Memot in the Fishhook region. American casualties totaled 13 killed and 60 wounded. Enemy losses were estimated at nine killed. The U.S. command reported June 14 that 287 Americans had been killed and 1,245 wounded since the start of the Cambodian operations May 1. South Vietnamese losses were put at 679 killed and 3,064 wounded in all the operations in Cambodia since March 20. Communist fatalities were reported to total 11,376.

■South Vietnamese marines were reported June 15 to have killed 110 North Vietnamese in three battles around Preyveng, 30 miles east of Pnompenh. Twelve South Vietnamese were killed and 37 wounded.

Newsmen killed or captured. Eight TV newsmen, including three Americans, were reported missing and believed captured or killed by the Viet Cong after their three vehicles were ambushed May 30 near Takeo, 32 miles south of Pnompenh. The death of one of the victims was confirmed June 3. He was identified as CBS correspondent George Syvertsen, 38, whose body was found in a shallow grave near a burned jeep at the scene of the reported ambush. Among those accompanying Syvertsen were NBC correspondent Welles Hangen and CBS producer Gerald Miller.

The bodies of two of the missing newsmen were reported June 12 to have been found in graves 34 miles southwest of

Pnompenh. The victims were Gerald Miller and CBS cameraman Ramnik Lekhi, an Indian.

Three American correspondents, captured by the Viet Cong in Cambodia May 7, were released June 15 and arrived in Saigon the following day. They were Richard Dudman of the St. Louis Post-Dispatch, Elizabeth Pond of the Christian Science Monitor and Michael D. Morrow of Dispatch News Service.

A Cambodian army officer charged June 22 that as a result of the previous week's fighting in Kompong Speu, "the population now has more fear of the South Vietnamese than of the Viet Cong." Maj. Soeung Kimsea, commander of the 22nd Infantry Battalion, asserted that after South Vietnamese forces recaptured the city from the Communists June 16 the Saigon troops went on a looting rampage, taking "everything—furniture, radios, money. They even broke open safes," and "looted homes of Cambodian officers. Monks were robbed, too."

The South Vietnamese troops which moved into Kompong Speu looted abandoned stores and robbed returning civilians. The South Vietnamese commander forced the soldiers to surrender the loot, but no attempt was made to have them give up the valuables stolen from the civilians.

Battle for Kompong Speu. Allied and Communist forces fought a savage battle June 12–16 for the provincial capital of Kompong Speu, 30 miles southwest of Pnompenh. The strategic city was captured by Viet Cong and North Vietnamese forces June 13 and retaken by Cambodian and South Vietnamese soldiers June 16. Kompong Speu was located on route 4, which linked Pnompenh with the port of Kompong Som (formerly Sihanoukville). Cambodia received all its petroleum through Kompong Som where its only oil refinery was located.

The allied forces that broke into Kompong Speu June 16 found that the large enemy force of about 1,400 men had escaped. A total of 4,000 South Vietnamese and 2,000 Cambodians were committed to the battle. In joining the attack, Saigon's forces made their deepest penetration into Cambodia. Kompong Speu was 50 miles from the South Vietnamese border. South Vietnamese authorities reported that their forces had killed 183 Communists and captured three, while losing four men killed and 22 wounded. Casualties among the civilians who remained in Kompong Speu were high; 40–50 were reported killed.

Communist troops renewed assaults against Kompong Speu June 24–26 but failed to take the city. The Communists penetrated to within the city's main pagoda June 24, but were thrown back by a Cambodian counter-attack. Fighting in the area June 26 blocked Route 4 to the port of Kompong Som.

Red pressure on Pnompenh. North Vietnamese and Viet Cong attacks north of Pnompenh June 17–21 were said to have almost isolated the Cambodian capital. Communist troops operating in the areas were striking almost at will and all the roads leading to the city were considered unsafe. Cambodian troops ringed the airport and other key installations in preparation for a possible Communist attack on Pnompenh itself. The principal fighting raged in and around Kompong Thom, 80 miles north of the capital [see above], while similar Communist pressure was being applied along the Mekong River.

The latest phase in the fighting was regarded as a Communist effort to seize the upper reaches of the Mekong River and increase the flow of soldiers and materiel into Cambodia.

Communist troops June 17 severed Cambodia's last working railway line when they seized a freight train carrying more than 200 tons of rice and other food supplies at a station at Krang Lovea, about 40 miles northwest of Pnompenh. The line ran northwest from the capital to the border with Thailand. The capture of the line reduced Cambodia's surface transport to only a few passable roads.

Two of those roads, major arteries, were cut by the Communists June 18. They severed Highway 1, linking Pnompenh with Saigon, 30 miles southeast of the capital, and Highway 4, leading southwestward to the port of Kompong Som. The Highway 1 attack consisted of a mine and mortar assault on the village of Koki Thom. The road was a key route for bringing South Vietnamese troops and supplies into Cambodia. The cutting of Highway 4 virtually stopped work on Cambodia's biggest dam development project 40 miles west of Pnompenh.

Kompong Thom came under heavy Communist assault June 17 and 18. By June 19, the Communists approached to within 200 yards of the city and were reported June 21 to have entered the provincial capital, gaining control of at least half the city. Cambodian military spokesmen reported June 22 that the enemy forces had withdrawn from Kompong Thom.

Heavy fighting also raged east and south of the city, at Kompong Cham, Tonle Bet, Skoun and Preyveng. South Vietnamese troops reported June 21 killing 32 enemy soldiers in an ambush of a North Vietnamese convoy just south of Preyveng.

A new South Vietnamese thrust into Cambodia was carried out June 20 but little enemy resistance was encountered. The action, involving 4,000 troops, occurred in the Se Bang Valley not previously swept in the allied offensives. The new Saigon force increased to 34,000 the number of South Vietnamese troops operating in Cambodia, Meanwhile, American forces in the country continued to be reduced as the June 30 withdrawal deadline approached. Two battalions were pulled out of the Cambodian border region June 22, decreasing the American force to 9,700 combat troops.

Communist forces June 23 captured Prek Tameak, on the Mekong River 15 miles north of the capital. Government counterattacks forced the Communists to withdraw and the strongpoint was occupied by South Vietnamese marines who landed there June 28.

Five thousand South Vietnamese troops launched a new assault in northeastern Cambodia June 24 in an effort to clear Highway 19 and evacuate Vietnamese refugees. The troops reportedly evacuated to Pleiku, South Vietnam 4,250 Vietnamese refugees from the towns of Labansiek and Bo Kheo along the highway.

The U.S. command reported June 25 that American combat deaths in Indochina June 14–20 reached their lowest level since March. Eighty Americans were killed, 20 in Cambodia, and 643 were wounded. The figures compared with 130 killed and 364 wounded the previous week.

U.S. jet raids deep in Cambodia. The U.S. Defense Department June 22 acknowledged that American planes had been bombing Communist infiltration routes deep inside Cambodia. The Washington Post quoted other sources as saying that the attacks' ranged as far as 100 miles inside the country, well beyond the 21.7 mile limit established by President Nixon for U.S. ground forces. A New York Times dispatch from Saigon June 21 said the deep raids had been in progress since the start of allied operations in Cambodia April 30. Nixon Administration officials had repeatedly said that the U.S. would not provide air combat support for South Vietnamese forces beyond the 21.7 mile limit.

Pentagon press spokesman Jerry Friedheim said June 22 that the air strikes had been launched the previous week and were aimed at new enemy supply lines posing a threat to U.S. forces in South Vietnam. He identified the targets as principally Se Kong and Mekong River supply routes west of the Communist border sanctuaries that had been overrun by allied forces. He said these raids might continue after American troops withdrew from Cambodia June 30. Friedheim refused to comment on a UPI dispatch from Saigon that American planes had flown support missions for Cambodian troops as far west as Kompong Thom, 80 miles north of Pnompenh. He would say only that "our organized [air] campaign is not a campaign to save Cambodia."

The Times June 23 quoted military witnesses as saying that American planes bombed Communist positions at Kompong Thom that day for the second consecutive day. The raids were followed by South Vietnamese jet attacks and apparently were designed to mark enemy targets for Saigon's pilots.

Secretary of State William P. Rogers said June 25 that after the U.S. troops left Cambodia "the main thrust of our policy is to use our air force for the purpose of interdicting supply lines and communication lines to protect Americans in South Vietnam." He added that the policy "may have a dual benefit—it may serve our purposes and at the same time serve the Cambodian government." Asked if he could say that U.S. planes "will not fly close air support" in Cambodia, Rogers replied "no."

In San Francisco June 29, Rogers said the North Vietnamese were "attempting to use Cambodian territory to re-establish their disrupted lines of supplies and communication to carry on the war in South Vietnam." "American air power is being used to frustrate these efforts," he said, and the Saigon government "has said that South Vietnamese forces may continue to engage the enemy in Cambodia." "Thus the enemy," he continued, ". . . can no longer count on the safe haven in Cambodia" and would "have to face Thai and South Vietnamese troops and possible interdiction of the American air power."

As for negotiations, Rogers said "at some point we believe it is possible that the Communists decide that it is in their best interests to negotiate an agreement which gives them representation proportionate to their numbers."

Cambodia abandons 4 provinces. All Cambodian troops were reported June 27 to have withdrawn from the province of Ratanakiri, virtually leaving the northeastern part of the country under Communist military control. The adjacent provinces of Mondulkiri, Kratie and Stung Treng had been abandoned previously by Cambodian troops. Some South Vietnamese troops were said to be in Kratie.

In a fifth northern province, Preah Vihear, a small government garrison remained in the provincial capital of Thbeng Menachey. Maj. Am Rong, a spokesman for the Cambodian military command, indicated that U.S. planes had evacuated two government garrisons at Lebansiek and Bo Kheo in Ratanakiri.

The withdrawal of Cambodian troops from the four provinces allowed the government to concentrate most of its 50,000 soldiers in the area around Pnompenh and east to the South Vietnamese border, where most of the fighting was centered.

In the latest action, North Vietnamese and Viet Cong troops launched heavy attacks June 25-29 at Longvek, site of an arms depot, 35 miles north of Pnompenh.

U.S. arms to Cambodia. The U.S. embassy in Pnompenh disclosed June 24 that the U.S. had stepped up the shipment of arms to Cambodia and that all of the $7.9 million in arms aid promised for the current fiscal year either had arrived or would arrive shortly.

Jonathan F. Ladd, political-military counselor at the embassy, said the equipment already received included 20,-000 M-1 rifles and M-2 carbines, some pistols, some 30-caliber light machine guns, and ammunition. Ladd disclosed that the Pnompenh government was also charged with the cost of repair and maintenance of Cambodia's 10 T-28 trainer planes converted into fighter-bombers and with the outfitting of 2,000 Khmer Krom, the ethnic Cambodian Special Forces who had been fighting in South Vietnam and who were brought into Cambodia May 1.

The U.S. was reported June 27 to be recruiting more ethnic Cambodians in South Vietnam for fighting in Cambodia. Col. Richard W. Ellison, senior American adviser in the Mekong Delta's Vinhbinh Province, said 230 Cambodian militiamen had been shipped out the previous week. About 200 of them were described as either members of or sympathizers with Khmer Serai, a Cambodian rightist movement. Ellison said the recruiting drive came to a halt when the province chief complained to President Nguyen Van Thieu that the men were being enrolled without his knowledge. Other American officials said recruitment of Cambodians was continuing in other delta provinces.

Thieu vows aid to Cambodia. South Vietnamese President Nguyen Van Thieu said June 27 that Saigon's troops would help Cambodia defend itself against Communist attacks.

U.S. Defense Secy. Melvin R. Laird had said at a London news conference June 23 that the South Vietnamese would be free to operate in Cambodia in the sanctuary areas in a combat role and that the sanctuary areas could be anywhere in Cambodia. "I can't state what areas will be used as havens by the North Vietnamese or the Viet Cong," he said. "But

I would not want to draw up any limit on South Vietnamese ground forces so far as attacking any sanctuaries that now exist or may come into being. . . . "

Thieu said his government had no intentions of maintaining a permanent military presence in Cambodia but that "a minimum number of troops" would stay to guarantee the continued evacuation of Vietnamese to South Vietnam. He said 115,000 refugees already had been brought into South Vietnam and another 64,000 awaited repatriation in camps in Pnompenh.

Thieu disclosed that two days after Prince Norodom Sihanouk had been overthrown March 18 as chief of state of Cambodia, he had authorized the South Vietnamese army in the Mekong Delta to "give help to the Cambodians in defending their border outposts and to start joint Vietnamese-Cambodian military operations to destroy the Communists along the border." Thieu said he ordered his troops into the Parrot's Beak April 29 after receiving Cambodian agreement on the operation.

U.S. troops quit Cambodia. U.S. combat troops completed their withdrawal from Cambodia June 29, ending two months of operations against the Communist border sanctuaries that had started May 1. The pullout came one day ahead of the June 30 deadline set by President Nixon for the total removal of all American ground forces from the country. The last of American advisers assigned to South Vietnamese units withdrew June 30.

The last troops to return to South Vietnam's Central Highlands through Cambodia's Fishhook region were 1,800 men of the First Cavalry Division (Airmobile). American forces in Cambodia had totaled 18,000 at peak strength. The number had dropped to less than 10,000 in the past two weeks as the withdrawal rate accelerated. A total of 34,000 South Vietnamese troops remained in Cambodia and were expected to stay there indefinitely in assisting the 50,000 Cambodian soldiers in their fight against the Communist invaders. Most of Saigon's troops were posted near Pnompenh.

U.S. casualties during the entire Cambodian operation totaled 354 killed and 1,689 wounded. South Vietnamese losses as of June 29 were put at 866 killed and 3,724 wounded. Allied military sources claimed Communist losses were 14,488 slain and 1 427 captured.

As the American troops left, Cambodian Premier Lon Nol June 29 expressed hope that the U.S. soldiers would return if his country's military situation deteriorated further. Lon Nol confirmed that the U.S. had been providing Cambodian ground troops with direct tactical air support. According to Lon Nol, he had been assured by the U.S. Defense Department that this assistance would continue after the American withdrawal deadline.

The premier's statement appeared to corroborate a report from Pnompenh June 27 that U.S. jets would provide close air support for Cambodian troops engaged in combat anywhere in the country. Military sources were quoted as specifically mentioning "the area all around Pnompenh" and the provincial capital of Siemreap in the northwest.

Nixon reports: 'successful.' President Nixon June 30 announced the "successful" completion of the U.S. military mission in Cambodia. In a written report announcing that the pullout deadline set by the Administration on American troops had been met, the President said the destruction of enemy base areas along the Cambodian-South Vietnam frontier had enabled the Vietnamization program to proceed on schedule, reduced potential U.S. and allied casualties, gained time for the South Vietnamese to take over the combat role in Vietnam, and enhanced American credibility with the enemy and the prospects "for a just peace."

Renewing his appeals to North Vietnam to enter into serious peace negotiations, Nixon said "there is no military solution to this conflict" and peace could come "through a negotiated settlement that is fair to both sides and humiliates neither. . . . We would hope that Hanoi would ponder seriously its choice, considering both the promise of an honorable peace and the costs of continued war." He also repeated his view that any "fair solution" would require formation of a postwar government reflecting "the existing relationship of political forces."

He pledged to accept any solution formulated by the South Vietnamese themselves.

Nixon also pledged that "there will be no U.S. ground personnel in Cambodia except the regular staff of our embassy in Pnompenh." The prohibition extended to combat personnel and advisers to Cambodian and South Vietnamese forces. As for air power, he said the U.S. would not provide air or logistical support for South Vietnamese forces in Cambodia but would continue bombing enemy personnel or supply concentrations "with the approval of the Cambodian government." The U.S. would also continue to supply Cambodia with small-arms assistance, he said.

Nixon indicated that without the American presence Cambodia would become a testing ground for the Nixon Doctrine to help Asians defend themselves. Urging Cambodia's allies to join the effort, Nixon volunteered to subsidize efforts of "third countries who wish to furnish Cambodia with troops or material."

The report contained a chronology of events prior to the President's decision to send U.S. troops into Cambodia plus an inventory of enemy arms and supplies captured or destroyed. He said the enemy had suffered "significant" losses during the operation—11,349 of the enemy killed, a year's supply of ammunition captured, more than a year's supply of mortar rounds, rockets and recoilless-rifle rounds captured and numerous weapons, vehicles and installations found or destroyed.

In his chronology, Nixon denied U.S. involvement in the overthrow of Prince Norodom Sihanouk as Cambodian chief of state in March, asserted that the U.S. could have abided a continued Communist presence in the sanctuaries if the enemy had not expanded them, and confirmed reports of a U.S. diplomatic effort to preserve the status quo in Cambodia, which was rebuffed.

Declaring that he had been concerned about the Cambodian developments well before April 20, when he had announced a U.S. troop withdrawal from South Vietnam by spring of 1971, Nixon emphasized that he had taken the Cambodia step to foil an obvious attempt by the enemy to move out of their sanctuary areas to seize the 600-mile South Vietnamese-Cambodian border.

Nixon, in his report on the completion of the Cambodian operation, listed these Communist losses from April 30 to June 29 as a result of the U.S.-South Vietnamese strikes against the sanctuary areas:

Personnel killed in action—11,349; POW's (including detainees)—2,328.

Individual weapons captured—22,892; crew-served weapons—2,509; bunkers and structures destroyed—11,688; machine-gun rounds—4,067,177; rifle rounds—10,694,990; grenades—62,022; mines—5,482; antiaircraft rounds—199,552; mortar rounds—68,539; large rocket rounds—2,123; small rocket rounds—43,160; recoilless rifle rounds—29,185.

Miscellaneous explosives, pounds (includes 1,002 satchel charges)—83,000; vehicles—435; boats—167; radios—248; generators—49; medical supplies, pounds—110,800; documents, pounds—12,400; rice, pounds—14,046,000; man-months (of rice)—309,012; total food, pounds—14,518,000.

Reds score U.S. withdrawal as trick. North Vietnam charged July 1 that despite the complete withdrawal of American troops from Cambodia, the U.S. was "prolonging and expanding the war in Cambodia through the service of the mercenary clique supplied by the reactionary authorities in Southeast Asia."

Hanoi radio said American aid to Cambodia and other countries sending their forces to fight there represented "an implementation of Nixon's doctrine of making Asians fight Asians for the realization of United States neocolonialism in Asia." The broadcast called the American operation in Cambodia "a disastrous failure" that belied Nixon's June 30 report "about military wins which have never existed."

The Soviet Union July 1 also characterized the American operation as a failure. The news agency Tass said this was evidenced by the fact that Communist forces still controlled large areas of the country. "Washington's miscalculations in Cambodia are evident, and no bragging in the President's [June 30] report can conceal them." Tass said.

Communist China charged in an article published July 2 that the U.S. had announced the expansion of bombing raids on Cambodia "while playing with the trick of troop withdrawal." The Communist Party newspaper Jenmin Jih Pao said the purpose of this action was to enable the U.S. to continue its "criminal scheme of making Asians fight Asians."

Allied meetings on war. The Southeast Asia Treaty Organization (SEATO) held its annual Ministerial Council meeting in Manila July 2–3. The seven-nation parley was followed by the yearly meeting of representatives of the six Vietnam war allies in Saigon July 5. The conferences dealt with the Indochina war in general but particularly stressed the situation in Cambodia. No specific decisions were announced at either conference.

A SEATO communiqué issued July 3 said the council meeting had noted that "overt military aggression against South Vietnam, Laos and Cambodia was accompanied by other forms of aggression —subversions, externally instigated insurgency, infiltration and terrorism— which continued to be a serious threat to peace and security in the area." The council refrained from offering direct aid to Cambodia on the ground that it was not a member of SEATO. The statement said "the council confirmed its intention to keep the situation under review and expressed its support for the cooperative efforts of states in the area to meet the threat."

The communiqué was signed by the foreign ministers of the Philippines, Thailand, Australia, New Zealand, Britain and the U.S. Pakistan refused to take part in the drafting of the treaty as it had done on two previous occasions, and France continued its boycott.

Thailand Foreign Minister Thanat Khoman and South Vietnamese Foreign Minister Tran Van Lam, who attended as an observer, expressed disappointment over the meeting. Thanat told newsmen after the conference that "I know SEATO better than to expect collective action" to oppose Communist moves in Indochina and to counter threats against Thailand. Lam said he had hoped for a "stronger, more direct

and quicker action by SEATO" when the Cambodian crisis erupted in March.

Secretary Rogers and South Vietnamese Premier Tran Thien Khiem urged the four other members of the Allied Nations Ministers Conference meeting in Saigon July 5 to provide aid to Cambodia. There was no immediate response from Thailand, South Korea, Australia and New Zealand.

(Washington's efforts to get Thailand to commit itself to dispatch troops to Cambodia were reported July 6 to have bogged down over Bangkok's insistence that the U.S. undertake a major share of financing such an operation. An unidentified U.S. official had discussed the matter with Thai officials in Bangkok for two days the previous week, but made no progress. Thai officials were told that potential budget cuts in American military spending and the Nixon Doctrine stressing Asians' self-defense responsibilities precluded meeting Thailand's request.)

A conference communiqué said the ministers had "suggested that the free nations examine what assistance they could give Cambodia in response to its requests." The statement noted "the steady improvement of the military situation" in South Vietnam.

Rogers vowed continued American air strikes against Communist forces in Cambodia and said the U.S. would provide the Pnompenh government with military and economic assistance.

Thailand's reluctance to provide military assistance to Cambodia and Pnompenh's pressing need for such aid was the topic of discussion between Rogers and Cambodian Foreign Minister Koun Wick in Saigon July 6. Koun Wick was said to have stressed the necessity of equipping 85,000 men of Cambodia's newly-expanded army of 120,000 with arms and uniforms.

Rogers sees Peking gains. Secretary of State William P. Rogers said July 13 that the Chinese Communists had "increased their influence with Hanoi as a result" of the U.S. and South Vietnamese incursions into Cambodia.

Rogers' remarks were recorded in a radio interview in London before he returned to Washington the following day from a two-week tour of Asia. The secretary's statement was an amplification of a comment he had made in Tokyo July 9 that China was the "key to the future of Indochina" and that if Peking would "talk sensibly," Washington believed that an Indochina peace settlement could be achieved "very quickly."

In his London statement, Rogers added: "We think that the Soviet Union's influence has decreased" to the advantage of Communist China. The U.S. doubted whether China had "any reason to bring an end to the war. We think it serves their purpose to have the war continue. In effect, they use Hanoi as their instrumentality for causing trouble. We don't at the moment expect the Communist Chinese will get directly involved in the conflict, but one never knows for sure."

Rogers said there was a possibility that "the war will continue to de-escalate and be more limited in nature" with the Communists relying largely on guerrilla and terror attacks. This, he said, could result in "a situation of no war and no peace."

Fighting in Vietnam & Laos

Increase in fighting. The allied thrust into Cambodia was preceded and followed by a sharp flare-up of fighting in South Vietnam and Laos.

A North Vietnamese regiment April 30 captured three of five hamlets in the district refugee resettlement town of Hiepduc in Quangnam Province, 40 miles south of Danang. U.S. and South Vietnamese attempts to recapture the village in fighting through May 3 resulted in the death of 219 North Vietnamese, seven Americans and about 12 government troops. Allied forces surrounded Hiepduc but refrained from using air and artillery strikes to avoid destroying the village.

Communist forces in South Vietnam May 2–3 carried out the heaviest attacks since launching their major offensive April 1. The U.S. command reported enemy rocket and mortar attacks, half a dozen ground assaults.

South Vietnamese troops, assisted by U.S. B-52 bombing attacks, reported killing 215 North Vietnamese troops 17 miles south of the demilitarized zone in the Dakrong Valley May 8. In other action May 8, 64 South Vietnamese towns and bases, including 17 American installations, were shelled by a coordinated Communist strike in the provincial capitals of Tamky and Hoian.

Maj. Gen. John A. B. Dillard, 50, head of the U.S. Army Engineer Command in South Vietnam, was killed in action May 13, the sixth American general to die in the war. He was killed when the helicopter in which he was flying was shot down by Communist ground fire in the Central Highlands of South Vietnam. Eight other Americans aboard the 'copter, including officers, also were killed. One American survived.

More than 60 allied positions were shelled throughout South Vietnam May 19. An American and 10 South Vietnamese were killed. The shelling took place on the 80th birthday of Ho Chi Minh. Viet Cong broadcasts had called for stepped-up attacks to mark the birth of the late North Vietnamese president. The allies observed a 24-hour truce May 18–19 to mark the birth of Buddha. The Communists, who did not honor the cease-fire, were accused of committing 190 truce violations during the period.

Saigon military authorities reported May 19 that 456 South Vietnamese civilians had been killed in Communist terror attacks May 6–13, one of the highest weekly figures ever recorded. The previous week's civilian death toll was 99.

A North Vietnamese and Viet Cong force infiltrated Dalat May 30 and escaped May 31, slipping past hundreds of government soldiers encircling the resort city, 145 miles northeast of Saigon. An estimated 200 Communist soldiers

87

had attacked and occupied a number of points in and around the city, including the National Military Academy, a seminary, a convent church and part of the Catholic university. The guerrilla assaults, assisted by mortar and rocket barrages, also were directed at an airfield 14 miles south. Government forces refrained from shelling the occupied church buildings to spare the structures and the hostages inside. Hundreds of civilians had fled to the church and seminary when the attacks began. Although Dalat was defended by South Vietnamese militiamen and infantry units, later reinforced by 2,500 men, about 75 Communists managed to make their way out of the city May 31 under cover of darkness. Military officials placed the number of enemy dead at 47, most of them killed during the attack on the military academy. Government losses were put at 16 killed and two wounded.

The South Vietnamese press agency reported June 4 that Col. Lo Cong Danh would be replaced as mayor of Dalat. Announcement of his dismissal followed expressions of dismay by American officials over the loose security arrangements that permitted the Communists to infiltrate the city and then escape.

In fighting to the north, a South Vietnamese battalion of 500 men June 3 was flown by helicopter to Fire Base Tun Tavern, 21 miles south of the demilitarized zone, to relieve a government garrison that had come under heavy Communist attack. The defending force, originally numbering 500 men, was pulled out after losing 50 killed and 119 wounded in beating off North Vietnamese attacks June 1–3. The allies reported killing 83 of the 600 attackers and capturing three. Following the arrival of the reinforcements, about 30 U.S. B-52s and other planes pounded North Vietnamese positions around the base.

Developments in Laos. North Vietnamese troops captured Attopeu, Laos April 29–30. The Laotian Defense Ministry reported that 93 government troops were killed and 23 wounded, the highest toll for a single battle ever reported by the Vientiane regime. Attopeu, at the foot of

a plateau overlooking the Ho Chi Minh Trail to the east, had been under enemy siege for several years and was supplied by government airlift. Its capture marked the first time that North Vietnamese soldiers had crossed the 1962 cease-fire line to take an important town held by the government.

Meanwhile, North Vietnamese troops maintained pressure on two other government strongholds—Sam Thong and Long Tien. The Communist forces April 4 had pushed to within 200 yards of Sam Thong's airstrip and the base came under heavy fire.

U.S. forces suffered heavy losses in the air war over Laos. Four planes were downed April 21. The pilots of two of the aircraft were rescued. An AC-130 gunship was brought down by Communist gunfire April 22 with a loss of six crewmen. Four were missing and one was rescued. The loss of the plane brought to 29 the number of American aircraft downed over Laos since the U.S. began disclosing these losses March 9.

The Communists followed up their April 30 capture of Attopeu with a threat against Saravane, a provincial capital 70 miles north. They had surrounded the village for years, but were reported May 5 to have warned that they were about to launch an assault. The warning prompted the government to evacuate 2,500 civilians from Saravane May 8–13. They were flown to Pakse in American planes.

The Communists posed another threat against the royal capital of Luang Prabang. Col. Thong Phanh Knoksy, a Defense Ministry spokesman, said May 9 that three North Vietnamese battalions, totaling possibly 1,000 men, had advanced to within 18 miles of the strategic center on the Mekong River.

North Vietnamese forces May 9 seized Tang Nay, but the village was later recaptured by government troops.

A strategic government artillery post at Phou Saphong, five miles northwest of Attopeu, changed hands several times. The position was first captured by Communist forces April 27, retaken by Laotian government troops and seized again by the North Vietnamese in a counterattack May 7. Phou Saphong was only three miles from an airfield used by U.S. planes.

Communist advances were reported on the Bolovens Plateau, a rice-growing area in southern Laos. North Vietnamese forces, which were said to have moved in from Cambodia, had driven government forces out of Phou Luang Noi on the southern rim of the plateau, it was reported May 13. A government counterattack, assisted by artillery and air strikes, led to its recapture, military sources in Vientiane reported May 25.

Government troops May 31 recaptured Paktha following two days of air strikes. The village, two miles east of the Thai border, had been captured by a combined Pathet Lao-North Vietnamese force April 29.

Laos issue—The issue of allied incursions into Laos came up May 17 after disclosure by South Vietnam Foreign Minister Tran Van Lam at the .Southeast Asia conference in Jarkarta, Indonesia that South Vietnamese forces had pursued Communist troops into Laos from time to time. Appearing before the U.S. Senate Foreign Relations Committee's disarmament subcommittee May 18, Defense Secretary Melvin R. Laird conceded that U.S. advisers had gone into Laos with South Vietnamese troops in "hot pursuit," "protective reaction" and rescue missions. But he said the border crossings were only made "in connection with the running battle in South Vietnam" and said large-scale combat operations in Laos by Americans were prohibited. From the Florida White House came word that there were no American ground forces in Laos and "no change in our activities in Laos." From Saigon May 18, there was a denial that South Vietnamese ground forces had struck in Laos along the Ho Chi Minh Trail or that Lam had told anyone that South Vietnamese armed forces had entered Laos "in strength."

CIA role in Laos conceded—Dr. John A. Hannah, director of the Agency for International Development, acknowledged June 7 that the U.S. aid prógram was being used as a cover for Central Intelligence Agency operations in Laos. Indicating his disapproval of such undercover work through his agency, Hannah said the role was authorized in 1962 and Laos was the only country where this was being done.

The Symington panel April 19 made public testimony that U.S. air observers had been secretly stationed in northern Laos in 1966 to guide the bombing of Pathet Lao and North Vietnamese forces by Royal Laotian and U.S. planes. It represented the first official acknowledgement—the testimony came from State and Defense Department personnel—of U.S. involvement in the northern Laos ground war.

The data also contained reports that about 100 American civilian and military personnel had been reported killed in Laos since 1962—half the casualties were stationed in Laos, the remainder were Air Force pilots operating out of Thailand.

Laotion military operations. The key Laotian town of Saravane was captured by Pathet Lao and North Vietnamese troops June 9, but was reported taken by pro-government guerrillas June 12. Saravane's fall was first announced by Premier Souvanna Phouma June 9. He said the single battalion defending Saravane withdrew to the east. Its abandonment followed a Communist attack on one of six advance posts about two miles north. The government garrison at Saravane was said to have included 500 government soldiers, 300 armed officials and about 100 policemen.

The Laotian cabinet received a report June 10 that about 320 government soldiers were killed or missing in the fall of Saravane.

The Communists' evacuation was believed to have been prompted by heavy bombings by Laotian planes and by the massing of 2,000 pro-government guerrillas around the town.

Elsewhere in Laos, Communist troops attacked a government unit June 8 near the Plaine des Jarres, killing 64 soldiers and wounding 60. Twenty-three others were reported missing.

North Vietnamese troops July 1 attacked a Laotian refugee camp at Phoucum, 20 miles north of the Plaine des Jarres. A government report July 9 said 30 civilians and three Laotian soldiers were killed in the assault.

The Laotian Defense Ministry reported July 3 that government troops had recaptured Phou Kate mountain, seized by North Vietnamese soldiers June 19. The mountain, six miles southeast of Saravane, had been the site of a U.S. radar station overlooking the Ho Chi Minh Trail, North Vietnam's main infiltration route.

The southern Laotian town of Moulapamok, just north of the Cambodian border, was overrun by North Vietnamese forces July 13. Both sides were said to have suffered heavy losses.

Government troops July 18 threw back a combined Pathet Lao-North Vietnamese assault against Ban Hatsaikhoune, on the eastern bank of the Mekong River.

Vietnamese civilians slain. An estimated 114 civilians were slain in a Viet Cong attack June 11 on the South Vietnamese hamlet of Thanhmy (also known as Baren), 17 miles southeast of Danang. A total of 316 homes were destroyed and 50 were partly destroyed. It was one of the most costly single attacks on South Vietnamese civilians by the Viet Cong since the 1968 Communist Tet offensive.

A force of about 200 Viet Cong moved through the village, firing mortars and then rifles, explosive barrages and grenades. Government defenders finally forced the attackers out of the hamlet, killing seven of the Viet Cong. Their own losses were three killed and 19 wounded.

(Forty-six South Vietnamese civilians were killed July 3 when a boat struck a Communist floating mine on the Cua Viet River near Dongha, about nine miles south of the demilitarized zone. Four persons survived.)

Defoliation raids suspended. American defoliation raids in South Vietnam were reported June 22 to have been suspended in April. Since 1961 U.S. planes had sprayed chemical defoliants and herbicides to wipe out jungle growth and to kill rice crops in order to deprive

About a dozen C-123 transport planes involved in the operation were said to have been diverted since the start of allied operations in Cambodia to haul out captured Communist arms and ammunition. It was assumed the spraying operations in South Vietnam would resume, but on a limited scale, once the American operations were ended in Cambodia June 30, according to the report.

The U.S. command disclosed Oct. 23 that U.S. troops had employed a chemical defoliant in South Vietnam despite a Defense Department order banning its use. A spokesmen said an Army inquiry was under way to determine whether the troops, identified as members of a company of the Americal Division, knew they were defying the ban and whether their action had been carried out under higher orders.

The herbicide, known as 2, 4, 5-T, had been used on "several occasions" in May, July and August in the northern provinces of Quangtin and Quangngai, the American officials said. The Defense Department had banned the weedkiller April 15 following a study which showed that the chemical caused an abnormally high incidence of birth abnormalities in mice and rats. The herbicide, also known as Orange, constituted about 90% of the three principal defoliants used in South Vietnam since 1961 to spray crops to deprive the Communists of cover. The command statement said Orange was still being stored in South Vietnam "pending further evaluation of its chemical constitutents."

Two other defoliants, White and Blue, were still being used on crop destruction and deforestation missions, the command said.

U.S. plane bombs North Vietnam. A U.S. Navy escort plane bombed gun positions deep inside North Vietnam June 25.

The U.S. command reported June 26 that the attack, about 155 miles north of the demilitarized zone, occurred after the guns had fired on a reconnaissance plane the Navy aircraft was escorting. The command said "there was no damage to the U.S. aircraft."

The U.S. had lost 6,592 aircraft since the bombings began in Vietnam in 1964, according to Defense Department testimony made public June 29. The six-year plane loss through March was worth an estimated $5.2 billion, Lt. Gen. Otto J. Glasser, deputy chief of staff for Air Force research and development, told a hearing of the House Defense Appropriations subcommittee April 20.

U.S. deaths at low level. The U.S. command reported July 9 that 61 Americans were killed in combat June 28-

July 4, the lowest weekly toll in more than three and a half years. The number of wounded in that period totaled 463.

South Vietnamese casualties suffered June 28–July 4 were 371 killed and 1,027 wounded. Viet Cong and North Vietnamese losses were put at 1,395 dead. The Communist casualties were reported to be the lowest in 18 months, reflecting the general reduction in fighting.

U.S. general killed. Maj. Gen. George W. Casey, 48, commander of the First Cavalry Division (Airmobile), and six other U.S. officers and enlisted men were killed in a helicopter crash July 7 in Lamdong Province, about 120 miles northeast of Saigon.

The army command reported July 9 that Casey was last heard from when he and the six others had taken off in the helicopter to visit wounded members of the division in a hospital.

Casey's death brought to seven the number of American generals killed in the Vietnam war.

Reds battered at Khesanh. The U.S. command in Saigon reported July 13 that American troops had killed 384 North Vietnamese soldiers and wounded many more near Khesanh, in the northwest corner of South Vietnam, in an operation that started July 8.

In the initial attack, the enemy troops were said to have been caught in the open by rocket-firing helicopters as 101st Airborne Division troops launched the assault. The command reported that about 150 Communists were killed in the first day of fighting. The North Vietnamese, identified as members of the 304th Division, were believed to be inexperienced troops sent into the area from Laos to replace the 66th Regiment, which had suffered heavy losses in June in fighting around Fire Base Tun Tavern 20 miles south of Khesanh.

U.S. B-52s dropped 180 tons of bombs over the area July 9 in an attempt to trap the remnants of the enemy unit. South Vietnamese forces later joined the operation and July 11 reported finding 143 more North Vietnamese bodies. An additional 93 were found by the South Vietnamese the following day.

Allied drive near Laos. South Vietnamese forces launched two coordinated drives in the northwestern part of South Vietnam July 12 and 15, paving the way for a possible thrust against North Vietnamese concentrations in nearby southern Laos.

The first drive, in which 2,000 men participated, began west of Hiepduc, 35 miles south of Danang. The second thrust, 23 miles away, was carried out by 5,000 government troops and 1,500 U.S. Marines landed by Marine helicopters. The latter operation, in the vicinity of Thuongduc, was aimed at destroying two North Vietnamese base areas. Virtually no contact was made with the enemy in either operation.

As part of one of the sweeps, allied forces July 18 established a new combat base at Khamduc, an abandoned U.S. Special Forces camp 13 miles from the Laotian border. Khamduc had been abandoned in May 1968 under heavy North Vietnamese pressure. U.S. Air Force C-130 cargo planes began landing at Khamduc after Army engineers finished filling in shell craters and cleared the debris left on the airstrip by the 1968 battle. Meanwhile, U.S. B-52s dropped bombs 12 miles southwest of Khamduc and in nearby Laos against suspected Communist concentrations.

In other military developments, Communist forces July 20 shelled Saigon for the fourth time since Jan. 1. Two 100-pound rockets struck the center of the city, setting off explosions. There was some damage but no casualties were reported. In a previous Communist shelling of the capital, May 12, three 100-pound shells landed in the city. One struck the grounds of the Presidential Palace.

U.S. quits South Vietnam base. U.S. paratroopers July 23 abandoned Fire Base Ripcord near the Ashau Valley in northern South Vietnam in the face of three weeks of heavy North Vietnamese attacks.

During that period, 61 Americans were killed and 345 wounded. U.S. forces had suffered their heaviest losses for a single day in the area July 22 when 12 members of a paratrooper patrol were killed and 51 were wounded in a 6½ hour clash a mile from the base. Three more Americans were slain and 20 were wounded in the July 23 evacuation that came under heavy enemy fire.

A U.S. communiqué did not attribute the decision to evacuate Ripcord to the heavy enemy pressure. The announcement said "Ripcord's closing will provide additional troop units for offensive operations against the Viet Cong and North Vietnamese in Thuathien Province." The communique said the North Vietnamese had suffered heavy casualties in the fighting around Ripcord. Sixty-one Communists were reported killed July 22 in addition to 22 the previous week.

The evacuation of Ripcord was followed by concerted North Vietnamese attacks against Fire Base O'Reilly, an artillery stronghold 27 miles west of Hue, among other allied targets in the north in August. The battle for Fire Base O'Reilly erupted Aug. 9 and continued through Aug. 19. About 1,500 North Vietnamese were reported arrayed against the base which was defended by a 665-man battalion of the South Vietnamese First Division, supported by American B-52s, fighter-bombers and helicopter gunships. The allied ground and air forces repelled repeated North Vietnamese assaults.

In fighting elsewhere in the north, South Vietnamese militia forces claimed the killing of 125 Communist soldiers in more than 80 coordinated attacks 45 miles south of Danang Aug. 14–15. The operation, involving 5,000 men, also resulted in the capture of 125 of the enemy. At least four militiamen were reported killed and 11 wounded in the two-day operation.

Five allied bases near the demilitarized zone were shelled by North Vietnamese troops Aug. 16. Heavy enemy shellings also were reported against two other bases further south—Fire Base O'Reilly and Fire Base Barnett. In a move to take pressure off the attacked bases, U.S. B-52s carried out their heaviest raid against enemy targets in two years, dropping an estimated 1,500 tons of bombs on suspected enemy positions ranging from near the DMZ to an area 25 miles to the south. The B-52s pounded the same area again Aug. 17 in an attempt to block what some allied officers said might be a big enemy offensive. Despite the bombings by nearly 100 B-52s, the North Vietnamese continued to shell the seven allied bases struck the previous day.

Saigon troop role in Laos? Pathet Lao leader Prince Souphanouvong charged Aug. 13 that the Laotian government and the U.S. had introduced South Vietnamese troops into Laos in "a new act of war escalation."

In a message sent to Laotian Premier Souvanna Phouma (disclosed by the Pathet Lao radio Aug. 18), Souphanouvong said: "Following the dispatch of many Thai regular battalions to take part in the fighting in Laos, the sending by the United States of Saigon puppet army units to carry out operations in the Saravane area [Aug. 9] is a new act of war escalation taken by the United States and its henchmen." The U.S.-South Vietnamese purpose, the message claimed, was to "widen the war of aggression in Laos with the aim of turning Laos into a 'second Cambodia.'"

The U.S. State Department Aug. 18 described as untrue the Pathet Lao charge that the U.S. had moved South Vietnamese troops into Laos. A department spokesman said Aug. 21, however, that South Vietnamese troops accompanied by American advisers "may" have crossed into Laos in "protective reaction missions" earlier in August. The Washington Post Aug. 20 had quoted allied sources as conceding that clandestine "reconnaissance" units often enter Laos.

Some U.S. helicopter crewmen reported Aug. 21 that they had recently ferried about 400 South Vietnamese troops into landing zones at Khamduc, South Vietnam, just short of the Laotian border, and that the South Vietnamese then walked across the frontier. The soldiers returned a few days later, after looking for enemy supplies, the pilots said.

A state of emergency had been declared by the Laotian government in six southern provinces July 23. The provinces included Saravane and Attopeu. The Pathet Lao and North Vietnamese had seized Saravane Province and the towns of Saravane and Attopeu.

Cutbacks announced. The U.S. command in Saigon announced a series of cutbacks in fighting strength in the first weeks of September as North Vietnamese and Vietcong forces continued on the offensive.

The U.S. Sept. 2 transferred control of a 31-ship helicopter force of Army UH-1 copters (Hueys) to South Vietnam's air force. Gen. Creighton W. Abrams, commander of the U.S. forces in Vietnam, said at the transfer ceremonies that the South Vietnamese navy had been given the responsibility for coastal patrols. The ability of the South Vietnamese to defend themselves "has been greatly enhanced," Abrams said.

The U.S. command said Sept. 7 that U.S. troop strength in Vietnam had dropped below 400,000 for the first time in more than three and a half years. The announcement said that as of Sept. 3, U.S. troop strength totaled 399,500, a decrease of 2,800 over the previous week and the lowest overall total since Jan. 14, 1967 when the figure was 398,400.

In another disengagement move, U.S. forces Sept. 29 completed the transfer of their base at Anhoa, 20 miles southwest of Danang, to the South Vietnamese. The installation, one of the largest Marine strongpoints in the north, was the 57th American base turned over to the South Vietnamese since the U.S. withdrawal began in 1969. The U.S. turned over 40 jet attack-bombers to the South Vietnamese Air Force Oct. 1.

In other moves aimed at giving Saigon greater combat responsibilities, the U.S. Air Force Nov. 4 turned over the Soctrang air base in the Mekong Delta to the South Vietnamese air force. The move also involved giving the South Vietnamese 31 American helicopters, raising their 'copter force to about 250.

The Navy had announced Oct. 23 that 19 ships of the 7th Fleet were being withdrawn from service in Vietnam. The ships included three aircraft carriers and three destroyers. The withdrawal represented about 15% of the 130-ship, 60,000 man fleet and was part of President Nixon's cutback of American forces in Southeast Asia.

U.S. Indochina deaths at 4-year low. The U.S. command reported Aug. 27 that 52 Americans had died in combat in Indochina Aug. 16-22, the lowest weekly American fatality toll since the week ending Dec. 3, 1966. The pre-

vious low U.S. death toll of 69 in the Aug. 9-15 period reflected a decrease in fighting throughout the area in recent weeks.

The number of Americans wounded Aug. 16-22 totaled 358, a drop of 257 from the previous week. Other casualties during the period: South Vietnamese—247 killed and 745 wounded; North Vietnamese and Viet Cong—1,055 reported killed. The Communists' fatality loss was said to be their lowest since April 1967.

Casualty figures announced Sept. 3 listed 63 Americans killed in action for the week of Aug. 23-29. The battlefield toll for the nine-week period totaled 623, the lowest for such a period since February 1966.

Late summer developments. Among military actions in late August and September:

U.S. B-52s staged saturation raids near the demilitarized zone Aug. 24 in an attempt to prevent a suspected North Vietnamese buildup. Most of the air strikes were carried out within 20 miles of the Laotian border. One B-52 attack occurred near the Cambodian border, 82 miles northeast of Saigon.

Viet Cong mortars Aug. 26 shelled the Mekong Delta village of Bachuc in Chaudoc Province, killing 11 persons and wounding 42 others. All but one of the victims were civilians.

American artillery Aug. 26 accidentally shelled a U.S. unit 100 miles northeast of Saigon. The mistaken attack killed two Americans and a Viet Cong who had defected, the U.S. command reported.

A U.S. helicopter was shot down by a Communist rocket grenade Aug. 26 near Khamduc in the north. Thirty Americans were killed and two survived. Another 'copter shot down that day resulted in the death of four Americans. The loss of the two aircraft brought to 3,998 the number of helicopters downed since January 1961. Of this figure, 1,777 were lost to enemy ground fire.

The first helicopter was lost during the completion of the closing down of the temporary base at Khamduc. The base, 13 miles from the Laotian border, had been used during a U.S.-South Vietnamese operation to disrupt a North Vietnamese buildup along the northern frontier. U.S. officers said the mission had been accomplished.

Actions reported Aug. 29 included the ambush of a convoy of U.S. infantrymen on a main highway in the Central Highlands, leaving six dead, and the mistaken shelling of a hamlet 40 miles east of Saigon by U.S. forces, in which three Vietnamese civilians were killed and 13 more wounded.

Fifty-five South Vietnamese were killed and 140 wounded Aug. 30 in a co-ordinated series of attacks by North Vietnamese and Vietcong forces across South Vietnam. Observers saw the overnight attacks as a buildup geared to the South Vietnamese elections.

South Vietnamese forces Aug. 31 reportedly killed 56 Viet Cong in an eight-hour battle near Phanthiet, 120 miles northeast of Saigon. The government force, aided by American tanks, helicopter gunships and jet bombers, blocked 100 Communist troops from crossing Route 1. One American was killed and a U.S. helicopter was shot down during the fighting.

The Viet Cong Sept. 4 attacked a civil self-defense training center in coastal Bindinh Province in what appeared to be a drive to wreck the Saigon government's pacification program there. The attack left 14 South Vietnamese dead and 26 wounded.

North Vietnamese commandos Sept. 8 attacked two bases south of Danang, reportedly killing 34 South Vietnamese soldiers and wounding 42. An American adviser was also killed. The setback to government troops occurred at the Trabong district headquarters and ranger camp, part of the frontier defense for Quangngai City on the coastal lowlands.

Three South Vietnamese civilians were killed and 14 captured for interrogation after they were discovered in a restricted zone, it was announced Sept. 13. The shooting at Phanthiet was authorized by the South Vietnamese after the civilians began to run when they were seen in the area.

South Vietnamese field commanders announced Sept. 15 that they were withdrawing from two northern bases because it would be difficult to resupply them during the monsoon season. Fire Base Barnett was in process of being evacu-

ated, the announcement said, and Fire Base O'Reilly would also be closed.

A Sept. 17 report said nine U.S. helicopters had been destroyed the previous six days. Four Americans were killed and six wounded in the actions, which occurred in the Mekong Delta, the Central Highlands, the northern sector of South Vietnam and the jungles of southeastern Laos. The helicopters were engaged in airlift and transport action.

Eleven Americans were killed and 11 others wounded Sept. 20 when North Vietnamese gunners shot down a U.S. helicopter trying to land a reconnaissance team, then shelled an armored relief force. The action, the most serious since Aug. 26, occurred a mile south of the Demilitarized Zone. Nine of the dead were aboard the UH-1 helicopter that was shot down; one person survived the crash. Two other Americans were killed when armored personnel carriers came under a mortar barrage resisting the North Vietnamese action.

The U.S. command announced Sept. 24 that 52 Americans had been killed in the Vietnam war the week of Sept. 13–19. This was the lowest U.S. death toll since the week ending Dec. 3, 1966.

South Vietnamese spokesmen said 195 government troops had been killed and 464 wounded the week ending Sept. 19.

The U.S. command said Sept. 14 that 3,200 servicemen had been withdrawn from Vietnam in the previous week. The withdrawal reduced total U.S. troop strength in the war zone to 396,300. This figure did not include 23,100 Navy and Coast Guardsmen offshore or 45,000 airmen stationed in Thailand and directly involved in Indochina operations

U.S. death toll continues to fall. The U.S. command in Saigon reported Oct 8 that 38 Americans had died in combat in Indochina Sept. 27–Oct. 3. It was the lowest weekly American fatality toll since the week ending April 23, 1966. The number of wounded totaled 666, an unusually high figure said to be the result of an accumulation of minor casualty reports.

Viet Cong and North Vietnamese combat deaths during the week ended Oct. 3 were listed by allied sources as 1,468.

The relatively light allied and Communist casualties reflected a drop in war activity.

A force of about 100 Viet Cong Sept. 26 attacked Pleikrong, a Central Highlands hamlet 11 miles northwest of the provincial capital of Kontum. One civilian and five South Vietnamese militiamen were reported killed. Two other South Vietnamese were slain in Viet Cong assaults on two villages 5 and 15 miles southwest of Saigon.

A U.S. helicopter crashed 50 miles east of Saigon Oct. 3, killing six Americans and a Communist defector aboard.

An increase in fighting Oct. 3 resulted in the killing of 108 Communist soldiers in scattered clashes in the northern provinces and the Central Highlands, according to allied reports. In one action, 11 North Vietnamese were slain by U.S. and South Vietnamese defenders of an outpost south of Danang. Three Americans were killed and four wounded in the clash.

The Communists carried out at least 84 mortar and rocket assaults Oct. 4–6, mainly in the central and northern coastal provinces. The worst shelling was said to have been directed at a refugee resettlement center near Phumy on the central coast. Seven civilians were reported killed and 52 were injured in a barrage that also destroyed 40 houses.

South Vietnamese infantry Oct. 8 abandoned Fire Base O'Reilly, under North Vietnamese shelling and ground pressure for two months. The pullout was said to have been prompted by monsoon rains.

The U.S. command reported Oct. 13 that 10 Americans and at least 38 Communists had been killed in two days of fighting. Both actions occurred in northern Quangngai Province.

The U.S. command disclosed Oct. 14 that eight South Vietnamese soldiers had been killed and 23 wounded Oct. 11 when they were accidentally bombed by a U.S. helicopter gunship. The incident occurred 132 miles southwest of Saigon. In another accidental raid reported by the command Oct. 30, nine South Vietnamese civilians were killed, 25 were wounded and 15 were missing when American helicopter gunships fired on a group of fishing boats June 20. The command said an investigation

showed that U.S. and South Vietnamese army units "share responsibility" for the incident.

Allied forces reported Oct. 21 that in the first two days of a new offensive 26 miles south of Danang, 163 Viet Cong had been killed and 20 captured. Many of the Communists were said to have been killed by bombers, helicopter gunships and artillery. The fighting centered around a Special Forces camp and the district town of Thuongduc, which had come under Communist rocket and mortar attack.

U.S. deaths at 5-year low. The U.S. command reported Nov. 5 that 24 Americans had died in combat in Indochina Oct. 25–31. It was the lowest weekly American fatality toll since the week ending Oct. 23, 1965 when 14 men were killed. It also was the fifth consecutive week that the American death toll had been below 50.

The number of U.S. soldiers wounded in the Oct. 25–31 period rose to 431, compared with 279 the previous week. The increase reflected the low level of fighting, in which most of the American casualties resulted from booby traps, sniper fire and mortar attacks, which more often wound than kill. South Vietnamese battle deaths that week increased to 309, up from 215 the previous week. North Vietnamese and Viet Cong deaths were put at 909, compared with 1,628 the week before. It was the lowest Communist fatality total since the first week of January 1967.

Fighting in South Vietnam's five northern provinces came to a virtual halt as the worst rain storm in six years struck the area Oct. 30–Nov. 1. The resultant floods killed at least 293 persons; more than 204,000 were left homeless, nearly 6,000 homes were destroyed and 80% of the rice crop was damaged. The heaviest death toll occurred in Quangnam Province, where 101 persons died.

The Communists Nov. 2 fired four rockets into Saigon, killing seven civilians and wounding 25 others. The attack on the capital was the first since July 20.

Sharp fighting resumed in the northern provinces Nov. 5. U.S. troops killed seven North Vietnamese in a clash 17 miles southwest of Hue, while suffering three killed and three wounded. In another engagement, 17 miles southeast of Danang U.S. Marines reported killing 20 North Vietnamese while losing one man.

The Bienhoa air base, 20 miles northeast of Saigon, was struck by more than a dozen Communist rocket shells Nov. 17. Casualties and damage were reported light.

The U.S. command reported Nov. 13 that there had been no American combat fatalities in Indochina Nov. 10 and 11. This was the first time in five years that American troops had gone through two days without a death. The U.S. fatality toll for the week of Nov. 8–14, however, reached 44, the highest seven-day total in five weeks.

Nineteen Americans were killed in the crash of three helicopters Nov. 18–19. Fifteen of the fatalities occurred Nov. 18 when a Marine Corps CH-46 crashed in the Queson Mountains 22 miles southwest of Danang. The 'copter was returning to its base with a reconnaissance patrol it had just rescued when it became lost in a fog.

The other four crewmen died when their two helicopters were shot down by enemy gunfire Nov. 19. One was downed on the coastal plain 286 miles northeast of Saigon, the other in the northwestern part of South Vietnam, 11 miles from Laos.

Nine civilians were killed and 43 were wounded Nov. 19 when a guerrilla grenade was thrown into an open-air movie at Congthanh, 20 miles northeast of Saigon.

U.S. battle deaths Nov. 22–28 were listed as 32 and those the following week totaled 27. U.S. fatalities Nov. 15–21 had reached 65, more than twice the number reported the previous week, but the increase was not attributed to increased fighting. Fifteen of the deaths resulted from a helicopter crash Nov. 18.

Two American planes carrying 123 persons disappeared Nov. 27 and 29 and were presumed to have crashed. It was confirmed that the second plane, a C-123 transport carrying 32 Americans and 12 South Vietnamese, crashed into a mountainside near Camranh Bay. The U.S. command reported Dec. 5 that only two survivors, both Air Force sergeants, had been rescued by helicopter. The plane had been on its way to the U.S. The other missing aircraft, also a C-123, carried six Americans and 73 Viet-

namese and was believed to have gone down in the same area.

In other plane losses: a helicopter carrying South Vietnamese troops collided Nov. 24 with a U.S. light plane over the Mekong Delta, 80 miles south of Saigon, killing all 17 persons aboard both planes. The crash of a U.S. helicopter Dec. 1 in the Central Highlands resulted in the death of four Americans. Two U.S. Army helicopters were shot down by Communist ground gunners near Phuoclong Dec. 14. One crewman was killed and two were wounded.

In ground action, South Vietnam reported the killing of 33 Viet Cong Nov. 27 in the Rungsat special zone, 23 miles southeast of Saigon. The communique said government troops also had destroyed 30 bunkers and 19 sampans in the zone, long a Viet Cong sanctuary.

A Saigon report Nov. 30 claimed the killing of 54 North Vietnamese and Viet Cong soldiers in a half dozen clashes that day two miles from the Central Highlands resort city of Dalat. Government losses were said to have totaled seven killed and six wounded in one of the engagements.

A 7,000-man South Vietnamese force Dec. 1 launched a major drive against a suspected Communist force of 3,000 in the U Minh Forest in the Southern part of the Mekong Delta. A Saigon communique Dec. 8 claimed 144 Viet Cong had been killed in the first eight days of the operation. Eight South Vietnamese soldiers were killed and 71 wounded, according to the communique. U.S. B-52s had pounded the area in two raids before the start of the ground operations. The U Minh Forest had been a major Viet Cong base since 1960, but repeated attempts to drive out the enemy had failed.

Communist rocket barrages struck 22 allied military installations in the 24-hour period ending Dec. 2. The targets included three air bases, three provincial capitals and two district towns. The Communists had carried out nearly 100 mortar and rocket attacks in the previous four days. One such shelling Nov. 30 struck a U.S. medical dispensary at Chulai, killing or wounding the entire staff.

Saigon came under Communist attacks Dec. 15, 16 and 19. Viet Cong grenades and bombs were directed at two U.S. military housing billets in the city Dec. 16, killing two American servicemen and one South Vietnamese civilian. Two Americans and two Vietnamese civilians had been slightly wounded in a Viet Cong bomb explosion at a U.S. officers' billet in Saigon Dec. 15.

Two Communist rockets struck a populous district in Saigon Dec. 19, killing six civilians.

Allied commands reported that 99 Viet Cong had been killed Dec. 19–20 in eight clashes ranging from the U Minh Forest in the Mekong Delta to the northwestern part of the country near the Laotian border. Allied planes also took a heavy toll of the enemy. In the same period, Communist rockets and mortars struck four allied positions, four American planes were downed and a U.S. convoy was ambushed. Five Americans were killed in the two days of fighting.

U.S. losses in Laos reported. An Associated Press dispatch from Saigon Oct. 25 reported that U.S. Special Forces troopers leading secret operations in Laos had suffered losses in recent months that had never been publicly disclosed.

The report drew an immediate denial from the Defense Department in Washington, which insisted that "all casualties for all of Southeast Asia have been reported on a regular basis." The Administration had announced a new policy March 9 of listing U.S. casualties and aircraft losses in Laos in response to Senatorial criticism of the growing American involvement in that country.

The American casualties incurred in Laos were said to be listed among the "cumulative figures for Southeast Asia," which included casualties in South Vietnam and in Cambodia during the U.S. incursion in May and June.

AP quoted a source as saying that the Special Forces "operating out of South Vietnam were losing one or two killed in Laos every month and anywhere from three to 10 wounded."

In one of the largest operations in southern Laos in September, according to AP, U.S. Special Forces men accompanying 150 mercenaries drew two North Vietnamese battalions out into the open where they were pounded by American bombers. More than 500 of the enemy were said to have been destroyed by the air strikes. Two Americans were wounded in the operation and a dozen of the mercenaries were killed. The operation was said to have been supported by U.S. troop-carrying helicopters, two of which were shot down.

The AP dispatch said U.S. helicopters from bases in South Vietnam were participating in other ground operations in Laos. The U.S. command had reported the shooting down of one 'copter in southern Laos Oct. 24, but did not disclose the aircraft's mission.

Squads of mercenaries and U.S. Special Forces men were operating in Laos on a regular basis, observing the Ho Chi Minh Trail and attempting to capture enemy soldiers for intelligence purposes, according to the AP report.

The U.S. command reported Dec. 13 that an American B-57 bomber carrying top secret intelligence equipment had been shot down the previous day over the Ho Chi Minh trail in southern Laos by Communist ground fire. The plane crashed and its equipment was believed destroyed. Two crew members were rescued. It was the 75th U.S. aircraft reported downed over Laos since the U.S. command began reporting losses there March 10.

The B-57 was one of about 20 such aircraft that had started secret combat missions over Laos Oct. 20. The planes were equipped with electronic aids, sensors, radar and navigational and weaponry systems. They were stationed at a base at Udon, Thailand, 40 miles from the Laotian border.

U.S. pays for allied fighters. A Senate subcommittee disclosed June 7 that the U.S. was paying Thailand $50 million a year for sending a combat division to South Vietnam. The total of such aid since 1966 was put at $200 million.

The disclosure was at variance with Thai government statements denying U.S. payments for support of Thai combat units for Vietnam.

The information—testimony taken in November 1969 from State and Defense

Department officials—was made public by the U.S. Security Agreements and Commitments Abroad Subcommittee (of the Foreign Relations Committee), headed by Sen. Stuart Symington (D, Mo.).

The U.S. aid to Thailand for the Viet units included equipment, training, logistic support and extra pay and allowances. U.S. military assistance was to be increased by $30 million for two years and Thailand would receive a battery of Hawk antiaircraft missiles. Total U.S. economic and military aid to Thailand since 1949 was said to total $2.2 billion. Since 1949, the U.S. also had invested $702 million in construction of military bases in Thailand.

The U.S. State Department announced Aug. 28 that Thailand had informed Washington it planned to withdraw its entire 11,000-man force from South Vietnam.

State Department press officer John F. King said the U.S. had "raised no objections" to the Thai "decision in principle" and "understands the reasons cited by Thai Prime Minister [Thanom Kittikachorn] for the withdrawal."

Thanom had said in Bangkok Aug. 27 that Thailand needed "as many as possible, if not all" of its troops stationed in South Vietnam to help defend its borders with Laos and Cambodia.

South Korean soldiers fighting in South Vietnam cost the U.S. more than $1 billion during the last five years, according to testimony of Administration officials before the Symington subcommittee. A transcript of the testimony, given during hearings in February, was released Sept. 12.

The U.S. support—for overseas allowances, arms, equipment, rations, etc.—totaled $1,052,500,000 from September 1965, when the South Koreans arrived in Vietnam, through June 30. The annual cost to the U.S. of maintaining a South Korean soldier in South Vietnam was said by the Pentagon to be about $5,000, compared to the $13,000 annual cost to maintain a U.S. soldier in Vietnam (a figure not previously released by the Pentagon).

The transcript included a Symington comment that U.S. citizens had been "deceived as to the degree of the desire

[of South Korea] to participate in the South Vietnamese venture."

According to South Korean data, as of the first week in September, its 50,000-man force in South Vietnam had mounted 471 battalion-sized operations of about 500 men; 152 regimental, multi-battalion operations; 22 divisional operations involving about 15,000 troops and six operations involving its entire force. Operating independently of the U.S. or South Vietnamese command, the South Koreans covered a hostile area 275 miles along the coast from Danang to Nhatrang and inland to the mountains and jungle. They reported killing more than 32,000 enemy soldiers while losing 2,902 Koreans in action.

The Senate, by voice vote Aug. 20–21, approved proposals to forbid U.S. allowances to allied troops in Vietnam higher than those paid U.S. troops, and to bar U.S. pay to foreign troops fighting in support of Cambodia and Laos. Both proposals were presented by Sen. J. W. Fulbright (D, Ark.), head of the Senate Foreign Relations Committee, as amendments to the military procurement bill.

In offering the first proposal Aug. 20, Fulbright cited revelations in 1969 hearings that the U.S. was paying allowances to allied troops that were about double those paid U.S. troops. He contended that the allied units in Vietnam were there more for propaganda than fighting value, and that Defense Department reports submitted to Congress underestimated the cost of such assistance. A General Accounting Office report to his committee, he said, estimated U.S. aid to the Philippines at $40.8 million from fiscal 1966 through the second quarter of 1970, while the Pentagon reported providing $17.3 million.

Fulbright said it was time "to stop making mercenaries out of allies and allies out of mercenaries."

Armed Services Committee Chairman John Stennis (D, Miss.) agreed with the argument and was in favor of "some adjustment...consistent with our honor."

The purpose of the second amendment, Fulbright explained Aug. 21, was to "prevent the South Vietnamese or the Thais, with our money, from going in... and building a full-fledged partnership with the government of Cambodia and drawing us in." South Vietnamese border areas were excluded from coverage under the amendment.

Red supply buildup. U.S. Air Force Secretary Robert C. Seamans Jr., ending a three-day visit to Saigon, reported Nov. 5 a huge supply buildup in the southern provinces of North Vietnam.

U.S. military sources said the massing of the supplies was about 40–50% more than at the same period in 1969. Seamans said the U.S. Air Force was entering a "very, very crucial time" in its drive to prevent those supplies from being moved down the Ho Chi Minh trail in Laos toward Cambodia and South Vietnam. Heavy rains had prevented the North Vietnamese from using the trail "so we are just at the beginning of a critical period," Seamans said.

U.S. B-52s had bombed the trail daily from Oct. 10 until Nov. 2, suspending all missions against Communist targets in South Vietnam.

North Vietnam downs U.S. plane. An unarmed U.S. reconnaissance plane was shot down over North Vietnam Nov. 13 and its two crewmen apparently were killed, the U.S. command in Saigon reported. The incident prompted Defense Secretary Melvin R. Laird to warn of retaliation if the North Vietnamese continued to fire on American reconnaissance aircraft.

The plane, an RF-4C, was on an observation mission about 100 miles north of the demilitarized zone and 42 miles south of Vinh when it was shot down by North Vietnamese gunners. The plane was believed to have been checking reports of a buildup of supplies to be sent to Communist forces in Cambodia and South Vietnam. It was the 13th American plane downed over North Vietnam since the Nov. 1, 1968 bombing halt of the North. The U.S. had flown more than 60 "protective raids" over the North since then to "prevent or silence enemy fire."

In his comment on the incident, Secretary Laird said "we remain ready to take appropriate action in response to attacks on our armed aircraft." Laird said the attack was a violation of "certain understandings that we arrived at" with the North Vietnamese in exchange for the bombing halt. The U.S. had in-

sisted there was a tacit agreement that North Vietnam would not interfere with American reconnaissance flights or carry out military incursions across the demilitarized zone. Laird said the bombing halt also "was predicated on the fact that the North Vietnamese would negotiate in good faith" at the Paris peace talks. "To date," he said, "the North Vietnamese have chosen not to negotiate in any substantive way."

North Vietnam Nov. 14 again denied it had accepted any conditions in exchange for the bombing halt. Nguyen Thanh Le, spokesman for the Hanoi delegation at the Paris talks, rejecting Laird's statement, said the U.S. "must bear the entire responsibility for its hostile acts." Le insisted that "there is absolutely no tacit accord. Mr. Laird once again furnishes proof that the Nixon Administration has consistently resorted to acts of provocation and reveals even more its plans to undertake new acts against the sovereignty" of North Vietnam.

Air raids on North. The war in Indochina suddenly intensified as American planes carried out widespread attacks on North Vietnam for a 24-hour period Nov. 21–22. The raids, described as retaliatory, were followed by the disclosure that a U.S. task force Nov. 21 had landed 23 miles from Hanoi in an unsuccessful attempt to rescue American prisoners of war believed held captive at a camp there. North Vietnam assailed the bombings and announced that it would boycott the Nov. 25 session of the Paris peace talks in protest.

The raids on North Vietnam were followed by heavy American air attacks Nov. 21 on Laos and Cambodia. About 400 Air Force and Navy planes were said to have taken part in the strikes.

The bombings of North Vietnam were the heaviest and the most sustained since the halt in American air raids over the North Nov. 1, 1968. U.S. Secretary of Defense Melvin R. Laird announced Nov. 21 that the raids were directed against missiles and antiaircraft gun sites south of the 19th Parallel. He added that they were of a limited duration and were a "protective response" to the downing of a U.S. reconnaissance plane over North Vietnam Nov. 13 and to attacks on other American observation planes over the North. Although the announced purpose of the raids was to suppress antiaircraft fire against American reconnaissance planes, the Nixon Administration later indicated that the principal purpose of the assaults was to destroy war stockpiles in North Vietnam to prevent a possible Communist offensive in the coming months.

Laird said he had noted "erroneous reports from Hanoi that in connection with our protective reaction strikes we have bombed prisoners of war camps." Asserting that such reports were false, Laird warned that "we will continue to hold the other side fully accountable for the safety and well-being of our prisoners of war."

The U.S. contended that the attacks were limited to Hatinh and Quangbinh Provinces, between the 19th Parallel and the demilitarized zone that divided North and South Vietnam. A North Vietnamese broadcast Nov. 21 claimed the raids were conducted as far north as the Hanoi-Haiphong area, that a prisoner of war camp had been struck, resulting in a "number of United States prisoner of war casualties" and that a number of civilians had been killed.

A Hanoi broadcast said six American planes had been shot down by North Vietnamese defenders. A government communique called the raids "an extremely serious act of war which infringes upon the sovereignty and security" of North Vietnam.

An Agence France-Presse report from the North Vietnamese capital Nov. 21 said the city was shaken by the blast of bombs that fell on surrounding towns 25 miles away. The North Vietnamese news agency was quoted as saying that the attacks were aimed at Haiphong harbor, the Quangminh mine complex and the Hatay and Hoabinh areas. Hanoi itself had been placed on an air alert as the American planes approached the city.

The raids were first announced by North Vietnam. Laird's announcement followed, the text of which was released by the Defense Department. It said:

"As part of our publicly announced policy and determined effort to protect American lives we are conducting limited duration protective reaction air strikes against missiles and antiaircraft gun sites and related facilities in North Vietnam south of the 19th parallel.

"These protective reaction strikes are in response to attacks on our unarmed reconnaissance aircraft. When the U.S. halted the bombing of North Vietnam on Nov. 1, 1968, it was with the understanding of the fact that unarmed reconnaissance would continue.

"These protective reaction missions are designed to protect the lives of U.S. pilots flying unarmed reconnaissance missions over North Vietnam and pilots flying missions associated with interdiction of North Vietnamese military supplies throughout southern Laos moving toward South Vietnam.

"To comment further could jeopardize the safety and security of Americans. Therefore I have nothing to add at this time."

In providing further information on the air strikes, Deputy Assistant Defense Secretary Jerry Friedheim disclosed Nov. 23 that about 200 fighter-bombers and about 50 support planes had participated. He said the raids were directed against military targets around the "approach routes" to the Mugia and Bankarai Passes (a funnel for Communist supplies) and at the northwestern edge of the demilitarized zone. Friedheim reiterated that missile and antiaircraft gun sites were singled out. "Related facilities" also came under attack, he said. These, according to Friedheim, might have included trucks, ammunition dumps, petroleum storage facilities, missiles and even troop barracks in "proximity" to air defense sites.

In response to questioning about initial pilot reports that about 100 North Vietnamese trucks had been destroyed by the raids, Friedheim said this might "hamper" Communist offensive operations in South Vietnam.

Friedheim said "appropriate" members of Congress had been apprised of the air strikes as they "were occurring," but he did not identify the legislators.

U.S. Senate aroused by raids—The U.S. bombing raids in North Vietnam aroused alarm in the Senate Nov. 21 over their policy implications. Many senators also expressed surprise and concern about the Administration's failure to consult Congress prior to the raids. The Senate Foreign Relations Committee, whose members had not been informed, immediately scheduled hearings and confronted Defense Secretary Melvin R. Laird in a nationally televised session Nov. 24. Laird also testified that day at a closed session of the Senate Armed Services Committee.

Sen. George D. Aiken (Vt.), ranking Republican on the Senate Foreign

Relations Committee, expressed concern Nov. 21 over the bombing. As far as he knew, no member of Congress had been consulted prior to the raids. He also questioned whether the U.S. had a "right" to fly intelligence planes over North Vietnam. On the Senate floor Nov. 24, Aiken deplored the prisoner rescue effort as well as the lack of consultation with Congress. The prisoners, he said, "may never be returned to us if we cannot combine resolve and restraint now." As for consultation, "no president in these times can ever hope to fashion foreign policy in the inner sanctum of the White House without risking grave repercussions at home and abroad."

Senate Democratic Leader Mike Mansfield said Nov. 21 "no matter how you look at it, it means a resurgence of activity, a renewed involvement and possibly a delay in settlement."

Other senators also commented Nov. 21: Sen. Edmund S. Muskie (D, Me.)—The raids indicated a "renewed reliance on military pressure" and a shift in policy "to force a settlement on the other side."

Sen. George S. McGovern (D, S.D.)—The bombing raids were "almost beyond belief. It is sheer folly to believe anything can be accomplished by renewing them."

Sen Claiborne Pell (D, R.I.)—Retaliatory bombing was "counterproductive to an ultimate peace settlement and to our national interests."

Sen. Mark O. Hatfield (R, Ore.)—Past history showed "such action tended to lengthen rather than shorten the war."

Sen. Jacob Javits (R, N.Y.)—Renewed bombing was the kind of incident that was "bound to occur so long as we do not determine to pull our troops out of Vietnam on our own timetable." "Vietnamization has the danger that we can always be drawn deeper in, as this incident indicates."

The raids drew support from some senators. Sen. Peter H. Dominick (R, Colo.) saw them as "part of our pattern to show North Vietnam they can't use our unarmed planes for target practice."

Sens. John Sherman Cooper (R, Ky.) and John J. Sparkman (D, Ala.) agreed about the probable necessity for the raids to protect intelligence planes. Sen.

Howard H. Baker Jr. (R, Tenn.) supported the raids as proper retaliation.

The prisoner rescue mission was upheld Nov. 23 by Sen. Henry M. Jackson (D, Wash.). He called it "fully warranted in the light of the North Vietnamese government's failure" to live up to the terms of the Geneva convention on prisoners of war.

Senate Foreign Relations Committee Chairman J. W. Fulbright (D, Ark.) commented Nov. 23 on the bombing raids—"It would seem that the actual policy is to escalate the war and to seek a military victory"—and the rescue mission—It had "implications of a much wider war" and the mounting of a physical invasion was "certainly a very provocative act."

Laird testimony—Defense Secretary Laird told the Fulbright Committee during its televised hearing Nov. 24 that while the basic policy of seeking a negotiated settlement had not changed as a result of the recent raids, he would recommend to President Nixon resumption of full-scale air attacks on North Vietnam if the enemy committed major violations of a tacit understanding with the U.S. that halted the bombing two years ago.

This tacit understanding, Laird said, included the U.S. obligation to halt the bombings and North Vietnamese acceptance of flights by unarmed reconnaissance craft, agreement to refrain from shelling major South Vietnamese population centers, from infiltration through the demilitarized zone and to permit the sitting of the South Vietnamese delegation at the Paris peace talks.

Laird said the recent bombing attacks were retaliation for the recent shellings of Saigon and Hue and the downing of the reconnaissance aircraft. The prisoner-rescue effort was undertaken, he said, after the Administration learned that six prisoners had died in the North Vietnamese prisons. Subsequently, he said, there were "unconfirmed" reports of the death of 11 more prisoners.

The U.S. had given Hanoi "a message" a week before the bombing strikes of its belief that the tacit understanding was being violated by Hanoi, Laird said, He insisted that the bombing raids and the rescue mission were separate isolated actions. He said the air strikes represented "a signal that we would not tolerate the setting aside of the understanding on the cessation of bombings" and the rescue effort was a signal that "we are concerned" about the prisoners and "we shall have rather unusual means to assure that they will return as free men."

While acknowledging that the U.S. was considering other action to gain release of the prisoners, Laird declined to go into details.

Fulbright criticizes Laird—Secretary Laird's testimony before the Senate Foreign Relations Committee Nov. 24 on the extent of the American bombing of North Vietnam was branded Nov. 29 by its chairman, Sen. J.W. Fulbright (D, Ark.), as a misrepresentation of the facts.

Appearing on the CBS program "Face the Nation," Fulbright charged that the American raids were further proof that the Defense Department had displaced the State Department as the principal formulator of foreign policy, particularly in Southeast Asia. This was part of "the process" by which "the military establishment runs nearly the whole country," Fulbright said. The influence of Laird and Presidential advisor Henry Kissinger far outweighed that of Secretary of State William P. Rogers in formulating foreign policy, Fulbright said. As a result, the senator asserted, Rogers' ability to devise foreign policy had become "subsidiary" and the diplomatic complications that emanated from a raid such as the one on Sontay were seldom considered.

In reply to Fulbright's criticism, Assistant Defense Secretary Henkin said that in Laird's Nov. 24 testimony the secretary had given "a factual report of what happened."

Responding to Fulbright's complaint that he had not mentioned the air strike carried out in conjunction with Sontay raid in his testimony, Laird said Nov. 30 that members of the Senate Foreign Relations Committee had not questioned him closely enough. Laird explained: "I've been as forthright as possible in answering all questions. Perhaps members of the committee did not ask.

That is not my responsibility. Now, I answer questions, but I only answer the questions that are asked."

Laird had told a closed hearing of the Senate Armed Services Committee Nov. 24 that American planes had fired 12–14 Shrike missiles against North Vietnamese missile sites. Laird said Nov. 30 he had been in error, that only 11 Shrikes had been fired.

U.S. attacks war prisoner camp—The Nov. 21 assault on the prisoner of war camp in North Vietnam was described by Secretary Laird at a news conference Nov. 23. He said a raiding party made up of an undisclosed number of Army and Air Force men landed in helicopters at the site of the compound at Sontay, about 23 miles west of Hanoi. The commando-type raid, he said, was launched about an hour before the massive American air strikes on North Vietnam and both operations were unconnected.

President Nixon had approved of the commando raid after he was informed earlier in November that some prisoners were dying, Laird said. According to Laird, the American raiders at Sontay "successfully returned to safety without suffering a single casualty" after discovering that the prisoners had been removed. During the operation, one American was slightly wounded by enemy rifle fire and one helicopter was deliberately destroyed after it crash-landed at the prison site, he said.

Four officers and men involved with the Sontay raid were honored by President Nixon at ceremonies at the White House Nov. 25. Air Force Brig. Gen. Leroy J. Manor was awarded the Distinguished Service Medal for planning the mission and Army Col. Arthur D. Simons was given the Distinguished Service Cross for leading the raiding party. Nixon also awarded the Distinguished Service Cross to Sgt. 1. C. Tyrone J. Adderley of the Army and the Air Force Cross to helicopter crewman T. Sgt. Leroy M. Wright for their role in the operation.

In making the awards, Nixon pledged that the U.S. would do all it could "at the diplomatic table and in other ways" to free American prisoners. He described the Sontay raid as a "mission of mercy."

Details of Sontay raid. These details of the aborted commando raid on the North Vietnamese prisoner of war camp at Sontay emerged from interviews with American officials:

About 50 men landed at the camp site in 10 large helicopters from a base in Thailand. Several of the 'copters were empty in expectation that 70–100 Americans believed held captive in the camp would be rescued. The assault force was escorted by several F-105s, which broke away from the helicopter fleet to attack enemy troop positions and antiaircraft sites outside the camp. These raids were carried out within two miles of the camp. Moments before this attack, Navy planes from aircraft carriers in the Gulf of Tonkin dropped flares and pretended to head for the mainland to give the North Vietnamese the false impression that the attack was coming from the coast.

One troop-carrying helicopter crash-landed in the compound of the prison camp to give the raiders fire power. This helicopter was destroyed by the men as they left. The other helicopters landed outside the camp to block enemy attacks on the ground. The commandos emerged from the aircraft and began their futile search for the American prisoners. In the ensuing gunfire, about 25 of the prison guards were killed. The raiders returned to their helicopters within 40 minutes. On the way back to Thailand, the commandos rescued an American pilot who had been shot down while flying cover for the Sontay mission.

Brig. Gen. Leroy J. Manor, who had led the Sontay raid, disclosed Dec. 2 that the camp had been empty for some time when his commandos reached it. He said: "It is very difficult to say exactly how long the camp had been vacated, but it was from several weeks to three months." He denied that intelligence was faulty since the camp "had been identified some time ago as a POW facility. Unfortunately, we weren't able to tell exactly when they moved the prisoners." As a matter of fact, the intelligence was "excellent because we knew how to approach the camp," Manor said. He lauded the operation as "a complete success with the exception that no prisoners were rescued."

Hanoi assails U.S. raids. The North Vietnamese delegation to the Paris peace talks announced Nov. 23 that it would not attend the Nov. 25 session in protest against the American air attacks on North Vietnam Nov. 21–22. The delegation said it would be present at the next scheduled meeting Dec. 3. The Viet Cong representatives similarly announced their refusal to attend.

In announcing Hanoi's views, North Vietnamese chief delegate Xuan Thuy charged that the American air strikes were "extremely serious acts of war [that] threaten the work of the Paris conference." "This is the argumentation of colonialist aggressors who rely on force," he said.

Thuy denounced the U.S. argument that the raids were in retaliation for North Vietnamese attacks on U.S. observation planes. He said that as a pretext for "acts of war," Washington authorities "have invented the so-called understanding" between North Vietnam and the U.S. "under which the United States would be allowed to carry out reconnaissance flights over North Vietnam" in exchange for a halt to the bombing of the North.

A statement by the North Vietnamese delegation Nov. 21 had asserted that the American raids constituted "a flagrant violation of the United States commitment to cease definitively and unconditionally all bombardments and all other acts of war" against North Vietnam. North Vietnamese spokesman Nguyen Thanh Le said that since the official bombing halt of North Vietnam Nov. 1, 1968, 127 American planes had been downed over the North. The U.S. had flown 7,970 missions over North Vietnam in 1969 and 11,180 between January and October 1970, Le said.

American reconnaissance flights over North Vietnam had been the subject of a sharp U.S.-Communist exchange at the Paris talks Nov. 19. Le said after the meeting that if "the Nixon Administration continues to make flights in violation of the sovereignty and security" of North Vietnam, "the people and the army will hand out the punishment they deserve and Mr. Nixon will have to bear full responsibility for the consequences."

Chief American delegate David K. E. Bruce reiterated the U.S. conditions for the bombing halt. He said: "At the time, the United States agreed to stop all bombing and acts involving the use of force over North Vietnam. Aerial reconnaissance is not an act involving the use of force. Reconnaissance flights are essential to the safety and security of our forces in South Vietnam."

At the Nov. 5 session, Xuan Thuy had charged that President Nixon "has lied to the American people and the reactionary policy that he practices is tied to the prolongation and the extension of the war in Vietnam." Bruce assailed the statement as a "personal insult" to Nixon.

Hanoi confirms prison raid. The American commando strike against the Sontay prison camp was confirmed by Hanoi Nov. 25.

The Communist party newspaper Nhan Dan broke the government's silence on the incident by stating that the bombing that followed the prisoner rescue attempt was "an extremely grave act of war." The newspaper added that "The Nixon Administration also rashly organized attacks of pirate commandos deep inside our territory." Nhan Dan said the bombings had been prepared in advance and approved by President Nixon at a National Security Council meeting Nov. 19.

The North Vietnamese delegation to the Paris peace talks Nov. 25 accused Defense Secretary Laird of lying when he implied that casualties in the Hanoi-Haiphong area Nov. 21 had been caused by North Vietnamese missiles that fell back to the ground. The delegation statement said: "We wonder then why the 'North Vietnamese missiles' are of the [U.S.] Shrike types, one of which bears the number SK42L and another SK51L. Let Mr. Laird answer these questions."

North Vietnamese delegation spokesman Nguyen Thanh Le said Nov. 26 that among the 49 civilians killed in the Nov. 21–22 raids in the Hanoi-Haiphong area, 28 had died in the bombing of a restaurant in Hatinh, just below the 19th Parallel, and six had died in the bombing of a sanatorium in Hatay Province near Hanoi. Le also said three schools in Quangbinh Province were hit, a day

care center in Hatay Province was struck by phosphorous bombs and burned, 100 homes had been destroyed and that Shrike missiles had fallen around Hanoi, one of them six miles north and another about four miles west.

Le made no reference to the Sontay attack, speaking only in general terms of "acts of war."

North Vietnam raid aftermath. Further details on the American air raids on North Vietnam Nov. 21–22 and the aborted U.S. commando attack on a prisoner of war camp at Sontay near Hanoi Nov. 21 were provided by U.S. and North Vietnamese officials Nov. 25–27. In the wake of the aerial and commando assaults, the U.S. Nov. 30 carried out another "protective reaction" attack on a North Vietnamese gun site.

The U.S. command, reporting on the latest air strike, said a U.S. fighter-bomber, an F-105 Thunderchief, bombed a radar-controlled gun site in North Vietnam $5\frac{1}{2}$ miles north of the demilitarized zone, near the Laotian border. The jet had not been fired on, but the North Vietnamese radar installation reportedly was zeroing in on the F-105 and other U.S. aircraft in preparation for firing, it was said. A command spokesman would not disclose the mission of the F-105 but it was believed to have been taking part in an operation with the other jets on a bombing run against North Vietnamese supply routes.

In announcing the attack, the command said "protective reaction is the inherent right of self-defense."

U.S. admits raids near Hanoi. The U.S. Defense Department confirmed Nov. 27 that the air strikes on North Vietnam Nov. 21 were aimed at military targets near Hanoi, but that the attacks were directly connected with the commando raid on the prisoner of war camp at Sontay. The department attempted to draw a clear distinction between the "protective" operations around Sontay and the wider bombings of North Vietnamese targets Nov. 21–22. Those attacks, the U.S. had said, were below the 19th Parallel. North Vietnam, however, again insisted Nov. 26 that the Nov. 21–22 air raids were far above the 19th Parallel and that

49 civilians had died in the raids and 40 had been wounded.

Assistant Secretary of Defense for Public Affairs Daniel Z. Henkin disclosed Nov. 27 that U.S. planes flying cover for the helicopter commando force about to land at Sontay had used "appropriate" ordnance against North Vietnamese antiaircraft, missile and artillery positions and troops in the vicinity of Sontay. A later department statement described the ordnance as "about a dozen" Shrike missiles, which had been launched near Sontay during the "protective" mission.

Henkin said the purpose of the accompanying air strikes had been designed "to draw fire away from the central operations" in "the immediately adjacent area of the camp." "There were some antiaircraft installations in the area, which we knew about, and there were some troops in the area, which we knew about," he said. Referring to the commandos, Henkin said, "We obviously were not going to send them in there without arranging for their protection."

Henkin contended that the casualties which the North Vietnamese claimed had been inflicted by the American planes actually had been caused by the "indiscriminate firing" of 30 of the enemy's own missiles at the American helicopters as they were landing.

Testifying before the Senate Foreign Relations Committee Nov. 24, Defense Secretary Melvin R. Laird had said that during the Sontay attack "we had some flares dropped by Navy diversionary planes . . . to illuminate and divert the radar system, the antiaircraft system, to that side." In first disclosing the Sontay attack Nov. 23, Laird had denied that any "ordnance" had been used.

Laird told the House Foreign Affairs Committee Nov. 25 that the Sontay raid was disclosed to preserve the Defense Department's "credibility." Laird explained: "We were being accused of something we had not done. We were accused of sending wave upon wave" of attacking planes against the Hanoi-Haiphong area. "It was not my plan to bring [the raid] to the public attention, necessarily," but to have let Hanoi's claims go unchallenged "would have created a tremendous problem in the United States" because it would have

conflicted with Nixon Administration contentions that it was winding down the war.

Laird contradicted a statement made by Vice President Agnew Nov. 24 that the Sontay raid had failed because of "faulty intelligence." Laird said "I regret that the vice president was not present for a briefing." When Agnew returned from Palm Springs, Calif. (where he had made the statement), "I hope to have the opportunity to give him a briefing," Laird said.

Secretary of State William P. Rogers, who also testified before the House Committee, said the American attacks on North Vietnam "will have no effect one way or another" on the Paris peace talks. "The fact is," he said, "no progress has been made" at those negotiations. In assessing prospects for success at Paris, Rogers said "in the absence of interest, negotiations in themselves have no urgency."

U.S. threatens to bomb North Vietnam. Warnings that the U.S. might order further bombings of North Vietnam were voiced by President Nixon Dec. 10 and by Defense Secretary Melvin R. Laird Dec. 11.

Speaking to a nationally televised news conference at the White House, Nixon warned that if he felt North Vietnamese infiltration into South Vietnam was enough to "threaten our remaining forces" and if the enemy increased "the level of fighting in South Vietnam, I will order the bombing of military sites in North Vietnam, the passes that lead from North Vietnam into South Vietnam, the military complexes and the military supply lines."

Nixon also warned of retaliatory air strikes if the Communists continued to fire on American planes flying reconnaissance missions over North Vietnam. The President rejected Hanoi's claims that American agreement to halt the bombing of North Vietnam in 1968 was unconditional, that there was "no understanding that [U.S.] reconnaissance planes are to fly over North Vietnam." Nixon insisted that the understanding for conducting such flights had been made clear at the time by President Johnson, Clark Clifford, then secretary of defense, and Cyrus Vance, chief U.S.

negotiator at the Paris peace talks in 1968.

Nixon reiterated the need for continuing the observation missions "as we are withdrawing our forces" to determine "whether or not there's any chance of a strike against those forces that remain." If the North Vietnamese fire on an American reconnaissance aircraft, he asserted, "I will not only order that they return fire, but I will also order that the military complex around that site be destroyed by the bombing."

On the matter of the Paris peace negotiations, Nixon said he had not abandoned hope for success. But he noted that North Vietnam's failure to accept a U.S.-South Vietnamese offer for an even exchange of prisoners made in Paris "pinpointed something that is pretty generally getting known around the world, and that is that this nation [North Vietnam] is an international outlaw."

Questioned about the abortive Nov. 21 American commando raid on the prisoner of war camp at Sontay, North Vietnam, the President explained that Congress had not been consulted about the mission "because of the high risk involved of the men who were participating." The information released on the raid afterwards had been complete; "there's been no attempt to withhold anything," Nixon said.

On American aid to Cambodia, the President said the additional $250 million he had requested to supply that country with small arms and other assistance was "probably the best investment in foreign assistance that the United States has made in my political lifetime." The additional funds, Nixon said, would help Cambodia defend itself against "a foreign aggressor," the North Vietnamese, who would "be over there killing Americans" if they weren't in Cambodia.

Laird sees raids if talks lag—Secretary of Defense Melvin R. Laird told the Senate Foreign Relations Committee Dec. 11 that the U.S. might resume the bombing of North Vietnam if the Communists failed to negotiate seriously in Paris. Laird said North Vietnam's readiness "for serious negotiations" in addition to its pledge to respect

the demilitarized zone, refrain from shelling South Vietnamese cities and permit American reconnaissance flights over the North were part of the 1968 understanding that led to the American bombing halt.

Two committee members interpreted Laird's testimony as a Nixon Administration decision to step up the war. Sen. Stuart Symington [D, Mo.] told Laird "It is clear as light to me that we have now decided to escalate the war over North Vietnam." Committee Chairman J. W. Fulbright [D, Ark.] called the retaliatory bombings of the North, military aid to Cambodia and the Sontay raid "a reversal of policy" and "a resumption of the warfare conducted" by the Johnson Administration. Like the Johnson Administration, the Nixon Administration appeared to be seeking a Vietnam settlement "through application of superior force on North Vietnam," Fulbright said.

Fulbright engaged in a sharp exchange with Laird over the Sontay raid. The chairman suggested that the Defense Department had been aware there were no American prisoners in the camp when the assault was launched. Laird took issue with what he called Fulbright's innuendoes about his truthfulness. The secretary said the commando attack had been carried out with the expectation that there was "a 50-50 chance of returning the prisoners of war."

Laird disclosed that preparations for the Sontay raid had started in mid-August, but that orders for its execution had not been issued until Nov. 21—the day of the actual attack. Fulbright said Central Intelligence Agency Director Richard Helms had informed him that he (Helms) had not been consulted beforehand on the operation. But Laird said "all intelligence agencies" had been apprised of the decision and that Helms had been "fully briefed and advised" "four or five weeks" before the raid.

Hanoi scores Nixon threat—North Vietnam Dec. 12 denounced President Nixon's news conference statements, charging they were a threat to step up the war. The army newspaper Quan Doi Nhan Dan denied Nixon's claim of an understanding to permit U.S. reconnaissance planes to fly over North

Vietnam. The newspaper asked: "Is there any independent and sovereign nation in the world which tolerates a tacit accord permitting its enemy to spy over its territory?"

The North Vietnamese Communist party newspaper Nhan Dan asserted that "The tacit agreement invoked by the American Administration for observation flights over the North, renunciation of artillery bombardments of cities or reinforcement of military potential in southern North Vietnam is sheer invention." The purpose of the latest upsurge of American military action against North Vietnam was "to save Vietnamization of the war in the South," Nhan Dan said.

Nhan Dan warned that North Vietnam would fire at all intruding planes invading its territory, "whether they are reconnaissance aircraft or fighters."

North Vietnamese Defense Minister Vo Nguyen Giap Dec. 22 called the alleged understanding on the American surveillance flights "the logic of pirates" and warned that his country reserved the right "to shoot down American aircraft of any type if they encroach upon our air space." Speaking to a mass meeting in Hanoi, Giap said North Vietnam was "a sovereign independent country, and no sovereign independent country will allow its enemy to spy freely upon it."

Russia criticizes U.S. threat. The Soviet Union Dec. 16 assailed President Nixon's threat Dec. 10 to resume the bombing of North Vietnam.

Moscow's statement, issued by Tass, said: "The Soviet government will draw the appropriate conclusions from the new provocations and threats to extend aggression against their fraternal Socialist state." A "continuation of the provocation against" North Vietnam and "attempts to carry out new military threats against the peoples of Indochina will lead to even greater complication of the situation in Southeast Asia and the Far East," the statement said.

The Soviet statement added: the Nov. 21 "barbaric raids by American aviation on populated localities" of North Vietnam "as well as the latest news conference by the United States President containing direct threats to resume the bombings . . . cannot but evoke wrathful con-demnation by all those who treasure peace and security."

The U.S. State Department Dec. 17 called the Soviet statement "misdirected." The department said "it should have been addressed to North Vietnam along with the suggestion to cease attacks" on unarmed U.S. reconnaissance planes flying over North Vietnam and to "start negotiating seriously in Paris."

U.S. bombing policy explained. Secretary of State William P. Rogers said Dec. 23 that President Nixon's Dec. 10 threat to resume the bombing of North Vietnam did not constitute a change in Administration policy. Speaking at a news conference, Rogers acknowledged that Nixon had gone beyond the 1968 terms that led to the bombing halt of North Vietnam, but he insisted this was because the situation had changed by American troop withdrawals.

Rogers noted that the President had warned of possible raids on North Vietnamese military targets "to protect the lives of Americans who are withdrawing from South Vietnam. . . . he didn't say that was any part of the understanding [for the bombing halt]. Obviously, it couldn't be part of the understanding. At the time the understanding was reached, there wasn't any Vietnamization program. Americans were not being withdrawn from South Vietnam. So it's quite a different situation."

Rogers took issue with press interpretations of Defense Secretary Melvin R. Laird's remarks that the Nixon Administration was suggesting that lack of progress at the Paris peace talks could be another justification for the resumption of the bombings.

"That's not the premise on which we're operating," Rogers said. The secretary said that at Laird's appearance before the Senate Foreign Relations Committee Dec. 11, Laird had read a statement by former Defense Secretary Clark Clifford, who was among those who had arranged the 1968 bombing halt, that "did convey the thought that one of the conditions of the bombing halt was the continuation of good-faith negotiations in Paris."

In a briefing on the bombing halt, Clifford had indicated Oct. 31, 1968 that Communist compliance with the two conditions for the cessation of the raids—an absence of military movement across the demilitarized zone between North and South Vietnam and a stop to the Communist shelling of South Vietnamese cities—constituted demonstrations of "good faith in negotiations" at Paris.

In an interview Dec. 23, Clifford denied Rogers' contention that the American bombing policy under Nixon remained unchanged. Clifford insisted that Nixon had departed radically from the understanding worked out by the Johnson Administration by adding "two new elements"—the threat to resume the raids on the North if combat activity increased in the South and the threat to destroy North Vietnamese missile sites and military complexes around them if U.S. reconnaissance planes were fired on from those positions.

Holiday truce plans. Communist and allied forces announced plans for ceasefires during the Christmas and New Year's holidays and Tet, the Vietnamese lunar new year, but the truces proposed by the two sides varied in length.

The Viet Cong's Provisional Revolutionary Government announced Nov. 30 that its forces in South Vietnam would unilaterally stop fighting for Christmas from 12:01 Dec. 24 to midnight Dec. 27, for New Year's from midnight Dec. 31 to midnight Jan. 3, 1971, and for Tet from midnight Jan. 26 to midnight Jan. 30.

The Viet Cong said it would not extend the truce into a permanent one because of U.S. refusal to announce a timetable for the withdrawal of American troops from Vietnam and because the current Saigon regime would not step down.

The U.S. Dec. 7 expressed interest in prolonging the holiday truce, but the South Vietnamese government announced Dec. 9 that it would observe only 24-hour truces for each of the three holidays.

Washington's interest in an extension of the truces had been prompted by a suggestion by Sen. Henry M. Jackson (D, Wash.) Dec. 6 that the temporary halt in the fighting be used to negotiate a permanent standstill cease-fire. Jackson, speaking on NBC's "Meet the Press" program, said he had not discussed his recommendation with Secretary of State William P. Rogers, but a State Department spokesman said later Dec. 6 that Rogers had heard the broadcast and had telephoned Jackson to inform him the Administration had been considering an extension and intended "to pursue it."

A follow-up statement by the State Department Dec. 7 said the U.S. and South Vietnam were discussing the possibility of extending the truce, "but for anything like this to have meaning it would have to be strictly observed by both sides."

Both South and North Vietnam Dec. 10 ruled out any extended truce. A Saigon Foreign Ministry spokesman said "If we agree on a five-week cease-fire beginning at Christmas, we must be certain that the enemy accepts the same period."

A Hanoi broadcast Dec. 10 charged that the proposal for an extended ceasefire was "a new treacherous trick by the Nixon Administration aimed at advertising the so-called cease-fire proposal by Nixon last Oct. 7."

Christmas, New Year's truces. Sporadic but light clashes continued in South Vietnam despite cease-fires of varied lengths declared by allied and Communist forces for the Christmas and New Year's holidays.

The U.S. and South Vietnamese commands reported that their 24-hour truce which lasted until 6 p.m. Dec. 25 had been marred by 81 Communist-initiated incidents, with 17 South Vietnamese and 30 Communist soldiers killed. This compared with 116 incidents initiated by the enemy during Christmas 1969 when the allies had similarly observed a one-day crease-fire.

The Communists had announced earlier that their forces would observe a 72-hour Christmas cease-fire starting at 1 a.m. Dec. 24.

Two hours before the start of the allied Christmas standstill, U.S. artillery had accidentally fired a 105-mm. shell into a group of soldiers of the 1st Brigade, 101st Airborne Division 11 miles south of Hue. Nine American soldiers were killed and nine wounded.

A Saigon military spokesman reported Dec. 31 that 90 minutes after the 24-hour allied New Year's truce, which had begun at 6 p.m. the previous day, Communist forces attacked Baudien hamlet in Haunghia Province, 24 miles northwest of Saigon. Nineteen members of the hamlet's defense force were reported killed. The Communist truce started at midnight Dec. 31 and was to end at midnight Jan. 3.

The Viet Cong ended their 72-hour Christmas truce Dec. 27 with a mortar attack on an allied naval base in the Mekong Delta.

Cambodia After U.S. Exit

Fighting continues. North Vietnamese, South Vietnamese and Viet Cong forces as well as Cambodian troops continued to fight on in Cambodia after U.S. troops were pulled back to South Vietnam June 29.

About 3,000 South Vietnamese troops June 29 lifted a siege of an arms depot at Longvek, 23 miles north of Pnompenh. Cambodian troops had been trapped in the town by Communist soldiers since June 25.

More than 5,000 South Vietnamese troops launched a sweep of areas north of Pnompenh July 1 but made no significant contact with the enemy. Meanwhile, more than 800 Khmer Krom, ethnic Cambodians, arrived from South Vietnam to bolster the defense of Pnompenh. The reinforcements, trained by U.S. Special Forces, joined 4,000 other Khmer Krom from Vietnam assigned to the defense of the capital.

North Vietnamese and Viet Cong July 5 entered the town of Saang, 20 miles south of Pnompenh, but began pulling out later in the day after the arrival of Cambodian reinforcements in the area. The Cambodians surged into Saang July 6, cleaned out the remaining Communist troops and retook complete control of the town.

The Saigon command reported July 5 that its troops killed 34 Communists in repelling attacks on South Vietnamese positions near Svayrieng, Cambodia and along Route 7 west of the Chup rubber plantation, close to the Vietnamese frontier. South Vietnamese losses were given as eight killed and three wounded.

The withdrawal of Communist troops from the ancient temple ruins at Angkor was reported July 6. Cambodian patrols that entered Angkor reported no damage to the country's greatest cultural shrine after a Communist occupation of more than a month. There was no explanation as to why the Viet Cong, the North Vietnamese and Khmer Rouge troops had abandoned the area, where they had set up supply dumps and fortified positions. The entire Angkor area had been treated as an "open city" by the Cambodians, who made no effort to attack the Communist positions there.

The Saigon command July 8 reported completion of a six-week drive in the Parrot's Beak, in southeastern Cambodia. The offensive, the command claimed, resulted in the killing of 1,119 Viet Cong and North Vietnamese and the capture of 8,427 rifles and 158 heavy weapons. South Vietnamese losses were listed as 878 killed and 3,832 wounded.

About 2,000 South Vietnamese irregulars had been withdrawn from Cambodia, reducing Saigon's forces there to 18,000 men, it was reported July 8.

Communist forces July 11 captured a Cambodian military base at a mountain top resort at Kirirom, 50 miles west of

111

Pnompenh, after routing 400 government defenders. Kirirom was astride vital Highwʌ 4 linking Pnompenh with the port oi Kompong Som on the Gulf of Siam. Cambodian counterattacks were assisted by South Vietnamese air strikes. Two battalions of Khmer Krom were sent from Pnompenh July 12 to capture the road leading to the summit of the mountain, but they were halted about three miles from the top by heavy Communist fire and withdrew to Highway 4. The ethnic Cambodians staged new diversionary attacks July 13 and reported killing 50 of the estimated 1,000 North Vietnamese and Viet Cong. Cambodian troops recaptured Kirirom July 16.

Assistance to the hard-pressed Pnompenh government was the subject of a high-level meeting of South Vietnamese and Cambodian officials in Neak Leung, Cambodia July 17. After meeting for two hours with Lon Nol, Deputy Premier Sisowath Sirik Matek, and Chief of State Cheng Heng, South Vietnamese President Nguyen Van Thieu said: "The most important thing that we agreed together was that the other nations of the free world should come as rapidly as possible to help Cambodia and not permit the Communists to take the initiative." Thieu dismissed a recent suggestion by Vice President Nguyen Cao Ky that Cambodia, Thailand and South Vietnam form a joint anti-Communist front in Southeast Asia. Thieu said the idea was "not feasible" because "we don't need a classical or rigid alliance."

A force of 2,500 South Vietnamese troops moved into Cambodia July 26 on a new search and destroy mission, raising Saigon's forces in the country to about 20,000 men. The troops were flown by U.S. helicopters to a staging area at Donphuc in South Vietnam's western Mekong Delta, three miles from the Cambodian border. From there, the South Vietnamese pushed across the border six miles east of Kompong Trabek on the main Saigon-Pnompenh highway. The South Vietnamese reported killing 35 Communist soldiers in their initial contacts with the enemy and finding the bodies of 26 Communists killed earlier by allied air strikes southeast of Kompong Trabek.

Cambodians recapture Skoun. Cambodian troops Aug. 7 recaptured the town of Skoun, seized by North Vietnamese and Viet Cong forces Aug. 1. Skoun, located at a key intersection 40 miles northeast of Pnompenh, had been retaken briefly by government soldiers Aug. 2 but the Communists later swept back into the village.

A Pnompenh military spokesman reported that Cambodian soldiers re-entering Skoun were assisted by allied air strikes. Although the spokesman did not specify whether the planes were American, the announcement called attention to a growing controversy over whether stepped-up U.S. air strikes in Cambodia were in direct support of Cambodian troops or were intended only to interdict Communist supplies.

U.S. air support controversy. Eyewitness reports by American journalists that U.S. planes were flying bombing missions in direct support of Cambodian troops were denied Aug. 6 by Defense Secretary Melvin R. Laird.

Laird said that bombings by U.S. jets Aug. 5 in front of a battalion of Cambodian troops fighting at Skoun were part of a general interdiction campaign to prevent the Communists from reopening sea supply routes through Cambodian coastal towns. Laird emphasized that the Administration's policy of conducting only interdictory attacks against Communist forces in Cambodia to protect American troops applied to virtually all of Cambodia, particularly "along the sanctuary areas, or along the river route." He conceded that such raids would provide the Cambodians with "ancillary benefits," but he did not specify what these benefits would be.

In explaining the distinction between "ancillary benefits" and direct air support, Defense Department spokesman Jerry Friedheim said Aug. 6: "The difference is how it looks to the Cambodians and how it looks to us. How it looks to the Cambodians is that ancillary benefits are direct support for his troops. It looks to us like an interdiction campaign conducted in the context of our interdiction operations aimed at protecting the safety and security of our forces in South Vietnam."

Cambodian military spokesman Maj. Am Rong confirmed Aug. 6 that "American air intervention is being carried out in Cambodia to interdict supply routes and to protect the lives of Americans in South Vietnam."

Laird's remarks were a reiteration of a White House statement Aug. 4 denying any change in President Nixon's June 30 announcement that American air attacks would be limited to Communist troops and supplies that endangered U.S. forces in South Vietnam.

An AP report on the Aug. 5 fighting at Skoun had said that seven American planes provided direct air support to Cambodian ground troops. The attacks were directed by a Cambodian ground controller trained by U.S. Special Forces, according to the report.

A U.S. military command directive issued Aug. 6 advised all unit commanders to restrict their comments about American air involvement in Cambodia. The statement, whose contents were made public Aug. 8, said when asked about these operations, the commanders only were to reiterate that the purpose of the bombings was "to protect Americans in Vietnam, the Vietnamization program, to enhance continuing American withdrawals and to reduce American casualties."

Senate Majority Leader Mike Mansfield (D, Mont.) Aug. 7 questioned whether President Nixon had gone back on his pledge to limit American air involvement in Cambodia. Mansfield said: "I think we better call things what they are. It seems to me their reasoning is a bit tortured."

Mansfield had warned Aug. 5 that U.S. air support of Cambodian troops could lead the U.S. into "a full-fledged war."

Informed Saigon sources said Aug. 22 that U.S. pilots were free to go anywhere in Cambodia and attack enemy troops and supply lines. But the informants insisted this represented no change in policy. The pilots could attack whenever military officials believed enemy troops might pose a threat to forces in South Vietnam, the sources said. Final judgment on a threat rested with Gen. Creighton W. Abrams, commander of the U.S. forces.

Military spokesmen said American B-52 bombers had crossed into Cambodia Aug. 23 to bomb North Vietnamese infiltration routes and suspected troop concentrations.

(Secretary of Defense Melvin Laird had announced Aug. 20 that the average monthly number of B-52 sorties in Indochina would be cut to 1,000 [from a reported 1,200].)

Cambodia gets U.S. military aid. Under a pact concluded in Pnompenh Aug. 19, the U.S. agreed to provide Cambodia with $40 million worth of military equipment.

The military assistance agreement, confirmed by the U.S. State Department Aug. 24, would furnish Cambodia with small arms, ammunition, communications equipment, spare parts and training funds. The funds were to cover the fiscal year ending June 30, 1971. Cambodia had received $8.9 million in emergency military aid from the U.S. in May-June. Additional military funds to be given Cambodia during the current fiscal year depended on the progress of the fighting, State Department officials said.

In previous action aimed at helping Pnompenh fight the Communist invaders, the U.S. State Department Aug. 14 had confirmed a "tentative" agreement to provide American aid to the 5,000 troops being recruited or trained in Thailand for operations in Cambodia.

"The nature and extent of whatever support we may provide will depend in part on arrangements, including the training and disposition of the troops involved," the department said. According to the department, "no final overall agreement on U.S. support for troops recruited or trained in Thailand" had yet been reached. The agreement covered 3,000 Thai troops described as "ethnic Cambodians" and about 2,000 Cambodians being trained in Thailand.

Sen. Frank Church (D, Idaho) charged Aug. 14 that if Washington implemented the Cambodian-Thai troop aid arrangement it "would represent the second violation of the Senate-approved Cooper Church amendment within a week's time." The "first" violation," Church said, "was the disclosure that direct air support is now being extended to Cambodian troops."

In another development, the U.S. turned over six new UH-1 helicopters

(Hueys) to Cambodia Sept. 6. Another shipment was confirmed Sept. 10.

Communists near Pnompenh. Cambodian soldiers fought Communist troops seven and a half miles from Pnompenh Aug. 20 in the nearest battle to the capital since the Cambodian war began in April.

A force of 1,500 Viet Cong and North Vietnamese struck out at a 700-man government unit at Puk Rusey on the eastern bank of the Mekong River, breaking a 10-day lull in the fighting. The nine-hour clash was followed by a Communist mortar attack on government positions at Arey Ksach on the eastern bank of the Mekong below Puk Rusey, only one mile from the center of Pnompenh. The brief shelling, nearest the capital since the war began, was reported to have caused no damage or casualties.

According to government estimates, about 300 Communists had been killed in the fighting at Puk Rusey, while Cambodian losses had totaled 19 killed and 124 wounded.

Cambodian troops carried out clearing operations in the vicinity of Puk Rusey Aug. 22 in an attempt to uncover enemy soldiers left behind after the Aug. 20 fighting.

Among other military developments in Cambodia:

A 4,000-man South Vietnamese force Aug. 21 opened a new drive against Communist troops in an area 12 miles southeast of Neak Luong near the main highway linking Pnompenh and Saigon.

In a report on completion of a 10-day campaign, Saigon authorities announced Aug. 22 that an 1,800-man South Vietnamese ranger force had killed 47 Communists.

A Cambodian military spokesman disclosed Aug. 24 that 500 North Vietnamese and Viet Cong troops had been killed by allied air strikes Aug. 9–11. The Communist troops were pounded while operating in a sanctuary along the South Vietnamese border near Kompong Trach, 67 miles southeast of Pnompenh. The raids also destroyed a Communist command post and a weapons factory. The Cambodian command said it had only learned of the attack Aug. 23 in information received from villagers and Cambodian troops operating near the area. The Cambodian military spokesman declined to identify the allied planes involved in the air strike.

Agnew visits Cambodia. U.S. Vice President Spiro Agnew visited Cambodia during an Aug. 23–30 tour that took him also to Thailand, South Vietnam, South Korea and Taiwan.

The visit to Cambodia, unannounced beforehand because of security considerations, was a flight into Pnompenh Aug. 28 for a meeting with Premier Lon Nol and Chief of State Cheng Heng. Agnew had said at the outset of his tour that the Administration would do everything it could to help the Lon Nol government and that it would be impossible to proceed with the U.S. disengagement program in Vietnam if Cambodia fell.

After the consultations with Cambodian leaders, Agnew modified his stand, saying that he had "made no commitments whatsoever" to expand the U.S. presence in Cambodia. "If my presence gave a message to the Communists that we are not going to stand idly by in the sense of rendering economic aid and material assistance when free nations are invaded," he said, "that's exactly what we had in mind."

His message to Lon Nol, he said, was that the U.S. "would not become militarily involved" in Cambodia, that the U.S. would contribute money and arms to the defense of Cambodia but not U.S. troops. As for what would happen to the Vietnamization and withdrawal program in Vietnam if Cambodia fell, Agnew said that would cause a "considerable stretchout" but he "wouldn't go so far as to say we'd never get out of Vietnam."

On the return flight to Hawaii Aug. 30, Agnew told newsmen the U.S. withdrawal timetables "might not be as ambitious" as the Administration desired if the South Vietnamese had to come to grips with a Communist-controlled Cambodia along their joint 600-mile border.

But Agnew said the overall situation in the area he visited was "quite a bit more stabilized" than it was during his first Asian tour in January. More than half the Communist combat forces in Cambodia "have been eliminated," he said, the enemy was not capable of mounting a major offensive in South Vietnam, according to Gen. Creighton W. Abrams, the U.S. commander there, and the Asian allies were prepared to accept the Nixon doctrine of replacing direct U.S. combat assistance with self-defense efforts supported by U.S. military and economic aid.

Agnew told newsmen at the Western White House in San Clemente, Calif. Sept. 1, after briefing President Nixon on his trip, that "the Cambodian situation seems to be developing very well," that "a nation that had virtually no chance before the cleaning out of the sanctuaries now has at least a fighting chance for survival." Agnew said the U.S. regarded the Lon Nol government of Cambodia as that of a neutral, not an ally.

Agnew visited Saigon Aug. 27 and reviewed with South Vietnamese President Thieu the "progress" of pacification and Vietnamization and the "factors relating to the economic situation in Vietnam as well as U.S. economic assistance."

He completed his tour with a visit Aug. 28 and 29 to Bangkok and conferences with Premier Thanom Kittikachorn and other Thai leaders, who saw "in principle . . . eye to eye completely" with him, according to Thai Foreign Minister Thanat Khoman Aug. 29.

Thanat affirmed an Agnew assurance to "leave no stone unturned" to insure that implementation of the Nixon doctrine was not blocked by American critics. As for the Thai attitude toward that doctrine, the Agnew trip was unnecessary on that score, he said, since "we have been practicing the Nixon doctrine for five or six years already."

Government offensive stalled. A government offensive that began Sept. 7 was reported stalled along Highway 6 less than two weeks after it had started.

Provincial capital Kompong Thom, goal of the offensive, was reportedly reached by a flotilla of patrol boats Sept. 9. The Cambodian command announced that the arrival had broken a three-month siege by Communist forces. Ground forces, however, were reported to be 36 miles from the city, having moved about 10 miles in the first three days of the offensive.

Cambodian military spokesmen acknowledged Sept. 12 that the eight-battalion force was stalled at that point, while army engineers attempted to repair a bridge along the route. Sharp fighting was reported Sept. 13 as the Viet Cong attacked the government advance.

Senior Cambodian commanders directing the government offensive were reported in Pnompenh Sept. 16 for urgent talks with the high command. A relief force of about 1,500 government troops was moving toward the main concentration of stalled troops Sept. 17 in an attempt to cut off the enemy forces that had moved in behind the lines. (Meanwhile, Saigon sources reported U.S. fighter-bombers were flying raids along Route 6 Sept. 17. One plane was lost in the raid, the first such loss in more than two months.) The relief troops linked up with the main force Sept. 18.

Both government and Communist forces moved up reinforcements Sept. 19 in what appeared to be preparations for a showdown battle. U.S. air support continued. The expected government advance did not take place, however, as enemy troops blew up the newly-constructed bridge virtually in the midst of the government force.

Government troops Sept. 21 began a flanking move with three battalions of paratroops swinging east from Route 6 behind Tangkok. Other battalions moved west in a pincer operation against the estimated 3,500 guerrillas deployed in and around Tangkok.

Sharp enemy resistance prevented government forces from penetrating Tangkok itself; unofficial reports Sept. 25 said Vietcong guerrillas holding the town had forced back an assault by 10,000 government troops.

In other developments, a Sept. 4 report said 1,000 South Vietnamese rangers had moved across the border into Cambodia's Fishhook area. The Vietnamese met with little resistance. The drive brought the number of South Vietnamese troops in Cambodia to 17,000.

In other developments, new fighting was reported Sept. 8 near the ruins of the temples at Angkor Wat. Enemy troops were reported Sept. 11 to be about 500

yards from the southern edge of Siemreap, just south of Angkor. The enemy
was also threatening the Siemreap airport.

A South Vietnamese naval task force
Sept. 19 launched a major operation in
Cambodia along the Bassac River 35
miles southeast of Pnompenh. The force,
made up of 200 vessels and more than
1,500 Vietnamese marines, was aimed at
destroying enemy base areas between the
Bassac and Mekong Rivers.

The South Vietnamese command reported Oct. 6 the completions of a three-
month operation in southeast Cambodia
around Neak Luong and Takeo and the
withdrawal of the Saigon force involved.
The communique said 453 North Vietnamese and Viet Cong had been killed
in the operation. South Vietnamese losses were said to total 93 killed and 642
wounded. The withdrawal reduced to
12,000 the number of South Vietnamese
troops in Cambodia.

Republic proclaimed. Cambodia was
formally proclaimed a republic Oct. 9.
In a ceremony held in the National Assembly, the chamber's president, In
Tam, declared that "Cambodia is from
this hour a republic, one and indivisible,
bearing the official name of the Khmer
Republic."

The move to replace the country's ancient monarchy with a republic had
been unaimously approved by the
assembly and the Senate Oct. 5.

Exiled Prince Norodom Sihanouk
called on other countries not to recognize the Cambodian republic, the Chinese Communist news agency Hsinhua
reported Oct. 11.

Vietnam opens new Cambodian drives.
South Vietnamese forces opened two
separate offensives in Cambodia Oct. 24
and 25.

The Oct. 25 offensive involved a force
of 6,000 South Vietnamese troops that
crossed the border into Cambodia's
Fishhook area and captured the abandoned town of Snoul Oct. 26. The drive,
which had encountered little Communist
resistance, brought the number of South
Vietnamese troops in Cambodia to about
17,500.

The attacks were aimed at offsetting
North Vietnamese pressure against the
Saigon area. It was supported by American artillery operating from bases in
South Vietnam. The invading troops
fanned out along three key highways used
by the North Vietnamese as supply and
infiltration routes into the southern half
of South Vietnam.

The Oct. 24 drive was centered in the
Fishhook and the Parrot's Beak regions. The operation was aimed at lifting
a North Vietnamese threat to Saigon and
11 surrounding provinces, a region from
which U.S. forces were being withdrawn
rapidly.

Lt. Gen. Do Cao Tri, commander of
the Oct. 25 drive, said the following day
that his forces would push deeper into
Cambodia to force the North Vietnamese
to fight.

South Vietnamese forces had fought
sharp engagements with Communist
troops at three points along the Cambodian frontier Oct. 13. Two of the
clashes occurred just inside Cambodia
and the other in South Vietnam. The
largest battle was fought in the Seven
Mountains area just inside South Vietnam.

Two United Press International
newsmen were found slain Oct. 29 about
20 miles south of Pnompenh. They were
Frank Frosch, 28, chief of the UPI bureau
in Pnompenh, and Kyoichi Sawada, 34, a
photographer. Their car was believed to
have been ambushed by Communist
troops on Route 2. Their deaths brought
to seven the number of journalists known
killed in the Cambodian fighting.

Hundreds of Saigon militiamen
crossed into Cambodia Nov. 2 about 100
miles west of Saigon and launched attacks along the eastern bank of the Mekong River, 50 miles southeast of Pnompenh. Saigon claimed the killing of 43
North Vietnamese and Viet Cong in the
attacks.

In an area more than 100 miles to the
northeast, other South Vietnamese
troops reported finding 65 North Vietnamese bodies near Snoul. Most were
reported killed by air and artillery
strikes.

A 6,000-man South Vietnamese task
force swept into southeastern Cambodia Nov. 6. But the invading units
were reported Nov. 11 to have withdrawn after making contact with the
enemy but failing to trap part of the 5th

Viet Cong Division in the Fishhook area. The purpose of the drive reportedly was aimed at countering North Vietnamese attempts to bring reinforcements and supplies to the Seven Mountains region in southeastern South Vietnam.

Saigon troops came under heavy Communist shelling during fighting Nov. 8. About 500 enemy shells struck bases and posts along the frontier. In the ground clashes, the Saigon command reported that 62 Communists and one South Vietnamese had been killed in six clashes along Routes 1 and 7. The heaviest fighting was said to have occurred two miles north of Snoul, about five miles inside Cambodia. Forty-one North Vietnamese were reported slain in this action.

A force of 7,000 South Vietnamese and Cambodians was reported Nov. 8 to have launched a combined operation between Routes 2 and 3, 24 miles south of Pnompenh. A Cambodian spokesman said little contact with the enemy was expected. The principal purpose of the drive was to re-establish government control in the area, the spokesman explained.

Cambodian military positions and towns northeast of the capital were subjected to heavy Communist attacks Nov. 9. A command spokesman said five Cambodians had been killed and six wounded in an assault on the airport at Kompong Cham, 50 miles northeast of Pnompenh. The government reported five Cambodians and 85 Communists killed. Fifteen North Vietnamese were reported killed in fighting around Skoun, a command center for a large Cambodian force, west of Kompong Cham.

Launching a new offensive Nov. 9, North Vietnamese and Viet Cong troops attacked and isolated Kompong Cham and assaulted fortified towns nearby. The Cambodian high command reported it had lost contact with Troeung, eight miles west of Kompong Cham. The attack on Kompong Cham cut the city's road links with Pnompenh, 50 miles northeast. Skoun, halfway between Pnompenh and Kompong Cham, was hit by the Communists, but the Cambodian defenders repulsed the attack and killed 15 Viet Cong.

Two elements of a 20,000-man Cambodian task force were reported Nov. 16 to have been battered by North Vietnamese troops 50 miles north of Phompenh. A high command account of the action said 13 soldiers had been killed and 49 wounded. Seven North Vietnamese were reported killed.

A force of 4,500 South Vietnamese soldiers crossed into Cambodia's northern-most Ratankiri Province bordering Laos Nov. 17. It was the first time that Saigon's soldiers had crossed the Cambodian frontier in that area in six months. The operation centered 36 miles east of Lomphat, the provincial capital. The South Vietnamese drive, however, made little contact with the enemy, but uncovered big food and equipment dumps. Four caches containing 254 tons of ammunition were found Nov. 17. The South Vietnamese command reported Nov. 18 that since then 20 houses, 20 bunkers and five acres of crops and a base camp had been destroyed as the task force probed deeper into the province.

Another South Vietnamese task force, comprised of 1,000 men, crossed into Cambodia Nov. 19, about 15 miles northeast of the Vietnamese border town of Boduc. This force, too, failed to meet any enemy resistance.

Communist forces renewed their attacks Nov. 23, but this time directed their assaults south of Pnompenh. They forced the destruction of Cambodia's only munitions factory and seized a six-mile stretch of Highway 4, the country's supply lifeline to the Gulf of Siam. The munitions factory, at Stung Chral, 60 miles southwest of the capital, came under heavy enemy rocket, mortar and machine gun fire, forcing a government battalion in the building to withdraw. Before pulling out, the Cambodian defenders blew up the factory and the munitions stocks.

The Communists' southward drive toward Pnompenh was renewed Nov. 27 with a five-hour attack on government positions 10 miles northeast of the capital. A Cambodian military spokesman said the enemy had taken control of Route 6 on the northern bank of the Mekong River and had captured the vital ferry point at Prek Khdam on the Tonle Sap River, 20 miles north of

Pnompenh. The ferry was the only connection to the land route to the northern area of Cambodia.

Cambodian forces recaptured the Prek Khdam ferry point Dec. 1. The new government drive reportedly was led by a Cambodian battalion recruited and trained in South Vietnam. Prek Khdam was the southernmost penetration thus far of the Communist offensive.

A South Vietnamese task force operating in southeastern Cambodia came under North Vietnamese attack Nov. 27 near the town of Krek. The Saigon forces repelled the assault on the headquarters of the 52nd Task force, killing 48 North Vietnamese. The South Vietnamese command listed its losses as 10 killed and 20 wounded.

A Cambodian military headquarters about 40 miles east of Pnompenh was overrun by Communist forces Dec. 6. The headquarters was at Peam Chikang on the northern bank of the Mekong River. A Cambodian spokesman said a battalion of government defenders and the attackers had both suffered heavy losses. The fighting raged in the area of Route 7, where according to Pnompenh's Dec. 4 report, 8,000–10,000 Viet Cong had been operating along a 32-mile stretch of Route 7 between Pnompenh and Kompong Cham, isolated by the Communists since September. A government report Dec. 21 said Cambodian troops had ousted the enemy from the road and that it was now under Pnompenh control.

The Pnompenh military command claimed that 217 North Vietnamese and Viet Cong were killed Dec. 8 in a five-hour battle north of Svayrieng, an area rarely challenged by the Communists since the allied incursion in the spring wiped out enemy bases in the sector. The Communists suffered the heavy casualties after opening a strong assault against the government's northern defense line.

A Saigon communiqué reported Dec. 10 that South Vietnamese forces had suffered 30 killed and 41 wounded in the Fishhook area just inside Cambodia the previous day during a Communist rocket and mortar assault. The shelling also destroyed several trucks. The communiqué claimed that the defenders had killed 48

of the 200-man North Vietnamese force in repulsing the attack.

Cambodian forces Dec. 9 recaptured the northwestern district town of Puok, held by the North Vietnamese for more than a month. The North Vietnamese defenders were driven out after fierce street fighting, Premier Lon Nol's office reported.

A force of 3,000 South Vietnamese troops was reported Dec. 15 to have been airlifted to Kompong Cham in 40 helicopters. The troops were brought in as a result of a personal appeal by Premier Lon Nol to President Nguyen Van Thieu. The Saigon forces were said to have moved into an area believed to contain at least 6,000 North Vietnamese and Viet Cong soldiers.

Foreign newsmen who visited Prey Totung Dec. 17 reported that the village, 44 miles north of Pnompenh, had been destroyed by U.S., South Vietnamese and Cambodian air attacks. South Vietnamese forces had linked up with the remaining Cambodian defenders in the village after the allied air strikes.

The Cambodian command reported Dec. 27 fierce fighting with Communist forces at Chambak and Tram Khnar, two towns close to the main supply corridor in southern Cambodia. Thirty North Vietnamese and Viet Cong were said to have been killed at Chambak, 22 miles south of the capital.

Cambodia-Vietnam border dispute. A Cambodian official charged Dec. 9 that more than 400 South Vietnamese peasant families had moved at least seven miles inside Cambodia and had taken over farms and ricelands abandoned by Cambodian war refugees. Lt. Col. Koh Chhuon, the commander of Svayrieng Province, said the affected area was along a 60-mile stretch from Kompong Trach in the north of Svayrieng to Samraong at the tip of the Parrot's Beak in the south.

Chhuon said the squatter movement had started in September and charged that the Saigon government had ignored repeated Cambodian protests. The officer said that in one note handed the South Vietnamese ambassador in Pnompenh Nov. 25 South Vietnamese soldiers were accused of assisting the infiltrators into the abandoned homes.

A Cambodian intelligence officer reported Dec. 9 that Viet Cong and North Vietnamese were "in effect" cooperating with the Saigon troops in settling the Cambodian areas in South Vietnam. He said that former Cambodian Communists who had defected to the government side had reported that Viet Cong and North Vietnamese commanders in the area had ordered their troops not to fire on South Vietnamese soldiers in the Parrot's Beak, but to concentrate instead on killing Cambodian government troops.

The Cambodian Foreign Ministry was reported Dec. 5 to have filed another protest with Saigon, charging that South Vietnamese troops had burned the houses of Cambodians and permitted Vietnamese civilians to take up residence in Cambodia.

The $255 million program for Cambodia was approved Dec. 14 by the Senate Foreign Relations Committee, but the committee appended a restriction prohibiting the President from sending American ground troops or advisers into Cambodia. The committee also added a stipulation that the aid should not be construed as a commitment by the U.S. to defend the Cambodian government.

U.S. aid to Cambodia debated. The U.S. House of Representatives passed by 249–102 vote Dec. 9 a bill authorizing $550 million in supplemental foreign aid for fiscal 1971, including $255 million for Cambodia.

The Senate panel approved the total foreign aid authorization by an 8–4 vote, the opposed votes being cast by committee chairman J. W. Fulbright (D, Ark.), Senate Democratic Leader Mike Mansfield (Mont.), and Sens. Stuart Symington (D, Mo.) and Albert Gore (D, Tenn.).

Defense Secretary Melvin R. Laird said after an appearance before the Senate Appropriations Committee Nov. 20 that the Cambodia aid program was a "good investment" and that if Congress denied the funds U.S. troop withdrawals from Vietnam could be slowed.

The same day, Fulbright, announcing that staff consultants were being sent to Cambodia to prepare a first-hand report for his committee, recalled testimony April 27 by Secretary of State William P. Rogers that large-scale military as-

sistance for Cambodia could lead to the need for American military advisers and perhaps, eventually, troops.

Both Laird and Rogers appeared before a panel of the Appropriations Committee Dec. 8 to urge provision of the Cambodia aid. Rogers insisted a long-term aid program was essential for Cambodia and stressed the Administration's intention to avoid direct military involvement. "The idea this is a repetition of Vietnam is fallacious," he said, and "we have no intention of slipping into the mistakes of the past." However, Laird indicated the necessity of having in Cambodia a U.S. military mission to handle the military supplies, and Rogers indicated U.S. bombing support for Cambodian government forces.

Congress cleared for the President's signature Dec. 31 a $2.5 billion foreign aid appropriation and the Foreign Military Sales Act. The bills had been delayed by the dispute over the "Cooper-Church" amendment barring U.S. incursions into Cambodia which had been attached to the foreign military sales bill. This bill was delayed by opponents of the provision in the House, which approved putting a $200 million item in the foreign aid appropriation bill for the military sales credits.

After a separate version of the Cooper-Church amendment was put in another bill, the original language was deleted by the conferees from the Foreign Military Sales Act, which emerged from conference and was passed by both houses. This ended the objection to passage of the foreign aid funds, which included the $200 million for military sales, and that also was approved by both houses.

The military sales authorization called for $680 million in credit ceilings over a two-year period. It also repealed the Gulf of Tonkin Resolution and required that the new international Freedom Fighter plane, if sent to any country except Vietnam, be paid for out of foreign aid funds. President Nixon signed the foreign aid fund bill later Dec. 31.

The final version of the Cooper-Church curb on the President's war-making powers was incorporated in the $66.6 billion defense appropriation bill for fiscal 1971, approved Dec. 29 by 234–185 House vote and 70–2 Senate vote. (The total was $2 billion less than requested by the Nixon Administration.) The bill barred the introduction of ground troops into Thailand or Laos (a Senate attempt to extend the ban to Cambodia was deleted), and it stipulated that a $2.5 billion fund for

"free world forces" in Southeast Asia could not be used for military support to the government of Cambodia or Laos. The stipulation itself made clear that nothing in the restriction would prevent support of any action required to insure a safe withdrawal of U.S. forces.

Peace Efforts

Search for peace continues. The U.S. and South Vietnamese operations in Cambodia and the resumption of the aerial bombing of North Vietnam had relatively little effect on international efforts to find a solution to the problem of war in Indochina. Although the pro-Communist side reacted with expected anger, there was no long interruption in whatever negotiations had been taking place.

Communists boycott Paris talks. The Communist delegations to the Paris peace talks boycotted the 66th plenary session May 6 to protest the resumption of U.S. bombing attacks on North Vietnam. They proposed the next session be held May 14.

In a formal statement announcing the boycott, Nguyen Thanh Le, spokesman for the North Vietnamese delegation, warned that "if the Nixon Administration continues its bombing" of North Vietnam, "it must bear the entire responsibility for all the grave consequences arising from its acts." Le charged that, "while preparing the aggression in Cambodia," the U.S. in late April had carried out 42 bombing raids against North Vietnam in addition to about 2,000 reconnaissance flights. "Hundreds" of U.S. planes had bombed North Vietnamese population centers May 1-5, causing numerous deaths, Le said.

In the three previous sessions of the Paris peace talks, April 16, 23 and 30, the North Vietnamese and Viet Cong representatives focused their attacks on American involvement in Cambodia. The Viet Cong delegation said April 16 that American troops "continuously thrust deep into Cambodian territory to give a hand to the reactionary group of Premier Lon Nol . . . in opposing the Cambodian people and persecuting and massacring Vietnamese residents living in the country."

Philip Habib, U.S. acting chief delegate, reminded the Communists that "your regular armed forces are conducting combat operations in Cambodia and Laos and are using [those territories] as a base of operations against South Vietnam."

The Saigon representative explained after the April 30 meeting that the U.S.-supported South Vietnamese thrust into Cambodia the previous day was an act of "legitimate self-defense." Nguyen Thanh Le countered by accusing South Vietnam of "executing the orders of the United States" to spread the war to all of Indochina.

The American invasion of Cambodia May 1 prompted Le to say that day that the action would have a "bad influence" on the Paris talks. Hanoi radio said May 3 that the U.S. bombing of the North would "affect" the negotiations.

121

Xuan Thuy, chief North Vietnamese representative, left Paris for Hanoi May 11, declaring that a peace settlement could not be reached until President Nixon gave up "his policy based on a position of strength." Thuy had not attended the talks since Dec. 11, 1969, shortly after Henry Cabot Lodge had **departed as chief U.S. delegate.**

Habib complained at the May 14 session that the Communists' "intransigence" in Paris and their increased military activities in Indochina had become "intolerable." He warned that "we will act accordingly" if the situation continued. President Nixon's June 3 report on Cambodia was denounced at the June 4 session. Challenging the President's statement that the Cambodian operations insured the continued withdrawal of American troops from Vietnam, the Communist spokesman declared that no U.S. soldiers had been pulled out since April. Viet Cong press spokesman Ly Van Sau said after the meeting that American ground forces in Vietnam in fact had increased by 5,000 since April. The only troops to be withdrawn, he said, were casualties.

South Vietnam announced · at the June 11 meeting that it would repatriate 62 ill North Vietnamese prisoners of war and 24 captured North Vietnamese fishermen. Saigon delegate Pham Dang Lam said the men would be sent back to North Vietnam July 11. Unlike its previous offers to free Communist prisoners, South Vietnam did not insist that North Vietnam first formally accept the captives. A formal Hanoi acceptance of the offer would amount to north Vietnamese acknowledgment that its forces were fighting in the South.

The number of U.S. military personnel in Laos was a controversial topic at the June 18 session. North Vietnam charged there were more than 12,000 American military men in the country, 10,000 Thai soldiers, plus an undisclosed number of Central Intelligence Agency men. Citing recent White House announcements in support of lower figures, U.S. press spokesman Stephen Ledogar said there were 616 Americans in Laos, plus 424 on contract. The U.S. had always insisted that there were no American ground troops in Laos.

U.S.S.R. vs. Indochina parley. The Soviet Union June 17 reaffirmed its opposition to an international conference on Indochina.

Soviet Premier Aleksei N. Kosygin scored "American aggression" in Indochina and urged "strict respect for the right of the peoples of Vietnam, Cambodia and Laos to decide independently their own affairs."

Moscow's aversion to multi-nation parley was further stated later June 17 by Foreign Minister Andrei A. Gromyko at a meeting with a three-nation task force of Indonesian, Japanese and Malaysian officials led by Indonesian Foreign Minister Adam Malik. The group had been formed at a May 16–17 meeting of Asian nations seeking to restore peace in Indochina. The task force, which had arrived in Moscow June 16, received a negative reply from Moscow to its formula for ending the fighting, Malik said. Gromyko rejected the idea of a Geneva conference and blamed the U.S. for the trouble in Cambodia, Malik said.

The Jakarta conference was assailed June 19 by the Soviet news agency Tass. It charged that the 12-nation meeting "constituted an attempt to divert attention from the armed invasion of Cambodia by the United States. Naturally, it was met with a negative attitude by the majority of the countries of the world, including the Soviet Union."

(Increased Soviet military and economic aid to Hanoi had been announced in Moscow shortly before the Jakarta group arrived. A communiqué issued June 11 said the new aid, supplementing assistance provided in an Oct. 15, 1969 agreement, was being provided "at a time when American imperialists are intensifying the aggressive war in South Vietnam, when they are bombing some areas of North Vietnam, carrying out military escalation in Laos and waging an aggressive war in Cambodia." Additional military and economic aid from China to North Vietnam was announced May 27 and Oct. 7. The earlier agreement [signed May 24] provided for aid during 1970. The latter arrangement was for 1971. The unspecified aid was described as "nonrefundable.")

Other developments—The Jakarta conference task force discussed its peace formula with Indian officials in New Delhi June 19 but failed to receive its endorsement. Foreign Secretary T. N. Kaul told the delegation that India could not support a "piecemeal solution" relating only to Cambodia. In addition to proposing an international peace parley, the conference also had called for withdrawal of all foreign troops from Cambodia and reactivation of the International Control Commission.

Pnompenh had appealed to the Soviet Union June 13 to "use all its influence" to get Communist forces to withdraw from Cambodia to restore the country's neutrality.

U.N. Secretary General U Thant discussed the Indochina situation with Soviet officials in Moscow June 17-19. A Tass report on the discussions June 19 quoted Thant as saying his attitude on the war coincided almost completely with that of the Soviet Union.

A proposal by Thant June 11 for an international conference to end the war was rejected by North Vietnam June 13 and 16. Thant suggested that the participants include all the parties involved in the fighting, the Cambodian government of Premier Lon Nol and the forces supporting Prince Norodom Sihanouk, the ousted chief of state, the U.S., Britain, France, the Soviet Union, Communist China and the three members of the International Control Commission— India, Poland and Canada.

Nguyen Thanh Le, the North Vietnamese press spokesman at the Paris peace talks, denounced Thant's proposal as "sheer hypocrisy" June 13. Le said Thant had "lumped the usurpers of power in Cambodia together with the legitimate leaders of the country and placed them on the same footing. In effect, he has recognized the Lon Nol regime by this proposal, while we do not."

The North Vietnamese Communist Party newspaper Nhan Dan June 16 said Thant's plan was aimed at shielding "atrocious aggressive acts of U.S. aggression."

Nixon vs. imposed coalition. President Nixon declared at a news conference July 20 that he supported South Vietnamese President Nguyen Van Thieu's opposition to an imposed coalition government with the Communists. Thieu

had said in a television interview July 16 (broadcast July 19) that he remained opposed to a coalition regime with the Communists. He had criticized Secretary of State William P. Rogers and some U.S. senators for having created "some misunderstanding" about his position.

Nixon, addressing a hastily-summoned White House press conference, said he sympathized with Thieu's "indicated concern about the use of the word coalition." The term, the President said, was "a code word in international settlements" that usually meant eventual Communist control. Reiterating the views he said he had expressed June 30, Nixon asserted that in any future negotiations "there will not be an imposed coalition government on South Vietnam. The government of South Vietnam must be one that is chosen by the people of South Vietnam. It will be one and should be one that reflects the political forces in South Vietnam. Under no circumstances does this government [the U.S.] stand for the proposition that we would attempt to negotiate an imposed coalition government."

Nixon endorsed Thieu's position that the Communists could participate in free elections. But he added: "Once the election has been held, then what government comes out of the election is something to be worked out by the elected officials. But it should not be determined in advance of the people indicating what kind of government they want."

Commenting on the peace negotiations in Paris, Nixon said that David K.E. Bruce, the new chief American negotiator, was being given "great latitude to discuss all of the proposals we have made both in public and in private sessions with the North Vietnamese and the Viet Cong."

In his television interview (CBS's Face the Nation), Thieu had said: "Sometimes some declaration of Secretary Rogers and some senators create some misunderstanding, but for us our position is very clear. We never accept a coalition government imposed by anyone."

Thieu reiterated his July 1969 proposal for an internationally supervised election in which members of the National Liberation Front and Communists could participate. But he emphasized that it would be "anti-constitutional" for pro-coalition candidates to run for office. Thieu did not explain the seeming contradiction between his belief in free elections and his opposition to candidates favoring a coalition.

Thieu's remark about Rogers' misrepresentation of his views was in apparent reference to a statement made by the secretary June 29. Rogers had said then that the Viet Cong might decide "to negotiate an agreement which gives them representation proportionate to their numbers." But at a meeting with Rogers in Saigon July 4, Thieu had expressed objection to this arrangement.

In his television statement, Thieu also said he expected the fighting in South Vietnam to continue at least another year, but that by the end of 1971 U.S. troops would be required only in a support role. More than 50,000 American soldiers would be needed for this assignment, he said. Thieu acknowledged that the allied incursion into Cambodia might shorten the war, but he said it was still to early to tell.

Rogers July 15 amplified his previous views on the political effects of the allied campaign in Cambodia. As a result of their setbacks in that operation, Rogers said, the Communists would "not be inclined to negotiate." Therefore, prospects for serious peace talks "in the next couple of months are not too bright. But in the long run" the allied successes in Cambodia do "increase the probabilities that the enemy—somewhere along the line—will negotiate."

Since the allied drive into Cambodia began April 30, White House officials had taken the stand that the offensive would improve the prospects for serious negotiations. White House Press Secretary Ronald Ziegler pointed out July 15 that the views of Rogers and of the Administration were not at variance. He told newsmen: "It is wrong for you to draw the conclusion there is any lack of unanimity. There is not."

Thieu declared July 31 that South Vietnam remained opposed to any coalition government with the Communists, except one that might result from free, internationally supervised elections.

Thieu's reiteration of his peace terms, the most detailed he had delivered, was

made in a 45-minute television address. Thieu made clear that a cease-fire could be implemented as part of a general peace agreement or could be negotiated and put into effect before a peace settlement. But in any case, an agreement on a halt to the fighting must meet minimum conditions, he said. Thieu said: The cease-fire conditions would have to be worked out in negotiations. The truce must not be used by the Communists to rebuild their forces and must be conducive to a general settlement. The cease-fire must be fully implemented and respected and supervised.

Thieu said the Viet Cong could participate in any future elections by casting ballots and by helping tabulate the votes under international supervision. He said: "We do not ask them to surrender, but only to lay down their arms and accept democratic struggle."

Thieu had told a gathering of 11 Western correspondents in Saigon July 30 that a "residual force" of about 50,000 American troops might have to remain in South Vietnam after 1973 to "guarantee the peace." Thieu said he foresaw the need to keep some American combat soldiers in his country after 1971, but only to protect U.S. logistical and support troops. South Vietnamese forces, he said, would bear the burden of combat by then.

(Mrs. Nguyen Thi Binh, foreign minister of the Viet Cong's Provisional Revolutionary Government, had said July 22 that her side would accept a coalition government for South Vietnam as the basis of a general peace agreement. But she said that Thieu and Vice President Nguyen Cao Ky would not be acceptable as members of that government.

(Ky, an adamant opponent of a coalition with the Communists, had pledged acceptance of such a regime if it were the result of free elections. He had said July 4: "We would accept a Communist president if the Communists were strong enough to get him elected through really free, internationally supervised elections. There will be no coup against him.")

Nixon optimistic on talks. An optimistic view on peace negotiations was expressed by President Nixon July 30 in a televised press conference at the Century Plaza Hotel in Los Angeles. Nixon said:

The prospects for a negotiated peace "should be better now than they were before the Cambodian operation.... The enemy position is weaker than it was before we went into Cambodia. Their timetable has been set back. Time is no longer on their side." The U.S. had assigned "a senior negotiator" to Paris "with wide latitude in negotiation, and we hope that they will reciprocate by negotiating in good faith and try to bring the war to an early conclusion, as it could be by negotiation, rather than letting it be drawn to a conclusion through the longer path of Vietnamization, which we're prepared to do also."

South Vietnamese President Thieu's position on negotiation "is on all fours with ours. We have consulted with him and he with us before any negotiating positions have been presented." Thieu's position "with regard to a Communist not being on the ballot is purely a matter of semantics. Under the South Vietnamese Constitution, a Communist cannot run for office. On the other hand, President Thieu has specifically agreed that those who are members of the NLF, [National Liberation Front], who of course represent the Communists in South Vietnam, could run as members of the NLF on the ballot." Thieu's attitude on coalition government "is the same as ours. A coalition government should not be imposed upon the people of South Vietnam without their consent. If the people of South Vietnam by election elect people who then choose to form a coalition government, that is a matter of course that we will accept."

"We are opposed to a coalition government, negotiated or imposed. We are for a government which is consented to by the people of South Vietnam, and if that government happens to be one that has Communists in it, and it is their choice, we do not have an objection, and neither does President Thieu, as I understand it." When Thieu "speaks of victory" for his government and the people of South Vietnam, "he is referring ... to what will happen in Vietnam over the long haul, assuming there is not a negotiated settlement." If, after the U.S. had withdrawn, the South Vietnamese had not worked out a negotiated settlement, "then it is certainly up to the

South Vietnamese to determine whether they are going to negotiate with the enemy or seek a victory."

The problem of U.S. prisoners held in North Vietnam was "of enormous concern to us" and "will be very high" on the negotiating agenda.

Bruce enters Paris peace talks. David K. E. Bruce, the new chief American negotiator at the Paris peace talks, attended his first session Aug. 6.

In his opening statement, Bruce expressed hope "that we can avoid propaganda and harsh language and settle down to businesslike discussion of the issues." "It is also time," he said, "to set aside the language of preconditions and of demands for one-sided action." The Communist delegations declared at the end of the meeting that Bruce had offered nothing new.

North Vietnamese spokesman Nguyen Thanh Le said the Nixon Administration had "corrected an error" in appointing Bruce as chief negotiator. But Le said the Administration had committed "an arrogant act" in not immediately naming a successor to Henry Cabot Lodge, when he resigned as chief negotiator in December 1969.

Philip Habib, who had been serving as acting chief mediator since Lodge's resignation, had attended his last conference July 30 as acting head of the American delegation. That meeting, as previous weekly sessions since June 25, provided no progress.

Bruce did not attend the 80th session Aug. 20.

North Vietnam announced Aug. 24 that Xuan Thuy had left Hanoi Aug. 19 for Paris. The envoy arrived in Paris Aug. 26 after stopovers in Peking and Moscow. At a press conference upon his arrival, Thuy hinted that he was open to suggestions for a renewal of secret talks with the U.S.

Thuy remained away from the Aug. 27 session, the 81st of the talks. Ambassador Bruce attended, but a U.S. spokesman said "there was nothing of any interest" in the meeting.

The 82nd session Sept. 3 marked the first public meeting between Bruce and Thuy. Reports said the North Vietnamese delegation had delivered a 13-page statement that reiterated its position calling for U.S. withdrawal before negotiations could take place.

Informed observers saw some indications for optimism in the use of a less polemic tone during the Sept. 10 talks, the 83rd session.

14 senators urge cease-fire. President Nixon was urged in a letter from 14 senators Sept. 1 to make a standstill cease-fire in Vietnam the "next order of business" at the Paris peace talks. The signers included hawks and doves and the majority and minority leaders of the Senate.

The letter, drafted and circulated by Sen. Henry M. Jackson (D, Wash.), said the proposal was "a course of action that has not yet been tried" and "could present a new context for the Paris negotiations, give fresh and added meaning to our previous proposals and create a new impetus for the other side to respond."

The senators suggested that the President offer detailed proposals in Paris for "international peace-keeping machinery" to oversee the cease-fire, for free elections supervised by a mixed electoral commission having representatives of the South Vietnamese government, the National Liberation Front and other political and religious groups in South Vietnam, and for safeguards to assure freedom of speech, assembly and the press in South Vietnam after the cease-fire.

As part of the package, the senators also urged proposals on withdrawal of all foreign forces and on the release of all prisoners, political as well as military.

The senators' initiative was welcomed later Sept. 1 by White House Press Secretary Ronald L. Ziegler, who said the recommendations were "generally consistent" with the U.S. position. He added that "the President on numerous occasions discussed a willingness to discuss arrangements for a cease-fire and the establishment of an international body to supervise a cease-fire," but that the difficulty in Paris was that "the other side continues to show an unwillingness to engage in meaningful discussion."

The chief North Vietnamese negotiator in Paris, Xuan Thuy, commented Sept. 2 that the Viet Cong's 10-point peace plan also called for a cease-fire but only after the U.S. agreed to a complete withdrawal.

In addition to Jackson, the letter to Nixon was signed by Senate Democratic Leader Mike Mansfield (Mont.), Republican Leader Hugh Scott (Pa.), and Sens. Birch Bayh (D, Ind.), Alan Bible (D, Nev.), Robert J. Dole (R, Kan.), Barry Goldwater (R, Ariz.), Jacob K. Javits (R, N. Y.), Warren G. Magnuson (D, Wash.), Thomas J. McIntyre (D, N.H.), Charles H. Percy (R, Ill.), Winston Prouty (R, Vt.), Theodore F. Stevens (R, Alaska) and Milton R. Young (R, N.D.).

New Viet Cong peace proposals. The Viet Cong, with the support of North Vietnam, Sept. 17 presented an eight-point peace proposal at the talks in Paris. The proposal sought to establish a deadline for withdrawal of allied troops and offered immediate discussions on release of prisoners of war should the withdrawal proposal be accepted.

The plan, the first substantive initiative in the talks since May 1969, was described by a spokesman for the Provisional Revolutionary Government (PRG) as an "important peace initiative," but U.S. and Saigon officials were cool to the new move.

The plan was presented at the 84th session of the talks. It was the first time since December 1969 that the heads of all four delegations were present.

The chief delegate for the Vietcong, Mrs. Nguyen Thi Binh, returned to Paris Sept. 14 after a three-month absence and presented the proposal at the session three days later.

The new proposal:

(1) Withdrawal of U.S. and allied forces from Vietnam by June 30, 1971, with the Vietcong agreeing to "insure safety" for the withdrawal and begin talks on prisoners of war if the withdrawal were agreed to.

(2) The "Vietnamese parties themselves" to resolve the question of North Vietnamese troops in South Vietnam.

(3) An administration in Saigon purged of President Nguyen Van Thieu, Vice President Nguyen Cao Ky and Premier Tran Thien Khiem.

(4) Free elections to be held by an interim government.

(5) A provisional government to include members of the PRG, members of the current Saigon administration (excluding Thieu, Ky and Khiem) and "persons of various political and religious forces and tendencies."

(6) Gradual reunification of the two Vietnams.

(7) Decisions on implementation of peace measures to be agreed on by "the parties."

(8) A cease-fire to be arranged after agreement on all other points.

U.S. Administration officials commented Sept. 17 that there was "nothing new" in the proposals, which were just an "elaboration" of earlier formulas with added "bait" in the form of a promise of immediate talks on POWs.

The eight-point plan differed slightly from the 1969 proposals. The first new element was the offer to assure the safe departure of allied troops if the troops agreed to withdraw by June 30, 1971. Officials in Washington noted that the deadline was six months earlier than one presented by the McGovern-Hatfield amendment, which was defeated in the U.S. Senate. They said the offer was insignificant because the Viet Cong would not wish to fire on withdrawing troops who could, in any case, protect themselves.

However, the offer to begin immediate negotiations on the release of prisoners once the withdrawal was agreed to represented a shift of position for the Vietcong. In the 1969 10-point plan this question would have been part of an overall accord.

Nevertheless, the proposal was still far from the U.S. position calling for gradual withdrawal over 12 months following an agreement, with the remaining forces to withdraw as the North Vietnamese withdrew.

A second new element in the plan was the demand for a purge of South Vietnam's top three leaders—Thieu, Ky and Khiem.

What could be considered a new move by the Viet Cong was the mention of a cease-fire. The 1969 proposals did not include any comment on this question. But the Sept. 17 plan called for a cease-fire to be arranged after agreement on all other points.

Chief U.S. negotiator David K. E. Bruce said after the proposals were presented that they appeared to be "old wine in new bottles," but he said he would reserve final judgement until he had carefully studied the new plan.

A Sept. 18 Washington Post report said that reaction in the U.S. capital saw no substantial advance in the proposals.

(The Post reported that a Moscow broadcast of the Viet Cong proposal transmitted less than two hours after Mrs. Binh had presented her plan to the press in Paris, went even further in its language than the Viet Cong proposal on the question of prisoners. The Tass report said the Viet Cong would be "ready to set free all prisoners of war" once conditions for withdrawal were met.)

Nixon offers 5-point plan. In a major foreign policy address Oct. 7, President Nixon proposed a five-point peace plan for Indochina.

The plan, disclosed in a 12-minute television address to the nation, called for: (1) A "cease-fire in place," (2) an expanded peace conference that would seek to end the fighting in Laos and Cambodia as well as in South Vietnam, (3) American readiness "to negotiate an agreed timetable" for total withdrawal of U.S. troops "as part of an overall settlement," (4) efforts by the allied and Communist sides to "search for a political settlement that truly meets the needs of all South Vietnamese," and (5) the "immediate and unconditional release of all prisoners of war."

North Vietnam denounced the Nixon proposals Oct. 10. The plan drew similar opposition from the Soviet Union Oct. 10 and from Communist China Oct. 11.

Nixon Administration officials described the President's peace initiative as a new one aimed at replacing his original eight-point plan advanced May 14, 1969. The officials, however, made clear that Washington would continue to press for acceptance of some of the original proposals, including the one backing internationally supervised free elections to determine the composition of a future South Vietnamese government.

The only two new elements in the latest Nixon plan were the standstill truce and the expanded peace talks.

Details of the plan as outlined by the President:

Cease fire—The proposed truce, "put forth without preconditions," should "be the subject of immediate negotiations." To be effective, the truce must be "supervised by international observers, as well as by the parties themselves." The combat standstill "should cause all kinds of warfare to stop, including bombings and acts of terror" and should not be used by either side to improve its military position. Applying to all of Indochina combat zones, the truce should "be a part of a general move to end the war" in the region.

Peace conference—An international peace conference was necessary to "deal with the conflict in all three states of Indochina" (South Vietnam, Cambodia and Laos), since the fighting in those countries "has proved to be of one piece; it cannot be cured by treating only one of its areas of outbreak." (Administration officials suggested that the projected parley include not only the Paris peace talk parties—the U.S., North and South Vietnam and the Viet Cong—but also Cambodia, Laos, the Soviet Union and Communist China.) The Paris talks would remain "our primary forum for reaching a negotiated settlement until such time as a broader international conference produces serious negotiations."

Troop withdrawals—The U.S. was prepared to withdraw all its forces from Indochina "as part of a settlement based on the principles I spelled out previously and the proposals I am making tonight." The U.S. already had pulled out 165,000 troops from South Vietnam in the past 20 months and "during the spring of next year these withdrawals will total more than 260,000 men."

Political settlement—The U.S. stood by these three principles which governed its approach for solving the political aspect of the South Vietnamese problem: "We seek a political solution that reflects the will of the South Vietnamese people"; "a fair political solution should reflect the existing relationship of political forces in South Vietnam"; "and

we will abide by the political outcome of the political process agreed upon."

The U.S. rejected as "totally unacceptable" the Communists' "patently unreasonable demand" "to dismantle the organized non-Communist parties" in South Vietnam for the purpose of a Communist takeover.

Prisoner release—"I propose all prisoners of war, without exception, without condition, be released now to return to the place of their choice." The Communists must also release "all journalists and other innocent civilian victims of war." The freeing of the captives would not only "be a simple act of humanity" but would also "improve the prospects for negotiations."

Nixon said that his new peace initiative had been drawn up after a meeting in Ireland Oct. 7 with members of the U.S. delegation to the Paris talks. These discussions, he said, "marked the culmination of a government-wide effort begun last spring on the negotiation front." The President said the new peace plan had been discussed with the governments of South Vietnam, Cambodia and Laos and had received their support.

President Nixon expanded on his peace plan Oct. 8: "We made this proposal because we wanted to cover every base that we could. That is why we offered the cease-fire, a total cease-fire. That is why we offered a total withdrawal of all of our forces, something we have never offered before, if we had mutual withdrawal on the other side."

U.S. plan submitted to Paris talks. President Nixon's five-point peace plan was submitted to the Paris peace conference Oct. 8 by David K. E. Bruce, chief of the American delegation.

The Communist representatives responded by denouncing the proposal, but did not reject it outright. Xuan Thuy, head of the North Vietnamese delegation, called it "only a gift certificate for the votes of the American electorate and a coverup for misleading world

In press briefings after the talks, the Communist delegates assailed Nixon's proposal as "a maneuver to deceive world opinion" and reiterated their previous demands for unconditional and total withdrawal of American troops and overthrow of the South Vietnamese "puppet" regime. They complained that Nixon, in his new plan, had not "seriously answered" the Communists' Sept. 17 proposal.

The North Vietnamese delegation Oct. 10 denounced President Nixon's Oct. 8 amplification of his peace plan, calling it a repetition of "his unreasonable demand for mutual withdrawal from South Vietnam." The President, the Hanoi spokesman asserted, "now speaks of total withdrawal of United States troops but he still repeats his unreasonable demand for mutual withdrawal." Nixon's remarks, the statement said, "prove that hitherto he has never had the intention to withdraw all United States troops from Vietnam."

Hanoi opposes cease-fire. The North Vietnamese government's opposition Oct. 10 to President Nixon's Indochina peace plan centered on a reiteration of the Communist demand that a cease-fire be conditional on a political settlement.

Hanoi's Communist party newspaper Nhan Dan said that to accept Nixon's bid for an immediate truce would be to admit that that the U.S. had a right to be in Indochina. The journal argued that on the question of a military pull-out, Nixon "refuses to state a definite period for the withdrawal" of American troops. Under the current American withdrawal plan, 300,000 U.S. and 60,-000 allied troops would remain in Vietnam by the middle of 1971, Nhan Dan noted. The newspaper also complained that Nixon had ignored "the replacement" of the present South Vietnamese government "by an administration that favors peace, independence and democracy."

Congress backs Nixon plan. President Nixon's cease-fire proposal was warmly received by all sides in Congress—Democrat and Republican, hawk and dove, although one representative, Robert L. F. Sikes (D, Fla.) objected Oct. 8 that it was a "dangerous concession" to the Communists in Southeast Asia. A prominent hawk, Rep. L. Mendel Rivers (D, S.C.), chairman of the House Armed Services Committee, said the President's plan was a "good package" that "could work."

In the Senate Oct. 8, a resolution was adopted backing the Nixon peace initiative as "fair and equitable" and providing "the basis for ending the fighting and moving toward a just settlement of the Indochina war." Introduced by Sen. Charles H. Percy (R, Ill.), the resolution was cosponsored by such doves as Democratic Leader Mike Mansfield (Mont.), Frank Church (D, Idaho), John Sherman Cooper (R, Ky.), Mark O. Hatfield (R, Ore.), Harold E. Hughes (D, Iowa) and George S. McGovern (D, S.D.).

Mansfield called the Nixon plan "excellent" and predicted that the chance for a negotiating breakthrough in Paris "will be enhanced in the weeks ahead."

Sen. Edmund S. Muskie (D, Me.) said the Nixon proposals were "overdue but nonetheless welcome."

The initiative also gained the support of W. Averell Harriman and Cyrus R. Vance, head of the Paris negotiating team under President Johnson.

Nixon, touring in Georgia Oct. 8, said the bipartisan support for his proposals would "not go unnoticed by the North Vietnamese."

Secretary of State William P. Rogers said Oct. 9 that the domestic support given the plan "in all parts of the political spectrum" was "particularly important because we think the enemy has, over the years, relied on the division in our own society in the hope that that division would cause us to lose our resolve in carrying out our policies."

Other reaction. The Soviet Union Oct. 10 called President Nixon's peace plan "a great fraud" that would only "legalize and perpetuate the intervention of the United States in Indochina."

Moscow's reaction, appearing in the Communist party newspaper Pravda, said Nixon's proposed battlefront standstill would merely consolidate "the position of American interventionists in an alien land." Pravda instead repeated Soviet support for the Communist demand for withdrawal of all American forces and took issue with Washington's backing of "the most odious figures of the regime of Thieu-Ky." The Nixon plan, the newspaper said, did not "provide a proper basis for a cease-fire or for a political settlement."

Communist China charged Oct. 11 that the Nixon peace initiative was "a fraud and deceitful trick to legalize U.S.

aggression in the whole of Indochina."
Nixon had been prompted to submit the
new plan by foreign and domestic opposition to "the U.S. policy of aggression" and by the forthcoming American
Congressional elections, Peking said.

Prior to the Soviet Union's criticism
of the Nixon plan, the U.S. had appealed to Moscow Oct. 8 to persuade
North Vietnam and the Viet Cong to
accept it. This plea was followed by an
American call for North Vietnamese acceptance of the proposal through separate statements Oct. 9 by Secretary of
State William P. Rogers and Deputy Defense Secretary David Packard. Asserting that he was not discouraged by Hanoi's "knee-jerk" negative response, Rogers said Nixon "does not consider this
proposal as a proposal that is to be either
accepted or rejected." "We would hope
that it would provide a foundation on
which negotiations could begin," Rogers
said.

Packard expressed confidence that
the Communists would agree to a cease-
fire because they were losing militarily.

The South Vietnamese government
Oct. 8 gave its support to the Nixon plan
and coupled its approval with a reiteration of its offer of free elections supervised by a commission that would include
the Vietnamese Communists. At the
same time, Saigon urged North Vietnam to abandon its "demands for preconditions to be fulfilled by our side
which are tantamount to our surrender."

South Vietnamese President Nguyen
Van Thieu Oct. 9 called the Nixon plan
"constructive and practical" and said it
reflects a "sincere desire to end the
war and restore peace."

Hanoi rejects U.S. peace plan. North
Vietnam Oct. 14 formally rejected President Nixon's five-point plan for peace
in Indochina.

A statement issued by the Foreign
Ministry said the Vietnamese people and
the Hanoi government "severly condemn
and resolutely reject the deceitful peace
proposals" announced by Nixon Oct. 7.
It said North Vietnam was "entirely
unanimous with statements" of condemnation by the Cambodian government in
exile, the Laotian Communist Central
Committee and the Viet Cong's Provisional Revolutionary Government.

The Nixon plan, the ministry said, did
not "contribute to the peaceful settlement of the Indochinese problem but only
serves the scheme to prolong and expand
its aggressive war in Indochina." The
statement called the proposal to convene
an international conference on Indochina
"nothing but a cunning trick aimed at
fooling public opinion, hiding the fact
that the United States is obdurately
maintaining its aggressive stand against
Vietnam, Laos and Cambodia. The key
question is that the United States must
change its policy and end its aggression
against the three Indochinese states."

The Foreign Ministry called on the
U.S. to reply to the "concrete proposals"
advanced by the Viet Cong Sept. 17.

The Nixon plan was similarly turned
down by the Communist delegations at
the Paris peace talks Oct. 15. U.S. chief
negotiator David K. E. Bruce replied
that "we will not take your comments
today as your final position. We will continue to seek serious negotiations here in
which all proposals, yours as well as our
own, can be discussed meaningfully."

In answer to Bruce's statement, Hanoi spokesman Nguyen Thanh Le said
"our rejection is firm, total and categori-
cal." Viet Cong spokesman Duong Dinh
Thao accused Bruce of "a maneuver to
make people believe we have not yet
rejected the proposals."

The Communists centered their criticism on Nixon's proposals for troop withdrawals and the convening of an international conference on Indochina. They
opposed his plan on the ground that he
had failed to set a date for withdrawals
and continued to insist on a pullout of all
but South Vietnamese forces from South
Vietnam. Xuan Thuy, head of the North
Vietnamese delegation, called the conference proposal "deceitful" because,
he said, the U.S. had continued to oppose
the Communist peace plan, intensified
the war, hampered negotiations between
the Pathet Lao and the Laotian government and kept the Paris talks deadlocked.

A White House statement Oct. 15 expressed doubt that the Communist rejection of Nixon's peace plan was final.
Asserting that the Communist rebuff was
a "traditional bargaining technique,"
the statement said it was the Administration's belief that the Communists "should

and will continue to examine" the American offer, which it described as an attempt "to compromise the existing differences" between the two sides.

The Pathet Lao rejected the Nixon peace formula Oct. 14. A statement by the Laotian Patriotic Front called it a "maneuver of deception at the time of the Congressional election campaign." The statement also accused the U.S. of impeding contacts between the Laotian government and the Pathet Lao in their efforts "to seek a peaceful solution to the Laotian problem."

Reds again reject U.S. plan. President Nixon's five-point plan for peace in Indochina was again rejected by the Communist delegation at the Paris talks.

Nguyen Thanh Le, North Vietnamese press spokesman, told newsmen after the Oct. 22 meeting: "We reject categorically and definitively this so-called peace initiative because our analysis shows it aims not to rectify the problem but to prolong the war."

North Vietnam's chief delegate, Xuan Thuy, implied during the session that Nixon's proposal for a standstill ceasefire would put the Communist forces at a disadvantage. He said: "Nearly 300,000 American troops and 70,000 satellite troops will pursue their occupation of the country and consider this occupation legal."

Following the Oct. 29 session, Nguyen Thanh Le declared that Nixon's peace plan was "buried once and for all." He dismissed reports that Hanoi was giving it serious consideration, asserting that "this type of rumor is aimed only at sowing illusions in order to camouflage the shady designs of the Nixon Administration."

Thieu opposes coalition. South Vietnamese President Nguyen Van Thieu Oct. 31 reiterated his strong opposition to entering a coalition with the Communists. He assailed those who favored this action as "cowards and defeatist people" who must be eliminated.

Addressing a joint session of the National Assembly on the third anniversary of his presidency, Thieu said the Communists would "use coalition only as a ruse to fool innocent people and to achieve a silent takeover."

Thieu said there was no chance that a settlement of the war could be achieved at the Paris peace talks. He charged that the Communists regarded the negotiations as a way of gaining time to "continue their war of aggression and agitation leading to their ultimate purpose—that is, a takeover." The Communists, he said, had deliberately created a deadlock at the Paris talks to continue the war in South Vietnam and "to expand their war of aggression in all of Indochina." Thieu foresaw no peace even if the Communists signed a pact ending hostilities. "Countless past experiences have shown that the Communists never signed a peace agreement to honor it," he said.

Contending that the Saigon government now controlled 99.1 per cent of the people of South Vietnam, Thieu said a military victory was close at hand, "we are seeing the light at the end of the tunnel."

(Mrs. Nguyen Thi Binh, chief negotiator for the Viet Cong at the Paris peace talks, indicated Nov. 2 that her side might be prepared to deal with a South Vietnamese government headed by an acceptable replacement for Thieu. She said the Viet Cong had stated in the past that "we are ready to make contact with any person, except Thieu, [Vice President Nguyen Cao] Ky and [Premier Tran Thien] Khiem, provided that the person is for peace, independence, neutrality and democracy, with a view to discussing the problem of the cessation of the war and the formation of a coalition government.")

Hanoi gives terms on elections. North Vietnam indicated Nov. 30 that it might not oppose international supervision of elections in South Vietnam if they were conducted under a coalition government long advocated by the Communists.

Xuan Thuy, Hanoi's chief delegate to the Paris peace talks, said, "We are opposed to the maintenance by the United States of the present [Saigon] administration and the demand that it organize such elections."

The coalition regime envisioned by Thuy would be comprised of representatives of the present Saigon regime, but excluding President Nguyen Van Thieu, Vice President Nguyen Cao Ky and Premier Tran Thien Khiem, representatives of the Viet Cong and representatives of parties and groups inside and outside Vietnam who did not belong to the first categories.

The Viet Cong's eight-point peace proposal advanced at the Paris talks Sept. 17 was described by the Communists themselves as primarily a tactic "aimed at creating favorable conditions for the consolidation of our forces and for attacks on the enemy in all fields," it was reported by allied authorities in Saigon Nov. 22.

The Viet Cong's alleged explanation of its peace plan was said to have been contained in a directive captured by allied forces earlier in the week. The directive, distributed to local Viet Cong cadres in South Vietnam's Binthuy Province Sept. 17, said the peace plan was part of a "diplomatic offensive" that was "not designed to solve the problem of ending the war and bring about peace in Vietnam." According to the document, the proposals were "designed to coordinate with the American people's [antiwar] movement, to facilitate our revolutionary tasks, and to turn the tide in favor of our revolution."

Paris peace talks resumed. The Vietnam peace talks resumed in Paris Dec. 3 following a Communist boycott of the Nov. 25 session to protest the American bombing of North Vietnam Nov. 21.

U.S. chief delegate David K. E. Bruce proposed that North and South Vietnam permit their prison facilities to be opened to inspection and recommendation by an impartial group such as the Red Cross. Rejecting the proposal, the North Vietnamese and Viet Cong delegates asserted that the only way to settle the prisoner question was for the U.S. to agree to withdraw from Vietnam by June 30, 1971.

Bruce Dec. 1 had assailed North Vietnam's treatment of American prisoners and criticized its refusal to negotiate in Paris. Addressing a news conference, Bruce said the aborted American commando raid on the North Vietnamese prison camp at Sontay Nov. 21 reflected the grave concern for the fate of the missing and captured men. He said: "There is no issue on which the American people are more united and more determined. We intend to get those prisoners out by one means or another." Communist refusal to discuss the pris-

oner question until the the U.S. first agreed "to their basic preconditions to negotiation" represented "a crude and unacceptable attempt at blackmail," Bruce charged.

Bruce estimated that about 1,500 Americans were held prisoner by the Communists. Previously, other U.S. officials had placed the number of American captives held by North Vietnam at 378 with 958 missing, some of whom were believed to be in camps. Bruce took issue with North Vietnam's claim that the American prisoners were being well-treated. The chief delegate cited 13 articles of the 1949 Geneva Convention of war prisoners that had been violated by North Vietnam. The articles included information on the persons held, repatriation of the sick and wounded and information on camp locations.

U.S. vs. Red withdrawal plan. The North Vietnamese delegation at the Paris peace talks proposed a new plan Dec. 17 for the withdrawal of American troops, but the U.S. delegation rejected it, insisting on a pullout of all foreign forces from South Vietnam.

Xuan Thuy of North Vietnam said since the U.S. had turned down the Communist proposal for the withdrawal of American troops by June 30, 1971, Washington should come up with "a reasonable deadline" for the removal of the U.S. troops.

U.S. chief negotiator David K. E. Bruce replied that the U.S. was "prepared to negotiate a complete timetable for complete withdrawals as part of an overall settlement." Bruce added: "What can you tell us about your intentions as far as North Vietnamese withdrawals from South Vietnam, Laos and Cambodia are concerned?"

At the Dec. 23 meeting, the North Vietnamese repeated their proposal calling on the U.S. to withdraw its forces from Vietnam by June 30, 1971 or to suggest another date. Xuan Thuy introduced what he called a modification of his original proposal, but the U.S. representatives said they saw no change. The reported modification was contained in a statement by Thuy in which he said if the U.S. pulled out its troops at the prescribed time both sides "can also enter immediately into discussion of the total cessation of the cruel war that is now going on in Vietnam and of the respect of the fundamental national rights and the right of self-determination of the Vietnamese people." A North Vietnamese spokesman later affirmed that the rights referred to by Thuy implied replacement of the Thieu-Ky "puppet" government in Saigon, a demand repeatedly rejected by the U.S. Previously, the Communists had linked an American promise on troop withdrawal with the ouster of the Thieu-Ky regime as conditions for a cease-fire.

Paris peace talks end 2nd year. Allied and Communist delegates held another fruitless session Dec. 30 at their 97th session of the Paris peace talks. The meeting marked the end of the second full year of the negotiations.

U.S chief delegate David K. E. Bruce told newsmen after the meeting, "It is my unhappy task to report to you that 1970 comes to an end with prospects for a real negotiation . . . still frustrated by the intransigent position taken by the other side."

U.S. Dissent

Opposition mounts. Opposition to American policy in Vietnam appeared to grow throughout the U.S. during 1970, especially after U.S. forces were sent into Cambodia. This dissent was manifested in various ways. Students and other citizens marched and held rallies. Many draft-eligible youths refused induction, and some fled to Canada or other countries. Some servicemen deserted, a few of them seeking asylum in Sweden. Activists attacked draft board offices and ROTC installations. Members of Congress introduced legislation to withhold funds for the war.

Some citizens, however, supported the war effort and demonstrated against the dissenters. FBI Director J. Edgar Hoover, reporting Jan. 2 on FBI operations in 1969, said New Left and other dissident groups were "encouraged and inflamed from without" in violent attacks on the government. Hoover linked the massive Nov. 15, 1969 antiwar rally in Washington with "international Communist efforts."

4 students slain at Kent State. In one of the most emotionally shattering incidents of the U.S. antiwar movement, four students, two of them women, were killed at Kent State University in Ohio May 4 as 100 National Guardsmen fired their M-1 rifles into a group of antiwar demonstrators. Eleven other students were wounded.

Ohio Adjutant Gen. Sylvester T. Del Corso, in a statement May 4, said the troops, who had run out of tear gas, fired in reaction to sniper fire "from a nearby rooftop." However, Corso said May 5 "there is no evidence" of sniper fire. Reporters and students at the scene of the shooting said demonstrators had thrown rocks and pavement stones at the troops but that there were no shots before the Guardsmen suddenly fired on the students without warning.

The four victims were Allison Krause, 19, of Pittsburgh; Sandra Lee Scheuer, 20, of Youngstown, Ohio; Jeffrey Glenn Miller, 20, of Plainfield, N.Y.; and William K. Schroeder, 19, of Lorain, Ohio. None were described as radicals. Schroeder was second in his Reserve Officers Training Corps (ROTC) class at Kent State. The two girls, according to friends, were on their way separately to class when struck down.

The shooting occurred 20 minutes after the troops had used tear gas to disperse a student protest against the use of U.S. forces in Cambodia. Six hundred Guardsmen had been ordered onto the campus the day before after the university's ROTC building had been burned to the ground in the second night of disruptions by antiwar students.

A few students began throwing rocks at the Guardsmen as they retreated up a campus hill, and a couple of students threw back a tear gas canister. In all, about 20 rocks allegedly were thrown at the troops who were about 40 yards from the 500 to 600 students when they turned around, formed a skirmish line and began to fire. Witnesses said many students dropped to the ground but others remained standing, apparently believing the troops were firing into the air. One Guardsman was treated for injuries and released from the hospital. Another was admitted to the hospital suffering from heat prostration.

Maj. Gen. D. E. Manly, commander of the Ohio Highway Patrol unit that was working with the National Guardsmen, May 5 denied earlier reports by the Guards that his men, circling above the campus in a helicopter, had spotted snipers on a rooftop. Brig. Gen. Robert Canterbury, officer in command of the Guards, said May 5: "In my opinion, the fact that there is or is not a sniper is not important. . . . I think the reason the people fired was because they were being assaulted with rocks and concrete." He said there were no orders to open fire but the men had made "individual decisions" to shoot when they feared their lives were threatened.

Gov. James A. Rhodes called on FBI Director J. Edgar Hoover to investigate the shooting, and FBI men were on the campus May 5 making a preliminary study.

The Kent State Student Senate had accused Rhodes May 3 of political motivation when he ordered troops onto the campus. (Rhodes was engaged in a primary battle with Rep. Robert Taft for the Republican nomination for the U.S. Senate.) The Pentagon said May 5 it would not investigate the shooting because the troops were on non-federal status under the command of the state.

The campus was nearly empty of students May 5. Robert I. White, president of the university, had ordered the school closed May 4, and students were sent home. However, students on other campuses around the nation, continuing to demonstrate against the use of U.S. troops in Cambodia, protested against the events at Kent State and held memorial services for the four dead students.

Administration reaction—President Nixon, in a statement released by Press Secretary Ronald L. Ziegler May 4,

said the deaths at Kent State "should remind us all once again that when dissent turns to violence it invites tragedy."

Nixon said: "It is my hope that this tragic and unfortunate incident will strengthen the determination of all the nation's campuses . . . to stand firmly for the right which exists in this country of peaceful dissent and just as strongly against the resort to violence as a means of such expression."

Vice President Agnew said the incident was "predictable and avoidable." He said he had called attention to the "grave dangers which accompany the new politics of violence and confrontation" and that events at Kent State "make the truth of these remarks self-evident."

FBI criticizes shooting. The FBI found the Kent State shooting unnecessary, according to a copyrighted article in the Akron Beacon Journal July 23. The article was based on a 10-page Justice Department memo, which summarized a longer report on the findings of 100 FBI agents.

According to the article, the memo, signed by Jerris Leonard, chief of the department's civil rights division, said the shootings "were not necessary and not in order." It said that about 200 demonstrators who were heckling Guardsmen could have been repulsed by use of more tear gas and more arrests, that there was no hail of rocks thrown before the shooting, that no Guardsmen were hit by flying rocks or projectiles and that none was in danger of his life. The statements differed radically from previous accounts of the shootings by Ohio officials and Guard leaders.

The memo also said one Guardsman fired at a student making an obscene gesture and another fired on a student about to throw a rock. The memo said one hysterical Guardsman, after the shooting, ran around shouting, "I shot two teen-agers . . . I shot two teen-agers."

According to the Beacon Journal, the department listed the names of six Guardsmen who could be criminally charged for the shootings. Under Ohio law, such charges could not be brought unless the confrontation were classified as a riot. The summary had been prepared by the department for Ronald

Kane, prosecutor for Portage County, Ohio where the university is located.

A Justice Department statement confirmed July 23 that the memo contained options for prosecution but did not comment on the details published by the Akron newspaper. The statement said: "If Mr. Kane chooses to release such information, he must bear responsibility for it." Kane said July 23 that the FBI report was to be used in a grand jury investigation of the Kent tragedy. He said: "Nothing has been released about this from this office and nothing can until it is given to the grand jury."

The adjutant general of the Ohio National Guard said July 24 that the reported FBI assertions "are not factual. . . . They fail to include many facts which we provided." Maj. Gen. Sylvester T. Del Corso said that "the conclusions as stated in the paper by the reporter are just unbelievable . . . that there were no troops injured, that no stones were thrown and there was a question of whether there was even a riot."

Campus rioters called 'bums.' Prior to the Kent State incident, President Nixon May 1 had contrasted the "bums . . . blowing up the campuses" with the "kids" fighting the war in Vietnam, who, he said, were "the greatest."

Speaking informally with civilian employes at the Pentagon, where he attended a briefing on the Cambodia developments, Nixon said: "You see these bums, you know, blowing up the campuses. Listen, the boys that are on the college campuses today are the luckiest people in the world, going to the greatest universities, and here they are burning up the books, storming around about this issue. You name it. Get rid of the war there will be another one. Then out there [in Vietnam] we have kids who are just doing their duty. They stand tall and they are proud. . . . They are going to do fine and we have to stand in back of them."

At a televised press conference May 8, Nixon said he regretted that his use of the word "bums" was "interpreted to apply to those who dissent." He said "when students on university campuses burn buildings, when they engage in violence, when they break up furniture, when they terrorize their fellow students and ter-

rorize the faculty, I think bums is perhaps too kind a word to apply to that kind of person. Those are the kind I was referring to."

Student strike launched. The editors of campus newspapers in 11 major Eastern colleges agreed May 3 to run a common editorial calling for "the entire academic community of this country to engage in a nationwide university strike" to protest widening U.S. involvement in the war in Southeast Asia. The next day the presidents of 37 colleges and universities joined in a letter to President Nixon warning of "the incalculable dangers of an unprecedented alienation of America's youth" due to the U.S. invasion of Cambodia and renewed bombing of North Vietnam.

In the campus editorial that was published May 4, the students said a strike was necessary "to free the academic community from activities of secondary importance and open them up to the primary task of building renewed opposition to the war." According to a May 5 statement from Brandeis University (Waltham, Mass.), where a National Strike Information Center was set up, more than 115 schools across the nation were already on strike. The College Press Service estimated May 5 that 208 schools were closed or were planning to close, including Yale University, whose president and campus newspaper had opposed the strike May 3. The Yale campus had just returned to normal after a two-day massive rally in support of Black Panthers on trial in New Haven, Conn. [see p. 308A1]. Yale President Kingman Brewster, Jr., while attacking the spread of the war as a "dreadful policy," said he hoped students could find an alternative to the strike call "to demonstrate our distress."

The college presidents' letter had been drafted by Dr. James M. Hester, president of New York University, and included the signatures of the presidents of Princeton, Columbia, Radcliffe, Cornell, Stanford, Dartmouth and the Universities of Notre Dame and Pennsylvania. The presidents said they shared the "severe and widespread apprehensions on our campuses" and called on Nixon to "take immediate action to demonstrate unequivocally your determination to end the war quickly."

In Washington, D.C. May 4, leaders of the National Student Association (NSA) and the former Vietnam Moratorium Committee officially called for a nationwide strike of indefinite duration. The NSA and student body presidents from 10 campuses had called on the House of Representatives May 1 to begin impeachment proceedings against President Nixon. Sixty-eight members of the Cornell University faculty, in a May 1 resolution, had also called for Nixon's impeachment.

Among developments on specific campuses:

Princeton University (N.J.)—The faculty at Princeton, where immediate plans for a strike had been adopted by 2,300 students May 1, voted May 5 to approve a two-week recess immediately before the Nov. 3 national elections to permit students and faculty to work to elect antiwar candidates to Congress.

University of Wisconsin (Madison)—Madison Mayor William Dyke declared a state of emergency and Gov. Warren Knowles ordered National Guardsmen to stand by May 5 after about 3,000 students tried to raid a Selective Service office. Local police drove back the rock-throwing demonstrators with tear gas.

Stanford University (Palo Alto, Calif.)—At Stanford, where anti-ROTC demonstrators had been causing major disturbances since the beginning of April, a student and faculty strike began May 4 when whole departments, including the School of Law, voted to discontinue classes to protest Nixon's actions in Cambodia.

The students had voted by a slim majority to permit the ROTC program to stay on campus without academic credit in a two-day referendum, the results of which were announced April 17. Anti-ROTC protests continued, however, and fires caused $50,000 to $100,-000 damage to the Stanford Center for Advanced Studies in the Behavioral Sciences April 24. The university said the work of 10 visiting scholars was destroyed in the blaze, which followed an anti-ROTC sit-in at the campus's old student union building.

Forty-two persons were arrested April 30 after rock-throwing students, whom university officials said were "heated up" by the Cambodian crisis, confronted police. The violence followed a day-long peaceful sit-in at the old Student Union by anti-ROTC protesters.

University of Maryland (College Park)—Maryland Gov. Marvin Mandel declared a state of emergency on the campus May 4 and called in National Guardsmen after student demonstrators blocked traffic along a major highway for the second time in four days. The demonstrations had begun May 1 when students ransacked the university's ROTC office, causing $10,000 damage. The police used tear gas to disperse the protesters blocking the highway. Some students had thrown rocks at the officers. The confrontation May 1 resulted in 25 arrests and 50 injuries.

The demonstrations, in reaction to the President's decision to send troops into Cambodia, followed unrest over the arrest of more than 80 students March 24 after a building occupation to protest the school's refusal to grant tenure to two assistant professors. A special university court later dismissed charges against the students, but the protesters still faced state trespassing charges.

Student strike gains strength. The nationwide student strike movement, fueled by the use of U.S. troops in Cambodia and the deaths of the four students at Kent State University, continued to gain strength while governors in a number of states called out National Guard troops to meet violence by protesters. A student strike center at Brandeis University (Waltham, Mass.) reported as of May 10 that 448 universities and colleges were on strike or closed. The Brandeis center said May 12 that 286 colleges continued on strike "indefinitely" and that class boycotts continued at some of the 129 schools in 49 states that had officially reopened May 11.

Gov. Ronald Reagan ordered the nine campuses of the University of California and the 18 state colleges closed May 6 through May 10 to provide "time for rational reflection away from the emotional turmoil and [to] encourage all to disavow violence and mob action." Pennsylvania State University, with 18 campuses, was also closed May 6. The Pennsylvania campuses reopened May 7, but the 27 colleges of the University of Georgia system were shut down.

Gov. Louie B. Nunn had sent 250 National Guardsmen "with mounted bayonets and live ammunition" to the University of Kentucky May 5 where six students were arrested and 1,000 other protesters dispersed. Illinois Gov. Richard Ogilvy ordered 5,000 Guard troops on duty at various troubled campuses throughout the state May 6. At the University of Wisconsin, Guardsmen stood by with bayonet-tipped rifles to keep campus buildings open to students who wished to attend class. The troops used tear gas to disperse protesters; 20 persons were injured, including three policemen and two Guardsmen, and 25 protesters were arrested

Firebomb blasts were reported on a number of campuses May 6 and 7. Gov. Robert McNair dispatched 150 troops to the University of South Carolina May 7 where 36 students were arrested after a sitdown strike in a campus building. McNair declared a state of emergency on the campus May 11 after police and National Guardsmen confronted brick-throwing students.

A state of emergency was declared at Southern Illinois University (Carbondale) May 8 as National Guard troops hurled tear gas and advanced with fixed bayonets to rout protesters. Troops moved onto the University of New Mexico campus May 8, and a university information officer said there were reports that at least seven students had been wounded by bayonets. On May 6, three students had been reported stabbed in a flag-raising dispute at the university.

Troops were ordered on standby at the University of Iowa May 9, and state police arrested 68 protesters at the University of Virginia after an apparently spontaneous demonstration in Charlottesville. A Miami, Fla. circuit court judge ordered the resumption of classes at the University of Miami (Coral Gables) May 9 in a ruling on a suit brought by two law students. In another ruling, the State Court of Appeals in Albany, N.Y., held May 12 that law students must complete a specified

number of classroom hours and take final exams to be eligible for state Bar examinations. Law students at New York University (NYU) and at other campuses had voted to boycott classes, and an NYU spokesman had said students who elected to stay out of class could receive course credits.

In San Diego, a University of California student died May 11. George M. Winne Jr., 23, had set himself on fire May 10 while calling on God to end the war.

Colorado troops were alerted May 12 after demonstrations on the University of Denver campus. War protesters cashed in about $31,000 in U.S. savings bonds May 11 and 12 in Palo Alto, Calif., site of Stanford University, and in Madison, Wis., site of the University of Wisconsin campus. Students at the University of Massachusetts and Amherst College (Mass.) planned mass withdrawals of bank deposits May 12 in the hope of removing funds from war resources.

Campus lobbying efforts organized. Increasing numbers of students and faculty turned from street and campus demonstrations to mount an intensive lobbying effort in Washington, D.C. to persuade members of Congress to oppose the war in Vietnam and the use of U.S. troops in Cambodia. Almost the entire student body at Haverford College (Pa.)—accompanied by professors, administration members, employes and Bryn Mawr students—converged on Washington May 7 for a day of discussions with congressmen. A movement at Princeton University (N.J.) to involve the university community directly in politics began to expand to other campuses.

A law school lobbying effort against the war was under way May 6 following a meeting of student leaders from 12 Northeastern law schools the night before at New York University. Students and professors began converging on Washington to go to headquarters set up at George Washington University and seek meetings with virtually every member of Congress.

Columbia University professors began a telephone campaign May 6 to colleagues at campuses across the nation on behalf of a newly-organized Academic and Professional Lobby for a Responsible Congress. The group reported May 7 that so far, faculty delegations for antiwar lobbying had been set up at 13 schools, most of them in the Northeast.

Yale University President Kingman Brewster Jr. said May 7 that he would join a faculty-student delegation on a trip to Washington May 11 to meet with Yale alumni who were members of Congress. Brewster said the group would express the university community's opposition to the war to the 22 Yale alumni in the House and the seven alumni in the Senate. May 11 reports said that 1,000 students and 75 faculty members joined in the effort.

In an outgrowth of Princeton's decision to declare a two-week recess before the November elections for political activity, student and faculty representatives from 29 universities met in New York May 9 to form the Movement for a New Congress. The group formed a steering committee with headquarters at Princeton and planned campaigning efforts on behalf of peace candidates facing primary battles in a number of states.

Among college lobbying groups in Washington May 11 were 600 Brandeis University students, a delegation from the small Church of the Brethren school in Indiana, representatives from nine eastern Pennsylvania colleges, and groups from the University of California, the University of Minnesota, Colgate University and the University of Virginia.

Hickel's letter of dissent. A letter urging President Nixon to establish communication with the nation's youth was sent to the President by Interior Secretary Walter J. Hickel May 6. In the letter, Hickel suggested that Vice President Spiro T. Agnew end his attacks on youth and urged the President to consult with members of his Cabinet.

The letter, purportedly a private communication, was leaked to the press shortly after transmittal to the White House.

Hickel stressed that "youth in its protest must be heard." He warned that the Administration was "embracing a philosophy which appears to lack appropriate concern" for youth and that a de-

liberate attempt to alienate youth was wrong "politically or philosophically." "A vast segment" of the young people, he said, felt there was "no opportunity to communicate with government . . . other than through violent confrontation."

"Let us give America an optimistic outlook and optimistic leadership," Hickel urged. "Let us show them we can solve our problems in an enlightened and positive manner."

He suggested that the President meet with college presidents to talk about the campus protest situation. "We must win over our philosophical enemies by convincing them of the wisdom of the path we have chosen rather than ignoring the path they propose," he said. "In this regard," he continued, "I believe the vice president initially has answered a deep-seated mood of America in his public statements. However, a continued attack on the young—not on their attitudes so much as their motives—can serve little purpose other than to further cement those attitudes to a solidity impossible to penetrate with reason."

Hickel ended his letter with an appeal to the President to meet "on an individual and conversational basis" with members of the Cabinet. "Perhaps" then, he said, "we can gain greater insight into the problems confronting us all."

(President Nixon sent an aide, John C. Whitaker, to confer with Hickel May 7. Asked at his news conference May 8 about the incident, Nixon said that Hickel was "outspoken" and "courageous" and held "very strong views." That was why he was in the Cabinet and why the President had defended him when Hickel came under early attack, Nixon said. As for Hickel's advice, Nixon said he would, of course, "be interested" in it.)

Nixon talks with students. President Nixon, in sudden decisions, conferred May 6 and May 9 with student antiwar protesters. The first meeting was at the White House with six Kent State University students who had come to Washington to see their congressman, Rep. J. William Stanton (R, Ohio). The second meeting was a pre-dawn excursion to the Lincoln Memorial that "petrified" the Secret Service.

The Kent State students had met May 5 with Presidential Assistant John D. Ehrlichman after their meeting with Stanton, who had called the White House. The Presidential invitation followed. The students later reported telling the President the campus unrest was caused by opposition to the Vietnam war, the extension of it to Cambodia and a lack of communication between youth and college administrations and the federal government. They said the President promised a full report on the killing of the four Kent State students "to find out where the errors were made." He also suggested, they related, four basic goals that might "minimize" the student dissent—ending the war in Vietnam, avoiding similar overseas entanglements in the future, slowing the arms race and creating a volunteer army.

(Another student confrontation with high-level Administration personnel took place May 6—ten students and five faculty members from Stanford University met with Ehrlichman and Henry A. Kissinger, the President's adviser on national security affairs.)

The President's pre-dawn tour on the day of the student antiwar protest in Washington, May 9, lasted 3½ hours and involved an hour's chat with a group of youths, eight at the start and eventually about 50, on the steps of the Lincoln Memorial. Accompanied only by a valet and several Secret Service men, Nixon told a Washington Star reporter upon his return to the White House at 7:30 a.m. he had tried "to relate" to the students "in a way they could feel that I understood their problems." He asked them, he said, "to try to understand what we are doing," that "I know you think we are a bunch of so and sos —I used a stronger word to them. I know how you feel—you want to get the war over. . . . I know it is awfully hard to keep this in perspective. . . . Sure, you came here to demonstrate and shout your slogans on the Ellipse. That is all right. Just keep it peaceful. Remember, I feel just as deeply as you do about this."

Two Syracuse University students present commented later. Ronnie Kemper said: "It was unreal. He was trying so hard to relate on a personal basis, but he wasn't really concerned with why

we were here." Joan Pelletier said she hoped "it was because he was tired but most of what he was saying was absurd. Here we had come from a university that's completely uptight, on strike, and when we told him where we were from, he talked about the football team. And when someone said he was from California, he talked about surfing."

Nixon sees university heads. President Nixon met with the presidents of eight major universities May 7 and reportedly assured them that hostile attacks on students by members of his Administration would cease. The educators later said they found the President "an attentive listener" while they had spoken of "the deep and widening apprehensions on campuses everywhere and the reasons for them."

In a statement, they said they had given the President their "assessment of the distress, frustration and anger among students and faculty across the nation—reactions that result from the developments in Southeast Asia, hostile comments by members of the Administration about campus events and persons and the tragic incidents that have occurred on several campuses."

Harvard President Nathan Pusey, who read the statement, was asked if the President assured the group that the hostile statements would cease. He replied "yes."

In addition to Pusey, the university heads meeting with Nixon included Malcolm C. Moos (University of Minnesota), William C. Friday (University of North Carolina), Fred H. Harrington (University of Wisconsin), Alexander Heard (Vanderbilt), Charles J. Hitch (University of California), Edward H. Levi (University of Chicago), and W. Allen Wallis (University of Rochester).

At his news conference May 8, Nixon said the educators had "raised questions" about the vice president and "other people in the Administration, about the rhetoric," but he "did not indicate to them that I was going to muzzle" Agnew or "censor" him. He said he would not try "to tone" Agnew down and hoped that everyone in his Administration would keep in mind "a rule that I have always had, . . . when the action is hot, keep the rhetoric cool."

Nixon meets with governors. The Cambodian decision and campus turmoil were the subjects of a four-hour White House meeting May 11 with 46 state and territorial governors. In addition to President Nixon, the group also heard from Vice President Agnew, Secretary of State Rogers and Labor Secretary George P. Shultz.

The need for more and better communication between the government and the public, especially the campus community, and between the various levels of government, reportedly was stressed. According to Gov. Raymond P. Shafer (R, Pa.), "the problem of communication was discussed in great depth and it was suggested that channels of communication should be established by the governors. It is very clear most of the problems are based on a lack of understanding."

There were conflicting accounts of Agnew's role and language during the meeting. Some said he had an exchange with Gov. Frank Licht (D, R.I.). Others, including Licht, denied any "confrontation." Some said he spoke of the "anti-intellectuals" dominating many campuses and the need to restore "authority" and clear out the "radicals and rascals." White House Press Secretary Ronald L. Ziegler said he heard no such words. Agnew, he said, "referred to the fact that he would like to go on campuses and speak" and "to the fact that it is difficult to do so because of the problem of being heard."

Agnew focus of attention. Vice President Spiro T. Agnew remained a center of attention amidst complaints, specifically from the educators in their meeting with President Nixon, of hostile rhetoric. Another complaint came from Robert H. Finch, secretary of health, education and welfare.

Finch responded to student antiwar demonstrators in Washington May 9 by agreeing that the public rhetoric of Agnew and Gov. Ronald Reagan (R, Calif.) had "contributed to heating up the climate in which the Kent State students were killed." In a statement later, Finch stressed he had in no way indicated any direct link of any Agnew remark with the tragedy.

Agnew himself told TV interviewer David Frost May 7 (for later broadcast) that the National Guardsmen at Kent State had "overreacted." Asked if the guardsmen might not be held responsible for murder if it were established that no shots were fired at them first, Agnew said: "Yes, but not first-degree murder. There was no premeditation, but apparently an overreaction in the heat of anger."

Agnew also said the opinions of youth were being heard in the nation but that this did "not necessarily mean they must be heeded."

Following the President's denial at his news conference May 8 that he would "muzzle" Agnew, attention focused on some impending Agnew speeches. The first was delivered in Boise, Idaho May 8. In a prepared version released early, Agnew was quoted as inveighing against "a cadre of Jeremiahs—normally a gloomy coalition of choleric young intellectuals and tired, embittered elders" who speak up in times of national crisis. Speaking of Indochina, he said "we intend to reaffirm our credibility and decisiveness when these qualities have been sharply questioned, not only by Hanoi but by others."

However, Agnew departed from the prepared text, saying he wanted "in some small way" to help cool the temper of the nation. The speech he delivered was subdued.

Agnew told reporters on arrival in Boise May 8 that a Presidential aide had called him to inform him "the President wanted me to understand thoroughly he was not attempting to put any kind of muzzle on me and that he was not opposed to the kind of things I have been saying." Agnew added that he would continue to oppose "criminal conduct" in antiwar protests but said "we never meant to imply that a great majority of the students were involved in this kind of conduct." "Dissent," he said, "can be handled without violence."

Agnew also delivered a mild speech in substituting for Nixon at a dedication ceremony at Stone Mountain, Ga. May 9 for the unveiling of a monument—equestrian carvings on a granite outcropping—to Robert E. Lee, Jefferson Davis and Stonewall Jackson. He came, he said, "to reaffirm our faith in the fact that we are one nation—drawing strength from diversity and drawing even greater strength from our unity." "We must set aside the evils of sectionalism once and for all," he said. "Just as the South cannot afford to discriminate against any of its own people, the rest of the nation cannot afford to discriminate against the South." As for Cambodia, he said the U.S. troops were "upholding the standards of honor that make it possible for a great nation to bring some order to a threatened world." "Let no one here or abroad," he declared, "mistake disagreement with disunity. . . . We have paid too great a price for being one nation to let ourselves come apart at the seams."

New York developments. Helmeted construction workers broke up student antiwar demonstrations in New York City's Wall Street May 8. Seventy persons were injured in the fighting, including three policemen. The workers, yelling "All the way U.S.A." and "Love it or leave it," then stormed City Hall and forced officials to raise to full staff the U.S. flag that had been placed at half staff in mourning for four students killed May 4 at Ohio's Kent State University.

At a news conference May 9, Mayor John Lindsay, appearing with Police Commissioner Howard R. Leary, charged that New Yorkers had "witnessed a breakdown of the police as the barrier between them and wanton violence." He said violence by "marauding bands of construction workers" had been appalling and charged that police had failed to contain it.

Two thousand enraged construction workers and their supporters again marched through Wall Street May 11. Enough police were on hand to control the demonstration, but several bystanders were punched and kicked. The workers carried signs saying "Lindsay is a bum" and "Impeach the Red Mayor." Lindsay praised the police May 11 for acting "alertly, skillfully and professionally" to control the crowds.

Construction workers again gathered on Wall Street May 12 across police barricades from about 1,000 antiwar students from a dozen graduate business schools of Eastern universities. The students wore short hair, coats and ties and claimed they voiced opposition to the war from the "Establishment."

More than 100,000 helmeted construction workers, dockmen and office workers demonstrated around City Hall in New York City May 20 in support of President Nixon and his policies in Vietnam and Cambodia. Sponsored by the Building and Construction Trades Council of Greater New York, the crowd, numbering 60,000–150,000 according to various estimates, rallied to demonstrate "love of country and love and respect for our country's flag."

(In a similar demonstration in support of President Nixon, some 1,500 construction workers rallied May 20 in Buffalo, N.Y.)

In a smaller demonstration May 21, about 20,000 students and union members rallied near City Hall in New York to protest the war in Indochina. The protest was organized by the Labor-Student Coalition for Peace and was hailed by Victor Gotbaum, head of District 27 of the AFL-CIO American Federation of State, County and Municipal Employes, as "a beginning of an alliance between forces—between the academic community and the labor movement." Following the demonstration, a smaller group of youthful protesters began to march uptown, and nine demonstrators were injured as police suddenly dispersed the marchers.

Marchers back U.S. policy. Other groups also had opposed the antiwar dissenters and had supported U.S. policy in Vietnam.

Thousands of demonstrators advocating victory in Vietnam marched down Pennsylvania Avenue in Washington, D.C. April 4, led by the Rev. Carl McIntire, a fundamentalist preacher and anti-Communist radio commentator. Police estimated that 10,000–15,000 people participated in the march and rally, the largest Washington pro-war demonstration since America's involvement in Vietnam. McIntire's estimate of the crowd was 50,000, still far below the 250,000 figure reported for the November 1969 peace march in Washington.

The crowd included people of all ages, many of whom carried American and

Confederate flags, Bibles and pro-war and anti-desegregation banners. Their signs advocated escalation of the Vietnam war and prayers in schools. During a rally after the march at the Washington Monument, speakers called for an end to busing, sex education and legalized abortion. McIntire proclaimed a "holy crusade" and said: "May this be the great turning point in the worldwide crusade against communism." Georgia Gov. Lester Maddox charged that Washington officials were "telling us to forget your children, forget your country, forget your God." Another speaker, Rep. John R. Rarick (D, La.), denounced "the myth that America cannot win this war." He said the rally was "the first step to peace—we seek peace the American way, through victory."

McIntire said telegrams of support had been sent by Sens. Strom Thurmond (R, S.C.) and Barry Goldwater (R, Ariz.) and by former Alabama Gov. George Wallace. Among organizations represented by contingents of marchers were the American Legion, the Veterans of Foreign Wars and refugee groups from Cuba and Iron Curtain countries. Small delegations represented right-wing radical groups such as the Minutemen, National States' Rights Party and the National Youth Alliance.

Armed Forces Day parades and protests. Armed Forces Day observances were canceled at 23 military bases around the country May 16 because of planned antiwar demonstrations, but 50,000 people marched in a military parade in San Diego, Calif. and 10,000 people turned out for the parade in New York City. Police used tear gas to disperse antiwar protesters at Fort Dix, N.J., and police broke up scuffling between 500 antiwar demonstrators and 75 counter-demonstrators in Killeen, Tex. near Fort Hood.

The Fort Dix disturbance followed a peace rally attended by 3,000 persons.

Campus dissent continues. Campus protests against the war in Vietnam and the use of U.S. troops in Cambodia continued throughout the nation, and National Guard troops helped state and local police control demonstrators at some schools. A student strike center at Brandeis University (Waltham, Mass.)

reported strike activity at 281 colleges and universities May 19. News agency reports indicated that 15 institutions throughout the nation remained officially closed as of May 15.

Michigan Gov. William Milliken declared a state of emergency and a dusk-to-dawn curfew at Eastern Michigan University in Ypsilanti May 13 as police used tear gas to disperse antiwar demonstrators. At the University of Denver National Guardsmen moved onto the campus after antiwar protesters evacuated a shantytown commune that had been built on the campus. Two thousand college students gathered on the Kansas state capitol grounds in Topeka May 13 to petition Gov. Robert Docking to call a special session of the legislature to consider antiwar legislation. Northwestern University (Evanston, Ill.) resumed classes May 13 after students voted to end a strike, but five buildings were closed the next day because of bomb threats.

National Guard troops carrying unloaded rifles were brought back to the University of Maryland campus (College Park) May 14 as antiwar students continued to stage demonstrations to block a nearby highway. Martial law was declared May 15, but a midnight to 6 a.m. curfew was lifted May 19 on condition that no further trouble developed. A curfew was maintained at the University of South Carolina (Columbia) May 14. Gov. Robert E. McNair praised faculty and student leaders for helping to reduce tension. Assistant Dean George Turner of Illinois State University (Normal) was hospitalized with a head injury received during a battle between about 50 students and an equal number of police May 14.

Ohio University (Athens) was closed early May 15, and about 1,500 National Guardsmen with loaded rifles patrolled the campus after the second night of disturbances involving rock-throwing students and police armed with tear gas.

At the University of Pennsylvania in Philadelphia, about 500 students walked out of commencement exercises for 3,784 graduates May 18. The walkout was urged by an antiwar speaker. Protests and disruptions at a number of campuses May 19 led to arrests by state and local police: Northern Illinois University (De Kalb), 33 persons arrested; University of Alabama (Tuscaloosa), 37 arrests; Florida Memorial College (Opa-Locka), 46 arrests; and Michigan State University (Lansing), 132 arrests.

Some 5,000 college students campaigned in Pennsylvania May 18 for Norval D. Reece, an independent peace candidate seeking the Democratic nomination for the Senate in the state primary May 19. Other candidates around the nation who were receiving the support of antiwar student campaign workers were Rep. George E. Brown, who sought the Democratic senatorial nomination in California; the Rev. Andrew Young, an aide to the late Rev. Martin Luther King Jr. and an Atlanta, Ga. candidate for the House; Gary Hart, a Santa Barbara, Calif. candidate for the House; and Nicholas Lamont, candidate for the House from Philadelphia.

Sen. Eugene J. McCarthy (D, Minn.) May 19 endorsed a student move that began at Yale University (New Haven, Conn.) to have graduating students contribute money ordinarily spent for caps and gowns to the Congressional campaigns of peace candidates. Spokesmen for the movement, called the Peace Commencement Fund, said they hoped to raise about $1 million and had branches so far on more than 150 campuses.

Law students from 16 universities across the country appealed to the United Nations May 21 "for assistance in preventing the lawless expansion of the war in Asia." The students presented a 29-page legal memorandum to U.N. Secretary General U Thant saying that U.S. policies in Vietnam violated the "basic human rights of American youth." The students addressed the petition to the U.N. because the group was "despairing" of the Nixon Administration. The statement was endorsed by student bodies at seven New York law schools and by law students in schools in Massachusetts, Ohio, New Mexico, California, Colorado and Virginia.

Students from 61 schools met with Congressional candidates in New York City May 23 in a meeting organized by the Movement for a New Congress. The students endorsed eight peace candidates running in the New York primary June 23. In California May 25, students from 26 northern California colleges met with student leaders from other areas to coordinate antiwar activity. An organizer for the Movement for a New Congress said that the group planned activities "to channel the great activism and concern of the students into ways that would be politically effective."

The governing board of the 18-college City University of New York adopted a resolution May 25 to recess classes for two weeks before the November elections to allow students to take part in campaigns. The resolution was submitted by Chancellor Albert H. Bowker who had indicated in a speech May 22 that he thought political action was a more effective protest to the war than frequent school closings or strikes. The University Senate at Cornell (Ithaca, N.Y.) adopted a similar resolution May 25,

Lawyers plan peace lobby. Urged on by former Chief Justice Earl Warren and Mayor John V. Lindsay, 1,000 New York City lawyers planned to travel to Washington, D.C. May 20 to lobby for U.S. troop withdrawal from Indochina. A similar group of Washington lawyers planned a May 20 meeting in the capital to set up task forces for a long-term antiwar lobbying effort.

Warren told the New York group May 19: "You are inaugurating what I believe can become a rebirth of the tradition of active involvement by lawyers in pressing public problems." He said the war in Indochina "has brought to fevor pitch our crisis, already heightened by racial tensions, crime, poverty, inflation and pollution of the environment."

Mayor Lindsay declared that the war "has done to America what no enemy has done for a hundred years—it has turned our land into a battlefield." Among the lawyers listed as sponsoring the day of lobbying were Morris B. Abram, former president of Brandeis University; Ramsey Clark, former U.S. attorney general; Arthur J. Goldberg, candidate for governor of New York and former Supreme Court justice; and Francis T. P. Plimpton, president of the New York City Bar Association.

The Washington group, Lawyers Against the War (LAW), gathered May 20 to map out strategy in a meeting attended by at least a dozen Justice Department lawyers, former Defense Secretary Clark Clifford and former Assistant Attorney General John W. Douglas.

Protests in Washington. A variety of groups continued to protest in Washington—against the war and for other causes:

■Demonstrators demanding an end to the Indochina war, and an end to welfare inequities, staged sit-ins at the Health, Education and Welfare Department May 13–14. The first was a takeover of HEW Secretary Robert H. Finch's office for eight hours, ending with the arrest of 21 persons. The second was conducted, despite tightened security, by about 150 persons, who left after warnings of arrest.
■ A New York antiwar lobby that arrived in Washington May 20 had been organized by the staff of Rep. Richard L. Ottinger (D, N.Y.), a candidate for the U.S. Senate. It included some of New York's financial, business, fashion and cultural leaders.
■ Answering the call of 22 religious leaders, about 1,000 Protestant, Catholic and Jewish clergymen arrived in Washington May 26 to begin two days of lobbying. The effort was organized primarily by Clergy and Laymen Concerned About Vietnam. Another lobby group in the capital May 26 was composed of more than 325 Asian affairs scholars who called on Congress to halt American military intervention in Southeast Asia. The group bore a statement signed by 1,700 Asia scholars saying that "military intervention, if not terminated by Congressional action, can lead to an ever widening war in Asia and further deterioration in American society."
■Nearly 200 Roman Catholic priests, nuns and seminarians delivered a statement to Congress June 9 calling for the end to fighting in Southeast Asia, an end to repression of political dissent and efforts to restore confidence in the U.S. system of government.
■The Academic and Professional Alliance for a Responsible Congress, which had been organizing lobbying trips since May 14, brought 250 doctors, nurses and health officers from 19 states to Washington June 10 to urge passage of legislation to curb spending in Southeast Asia. A group of New York architects met with Housing and Urban Development (HUD) officials in Washington June 9 to protest the Cambodian involvement and to urge increased efforts to get more funds for the cities.
■More than 80 protesters were arrested in Washington, D.C. during daily peace masses celebrated on the Pentagon's shopping concourse June 15–18. The masses were part of an antiwar effort begun in 1969 by the Episcopal Peace Fellowship.

Sen. Hart's wife fined. Jane Hart, the wife of Sen. Philip A. Hart (D, Mich.), and seven other leaders of an ecumenical mass for peace conducted inside the Pentagon Nov. 13, 1969 were each fined $25 April 28 in Alexandria, Va. for violating federal regulations governing the use of the Pentagon. The defendants, arrested along with 178 other protesters, were charged with creating a "loud and unusual noise" and obstructing and impeding Defense Department employes.

The trial had opened Jan. 14, and in testimony Jan. 16, Mrs. Hart said she agreed with the motives stated by her co-defendant, the Right Rev. Edward Crowther of San Francisco—former Bishop of Kimberly and Kuruman, South Africa—that the mass was celebrated to show that "the means of nonviolence are open to those who would change our society through nonviolent methods."

The eight were found guilty by U.S. Magistrate Stanley King April 7. In addition to Mrs. Hart and Crowther, the defendants were the Right Rev. Daniel Corrigan, acting dean of Bexley Hall Theological Seminary of Rochester, N.Y.; Mrs. Corrigan; the Rev. Thomas Pike of Yonkers, N.Y., chairman of the Episcopal Peace Fellowship; Nathaniel W. Pierce, co-director of the fellowship; Thomas Quigley, staff member of the National Catholic Conference; and the Rev. William A. Wendt, rector of St. Stephen and the Incarnation Episcopal Church in Washington, D.C.

Debate in government. Dr. James E. Allen Jr., U.S. commissioner of education, May 21 stated his opposition to the Administration's war policy in Indochina. "I find it very difficult," he said, "to understand the rationale of going into Cambodia and continuing the war in Vietnam." "We must withdraw from there as rapidly as we can. The war is having a disastrous effect on the young people of this country."

Allen expressed his opinion—and he made clear it was a "personal" one —before a meeting of several hundred department employes. (Allen had convened the meeting to discuss causes of discontent within the office. His war policy remarks came in response to a question. In his opening remarks, Allen affirmed his intention to push forcefully for school desegregation although he conceded there were "differences of opinion on certain matters involving school desegregation" within the Administration. He said he would "keep fighting as long as I think there is hope.")

Presidential Press Secretary Ronald L. Ziegler denied May 25 that Allen had been asked to resign because of his dissent. "Non-support" by a member of the Administration after Presidential policy had been established, he said, was "an individual matter. The individual must determine on his own whether or not in good conscience he can remain and carry on his duties."

Among other developments:

■ Morton H. Halperin said May 11 that he had submitted a letter of resignation May 6 as a consultant to the National Security Council in protest against the Cambodian operation.

■ Democratic National Chairman Lawrence F. O'Brien May 14 announced establishment of a clearinghouse for youth and others interested in participating in political campaigns furthering their antiwar views.

■Chief Justice Warren E. Burger, speaking before a meeting of the American Law Institute in Washington, D.C. May 19, said the American system of justice was "durable enough" to meet the crisis of violence and turmoil in the nation. He said the legal system "must not give way to panic." Burger said: "In periods of stress there are always some voices raised urging that we suspend fundamental guarantees and take short-

cuts as a matter of self-protection. But this is not our way of doing things short of a great national emergency."

■The State Department confirmed May 20 that 50 Foreign Service officers who had signed a protest against the Cambodia operation had been informed by their superiors that they had a responsibility while in the diplomatic corps to support the President and his Administration.

■Sen. Eugene J. McCarthy (D, Minn.) accused the Administration May 24 of lacking a Vietnam policy "short of the objective of victory." A settlement should be sought, he said, "without regard for what such settlement shall be called—defeat, surrender, victory—and without regard for what history may say about any president of the United States."

■Petitions signed by 200 Peace Corps volunteers protesting what representatives claimed was an "expanded" war in Southeast Asia were presented to Peace Corps director Joseph H. Blatchford June 2. The petition, signed by volunteers in South Korea, Panama, the Dominican Republic and Guatemala, charged: "The government is using us as apologists for policies that run counter to the reasons for our service and the original reasons for the agency's existence."

■Nearly 300 Health, Education & Welfare Department employes protested the Indochina war in a Washington, D.C. rally June 24. Members of the group lobbied on Capitol Hill against the war earlier in the day and followed the rally with a march past the White House. Dr. Thomas Pollard, a Public Health Service officer, said: "We aren't here to protest just the war in Cambodia and Vietnam . . . but the Administration's entire foreign policy, which is taking money from necessary domestic programs."

Clothing union scores war. Jacob S. Potofsky and his AFL-CIO Amalgamated Clothing Workers of America denounced the Administration's war policy in Southeast Asia and called for U.S. disengagement May 24–27.

The antiwar stance also was at variance with that of AFL-CIO President George Meany. Meany was scheduled to speak at the ACWA's convention in

Atlantic City, N.J. May 26, but canceled following Potofsky's keynote address May 25 condemning the "further military adventures" by the U.S. "If we do not end our involvement in Southeast Asia, which is tearing us apart," he said, "our nation and the democratic processes are in danger of dying."

Potofsky said May 24 "Congress must exercise its Constitutional responsibility of not leaving the war-making decisions to the President alone."

A foreign policy statement approved by the delegates May 27 called for the withdrawal of U.S. combat forces from Cambodia and Vietnam by the end of 1970 and the withdrawal of all supporting forces by June 1971.

Three U.S. senators and former Assistant Defense Secretary Paul C. Warnke appeared at the convention May 25 to denounce the U.S. war policy in Southeast Asia. Warnke said "the threat to our security comes from continuation of the conflict" in Vietnam and not from whatever happened in Vietnam. America's role, he said, "should not be that of roving unilateral peacekeeper in Asia or anywhere else." Sens. Charles McC. Mathias Jr. (R, Md.) and Harrison A. Williams Jr. (D, N.J.) spoke of the domestic havoc caused by the U.S. war activity; Sen. Albert Gore (D, Tenn.) said the war had encouraged Soviet intervention in the Middle East.

The split with the AFL-CIO over the war policy was confirmed May 26 by ACWA Secretary-Treasurer Frank Rosenblum, who said "the labor movement has lost its image" and "is now thought of as part of the Establishment." "Once the defender of economic and social justice, in the vanguard of progressive movements," he said, "we now find the AFL-CIO endorsing the war in Vietnam. It has totally alienated our youth and antagonized others as well."

(Meany's support of the Vietnam war also was attacked in the June–July trade paper of the AFL-CIO Amalgamated Meat Cutters and Butcher Workmen. An editorial written by Secretary-Treasurer Patrick E. Gorman said "no rational segment in the makeup of America puts the stamp of approval on our war involvements.")

Nobel laureates urge end to war. Forty-three U.S. winners of the Nobel Prize declared that the health of the nation "depends on a swift disengagement" from the war in Southeast Asia. In a letter to President Nixon, dated May 28 and made public June 3, the Nobel laureates, most of them honored for contributions to the life sciences, said the Administration's military policies "have further aggravated the already severe and unhealthy political division within our country."

They called on the President to "rise to the heroism that these times demand and take swift and decisive steps to restore a unity of vision and purpose."

The signers represented three-fourths of the 57 Nobel Prize winners in science residing in the U.S. At a New York press conference to announce the letter, Edward L. Tatum, a 1958 Nobel winner in medicine, said he knew of no nonsigning Nobel laureate who disagreed with the substance of the letter. He said the letter was initiated by two Nobel laureates at the University of California in Berkeley—Owen Chamberlain and Charles H. Townes—who launched the appeal after the U.S. assault on Cambodia and the violence at Kent State University and Jackson State College.

■The board of directors of the American Civil Liberties Union (ACLU) announced June 3 that it had adopted a resolution to work for the "immediate termination" of the war in Southeast Asia. The board contended that the war deprived citizens of their civil liberties because it had not been declared by Congress. Identifying the move as a "major departure" from the organization's traditional role as defender of individual rights, ACLU executive director John DeJ. Pemberton said: "We have never before identified war itself as the cause of civil liberties deprivation." He said the union remained a nonpartisan organization.

■Thomas J. Watson Jr., chairman of the board of International Business Machines Corp. (IBM), told a Congressional committee June 3 that the Vietnam war was "a major obstacle" to the nation's economic health and threatened "irreparable" damage to the society. Another major corporate executive, E. I. du

Pont de Nemours & Co. Inc. President Charles B. McCoy, spoke out against the war and its effect on the economy June 4 at a White Sulphur Springs, W. Va. meeting of the Manufacturing Chemists Association. McCoy declared: "The Vietnam war is tearing at the whole fabric of our social and political and economic life."

■According to June 9 reports, the Massachusetts Conference of the United Church of Christ voted 418–388 to condemn the U.S. military involvement in Cambodia.

Other action. Among other developments in the continuing debate:

■An appeal to organize antiwar efforts among members of the publishing industry was announced June 14 by Christopher Cerf, an editor at Random House. Cerf said 5,000 persons had signed the Publishers for Peace appeal calling for a day of "positive action for peace" June 17. Cerf said several hundred in the industry had pledged a day's wages to the campaigns of peace candidates.

■The Universities Antiwar Fund, a national coalition of college educators formed in May, announced June 15 the endorsement of four candidates for the U.S. Senate and 14 candidates for the House. The group, organized to solicit campaign contributions for antiwar Congressional candidates, also announced an initial pledge of $50,000 for the primary campaigns of the candidates endorsed. James D. Barber of Yale, chairman of the fund, said fund-raising teams were already at work at 350 institutions with a goal of soliciting a day's pay from contributing faculty members. He said contributions were averaging $5,000 a day.

■Corporate Executives Committee for Peace, formed in May, sponsored a Washington lobbying effort June 24 by 100 executives, representing almost as many national corporations. Paul Woolard, executive vice president of Revlon Inc., said the lobbyists were "believers in and defenders of the system" and that they wanted to "end the war by Dec. 31, 1970."

■A resolution calling for immediate withdrawal of U.S. troops from South-

east Asia was approved June 25 by the American Newspaper Guild, holding its 37th annual convention in Seattle.

Pro-Nixon demonstrations. The following were among demonstrations and marches to honor the flag and support President Nixon's policies in Southeast Asia:

■About 1,000 Little Rock, Ark. residents marched at the State Capitol June 6 to support the war in Vietnam. After an address by the Rev. Carl McIntire, the crowd shouted approval of a resolution urging the President to take "decisive action" to destroy enemy "havens" in North Vietnam.

■From 20,000 to 45,000 members of trades unions and veterans groups marched in support of the Administration's policies in Southeast Asia in St. Louis, Mo. June 7. The marchers clashed with antiwar youths, and some 10 persons were arrested.

■A Baltimore, Md. march June 15 to celebrate Flag Day drew 10,000–15,000 participants, including helmeted construction workers and city firemen. The marchers carried signs saying, "Win in Vietnam," "America—Love It or Leave It" and "Respect Our Flag."

■About 5,000 persons marched in a Rome, Ga. parade to honor the American flag June 16. President Nixon sent a telegram to the march chairman expressing appreciation for "your support in the days ahead as we work to achieve [a] just and lasting peace."

Agnew attacks war critics. Vice President Spiro T. Agnew attacked eight antiwar critics June 20 as advocates of surrender.

Speaking at a Republican fund-raising dinner in Cleveland, Agnew singled out four men—Sens. J. W. Fulbright (D, Ark.), Edward M. Kennedy (D, Mass.) and George S. McGovern (D, S.D.) and Democratic National Chairman Lawrence F. O'Brien—as having "developed a psychological addiction to an American defeat." He cited three others—former Defense Secretary Clark M. Clifford and former Paris peace negotiators W. Averell Harriman and Cyrus R. Vance—as men "whom history has branded as failures." And he described

New York Mayor John V. Lindsay as one of the Republican Party's "summertime soldiers and sunshine patriots."

Agnew declared that "it is not President Nixon blocking the road to peace" but "Hanoi. And Hanoi's most effective —even if unintentional—apologists today are not in Paris; they are in the United States. They are in high places, and their prescription for ending the war amounts to surrender."

McGovern said on an ABC "Issues and Answers" broadcast June 21 he considered Agnew "a divisive, damaging influence on the people of this country" and a person who "has done more to divide and weaken the country, perhaps, than our enemies in Hanoi have done." Fulbright, asked on the CBS "Face the Nation" broadcast July 5 about Agnew's criticism of Harriman and Vance, responded: "I think it's disgraceful for these people to be subjected to this sort of criticism by an upstart man who has no standing in this comparable to the men he is criticizing."

Other Agnew remarks—Agnew told a GOP audience in Detroit June 15 he intended to continue to speak out "forcefully, factually and fearlessly" and with emotion. "No argument is fair that appeals exclusively to emotion," he said, but "no argument is realistic that rules out all emotion." He spoke in favor of "progressive partisanship" and "rational public persuasion" and against "emotionaries, a relatively small group of anti-intellectuals that has snatched the standard of dissent" from "rational dissenters."

Addressing the International Federation of Newspaper Publishers in Washington June 5, Agnew upheld freedom of the press but said his differences with "some of the news media" had arisen "not over their right to criticize government or public officials but my right to criticize them." He chided the news media in general for not "telling both sides of the story." He particularly objected to coverage of the Vietnam war, which he found "slanted against American involvement . . . without any attempt at balance."

At a GOP rally in Denver June 24, Agnew inveighed against "the Cassandras of the Senate" who were "trying to forge new chains upon the President's freedom of action" while the President was trying "to protect American lives in Vietnam." Upholding the President's authority to act in foreign affairs, he said the Senate was "not suited to crisis response."

Speaking in Washington June 17, the Vice President lauded the youth of America for their "unprecedented interest in political affairs" and their determination to change the governmental system.

(Agnew met in Washington June 4 with 11 University of Minnesota professors, including Walter W. Heller, former economic aide to Presidents Kennedy and Johnson, who appealed to Agnew to soften the tone of his public remarks. The gist of their message, according to Heller, was that the Vice President's rhetoric was "driving moderates into the arms of the extremists.")

Nixon advised on students. President Nixon's special advisers on campus unrest urged the President to "increase his exposure" to representatives of the campus and black communities and to improve his awareness of attitudes among students and minority groups. These and other recommendations were contained in a 40-page document, released by the White House July 23, which included a series of memoranda from Dr. Alexander Heard, chancellor of Vanderbilt University, who served as Nixon's consultant on campus problems from May 8 to June 30, and his co-adviser, Dr. James E. Cheek, president of Howard University.

"We do not believe that our national government really understands that a national crisis confronts us," Heard said in a June 19 memorandum, which pointed out the significance of student reaction to the nation's Cambodia involvement. He said the Cambodia action "exposed antiwar and social discontents" among a large body of normally conservative or moderate students and that problems on the campus should not be viewed as "a temporary, aberrational outburst" but as a "national emergency."

In a candid memorandum dated July 6, Heard discussed the problems the President and dissident students had "communicating" about Vietnam. Noting that he referred to views held by "significant numbers of activated students" although not by all such students, Heard said that "the President uses words that mean one thing to him but something different to many students." He said students thought that Nixon's dedication to "a just peace" and "self-determination for South Vietnam" probably meant continued American presence in Indochina and a pro-U.S. regime in Saigon—something quite different than "peace" as defined by these students, which Heard stated to be "an end to the killing immediately."

Heard said students gave "no real chance of success" to the President's chosen course in Vietnam. He said students seeking to avoid the draft "are not seeking to avoid personal danger. Rather, they abhor personal involvement in a war they perceive as 'immoral.'"

In the same memorandum, Heard said students construed Nixon's statements about "deep divisions" in the country as meaning "a serious disagreement in a stable society," whereas students perceived "not just differences of opinion, but rather the whole social order as being in a state of erosion." He said a "tendency toward an absolutist conception of moral values" made them view "any form of injustice and inequality . . . as an indictment of the entire social system, regardless of its improvements over the past or its relative superiority over other societies." Heard said students were obsessed with solving U.S. problems, had less fear of communism "than existed a decade ago" and did not share "attitudes derived from the Cold War." Thus, they did not seem as troubled as they might be over such things as the Soviet invasion of Czechoslovakia— they "tend to be suspicious of all national powers, including the United States"; "a generational loyalty appears to develop, a loyalty to young people internationally, that transcends national loyalties."

In a July 22 memorandum, Cheek, president of a predominantly black university, discussed "the special characteristics that differentiate the mood and posture of the black college community" from the academic community as a whole. He said Vietnam was "an additional issue that aggravates and intensifies feel-

ings already there," but that an end to the war "without some accompanying dramatic attention to their historic problems would increase their feelings of doubt" relating to the nation's "basic institutions." He said black students were seeking "new strategies" to achieve their goals and that they had "no strong allegiances to traditional political alliances."

Agnew attacks Senate doves. Vice President Spiro T. Agnew Aug. 17 attacked a Senate proposal to end U.S. combat operations in South Vietnam by a certain date as "a blueprint for the first defeat in the history of the United States and for chaos and communism for the future of South Vietnam." The proposal, known as the "amendment to end the war," was being offered by Sens. Mark O. Hatfield (R, Ore.) and George S. McGovern (D, S.D.). Attached to the military procurement bill being debated in the Senate, it would end U.S. combat operations in South Vietnam at the end of 1970 and bring U.S. troops home by mid-1971.

(After replying to Agnew's criticism later Aug. 17, McGovern said the amendment was being revised to win more support by moving the date for a final troop withdrawal back to Dec. 31, 1971. He said the amendment would call on the President to submit his proposals on the problems for carrying out such a withdrawal.)

Addressing a Veterans of Foreign Wars convention in Miami Beach, Agnew said the Hatfield-McGovern amendment would be a "lethal blow" to the Paris peace talks and would leave the South Vietnamese prey to a Communist slaughter, imperil all of Indochina with Communist rule and give the American people "national humiliation and disaster" for its Indochina effort.

"Are the isolationists content," he asked, "to let . . . Asia go by default to the Communists because they lacked the perseverance to see this through? Well, we are not, my fellow Americans and my fellow veterans—and the President is not—and together we shall see this war through to an honorable end that will do justice to the sacrifices of all our sons. Have the isolationists considered the impact of the abandonment of this one ally upon America's other allies around the world? Could any nation put trust in the word and capacity of the United States—if we slink home, defeated, from the battlefield of Southeast Asia?"

Agnew conceded that his charges were "among the strongest since I took office," but he said "no more dangerous" proposal had been presented to Congress "in those 19 months—or in 19 years for that matter." While Agnew did not question the patriotism of Hatfield and McGovern, he questioned "their wisdom, their judgment and their logic" and "their sense of justice." "One wonders," he said, "if they really give a damn" about the consequences of their proposal.

Agnew also assailed Senate efforts to limit the president's power to make war. President Nixon's decision to mount a U.S.-allied incursion into Cambodia, he said, represented "the finest hour in the Nixon presidency" and the Senate "should leave the President alone" to take the necessary steps to protect American troops.

Later Aug. 17, McGovern asked: "Is he [Agnew] really suggesting one-man rule? Is he advocating that the presidency become a dictatorship?" Agnew "totally misunderstands," he said, "the Senate's desire to share with the president the responsibility for systematically ending our military involvement in the affairs of the Vietnamese people." If, he added, "the Cambodian invasion was 'the finest hour in the Nixon presidency,' God save us from whatever may be the worst hour."

Hatfield told the Senate Aug. 18 Agnew's speech was "a direct attack on our constitutional process." Agnew "either fails to comprehend or simply disagrees with the provisions of our Constitution," he said.

Sen. J. W. Fulbright (D, Ark.), chairman of the Senate Foreign Relations Committee, said Aug. 18 he knew of no precedent for a vice president to mount a personal attack against members of the Senate. He said the attempt to intimidate senators was "a very dangerous perversion of the democratic process."

'Hatfield-McGovern' rejected. The Hatfield-McGovern "amendment to end the war" in Vietnam was rejected by the Senate Sept. 1 by 55–39 vote (34 R & 21 D vs. 32 D & 7 R). The amendment proposed that no more than 280,000 U.S. troops could be retained in South Vietnam after April 30, 1971 and that all U.S. troops would have to be withdrawn by the end of 1971.

In the event of an "unanticipated clear and present danger," the amendment provided that the President could keep the troops in Vietnam for 60 more days and submit to Congress a request for authorization of a new total withdrawal date.

Rejection of the amendment was seen as an Administration victory and Senate support for President Nixon's Indochina policy. But some doves voted against the amendment, including Sen. John Sherman Cooper (R, Ky.), who believed there would be a better chance for negotiations if the proposal were not adopted.

In arguing against adoption, Sen. John C. Stennis (D, Miss.) told the Senate prior to the vote that the move was constitutional and Congress had "the sole power to appropriate money" but he urged, "Let's not stampede, let's go on down the road with whatever power our chief executive has as a negotiator, as a man of discernment."

McGovern, in his final words, said "every senator in this chamber is partly responsible for sending 50,000 young Americans to an early grave and...for that human wreckage at Walter Reed [hospital] and all across this land— young boys without legs, without arms, or genitals, or faces, or hopes. If we don't end this damnable war those young men will some day curse us for our pitiful willingness to let the Executive [branch] carry the burden that the Constitution places on us."

The vote on the Hatfield-McGovern amendment climaxed the protracted debate on the $19.2 billion military procurement bill, which was approved later Sept. 1 by an 84–5 vote and sent to conference with the House.

During Senate consideration of the bill, an amendment to stop the defense use of herbicides in Vietnam to clear trails and camps and destroy enemy rice was rejected by 62–22 vote Aug. 26. Another amendment to bar use of herbicides on food crops in Vietnam was rejected by 48–33 vote Aug. 27. The Senate Sept. 1 also rejected a proposal to bar sending draftees to Vietnam against their will.

(During Senate action on the defense appropriation bill Oct. 8, a proposal to require the withdrawal of U.S. troops from Vietnam by June 1971 was rejected by a 65–23 vote. Proposals to cut off funds for U.S. combat operations in Vietnam after June 1971 and to impose a $15 billion ceiling on U.S. operations in Vietnam in fiscal 1971 were rejected by voice votes.)

Campus unrest hearings. An official of the Federal Bureau of Investigation told the President's Commission on Campus Unrest July 23 that if students were allowed to form an elite force above the law, the nation would become a totalitarian society. William C. Sullivan, assistant FBI director, testified that no permanent solution could be found for campus problems until students learned to discipline themselves.

Sullivan said there was "no centralized conspiratorial plot stemming from the Communist Party" behind unrest on the campuses but said the Communists had tried to exploit the unrest. He said the war in Vietnam was only one cause of the unrest, which he said was not limited to the U.S. He said dissident students in the U.S. compared notes and discussed tactics with their counterparts in Europe.

In testimony before the commission July 24, Edward Teller, a nuclear physicist from the University of California at Berkeley, said radical movements on the campuses posed a serious threat to scientific research related to national defense. He said recent events on the campuses had "practically cut the connection between the universities and defense-related industries" and warned that the U.S. would find itself "disarmed" in 20 years if students continued to be "indoctrinated" against entering careers in national defense work.

Commission finding: unparalleled crisis. The President's Commission on Campus Unrest warned Americans Sept. 26 of an unparalleled crisis on U.S. campuses that could threaten "the very survival of the nation."

Finding a "crisis of understanding" at the base of student violence and vio-lent reaction to campus protest, the panel appealed to President Nixon to "bring us together before more lives are lost and more property destroyed and more universities disrupted."

The panel's report, prepared during three months of hearings and study, was delivered by commission chairman William W. Scranton to President Nixon, who met with the nine commissioners before leaving for a European tour.

In its report, the commission cited divisions in American society "as deep as any since the Civil War." It described an emerging culture of young people opposed to the Indochina war, indignant over racial injustice and impatient with the university itself. The panel said there was a "growing lack of tolerance" among members of the new student culture and that "many Americans have reacted to this emerging culture with an intolerance of their own."

The commission appealed to the nation to "draw back from the brink" and observe a "cease-fire." Describing the threat to the nation's survival, the commission said: "A nation driven to use the weapons of war upon its youth is a nation on the edge of chaos. A nation that has lost the allegiance of part of its youth is a nation that has lost part of its future. A nation whose young have become intolerant of . . . all traditional values simply because they are traditional has no generation worthy or capable of assuming leadership in the years to come."

The panel described as criminals students "who bomb and burn" and law enforcement officials "who needlessly shoot or assault students."

"We utterly condemn violence. . . . We especially condemn bombing and political terrorism." But the panel warned that "much of the nation is so polarized that on many campuses a major domestic conflict or an unpopular initiative in foreign policy could trigger further violent protest and, in its wake, counter-violence and repression."

The commission urged President Nixon to "exercise his reconciling moral leadership as the first step to prevent violence and create understanding." The panel added, "To this end, nothing is more important than an end to the war in Indochina," which it said students saw as "a symbol of moral crisis" in the nation that "deprives even law of its legitimacy."

The panel cited the dangers of "divisive and insulting rhetoric" in the current political campaign and asked Nixon to "be aware of increasing charges of repression."

In recommendations addressed to government officials, law enforcement officers and university administrations, the commission urged cooperation and planning to handle campus disorders. The commission recommended special training for National Guardsmen and said lethal weapons "should not be used except as emergency eqiupment in the face of sniper fire or armed resistance justifying them."

The commission said it had been "impressed and moved by the idealism and commitment of American youth." It asked students to "face the fact that giving moral support to those who are planning violent action is morally despicable."

Agnew condemns report—At a Republican fund-raising luncheon in Sioux Falls, S.D. Sept. 29, Vice President Agnew criticized the commission report as "imprecise, contradictory and equivocal." He said the panel, in contending that "only the President can offer the compassionate, reconciling moral leadership that can bring the country together again," had indulged in " 'scapegoating' of the most irresponsible sort" and pointed out that campus unrest predated Nixon's election by at least four years.

Agnew, who spoke before 1,100 Republicans in behalf of Gov. Frank Farrar (R, S.D.) and two Congressional candidates, said the commission report "is sure to be taken as more pablum for the permissivists." He blamed "radical liberals" in Congress for fostering permissiveness and cited the voting record of Sen. George S. McGovern (D, S.D.) as "100% on the radical-liberal index."

Referring to the commission's condemnation of anti-student political rhetoric—a criticism some had assumed was directed at the vice president—Agnew said, "The suggestion that vigorous public condemnation of antisocial conduct is somehow, ex post facto, a cause of that conduct is more of the same remorseless nonsense that we have been

hearing for years." "Where it calls for a cease-fire," Agnew said, "the commission assumes a posture of neutrality as between the fireman and the arsonist."

Agnew maintained that the "primary responsibility" for preserving academic freedom on the campuses belonged "on the steps of the university administration building and at the door of the faculty lounge." He said President Nixon, by continuing to seek peace without surrender in Vietnam, by making "painful" decisions to curb inflation and by resisting pressure to "impose his will on college campuses," had demonstrated moral leadership "the likes of which this nation has not seen in many a year."

Commission on Kent State. In a supplemental report released Oct. 4, the President's Commission on Campus Unrest assailed the killings at Kent State University. The commission said, however, that "violent and criminal" actions by students had contributed to the Ohio tragedy. The commission emphasized that the tragedy was not unique. The panel said: "Only the magnitude of the student disorder and the extent of student deaths and injuries set it apart from the occurrences on numerous other American campuses during the past few years."

The panel said "indiscriminate firing" by National Guardsmen at Kent was "unnecessary, unwarranted and inexcusable." But the commission also asserted, "Those who wreaked havoc on the town of Kent, those who burned the ROTC building, those who attacked and stoned National Guardsmen and all those who urged them on and applauded their deeds share the responsibility for the deaths and injuries of May 4."

The report said "no one would have died" in Kent if the Ohio National Guard had followed recommendations by the National Advisory Commission on Civil Disorders and U.S. Army guidelines both advising against "general issuance of loaded weapons to law enforcement officers engaged in controlling disorders" that fall short of "armed resistance."

Repeating what one panel member said was the report's most important conclusion, the commission said, "The Kent State tragedy must surely mark the last time that loaded rifles are issued as a matter of course to Guardsmen confronting student demonstrators."

Much of the Kent report was a detailed chronology of four days of events that led to the shooting. The commission painted a picture of weary and frightened Guardsmen and students unsure of the permissible limits of dissent and hostile over the presence of troops on campus.

Kerr releases spring unrest survey. Dr. Clark Kerr, chairman of the Carnegie Commission on Higher Education, said Oct. 2 that results of a commission survey showed that campus reaction to President Nixon's decision to move troops into Cambodia was unprecedented in the history of higher education in the U.S.

Kerr, who released the survey results in Boulder, Colo., said, "No episode or series of episodes had a higher [campus] impact in all of our history than the events of last April and May."

The commission polled presidents of the nation's 2,551 colleges and universities on campus reaction to the Cambodia decision and the student deaths that followed at Kent State and Jackson State. Kerr said that among the 73% who responded to the survey, 57% reported some form of organized dissent on their campuses during the spring. Noting that normal academic activity was shut down at 21% of the campuses, Kerr said, "We have had nothing like that ever before."

Kerr said the net effect of the spring protests was "negative for higher education in the U.S." because they created a "very volatile" political issue. He said, "Everything possible must be done to stop terrorism, to stop disruption and to protect dissent."

Victory marchers rally without Ky. The Rev. Carl McIntire led thousands of demonstrators Oct. 3 in a Washington march calling for a military victory in Vietnam. Vice President Nguyen Cao Ky of South Vietnam, who had accepted McIntire's invitation to address the rally, had said Sept. 26 that he would not attend the march, a decision McIntire ascribed to "international political blackmail."

Ky, in a CBS "Face the Nation" interview televised Sept. 27, said the threat of violence between antiwar demonstrators and victory marchers rather than political pressure had persuaded him to cancel his appearance at the victory march. He said he still intended to visit the U.S.

Senate leaders Gordon Allott (R, Colo.) and Mike Mansfield (D, Mont.) had spoken out against Ky's proposed visit Sept. 17. Vice President Agnew had said Sept. 22 that he doubted that Ky's appearance would "serve a useful purpose."

A crowd that Washington park police estimated at 20,000 participated in the Oct. 3 march, which was led by McIntire, Rep. John R. Rarick (D, La) and the Rev. Billy James Hargis, leader of the Christian Crusade. Ky, in a short speech read by Tran Khoa Hoc, first secretary of the Washington Vietnamese embassy, said, "although I am unable to be with you, I feel that my voice must be among yours today."

In contrast with other rally speakers who attacked what was called President Nixon's "no-win" policy in Vietnam, Ky appealed for "continued assistance" and refrained from criticizing the Nixon Administration or its conduct of the war. He said the Vietnamese people were "firmly determined to keep up the fight in the task of stopping Communist aggression."

Some placards carried by the marchers, in addition to calling for a Vietnam victory, bore segregationist slogans and showed opposition to sex education, the Supreme Court and abolition of school prayers. The demonstrators carried American flags as well as numbers of Confederate, South Vietnamese, Czarist Russian and National Chinese standards.

A few antiwar protesters, among 1,000 youths gathered in the capital for a counter-demonstration and to attend a Yippie-sponsored rock concert, clashed with the marchers. Metropolitan police reported about 40 arrests but only minor disturbances.

Draft resistance organized. Antiwar students meeting at Princeton University (N.J.) May 21 called for open resistance to the Selective Service System at the end of a three-day conference called by the Union for National Draft Opposition (UNDO), an organization that originated at Princeton following the movement of U.S. troops into Cambodia. Some 250 voting delegates from 90 colleges and universities in 25 states voted to begin their campaign with a "national antidraft day" June 10.

The students resolved that the main purpose of UNDO would be "resistance, disaffiliation, and noncooperation within the military service, selective objection, direct action and full legal attacks on Selective Service." They voted overwhelmingly to gather signatures on an antidraft pledge which would commit the signer to turn in his draft card once 100,000 names were collected.

The "Charlottesville Pledge," named after the draft resistance group in Charlottesville, Va. that first proposed the idea, read in part: "I pledge that when 100,000 draftable men have signed pledges like this, I will return my draft card to my local or national resistance headquarters where it will be forwarded with the other returned cards to the proper authorities. I pledge that after that time I will cease to cooperate with any type of draft system in any way." The pledge also acknowledged that the signer recognized that he was in no way immune to federal prosecution for draft resistance.

(More than 100 antidraft protesters were arrested in Boston May 22 in one of a series of demonstrations where protesters attempted to block buses carrying Army inductees.)

'Milwaukee 14' defendant sentenced. Michael D. Cullen, the last of 14 antidraft protesters to stand trial for burning Milwaukee draft records in September 1968, was convicted in federal court March 22. Cullen was sentenced May 7 to a year and a day in prison on two counts of burning draft records and interfering with the administration of the Selective Service System.

'Catonsville 9' fugitives. Four of nine Roman Catholic antiwar protesters sentenced on charges arising from a 1968 attack on a Selective Service office in Catonsville, Md., refused to surrender to federal authorities in Baltimore April 9 to begin prison terms. A letter signed by one of the fugitives and sent to Baltimore radio and television stations proclaimed his intention to "seek the custody

of peace people and resist one last time before jail."

Two of the defendants, Thomas P. Lewis and John Hogan, surrendered April 9. Two others, Thomas Melville, a former priest, and his wife, Marjorie, a former nun, surrendered April 16 after completing courses at American University in Washington. One other, David Darst, had been killed in an automobile accident. The letter to the Baltimore stations was signed by the Rev. Philip Berrigan, who was arrested in a New York City church April 21. The letter was also signed by David Eberhardt, who was arrested with Berrigan. He had been sought on a fugitive warrant when he failed to surrender to serve a prison term in connection with a 1967 attack on a Baltimore draft office.

The Federal Bureau of Investigation announced May 18 that another of the missing Catonsville defendants, George I. Mische, had been arrested in Chicago two days before, leaving two defendants still at large: the Rev. Daniel Berrigan, brother of Philip Berrigan and former chaplain of Cornell University, and Mary Moylan, a former Washington nurse. Daniel Berrgian, in an interview printed in the New York Times April 26, had said that he would remain a fugitive from authorities as long as possible "to show them they can no longer lock people up on their order, any more than they can induct people into military service on their order." Berrigan, a Jesuit priest, said he was still in "full communication" with the Society of Jesus. He was interviewed in hiding in New York.

D.C. protesters sentenced. Nine antiwar protesters, all but one of them associated with Roman Catholic religious orders, were sentenced May 6 to terms ranging from a minimum of three months to a maximum of six years in jail for a March 22, 1969 raid on the Washington, D.C. offices of the Dow Chemical Co. The defendants, convicted Feb. 6 and 10 of malicious destruction of property and illegal entry, had been protesting Dow's production of napalm for use in Vietnam. They were charged with breaking windows and pouring what they said was human blood over company files.

The defendants, sentenced in Washington, D.C. by U.S. District Court Judge John H. Pratt, were Arthur Melville, a former Roman Catholic priest; Mrs. Catherine Melville, his wife and a former Catholic nun; Sister Joann Malone, a Catholic nun; the Rev. Bernard E. Meyer, the Rev. Robert Begin and the Rev. Dennis Maloney, all Catholic priests; Joseph O'Rourke and Michael Dougherty, both Jesuit theological students; and Michael Slaski, a draft resister from Detroit.

Philip J. Hirschkop, the defendant's lawyer, had been sentenced to 30 days in jail Feb. 11 for contempt of court. Judge Pratt cited him for using "insulting, derogatory and disrespectful language" and for "conduct which offended the dignity and decorum of this proceeding."

Draft ruling. The U.S. Third Circuit Court of Appeals, in a 2-1 decision Jan. 2, ruled unconstitutional a draft board action based on Selective Service Director Lewis B. Hershey's 1967 directive that local draft boards reclassify to 1-A (eligible for immediate induction) lawbreaking antidraft demonstrators. The court also ruled that local draft boards lacked statutory authority to reclassify antiwar protesters. The court's majority opinion said that reclassification constituted punishment without trial.

Nonreligious draft exemption backed. The Supreme Court ruled 5-3 June 15 that a young man who specifically disavowed a religious basis for his antiwar beliefs was nevertheless entitled to conscientious objector (CO) status if he sincerely objected to all wars. In a clarification of a 1965 ruling by the court—that the draft law did not limit CO status to those belonging to a religious denomination that opposed war—the court held in the case of Elliott A. Welsh 2d that the draft law exempted "all those whose consciences, spurred by deeply held moral, ethical, or religious beliefs, would give them no rest or peace if they allowed themselves to become a part of an instrument of war."

The court, in an opinion written by Justice Hugo L. Black and joined by Justices William J. Brennan Jr., William O. Douglas and Thurgood Marshall, made clear that the ruling was an interpretation of the draft law and did not consider constitutional questions about the law. Black's opinion also did not resolve the question of whether CO status should be granted to young men who objected only to the Vietnam war and not to war in general.

Justice John M. Harlan agreed that Welsh's 1966 conviction for refusing induction in California should be reversed but disapproved of Black's opinion, calling it a "remarkable feat of judicial surgery" on the draft law that did not face the constitutional issues involved.

In a dissent, Justice Byron R. White, joined by Chief Justice Warren E. Burger and Justice Potter Stewart, agreed with Harlan that Black's opinion stretched the draft law too far. The dissenters, however, affirmed the constitutionality of the draft law provisions that granted CO exemption to persons opposed to war "by reasons of religious training and belief" and specified that this did not include men opposed to war because of "essentially political, sociological or philosophical views or a merely personal moral code."

Black, in the prevailing opinion, said that in both the 1965 case, United States v. Seeger, and in Welsh's case, the Selective Service System denied CO status because of an absence of religious basis for the registrants' antiwar beliefs. Black continued that the present case was distinguished from the Seeger case because "Welsh was far more insistent and explicit than Seeger in denying that his views were religious" and because Welsh's objection to war "was undeniably based in part on his perception of world politics." Black said CO status should not be denied to a person "whose conscientious objection to participation in all wars is founded to a substantial extent upon consideration of public policy." He said the test for granting exemption should be that the registrant's antiwar beliefs must be "deeply held" and must not rest "solely upon considerations of policy, pragmatism or expediency."

In another Selective Service ruling June 15, the court held 8-0 that draft boards must consider a registrant's "non-frivolous" request for reclassification as a conscientious objector even if the man had already been classified 1-A.

The decision upset the conviction for refusing induction of Joseph T. Mulloy of Kentucky, whose draft board had ordered his induction without acting upon his request for reclassification.

Draft chief issues new standards—Selective Service Director Curtis W. Tarr announced draft guidelines June 16 that would require a CO applicant to demonstrate that his antiwar views were not only deeply held but were based on some kind of "rigorous training" and "system of belief" beyond purely personal moral code. In a Washington press conference, Tarr also said he would instruct draft boards, in line with the Supreme Court's June 15 rulings, to reopen cases of draft registrants who presented new claims to support reclassification.

Tarr said the court's ruling should not "open the door" to massive exemptions from the draft and that he did not believe that the Welsh decision would apply retroactively. In his guidelines for granting CO status, Tarr said there must be "no question" that the applicant's belief was sincere; that the applicant must be opposed to war in general and not just to the Vietnam war; that in forming his views against war, the applicant must have taken into account the thoughts of "other wise men" and must have consulted "some system of belief" beyond the scope of his own thoughts; and that the applicant's views must be the product of "some kind of rigorous training." When asked to specify portions of the Welsh ruling to support his requirement for "rigorous" training to qualify for CO status, Tarr replied that the court did not question the draft law's requirement for antiwar beliefs beyond "a mere personal moral code."

Roman Catholic wins CO discharge. An Army spokesman said Aug. 29 that 1st. Lt. John J. Forrest, 27, a Roman Catholic stationed at Fort Monmouth, N.J., had been discharged as a conscientious objector (CO). Mitchell Benjoya, who represented Forrest and specialized in draft cases, said the discharge was the first granted on grounds of conscientious objection based on Catholic theology.

Forrest, who was discharged Aug. 28, had contended that although objection

to war was not Roman Catholic dogma, such views were held by many clergymen and laymen in the church and constituted a viable minority position.

Muslim loses appeal—U.S. District Court Judge Frank A. Kaufman, in Baltimore Sept. 2, rejected the appeal of William H. Murphy Jr., a Black Muslim who contended he should be exempt from military service as a conscientious objector. Kaufman held that the Muslim faith represented a political rather than religious objection to war.

Church backs draft resistance. The Church of the Brethren, with a U.S. membership of 185,000, overwhelmingly approved an official church position endorsing nonviolent draft resistance at its 184th annual conference in Lincoln, Neb. June 27. The conference statement, approved 754–103 by the delegates, "commends" to draft age youths, their parents and counselors, the following alternatives to combat service: "constructive alternative civilian service work as a conscientious objector or open nonviolent noncooperation with the system of conscription." The delegates approved almost unanimously a second resolution criticizing America's military involvement in Southeast Asia.

Draft prosecutions increased. The Selective Service System reported Aug. 28 that prosecutions for draft evasion had increased to 10 times their level of five years ago. However, draft officials said that the percentage of draft cases ending in convictions had fallen in fiscal year 1969.

A Washington draft official explained that "one reason for the substantial reduction in the conviction rate is the policy of concluding the case without a guilty judgment if the defendant agrees to submit to induction." However, Selective Service officials also said that draft resisters flocked to California, a jurisdiction with a reputation for judges sympathetic to defendants in draft cases. The officials said they planned to ask President Nixon to tighten the rules governing transfers of inductions.

Among figures cited by the Selective Service System:

■The total number of draft evasion cases opened in the following fiscal years were: 1965: 369 cases; 1966: 642; 1967: 1,385; 1968: 1,698; and 1969: 3,455. During the first nine months of fiscal 1970, 2,950 draft evasion cases were opened.

■In fiscal years 1965, 1966 and 1967, 70% of the cases concluded ended in convictions. In fiscal 1969, the conviction rate dropped to 47%.

Rise in desertions reported. A Defense Department survey, reported Jan. 2, showed that 1,403 servicemen had deserted into foreign countries since July 1, 1966. Although desertion rates were far higher during the last years of World War II, the survey pointed to a high rate of deserters who crossed international boundaries.

The Defense Department said 371 of the deserters had returned, 468 others were aliens who deserted to their native countries and 349 had serious personal or financial troubles at the time of their departures. Only in 107 cases could the department find clear evidence that the desertion was a protest against the Vietnam war. The Pentagon said 576 American deserters lived in Canada as of Dec 18, 1969, 185 in Sweden and 88 in Mexico.

Sweden grants asylum to 18. Eighteen American soldiers and draft resisters were granted asylum in Sweden Jan. 20, bringing the total of Americans given asylum in Sweden since early 1968 to 357 persons. The Swedish government said the 18 Vietnam war opponents could remain in Sweden indefinitely but would not be considered political refugees.

AWOL, deserter rules set. The Pentagon announced a new set of rules Sept. 14 dealing with deserters and absent-without-official-leave (AWOL) servicemen. The regulations, signed Aug. 24 by Deputy Defense Secretary David Packard, for the first time brought all branches of the armed forces under a unified system covering absentees and deserters.

To facilitate the return of deserters and AWOL servicemen, the system provided a computer link between the armed forces branches and the Federal Bureau of Investigation National Crime Record System. Under the new rules, rewards of $15–$25 would be offered for the deten-

tion or return to military authorities of absentees, deserters or military fugitives.

The new regulations classified as a deserter any serviceman (1) AWOL for more than 30 days; (2) absent for any period when guilty of desertion under provisions of the Uniform Code of Military Justice; and (3) having sought asylum in a foreign country. A serviceman would not be considered AWOL if he were absent for less than 30 days.

Packard also asked the Defense Department and the separate services to report by the end of the year on measures to cut down on desertions.

Judge upholds Ft. Bragg order. A U.S. District Court judge in Clinton, N.C. Jan. 6 upheld as "constitutionally valid" an order prohibiting distribution of an underground GI newspaper at Fort Bragg. GIs United Against the War in Vietnam had brought suit charging that Lt. Gen. John J. Tolson, commander of the base, had violated the constitutional right of free speech when he denied requests for distribution of Bragg Briefs, an antiwar newspaper.

Antiwar soldiers arrested. Four antiwar soldiers at Fort Gordon, Ga. were arrested by military police after Army authorities Jan. 13 seized leaflets signed by the four privates announcing a "GI War Crimes Commission." One of the group, Pvt. Lawrence Joseph Czaplyski Jr., told a local radio station Jan. 13 that the self-appointed commission would collect information from returning Vietnam war veterans "concerning any atrocity they personally witnessed." He said the information would be sent to congressmen and to Jean-Paul Sartre, the French philosopher who was one of the founders of a 1967 "war crimes" trial in Stockholm.

The Army charged Czaplyski, Pfc. Terrance A. Kline, Pfc. Charles R. Horner and Pfc. Timothy P. Johnson with attempts to "promote disloyalty and disaffection among the troops."

Antiwar coffeehouse closed. South Carolina police closed down one of the nation's first antiwar GI coffeehouses Jan. 15. The action came two days after four officers of the club, the UFO Coffeehouse Inc. near Fort Jackson, had been indicted by a county grand jury on charges of operating a public nuisance. Judge E. Harry Agnew ordered the club padlocked in answer to a complaint filed by State Solicitor John Foard that the UFO was "detrimental to the peace, happiness, lives, safety and good morals of the people . . . living near and passing the said place."

Steve Essley, a spokesman for the arrested UFO officers, all of them civilians, had said Jan. 14 that the crackdown "is not an isolated incident, but a coordinated effort to shut down coffeehouses all over the country." Essley said police had closed other coffeehouses near Fort Dix, N.J., Fort Knox, Ky. and Fort Lewis, Wash. The solicitor's office said, however, that the action was "a strictly local effort."

About 300 demonstrators, including University of South Carolina students and a few uniformed soldiers, protested the closing of UFO in a march through Columbia, S.C. Jan. 18. Howard B. Levy, a former Army doctor who had served a jail term for refusing to train medics for service in Vietnam, told the protesters that the "government and the Army are panicking" over soldier dissent.

(Actress Jane Fonda and author Mark Lane were taken into custody at Fort Meade May 22 and were banned from the Maryland base. They had been part of a group attempting to gather the signatures of servicemen on antiwar petitions.)

Officers dissent. The Associated Press reported June 2 that 25 military officers based in Washington, D.C., most of them Navy men, had formed the Concerned Officers Movement to express what the group said was growing disillusionment with the war in Indochina.

In the first issue of a monthly newsletter, published in April, the group said U.S. policies had "turned an internal political struggle [in Vietnam] into a nation-destroying bloodbath." The organization's purpose was to "serve notice to the military and the nation that the officer corps is not part of a silent majority, that it is not going to let its thought be fashioned by the Pentagon."

The Pentagon confirmed June 5 that two members of the organization, Lts. (jg) Gordon Kerr and James Pahura, had been removed from intelligence posts in the office of the Chief of Naval

Operations "because of their association with the Concerned Officers Movement." Kerr and Pahura were released from service July 13, and a third member of the movement, Randall B. Thomas, was released July 13. They had lost federal court appeals against being removed from the Navy.

(Nineteen junior officers aboard the aircraft carrier Hancock, berthed at Alameda [Calif.] Naval Air Station, delivered through channels a letter opposing the Vietnam war to their commanding officer June 25. The Hancock had completed its fifth combat mission in Southeast Asia in April. The petition signers included half the carrier's complement of junior officers.)

West Point graduate seeks discharge. Lt. Louis Hall Font, 24, a West Point graduate, told a New York news conference March 17 that he had asked the Army to discharge him as a selective conscientious objector to the war in Vietnam. Font was believed to be the first graduate of the U.S. Military Academy to request conscientious objector status. He had placed 31st in the 1968 graduating class of 706 cadets at West Point.

In explaining his action, Font said: "I think that there is such a thing as being loyal to one's army and disloyal to one's country." His discharge application, prepared with the help of the American Civil Liberties Union, stated: "there exists no doubt in my mind that the Vietnam war is immoral and unjust." He told newsmen he would not serve in Vietnam "in any capacity."

According to Defense Department figures reported by the New York Times March 22, there were only five in-service applications for conscientious objector discharge from the Army in 1962, but in 1965, when the Vietnam buildup began, the number increased to 101. In 1969, conscientious objector discharges were requested by 943 Army servicemen, 34 of them officers, and 924 other soldiers asked for noncombatant status as conscientious objectors. Similar increases were reported in other service branches, but the percentage of approved applications decreased.

Cushing asks amnesty for protesters. Richard Cardinal Cushing, head of the

Roman Catholic Boston archdiocese, issued an Easter message March 28 calling for amnesty for all war protesters and young men who had chosen exile over military service. Cushing said such an "unprecedented" action would give alienated youth "the chance to make a new beginning."

The message, which was delivered March 29 at the Easter mass in Holy Cross Cathedral, contained the plea: "Would it be too much to suggest this Easter that we empty out our jails of all the protesters—the guilty and the innocent—without judging them; call back from over the border and around the world the young men who are called 'deserters'; drop the cases that are still awaiting judgment on our college youth?" Cushing spoke of "bewildered, confused, protesters against a world they are reluctant to inherit."

The cardinal's plea was endorsed April 4 by nine Protestant leaders in Boston, who urged the Massachusetts legislature to appeal to President Nixon for a grant of amnesty for political offenses related to the Vietnam war.

(New York Mayor John V. Lindsay, speaking April 29 at the University of Pennsylvania in Philadelphia, expressed "unending admiration" for those "heroic" enough to refuse to serve in Vietnam and willing to take the consequences. He stressed, however, that the course of justice would not be served "if we embrace revolutionary violence.")

GI news censorship denied. The U.S. command in Saigon said Jan. 28 that charges of censorship of GI radio and television news broadcasts over the Armed Forces Vietnam Network (AFVN) were "completely unfounded and unsupported." The statement came as a result of a probe that began after Spec. 5 Robert E. Lawrence, during a Jan. 3 AFVN TV broadcast, charged that the command censored news stories.

The command said investigators had studied 23 cases of alleged censorship covering a six-month period during which the military news service had screened 180,000 news items and had broadcast some 12,000. The investigators reported that some stories were withheld as a result of "editorial selections" and concluded: "This small percentage of contested news items did not constitute a pattern of censorship."

■According to a Jan. 8 report, Sen. Joseph D. Tydings (D, Md.) asked the Defense Department to put aside a punishment given to Air Force Sgt. Hugh Morgan, 24, of Rockville, Md. for "editorializing" in an AFVN broadcast. In a letter to Defense Secretary Melvin R. Laird, Tydings complained of an "incredible double standard" and said: "Our boys in Vietnam deserve a complete view of what is going on in the world." Morgan had lost his job as a Saigon newscaster after he had said during an AFVN radio broadcast that Columbia Broadcasting System commentator Eric Sevareid was one of those who had "earned [Vice President Spiro T.] Agnew's wrath."

Veterans stage 4-day peace march. One hundred antiwar veterans, organized by the New York-based Vietnam Veterans Against the War, staged a four-day simulated "military sweep" through the New Jersey and Pennsylvania countryside Sept. 4-7. At the end of an 80-mile march that began outside Morristown, N. J., the veterans joined 1,500 other antiwar demonstrators for a Labor Day rally at Valley Forge, Pa. The protesters demanded an immediate withdrawal of U.S. forces from Vietnam.

Along the route of the march the protesters staged simulated battle incidents to portray alleged American war atrocities in Vietnam. Al Hubbard, executive secretary of the veterans group, said Sept. 4 that the march "has been staged as realistically as possible without actually shooting anyone." In some of the incidents protesters, dressed in combat uniforms and carrying toy machine guns, abducted a woman for "interrogation," invaded a private home and terrorized its occupants and seized and manhandled two demonstrators posing as guerrilla soldiers. The victims of the simulated "combat patrols" had agreed earlier to participate in the demonstration.

Prisoners & Atrocities

Hanoi vs. U.S. prisoner list. North Vietnam declared Jan. 21 that it would refuse to publish the names of American pilots it held as prisoners of war. The assertion was contained in a statement issued by Vu Tien, North Vietnamese charge d'affaires in Vientiane, Laos. It was Hanoi's first public response to the submission by the U.S. at the Dec. 30, 1969 session of the Paris peace talks of a list of missing American servicemen and a request that the Communists provide the names of those imprisoned.

Tien said: "We do not consider the captured pilots prisoners of war. They are criminals . . . It is up to our law to judge them."

Tien issued the communique after conferring with the wives of three missing Americans who had come to Vientiane Jan. 17 to seek information about their husbands. The women had visited Moscow Jan. 10–12 in a similar effort to get news of their husbands, but were unsuccessful in attempts to meet Soviet officials.

The U.S. State Department Jan. 19 assailed as propaganda a Moscow radio broadcast that day of statements attributed to U.S. prisoners of war in North Vietnam. A U.S. protest delivered to the Soviet embassy in Washington asked that if Russia was able to get information on U.S. prisoners in North Vietnam "it be made available directly" to the U.S. government.

The U.S. command in Saigon had disclosed Jan. 17 that two U.S. soldiers captured by the Viet Cong Aug. 13, 1966 were later shot to death by their captors after being hauled from one village to another and placed on exhibit. The bodies of the two were discovered Dec. 24, 1969 in a shallow grave in Thuathien Province. They were identified as Capt. David R. Devers and Staff Sgt. John H. O'Neill.

A North Vietnamese official in Stockholm Jan. 18 confirmed an agreement announced Jan. 14 by the Swedish Vietnam Committee permitting captured U.S. airmen to send a postcard to their families once a month and to receive a gift parcel from home every other month. Bertil Svahnstroem, of the Swedish committee, had said Jan. 14 that two members of the American Friends Service Committee of Philadelphia had received approval of the plan in principle during a visit to Hanoi earlier in January.

The families of 70 American prisoners had received letters during the past four weeks from the captives for the first time, it was disclosed Jan. 21 by Frank A. Sieverts, special assistant for prisoner-of-war affairs to Undersecretary of State Elliot L. Richardson.

U.S. prisoners identified. A U.S. antiwar group, The Committee of Liaison with Families of Servicemen Detained in North Vietnam, released in

March-April the names of American prisoners held in North Vietnam. The committee had received the information from authorities in Hanoi.

The names of 14 captives were released by the organization March 3, 31 on March 11, 34 on March 26 and 81 more on April 7. The four groups of figures brought to 335 the number of Americans known by the committee to be held in North Vietnam.

Sweden announced March 7 that North Vietnam had provided it with a list of 14 captured American pilots. Sweden in turn passed the list on to U.S. officials.

Hanoi acknowledged that 320 Americans were imprisoned in North Vietnam, the Washington Post reported March 7. Most of the men were believed to have been previously identified. The Defense Department placed the number of American captives in North Vietnam at 433.

Texas billionaire H. Ross Perot returned to New York April 10 after making an unsuccessful attempt to meet with North Vietnamese representatives in Vientiane, Laos and in Paris to discuss the possible release of American prisoners. Perot had arrived in Vientiane April 5. He was accompanied on his private mission by the wives of five missing men or prisoners and 73 newsmen. North Vietnamese Chargé d'Affaires Vi Tien said in Vientiane April 6 that Perot's activities were "an act of propaganda" that had nothing to do with humanitarianism.

U.S. prisoner list confirmed. North Vietnam confirmed that it held 335 American servicemen as prisoners of war, it was reported June 25. The Defense Department June 26 dismissed the list as incomplete and inaccurate.

The roster, compiled by the Committee of Liaison With Families of Servicemen Detained in North Vietnam, was based on letters sent by prisoners to their families. The committee had delivered the list to Hanoi in April but the North Vietnamese did not indicate then that it was complete. Hanoi now insisted that it did not hold men who were not on the list.

In rejecting North Vietnam's account of the number of imprisoned Americans, the Defense Department asserted June 26 that the list "does not include the names of at least 40 men we carry as being captured." The department had said that 780 U.S. servicemen were either missing or held captive in North Vietnam. Of this number, 376 were listed as prisoners, or known captured, as of June 20. Americans missing or captured in North and South Vietnam and Laos totaled 1,551, with 454 believed to be prisoners.

The department statement said Washington wanted "a complete and official identification of all men who are prisoners, including civilian newsmen [totaling about 20], and a full accounting of all military and civilians who are missing."

The Committee of Liaison June 28 denounced the Nixon Administration for "systematically and deliberately using the prisoner issue to inflame the public." The committee insisted that no more than 335 Americans were held by Hanoi and discounted the additional 40 the Defense Department claimed were in North Vietnamese hands. Committee member David Dellinger said, "It is entirely possible that there are a few more—perhaps a handful—who will later turn out to be prisoners."

Red prisoners freed. A group of 62 sick and disabled Communist prisoners of war and 24 captured fishermen were released by South Vietnam July 11 and returned to North Vietnam.

The 86 men were taken in a South Vietnamese navy vessel and transferred to two motorized Communist junks six miles off the North Vietnamese coast. A total of 93 North Vietnamese and Viet Cong prisoners had been sent back to the North in four earlier repatriations between January 1966 and June 1967.

A letter bearing the signatures of 87 U.S. senators called on North Vietnam July 10 to end the "inhumane treatment" of U.S. war prisoners. The message, addressed to North Vietnamese Premier Pham Van Dong, said the legislators felt "compelled to personally express our outrage at the persistent callous attitude" of North Vietnam toward the American captives. The signers of the letter included both supporters and opponents of the Nixon Administration's Vietnam policy.

South Vietnamese authorities reported that 29 Communist prisoners of war escaped from their Phuquoc Island prison site in the Gulf of Siam Aug. 31. Military police reported killing nine and wounding two prisoners attempting to flee.

Hanoi says 6 U.S. captives died. North Vietnam reported the deaths of six U.S. prisoners and confirmed the identities of four additional American captives, a U.S. peace group disclosed Nov. 13. Hanoi transmitted the information to the New York-based Committee of Liaison with Families of Servicemen Detained in North Vietnam.

Committee cochairman Mrs. Cora Weiss refused to identify the names of the dead men because of what she termed family reasons. She said she had informed the families of the deaths. The six had been listed by the Defense Department as presumed captured. A State Department official Nov. 13 expressed "grave concern over the news, since no information has been supplied on the date or circumstances of the men's deaths."

The identification of the four new prisoners brought to 339 the number of American captives confirmed by Hanoi. The Defense Department had previously questioned the former figure of 335, asserting that its record showed 376 Americans were held by North Vietnam. U.S. officials said confirmation of the four new capitves "reopens the list and provides hope for the families of men whom North Vietnam still has not supplied any information about."

International Red Cross Committee President Marcel Naville Aug. 31 had criticized the treatment of prisoners by both North and South Vietnam. Naville charged that South Vietnam "grants prisoner-of-war status to only a small part of its detainees" and restricts Red Cross visits to "a large proportion of its other detainees." North Vietnam, he asserted, barred any Red Cross intervention "in favor of prisoners."

U.N. POW plea. The U.N. General Assembly's Social Committee Dec. 1 approved a U.S.-backed resolution aimed at insuring the protection and repatriation of prisoners of war. The committee coupled passage of the resolution, which did not refer specifically to Vietnam, with approval of a Soviet-supported condemnation of "aggressive wars" which asserted that "freedom fighters" in southern Africa and elsewhere were entitled to treatment as prisoners of war when captured.

The resolution on the POWs, sponsored by 11 other countries with the U.S., emphasized the rights of inspection of prison camps, humane treatment and repatriation of the ill and of those who "have undergone a long period of captivity." The six-point proposal urged that all prisoners "entitled to prisoner-of-war status" be subject to the provisions set forth in the 143 articles on treatment of prisoners in the 1949 Geneva accords. The resolution further urged Secretary General U Thant to continue in his "efforts to obtain humane treatment" for POWs in various conflicts.

The resolution was approved 60–16 with 34 abstentions. Communist and militant Arab countries opposed it. Most western European, Asian and Latin American countries supported it. France abstained.

A Hungarian initiative limiting the resolution to "innocent victims of war and armed aggression" was defeated 36–35, with 37 abstentions.

Viet Cong POW camp raided. A Viet Cong prison camp in the Mekong Delta was attacked by a joint U.S.-South Vietnamese raiding party Nov. 22. The operation resulted in the freeing of 19 Vietnamese prisoners. The incident was disclosed by the U.S. Navy Nov. 30.

The raiding party, composed of 15 Navy men and 19 South Vietnamese militiamen, broke into the camp, exchanged fire with the prison guards and suffered no casualties.

In addition to freeing the Vietnamese prisoners, the raiders took two Viet Cong as captives.

The raid increased to 48 the number of South Vietnamese reported to have been freed in similar operations in 1970.

Allies propose POW trade. The U.S. and South Vietnamese delegations to the Paris peace talks Dec. 10 proposed an immediate exchange of war prisoners with North Vietnam and the Viet Cong.

The Communist representatives rejected the offer and in turn suggested an immediate cease-fire in exchange for an American agreement to withdraw forces from South Vietnam by June 30, 1971. The allies turned down this proposal.

Chief U.S. negotiator David K. E. Bruce proposed that the two sides start meeting Dec. 11 to settle a prisoner swap by Christmas. The proposal, he said, "offers you the opportunity to obtain the release of some 8,000 men in exchange for far fewer on our side. It also offers you the opportunity to prove your claims of humanitarian concern for the prisoners you hold."

In rejecting this bid, the Communists termed it "a maneuver that seeks to camouflage American aggression and war crimes."

Chief Viet Cong delegate Mrs. Nguyen Thi Binh stated that if the U.S agreed to pull out its forces by June 30, Communist troops would refrain from attacking them as they were departing. This, she said, would pave the way for negotiations on security measures for the remaining American troops and for the release of the prisoners. Mrs. Binh offered the South Vietnamese army a truce as soon as there was agreement on the withdrawals and "a Saigon administration without Thieu, Ky and Khiem that stands for peace, independence, neutrality and democracy."

The allied delegations said they interpreted this proposal as similar to those rejected previously—U.S. withdrawal without any similar action on the part of North Vietnam, and elimination of the present Saigon government.

Bruce insisted that settlement of the prisoner question should not await a resolution of the military and political problems. "We do not accept this obvious attempt to use prisoners of war as a political pawn."

Hanoi issues POW list. North Vietnam Dec. 22 issued what it termed a final and definitive list of all the American prisoners of war it was holding. The U.S. dismissed the list as nothing new.

The information was delivered by North Vietnamese diplomats in Paris to representatives of Senators Edward Kennedy (D, Mass.) and J. W. Fulbright (D, Ark.). The representatives then turned over the data to David K. E. Bruce, chief U.S. negotiator at the Paris peace talks, who transmitted it to Washington.

The roster carried the names of 339 captives still being held, 20 who had reportedly died and nine previously released. It did not account for 10 airmen listed by the Defense Department as prisoners in North Vietnam and 412 other Americans listed as missing in action. The deaths of the 20 men had previously been reported by Mrs. Cora Weiss, co-chairman of the Liaison with Families of Servicemen Detained in North Vietnam.

The existence of the list was disclosed by Sen. Kennedy. At a news conference in Washington, Kennedy said that John E. Nolan, his representative in Paris, had been told by the North Vietnamese that the list was official and complete. Nolan, together with James G. Lowenstein, a member of Fulbright's Senate Foreign Relations Committee staff, had received the copies of the list with two letters from North Vietnamese President Ton Duc Thang. Kennedy and Fulbright had written Thang several months ago requesting that Hanoi make public the names of the prisoners it was holding.

In a statement issued later Dec. 22, Fulbright conceded that the names released by Hanoi might not be new but noted that "the government of North Vietnam declares this list to be final and definitive." "The families of the prisoners and the American people will appreciate this humanitarian gesture coming at the Christmas season," he said.

Defense Secretary Melvin R. Laird said that all of the names made public by Hanoi had been "reported previously through unofficial channels." He said the U.S. would press its efforts in "Paris and elsewhere to gain adherence by the other side to the provisions of the Geneva convention for all our prisoners of war held in North Vietnam, South Vietnam and Laos."

A State Department official discounted Hanoi's move as "a well-executed maneuver designed to divert attention from the fact that the North Vietnamese are not doing anything to relieve the plight of the prisoners this Christmas."

Secretary of State William P. Rogers expressed similar views at a news conference in Washington Dec. 23. He accused the North Vietnamese of "maneuvering with these prisoners in a way that is inhumane. They know the concern of the American people for these prisoners and they are diverting attention from their barbarism" by giving the impression that they were issuing a new list of names.

A North Vietnamese Foreign Ministry statement Dec. 23 said that American prisoners of war were being treated humanely. But it insisted that the captives had been taken "while perpetrating crimes against the Vietnamese people" and therefore were not covered by the 1949 Geneva convention on prisoners of war. Referring to the list given to the representatives of Kennedy and Fulbright, the ministry stated that "it is not incumbent upon the government of the Democratic Republic of Vietnam to hand over such a list to the United States government."

The Swedish Foreign Ministry had announced Dec. 11 that Hanoi had provided Premier Olof Palme with the names of 45 Americans held prisoner in North Vietnam. Palme had submitted a list of 203 names to Hanoi in November, requesting that the North Vietnamese check it. Hanoi's reply identified 45 men held captive and four who had died since capture. The North Vietnamese said nine of the names on the list could not be identified and the remaining 145 had never been held by North Vietnam.

South Vietnam announced Dec. 22 that it would release 30 disabled or incurably sick North Vietnamese prisoners of war Jan. 24, 1971 to mark Tet, the lunar new year. Foreign Minister Tran Van Lam said this offer was being made for "purely humanitarian reasons."

U.S. scores POW interview. An interview with two captive American pilots at a North Vietnamese prisoner of war camp on the outskirts of Hanoi Dec. 25 was criticized by U.S. officials Dec. 28 as "propaganda" and in violation of the 1949 Geneva convention on prisoners.

The interview, conducted by correspondent Michael Maclear of the Canadian Broadcasting Corp., was viewed on American television Dec. 27 and reported in newspapers the following day.

The two captives who spoke with Maclear were among seven prisoners who appeared on the televised program. They were Navy Commanders Robert J. Schweitzer and Walter E. Wilber. Both men said they had been captured in 1968 after being shot down over North Vietnam.

Maclear said the prisoners appeared alert, physically fit, well-clothed and apparently not underweight. Maclear was permitted to ask only four sets of questions which had been submitted to the prisoners a day in advance. They covered the prisoners' identities, mail privileges, daily routine and personal feelings about the war.

Wilber and Schweitzer both said "this war is bad" and called for its early termination. Schweitzer said the prisoners were given books by North Vietnamese authorities, all critical of U.S. policy in Southeast Asia. Wilber said the imprisoned Americans received "letters about every month and packages every two months" from home. He said "we eat three meals a day, have exercises" and were provided with recreation.

Maclear said North Vietnamese Premier Pham Van Dong had assured him before the interview earlier Dec. 25 that the list of names of 339 American captives provided by Hanoi Dec. 22 [see above] was a "full and complete account" of all those now held captive in North Vietnam. "I swear to you that these men are well treated," Dong said.

A U.S. official in Washington Dec. 27 said the interview had been conducted at "Hanoi Hilton," a "showplace camp" where numerous other journalists had been permitted controlled visits with selected individuals. Wilber and Schweitzer had been interviewed many times before by reporters visiting the camp, the official said.

Commenting on the interview, White House Press Secretary Ronald L. Ziegler said Dec. 28 that President Nixon "feels using prisoners of war for propaganda purposes such as this film is again evidence of the enemy's total disregard of the Geneva convention."

Defense Secretary Melvin R. Laird Dec. 28 called the film "cynical," noting that "there was no discussion, of course, of diet or medical treatment, of men who might be sick or who might be wounded."

"There was no idea of how many other camps there were or what they were like or even the condition of the people that were in the rest of the camp that was shown," Laird said.

Songmy (Mylai) massacre action. The U.S. Army during 1970 charged 11 more members of the Americal Division with complicity in the 1968 killing of more than 100 South Vietnamese civilians in the Songmy hamlet of Mylai 4. This increased the number of the accused to 14. But four of them were cleared before the year was ended. Fourteen officers (two of them among those charged with involvement in the killings) were accused of taking part in the suppression of information about the massacre, but three of them also were cleared several months later.

An account published Jan. 1 by the militant An Quang Buddhist faction had charged that almost 600 men, women and children had been slain at Songmy. The account appeared in a letter written by a former villager who said he had not been present during the alleged killings, but had witnessed the scene three hours after the American soldiers had left.

The South Vietnamese Senate Jan. 5 had adopted a resolution describing the Songmy affair as "an isolated act by an American unit and not the policy of the United States armed forces." The resolution, approved by 25 of the 29 senators present, upheld President Nguyen Van Thieu's position in the case and rejected a Senate Defense Committee minority report, which said that at least 47 men, women and children had been slain at Songmy. The report, read by Sen. Tran Van Don, committee chairman, charged that the Saigon government had failed to adequately protect the civilians at Songmy and that as a result Thieu "must bear full responsibility for the incident." Referring to the government's Nov. 22, 1969 statement saying that reports of a massacre were "totally false," Don said "the executive branch hid the truth and considered the case as closed. By doing so it demeaned the people and the armed forces."

Further Songmy area killings—NBC-TV news reported Feb. 18 that the U.S. Army panel's continuing investigation into the alleged massacre at Songmy had uncovered another incident nearby in which about 100 civilians were reported slain by American soldiers. The broadcast quoted several South Vietnamese survivors as saying that the civilians were slain at Mykhe 4, about 1½ miles away, and on the same day as the Songmy killings—March 16, 1968. The witnesses said that children in Mykhe had gone out to greet the Americans as they landed by helicopter. The soldiers were said to have shot the children on sight and killed other civilians with grenades as they hid in bunkers in the village.

New charges. Of the additional 11 accused in the Songmy case, these two men were charged Jan. 8 with premeditated murder: Pvt. Gerald Anthony Smith, 22, stationed at Ft. Riley, Kan., and Sgt. Charles E. Hutto, 21, stationed at Ft. Lewis, Wash. Smith was charged with premeditated murder and indecent assault on a Vietnamese female. Hutto was charged with premeditated murder, rape and assault with intent to commit murder. Both soldiers faced a military investigation to determine whether they were to be court-martialed.

An additional charge of assault with intent to murder a Vietnamese civilian had been filed against S. Sgt. David Mitchell, it was reported by Army authorities Jan. 13. Mitchell previously had been charged with intent to murder 30 Vietnamese civilians at Songmy. The Army announced Jan. 14 that Mitchell faced a further charge of committing an assault with intent to murder "upon an eight-year old Vietnamese male, . . . by shooting him with an M-16 rifle."

Charges of murder in the Songmy incident were preferred against Capt. Thomas K. Willingham Feb. 10, the day he was scheduled to be discharged from the Army. He was ordered to remain in the service pending investigation to determine whether he should be court-martialed. On the day of the Songmy attack, March 16, 1968, Willingham, then a 1st lieutenant, had been in charge of a platoon in Company B, 4th Battalion, 3rd Infantry, which was participating in the sweep of the entire area along with Company C, 1st Battalion, 20th Infantry. Although the Army did not specify details of its charges against Willingham, his attorney, Robert McKinley, said Feb.

13 that his client had been accused of killing 20 Vietnamese civilians.

The Army March 10 formally charged five more soldiers with murder and other crimes in connection with the Songmy massacre. The newly accused were Capt. Ernest L. Medina, commander of the company involved in the Songmy operation, Capt. Eugene M. Kotouc, 35, of Fort Omaha, Neb., S. Sgt. Kenneth L. Hodges, 24, of Dublin, Ga., Pvt. Max D. Hutson, 22, of Attica, Ind., and Sgt. Esequiel Torres, 21, of Brownsville, Tex. A new charge was filed in the case—against Medina and Kotouc—maiming, a legal term covering torture.

Details of the charges: Medina—charged with the "murder of two persons . . . , maiming and murder of one suspected enemy person, and murder of another, during their interrogation late in the day, and assault with a deadly weapon on a fifth individual while interrogating him on or about 17 March 1968"; Kotouc—charged with "assault, maiming and murder of one suspected enemy person, and murder of another, during their interrogation late in the day of about 16 March 1968"; Hodges—charged with rape, murder and intent to commit murder; Torres—charged with two murders and assault with intent to commit murder, one of which occurred in February or March 1968; Hutson—charged with rape, murder and intent to commit murder.

Kotouc had been an intelligence officer in the operation (Task Force Barker) against Songmy. The three enlisted men were members of Medina's company.

The Army announced March 25 that three more enlisted men had been charged with murder in connection with the Songmy incident. They were Cpl. Kenneth Schiel, 22, and Specialists 4 William F. Doherty, 21, and Robert W. T'Souvas, 20. They were charged with "murder in violation of the Uniform Code of Military Justice."

The Army April 1 filed new charges against Medina. Medina was held "responsible" for most of the Mylai murders believed to have been committed by the soldiers under his command. Army authorities said that the charges involved the 102 alleged victims of 1st Lt. William L. Calley Jr, the 30 civilians whom S. Sgt. David Mitchell was accused of killing and murders allegedly committed by at least five other men in the company commanded by Medina.

Medina was not accused of personally murdering any individuals but of being a "principal" in the case. A "principal," according to the Army, was "one who counsels, commands or procures another to commit an offense . . . whether he is present or absent at the commission of the offense."

In the face of the new accusations, Medina again proclaimed his innocence. Speaking at a news conference in Atlanta, Ga., April 1, he said: "I did not order a massacre and I did not see a massacre take place."

14 officers accused. Maj. Gen. Samuel W. Koster, superintendent of the U.S. Military Academy at West Point, and 13 other Army officers were accused by the Army March 17 of involvement in suppression of information dealing with the Songmy incident. All were either members of the Americal Division, 11th Infantry Brigade, which had participated in the operation against Songmy, or members of the U.S. Advisory Organization. Koster had been in command of the division at the time.

Koster, who had been serving in the West Point post since June 1968, immediately resigned.

The charges against the 14 officers were contained in a heavily censored version of a report issued by an Army panel that had been conducting a probe since December 1969 to determine whether a massacre had occurred and whether such killings had been deliberately concealed. The panel's head, Lt. Gen. William R. Peers, said at a Pentagon news conference, "Our inquiry clearly established that a tragedy of major proportions occurred there [at Songmy] that day." Peers said, "There was testimony and evidence" gathered at the 3½ months of hearings "to indicate that certain individuals, either wittingly or unwittingly, by their action suppressed information from the incident from being passed up the chain of command."

A statement issued simultaneously by the Defense Department said the panel's "report alleges that there were serious deficiencies in the actions of a number of officers holding command and staff positions in the Americal Division, 11th Infantry Brigade" and the U.S. Advisory Organization.

The Peers' panel report was heavily censored and the specific language of the charges were withheld on the ground that publication of the information might prejudice any future court-martial that might be held following further study of the case against the 14 officers. Two of the men had been previously charged and new accusations were filed against them. They were Captains Ernest L. Medina and Thomas K. Willingham.

The defendants and the charges (their positions at the time of the Songmy incident in parentheses):

Gen. Koster—failure to obey lawful regulations and dereliction of duty; Brig. Gen. George H. Young Jr. (assistant commander of the Americal Division)—failure to obey lawful regulations and dereliction; Col. Oran K. Henderson (commander of the 11th Brigade)—dereliction, failure to obey lawful regulations, making a false official statement and false swearing: Col. Robert B. Luper (commander of the Sixth Battalion, 11th Artillery)—failure to obey a lawful order; Col. Nels A. Parson (division chief of staff)—failure to obey lawful regulations and dereliction; Lt. Col. David C. Gavin (senior American adviser in the Sontinh district)—failure to obey lawful regulations, dereliction and false swearing; Lt. Col. William D. Guinn Jr. (deputy American adviser in Quangngai Province)—failure to obey lawful regulations, dereliction and false swearing; Maj. Charles C. Calhoun (executive and operations officer of Task Force Barker, the code name for the Songmy operation)—dereliction and failure to report possible misconduct to the proper authorities; Maj. Robert W. McKnight (operations officer of the 11th Brigade)—false swearing; Maj. Frederic Watke (commander B, 123d Aviation Battalion)—failure to obey lawful regulations and dereliction; Capt. Kenneth W. Boatman (artillery forward observer)—failure to report possible misconduct; Capt. Dennis H. Johnson (member of 52d Military Intelligence Detachment)—failure to obey lawful regulations; Capt. Medina—failure to report a felony; Capt. Willingham

—making false statements and failure to report a felony.

Massacre report diluted. The New York Times reported March 27 that the U.S. Army's still-secret Peers report, issued March 17, had concluded that the information on the killings had been diluted as it was transmitted from one command to another. According to American estimates, 175–200 South Vietnamese civilians had been slain by U.S. troops operating against Songmy. But by the time the account reached the headquarters of the Americal Division from each lower echelon, the death toll was reduced to an estimated 20–28 victims, the Times said. The Times reported that the Peers panel found that the report did not go beyond the Americal Division, the unit responsible for the operation.

Other findings of the Peers panel, as reported by the Times:

American soldiers in the village had committed individual and group acts of murder, rape, sodomy, maiming and assault. The troops were motivated by a "revenge element" injected into the operation by an officer, who apparently had referred to the heavy casualties suffered by other American units operating in the same area largely under Viet Cong control.

The Americans had killed the Vietnamese civilians in three groups. The people in each group were taken to a trench before they were shot.

Lt. Col. Frank A. Barker Jr., commander of the task force involved in the operation, had told his subordinates in a briefing before the attack that most of the civilians in the village would be away at market by the time the American troops were to sweep into the community. Those remaining in Songmy would only be Viet Cong and their sympathizers, Barker said. He was killed in a helicopter crash in a subsequent operation.

Vietnamese as well as Americans who had witnessed the slayings reported them to U.S. military channels. But Vietnamese authorities did not press the Americans to take action.

Willingham cleared. The Army June 9 dropped all charges against Capt. Thomas Willingham in connection with the Songmy killings. A preliminary investigation conducted at Ft. McPherson, Ga. ruled there was "a lack of evidence" to justify a court-martial for Willingham.

Willingham was in command of a platoon not involved in the attack on the hamlet of Mylai 4, the principal target of the Songmy operation. His unit instead conducted a sweep against the nearby hamlet of Mykhe. After hearing of the Army's action, Willingham said there had been no massacre at Mykhe and that he knew of no civilians being killed there. He said after searching Mykhe, his platoon had rounded up the residents and burned their homes along with a bunker and tunnel complex. Willingham speculated that the ejected villagers had "probably settled further south."

3 officers exonerated. The Army cleared three officers June 23 of charges that they had suppressed information dealing with the Songmy incident. Those exonerated were Brig. Gen. George H. Young Jr., Col. Nels A. Parson and Maj. Robert W. McKnight. The charges were dismissed because they "were unsupported by the evidence," the Army announced.

Army drops 2 cases. The Army dropped murder charges against two other men allegedly connected with the Songmy slayings on grounds of insufficient evidence. The dismissal actions were taken in the cases of S. Sgt. Kenneth L. Hodges Aug. 14 and Cpl. Kenneth Schiel Sept. 4.

Mitchell acquitted. An Army court-martial at Ft. Hood, Tex. Nov. 20 acquitted S. Sgt. David Mitchell of intent to commit the murder of about 30 South Vietnamese civilians at Songmy.

In the government's closing argument, Capt. Michael K. Swan, the trial counsel, said testimony by three prosecution witnesses who had seen Mitchell fire his rifle into a ditch at civilians pointed up the inherent incredibility of his own testimony that "he didn't see anyone shot." Mitchell officially issued his denial when he took the witness stand Nov. 19.

In the defense's summation, attorney Ossie B. Brown charged that Mitchell and others involved at Songmy were being accused by "some elements who are trying to undermine and destroy the military of this country. They'd love to gut the military because when you gut the military, you destroy the country."

In his opening argument Oct. 19, Capt. Swan declared that about 30 civilians in Songmy had been rounded up and pushed into a ditch by American soldiers who shot them to death.

One of the three witnesses testifying against Mitchell, Charles Sledge, told the court Oct. 19 that he had seen Mitchell and 2nd Lt. William L. Calley Jr., commander of the platoon at Songmy (C Company, First Battalion, 20th Infantry, 11th Infantry Brigade of the Americal Division), fire their rifles into the ditch where the civilians had been pushed. Another former member of the company, Dennis I. Conti, testified that he had observed Mitchell and Calley standing over the ditch, but had only seen Calley fire.

The third prosecution witness, Gregory Olsen, a machinegunner in the company, testified Oct. 20 that he had seen Mitchell pointing his rifle into the ditch, but under further defense questioning said he could not swear that Mitchell had fired.

Calley, who was being tried at Ft. Benning, Ga. for his role in the affair, was further implicated in the Songmy slayings in a sworn statement submitted at Mitchell's trial Nov. 18 by Paul D. Meadlo, a former rifleman in the company. Meadlo said he and Calley had gunned down one group of civilians and then both joined several other GI's and shot to death another group of men, women and children.

Calley trial begins. 1st Lt. William L. Calley Jr., who had commanded the platoon involved in the Songmy incident, went on trial before a court-martial at Ft. Benning, Ga. Nov. 12 on charges of murdering 102 Vietnamese civilians at Songmy.

Following selection of a six-man military jury, the government's case against Calley was presented in an opening statement delivered Nov. 17 by the chief Army prosecutor, Capt. Aubrey M. Daniel 3d.

Daniel charged: Calley and one of his platoon sergeants, Paul D. Meadlo, fired on a group of "unarmed, unresisting men, women and children" who had been ordered to sit down on a trail.

Some who "tried to run and didn't make it, were shot down in cold blood." A larger group of civilians, numbering more than 70, were shoved into an irrigation ditch and Calley "ordered them executed and they were." Calley left the scene briefly, then returned and ordered S. Sgt. David Mitchell (currently being tried at Ft. Hood, Tex.) to "finish off the rest" and he "executed those who escaped the initial volley of fire." A child observed running away from the ditch was caught and picked up by Calley, who "threw it back into the irrigation ditch, and shot and killed it." Two other members of Calley's platoon, Spec. 4 Dennis Conti and Pfc. James Dursi, defied orders to participate in the shootings.

At the Nov. 18 hearings, government witness Ronald L. Haeberle, a former Army photographer, said he had witnessed American troops kill 50–75 Vietnamese civilians in four separate incidents at Songmy, but had not seen Calley take part in the slayings.

The U.S. district court in Washington Sept. 25 had rejected a petition by Caley (filed July 20), requesting a civilian rather than a military trial. Calley argued that he could not receive a fair court-martial because publicity had made his name "synonomous with Mylai" and because high government officials "will influence all officers of the Army." The court upheld the government's contention that civilian federal tribunals had no jurisdiction in the case.

Calley suffered another setback at a pre-trial hearing Nov. 10 when Lt. Col. Reid Kennedy, a military judge, ruled that several key witnesses, including Haeberle, who had testified at a House Armed Services subcommittee investigation in April, would not be barred from testifying at Calley's court martial. The defense had sought to prohibit their appearance at the trial on the ground that the witnesses' subcommittee testimony had not been made available to them for examination. Kennedy ruled that the Jencks Act, which required government investigators to make available their questioning of prosecution witnesses, did not apply to closed hearings held by Congressional committees.

At the prosecution's unexpected request Jan. 20, Kennedy had dismissed two of the six counts against Calley, reducing the number of murders he was accused of having committed from 109 to 102.

At a Feb. 11 pretrial hearing, Kennedy dismissed these two defense arguments that the Army had no jurisdiction in the case: (1) Calley had been involuntarily held on active duty past his discharge date, Sept. 6, 1969, in order that he remain under Army jurisdiction. (The Uniform Code of Military Justice held that a soldier could be held on active duty past his discharge date if he had been charged with an offense that could lead to a court-martial. Calley had been charged Sept. 5 and was ordered to remain in the Army until action on his case was completed.) (2) A lack of a U.S.-South Vietnamese agreement covering criminal justice left the Saigon regime with the sole authority to try Calley.

In his opening statement for the defense, George W. Latimer, Calley's attorney, said Dec. 10 that his client had been ordered to "kill every living thing" in Songmy on the assumption that anyone encountered there were Viet Cong. The alleged "massacre," he said, had been witnessed by Calley's superiors who did nothing to stop it. Capt. Ernest L. Medina, Calley's company commander, had "ordered the village burned, the livestock killed, [and] the wells contaminated," Latimer said.

Former Chief Warrant Officer Scott Baker, a former helicopter pilot, told the court Dec. 11 that he had observed a large group of Vietnamese strewn along a road at the southern edge of Mylai who had been killed before any Americans reached the scene. Baker said the civilians might have been killed by artillery or helicopter gunships that he had seen strafing the village.

Five defense witnesses testified Dec. 14 that they had not seen Calley kill anyone at Songmy, but said they had the "impression" from a briefing given by Medina that he wanted every civilian killed in the village.

Another defense witness, Charles A. West, told the court-martial Dec. 15 that in a briefing the night before the American unit assaulted Mylai March 16, 1968, Medina had called on the men to "leave nothing walking, crawling or growing" in the village.

Among testimony heard before the prosecution rested its case Dec. 8:

Nov. 19—John Paul, one of Medina's radiomen, said the captain had shot to death a woman suspected of concealing a grenade. It was later discovered that the woman had been unarmed, Paul said. She had been lying in a rice paddy west of the village with the bodies of four other civilians who had been spotted by a helicopter search.

Nov. 24—Brian W. Livingston, who had piloted a helicopter at Mylai, testified that he had observed 'copters strafe civilians fleeing in panic from Mylai and that he had seen "bodies fall to the right and left of the road." Livingston, however, said this incident did not occur in the areas where Calley had allegedly killed or directed the killings of two large groups of civilians.

Dec. 1—Former Spec. 4 Robert Ear. Maples said Calley had ordered him to load his machine gun and fire into a ditch filled with women, infants and old men, but that he refused. Calley, joined by Pvt. Paul Meadlo, then fired into the ditch, Maples said.

Dec. 3—Meadlo, invoking the 5th Amendment against self-incrimination, refused to testify. Meadlo remained under subpoena and was to stay in the area of Fort Benning, Ga., where the court-martial was being held. Meadlo refused to testify at Calley's trial despite court assurances that a writ of immunity granted him earlier was an absolute safeguard against the possibility that he could be prosecuted by an American court for what he might tell the Calley court-martial.

Dec. 4—Dennis I. Conti said he had obeyed an order by Calley to round up about 30 civilians upon entering Mylai, but that he refused his later command to fire at the unarmed prisoners. Conti said Calley and Meadlo "stood side by side and fired directly into the people." Conti said later he had seen Calley along with Sgt. Mitchell "on top of a dike" firing into another group of civilians.

Dec. 7—Thomas Turner said that groups of civilians had been shoved into a trench by soldiers and that Calley, assisted by Meadlo, fired into the ditch. Calley also had shot down a Vietnamese woman pleading for her life, Turner said. Col. Reid W. Kennedy, the military judge, ordered reference to this incident stricken from the record because it was not included in the four counts the government had filed against Calley.

U.S. Marine massacre charged. Five U.S. Marines were arrested on charges of murdering 11 South Vietnamese women and five children Feb. 19 at Refugee Hamlet 4 of Sonthang village, 27 miles south of Danang, the Marine Corps command announced Feb. 26.

The men were all members of Company B of the 1st Battalion, 7th Regiment, 1st Marine Division, a combat patrol operating in the area at the time. They were identified as Lance Cpl. Randell D. Herrod, 20, leader of the patrol, Pfc. Thomas R. Boyd, 19, Pfc. Michael S. Krichten, 19, Pfc. Samuel G. Green, 18, and Pvt. Michael A. Schwarz, 21.

The killings were disclosed Feb. 20 when the villagers discovered the 16 bodies and notified a passing Marine patrol. A preliminary Marine investigation was begun the next day, leading to the arrest and jailing of the five men in Danang Feb. 23. Formal charges of murder under the Uniform Code of Military Justice were filed Feb. 24.

A seven-man Army military court in Danang June 21 convicted Schwarz of premeditated murder in the fatal shooting of 12 Vietnamese civilians at Sonthang. He was sentenced to life imprisonment, ordered to forfeit pay and allowances and was given a dishonorable discharge. Schwarz, whose trial had begun June 16, was found guilty of 12 counts of premeditated murder but was found not guilty of four other counts dealing with the slaying of four other civilians at Sonthang. The court rejected defense arguments that Schwarz had acted under orders and in self-defense during a five-man Marine patrol operation against the village in the belief that his unit was under Viet Cong attack. Capt. Franz Jevne, the trial prosecutor, said that although Schwarz allegedly had been ordered by patrol leader Herrod to fire at the civilians, the order was "patently unlawful" and should have been disobeyed.

Another member of the patrol, Lance Cpl. Michael S. Krichten, had testified June 19 that he had witnessed the slaying of the civilians and that Herrod had ordered them shot. Krichten said he had fired over the villagers' heads. He was originally charged in the case but was granted immunity.

Another member of the patrol charged in the Sonthang slayings—Pfc. Thomas R. Boyd Jr;—was acquitted of premeditated murder in a court-martial at Danang June 24. Cpl. Krichten testified that Boyd had fired over the heads of the villagers and "did not shoot anyone." Boyd testified that he had never killed anyone in combat.

The officer in command of the company involved, 1st Lt. Louis R. Ambort, 23, had received a reprimand and a $250-a-month pay cut for two months for making a false official statement about the incident.

U.S. officer convicted in slaying. A U.S. Army court-martial in Longbinh, South Vietnam March 29 convicted 1st Lt. James Brian Duffy, 22, of premeditated murder in the slaying of an unarmed Vietnamese civilian captured Sept. 5, 1969 as a suspected Viet Cong. The court reversed its decision after learning that the conviction carried a mandatory sentence of life imprisonment and handed down a lesser charge March 30 of involuntary manslaughter. Duffy was sentenced March 31 to six months in confinement and was required to forfeit $250 of his $534 monthly pay for six months.

Duffy, whose trial had started March 23, was accused of ordering one of his men, Sgt. John R. Lanasa, to shoot the prisoner, Do Van Man, who had been found hiding in a bunker. Specialist 4 David G. Walstad, a witness, had told of the killing in court testimony March 27. He said that after Lanasa had fired the fatal shot, he, Walstad, fired 12–14 shots at the fallen prisoner.

Hearings were being held to determine whether Lanasa should be tried for murder.

Four officers had testified March 27 that U.S. Army policy, as they understood it, was not to take prisoners in combat operations in Vietnam. A statement issued by the Defense Department later that day denied this, saying that Army policy was to take prisoners. To slay a captive or an enemy soldier about to be taken constituted murder, the department said.

2 officers accused re slaying. Two Army officers were charged with attempted murder May 28 "by ordering members of their command to fire into buildings used for human habitation" for the alleged purpose of "target practice." A South Vietnamese woman was killed and another civilian was wounded in the incident, which occurred June 15, 1969 near the Mekong Delta village of Caibe. The accused officers were Capt. Vincent M. Hartmann, 34, and 1st Lt. Robert G. Lee, Jr., 22. Hartmann had commanded a company in the Ninth Infantry Division at the time, and Lee was one of his platoon leaders.

The Army had begun an investigation in the fall of 1969 after receiving a report from Rep. Lionel Van Deerlin (D, Calif.). Van Deerlin had informed the Army that he had received a letter from Capt. J. L. Sugarman, a former medical officer with the Ninth Infantry, stating that another Army medic, since discharged, had told him about the shooting incident. Sugarman said he had given the Army a deposition and had been asked not to discuss it.

The eyewitness who had spoken to Sugarman, Gary Owen Nordstrom, confirmed the incident in an interview near San Francisco May 29. Nordstrom said he had given the Army his version of the episode in December 1969. Nordstrom, who had served with the Ninth Infantry, said Capt. Hartmann "definitely knew" that some huts were occupied by civilians when he ordered his 40-man platoon to fire into the structures during a search-and-destroy operation.

The firing lasted 30 seconds to one minute, Nordstrom said. He said Hartmann wanted the shooting as a "mad minute," which he described as an unplanned firing by the troops for target practice or to test their weapons. Nordstrom affirmed that he had informed Sugarman of the shooting soon after it occurred and that Sugarman in turn transmitted the information to the battalion commander.

The Army announced June 23 that Hartmann and Lee would be tried on charges of premeditated murder and assault with intent to murder.

Korean atrocities charged. A former director of a private research project in Vietnam said Jan. 9 his interviewers had turned up evidence that South Korean (ROK) soldiers had killed hundreds of civilians during military operations in South Vietnam's Phuyen Province in 1966. The disclosure was supported Jan. 10 by a member of another research group, Rand Corp., who told of "hearsay evidence" of alleged atrocities committed by ROK forces. U.S. Defense Secretary Melvin R. Laird Jan. 11 acknowledged receipt of "hearsay information" of the reported killings. He said the matter was not a U.S. responsibility; it should be handled by South Vietnam and South Korea.

The initial disclosure was made in Washington Jan. 9 by A. Terry Rambo, whose Human Sciences Research, Inc. of McClean, Va. had conducted a survey of refugees in Phuyen Province (240 miles north of Saigon), funded by the Defense Department. Rambo said the refugees had told of witnessing wanton slayings by ROK soldiers. Rambo added: When South Korean troops "passed a village and received sniper fire, they would stop and pull out people at random and shoot them in retaliation. For the Koreans, this was a deliberate, systematic policy." Rambo said the findings were based on more than 2,000 interviews of refugees conducted over a two-three month period in the spring and summer of 1966 by a team of U.S. students and Saigon University students.

Rambo said a U.S. Army officer in Saigon had told him not to continue his inquiry and to delete the findings from his report. Rambo ignored the suggestion and drew up two reports. One, "Korean Marine Behavior Toward Vietnamese Civilians in Phuyen Province," dated May, 1967, had not been made public. The other, "The Refugee Situation in Phuyen Province," dated July, 1967, was prepared under Defense Department contract. The department, however, said "the report has not yet been rendered."

Dale S. de Haan, chief counsel for the Senate Subcommittee on Escapees and Refugees, said Jan. 10 that the panel had been aware of Rambo's first report on Korean marine behavior, but had not been able to obtain it because it had been classified secret by the Defense Department.

Laird, appearing on the CBS-TV program "Issues and Answers," conceded Jan. 11 that his department had received "certain reports" of alleged atrocities by the South Koreans. But he said they "have not been substantial in the legal way."

Rand Corp. researcher Francis West, who had worked on a pacification research project in South Vietnam financed by the Defense Department, said Jan. 11 that he had received "hearsay information" of South Korean atrocities during several trips to Vietnam. He said he was "pretty convinced instances of brutality did occur." West, who had returned from Vietnam in December 1969, said he had been informed of the alleged killings by "at least 100 different people" among the several thousand refugees over a three-year period. West said that "at the direct urging" of an admiral and an assistant secretary of defense, he had filed a report in December to the "highest levels" of the Defense and State Departments and the National Security Council.

The South Korean Defense Ministry denied Jan. 15 that ROK forces had committed atrocities in Vietnam. The allegations, the ministry asserted, were "not substantiated by concrete evidence."

(Mrs. Nguyen Thi Binh, chief delegate of the Viet Cong's Provisional Revolutionary Government, asserted at the negotiations in Paris Jan. 22 that South Vietnamese and South Korean troops had massacred more than 700 civilians during an operation in the Thangbinh coastal district of Quangnam Province Nov. 11–16, 1969. Mrs. Binh charged that the troops were under "direct command" of the Americans and carried out their assault after U.S. bombing and shelling of the area. The U.S. and South Vietnamese delegations denied the charge.)

Other South Vietnam Developments

Political charges. In a New Year's address Jan. 8, South Vietnamese President Nguyen Cao Thieu denounced his political opponents in Saigon for supporting a coalition government with the Communists. He again assailed "the advocates of coalition and neutralism" Jan. 13, calling them "people-killers and traitors to the nation."

The South Vietnamese Senate Jan. 8 approved a resolution accusing Thieu and his government of inciting the Dec. 20, 1969 demonstration in which 600 persons had marched into the House of Representatives and disrupted proceedings there for a day. The resolution demanded a government trial for the "leaders and inciters" of the incident and called for disciplinary measures against the security officials for failing to take action against the demonstrators.

Military command shake-up. The South Vietnamese government Jan. 17 announced the replacement of two major army commanders in the Mekong Delta and 14 of 44 province chiefs. Another military command shift was reported Jan. 19. The changes were the start of a major shake-up aimed at improving military and civilian administrative efficiency.

Among the major changes announced Jan. 17: Brig. Gen. Nguyen Thanh Hoang was replaced as commander of the Seventh Division by Col. Nguyen Khoa Nam. Col. Vo Huu Hanh, the chief of Haunghia Province, replaced Brig. Gen. Pham Van Phu as commander of the 44th Special Zone, comprising three provinces in the western delta opposite the Cambodian border where North Vietnamese troops were reported massing for a possible offensive. Hoang and Phu were said to have been lax in preparing for that alleged enemy buildup.

The military reassignments reported Jan. 19 were said to involve three commanding generals and the replacement of four province chiefs. The command reshuffle covered central Vietnam, the Capital Military District, which included Saigon and its suburbs, and the 21st Infantry Division in the delta.

In fresh changes announced Aug. 20, Maj. Gen. Ngo Dzu, who had directed much of South Vietnam's military activity in Cambodia, was assigned to head Military Region II in the Central Highlands. Dzu's command in Military Region IV in the Mekong Delta was taken over by Maj. Gen. Ngo Quang Truong, commander of South Vietnam's First Infantry Division in the northernmost provinces. Lt. Gen. Lu Lan, former commander of the Military Region II, was named director of the armed forces' inspectorate.

Chau convicted, then cleared. Tran Ngoc Chau, a member of the South Vietnamese House of Representatives, was convicted by a five-man military court in

Saigon Feb. 25 and given a 20-year sentence at hard labor on charges of dealing with the Communists. A second House member, Hoang Ho, convicted at the same time on similar charges, was given a death sentence. After months of appeals, during which Chau was retried, reconvicted and resentenced, the Supreme Court finally annulled his sentence.

Both defendants were tried in absentia. Ho was believed to have fled the country and Chau refused to attend the trial, charging that President Nguyen Van Thieu had acted unconstitutionally in pressuring the House to lift his immunity against prosecution. The government had succeeded in obtaining by Feb. 1 102 of the House's 135 members to sign a petition authorizing Thieu to prosecute the two deputies. That figure met the constititional requirement of three-fourths House membership approval of such action.

Chau was arrested Feb. 26 in the National Assembly where he had been staging a protest sit-in since Feb. 23. His seizure provoked a wild melee. Minutes before his seizure, police had pushed and dragged about 50 newsmen from the room in which Chau had sought refuge.

Sixteen members of the House issued a statement condemning Chau's arrest as an illegal oppressive measure by the government.

Chau's imprisonment also was assailed in Washington Feb. 26 by Sen. J. W. Fulbright (D, Ark.,) chairman of the Foreign Relations Committee. He said that "the only reason for his arrest is that he's a possible rival to the present government of South Vietnam and that his policies might help promote a negotiated settlement of the war, which is against the policy" of President Thieu's regime.

Chau had been charged with pro-Communist activity in meetings with his brother, Tran Ngoc Hien, who had been sentenced to life in prison in July 1969 as a North Vietnamese intelligence agent. According to Chau's accounts, he had met with his brother eight times between 1965 and 1969 in an effort to get him to defect from the Communist side and to discuss the possibility of peace negotiations between Saigon and Hanoi. These contacts had been broken off by

Hien's arrest in April 1969. Chau claimed that these secret talks with his brother had been sanctioned by at least three U.S. officials in Saigon. He identified them as John Vann, now in charge of pacification in the Mekong Delta, and two CIA agents—Stuart Methune and Thomas Donohue. Chau complained that after Thieu had filed charges against him in 1969, U.S. Ambassador Ellsworth Bunker had "forbidden them to have anything to do with me."

Chau appealed his 20-year sentence and the government agreed Feb. 27 to grant him another trial.

A five-man military tribunal in Saigon March 5 convicted Chau for the second time on charges of having been in contact with the Communists. He was given a 10-year prison term, a reduction of 10 years from the previous 20-year sentence.

Chau again did not deny the charges that he had been in contact with his brother, Hien, on eight occasions between 1965 and 1969. Another brother, Tran Chau Khang, had acted as go-between. Both Khang and Hien had been jailed by Saigon. Chau said the most valuable information he had obtained from Hien was about a Communist plan to launch an offensive in South Vietnam late in 1967 or early in 1968 and that he had transmitted this intelligence to Ambassador Ellsworth Bunker and other U.S. officials in August 1967. The government prosecutor criticized Chau for having "persisted in not informing the Vietnamese leaders" about this "even after the Americans, who had their own position, chose not to believe Chau's expose."

Cao Van Tuong, a government liaison minister with the National Assembly, said March 6 that Chau could have avoided trial if the U.S. embassy in Saigon had confirmed publicly that he had worked with the U.S. Central Intelligence Agency. "Had we heard from these authorities" at the embassy, "then we might have adjusted or taken action accordingly," Tuong said. Bunker was reported to have urged Saigon privately not to prosecute Chau.

The South Vietnamese Supreme Court ruled May 5 that Chau's two trials were illegal. The court ruled that the military tribunal that had tried him operated unconstitutionally. The court did not actually overturn Chau's conviction, but its decision paved the way for an appeal of his 10-year sentence. The court held that the government had no legal right to bring Chau to trial without the required approval of three-fourths of the House of Representatives. A special committee of the Senate had concluded after a 10-day study March 23 that Chau should have been tried by a civilian court. The committee's report, adopted by Senate acclamation, was termed only an "observation" and had no force of law.

The Supreme Court Oct. 30 annulled Chau's 10-year sentence, although President Thieu had previously insisted that releasing Chau would be yielding to the Communists.

Land reform. Pres. Thieu signed a land reform bill March 26 aimed at giving every peasant the land he farmed. Under the program, the government would buy up more than two million acres and distribute it free to the one million families who had been working the land as tenant farmers for absentee landlords. The landlords would be given a 20% cash payment for their farms with the remainder to be paid in bonds redeemable over an eight-year period. The program was expected to cost $470 million over the next 11 years. The U.S. was to provide at least $10 million.

The land reform bill had been approved by the South Vietnamese House of Representatives Sept. 9, 1969 and by the Senate March 9.

Saigon newspaper seized. The March 12 issue of the Saigon newspaper Tin Sang (Morning News) was seized by South Vietnamese authorities that day because of an editorial and a news article critical of the government. The newspaper was permitted to resume publication the following day.

The editorial indirectly compared President Nguyen Van Thieu to the late dictator Ngo Dinh Diem. It accused the government of corruption and suppression and criticized its economic policy and recent imposition of austerity taxes.

Tin Sang had been shut down in February for criticizing the tax program and the use of defoliants in South Vietnam.

University strike. About 60,000 students at four South Vietnamese universities launched a boycott of classes April 5 to protest against the government's alleged suppression of civil rights by arresting student leaders and not bringing them to trial. The schools affected were Saigon University, a Buddhist college, and the universities in Hué, Cantho and Vanhanh.

In announcing the walkout April 3, a student spokesman in Saigon said the boycott would continue until the government brought the defendants to trial or released them. The students also demanded a halt to government violation of university autonomy.

The immediate cause of the strike was the arrest March 10 of Huynh Tan Mam, acting chairman of Saigon University's Student Union. He was accused of being a Communist and a Viet Cong agent. A leader of the Saigon University protest movement, Doan Van Toai, said April 6 that Mam was the 18th student leader arrested since 1967 and detained without trial.

Twelve Saigon University students had been arrested March 30 when they attempted to stage a hunger strike near the National Assembly to protest the arrest of another student. Their seizure brought to at least 40 the number of students arrested in the previous three weeks.

Saigon police April 5 occupied all branches of the university to prevent a mass protest meeting and a march on President Nguyen Van Thieu's palace. The police April 6 sealed off the offices of the student "struggle committee" which was directing the strike.

The protests were followed by a Saigon military court trial April 20 of Mam and 20 other students. The tribunal, however, granted a defense appeal to adjourn the proceedings pending a Supreme Court ruling on the court's constitutionality. Defense lawyers had argued that the military tribunal had no jurisdiction in the case and that the defendants had been beaten and tortured by the police.

Ten of the students, charged with "activities detrimental to the national security," were freed temporarily, the 11 others were sent back to prison.

The Supreme Court ruled April 29 that the military court trial April 20 of 21 students on charges of pro-Communist activity was unconstitutional because some of the defendants had been beaten and tortured to obtain confessions. The high court, however, did not pass on a defense request for a ruling on the constitutionality of the military court itself. The trial of the students had been adjourned the same day to permit the Supreme Court to rule on the defense appeal.

Saigon schools closed after riots. Widespread antigovernment riots and demonstrations by students and Buddhists, some of which were connected with the Cambodian crisis, prompted the government to close all schools and colleges in Saigon May 6 under a decree issued by President Nguyen Van Thieu. The city was placed under a stricter curfew, extending from 11 p.m. to 5:30 a.m.

The worst rioting occurred May 5. Government troops fired on about 600 students, monks and nuns who had been occupying Saigon's national pagoda since May 3. Government sources said two monks were killed in the clash. The Buddhists claimed 10 of their followers were slain. In another incident the same day, police, using tear gas, ejected about 100 students from the Cambodian embassy, which they had been occupying since April 24 to protest the alleged persecution of Vietnamese nationals in Cambodia.

Saigon police had used tear gas May 2 to disperse 300 students in front of the National Assembly, where they were protesting the treatment of Vietnamese civilians in Cambodia and the supplying of South Vietnamese arms to the Pnompenh government.

Veterans protest. Saigon police clashed April 5–7 with hundreds of disabled South Vietnamese war veterans demonstrating for increased welfare benefits, medical care and housing. The demonstrations were held near the presidential palace and the National Assembly. The former soldiers battled the police with stones, bottles and clubs. Police used tear gas to break up one of the demonstrations April 7 and later prevented a march on the assembly.

Veterans Affairs Minister Pham Van Dong April 6 presented proposals for a bill to be submitted to the National Assembly to improve veterans' benefits.

Anti-war rallies in Saigon. Buddhists and students held demonstrations in Saigon May 28–June 15 protesting the war and alleged corruption of and repression by the South Vietnamese government of President Nguyen Van Thieu.

About 600 hundred Buddhist monks and nuns of the militant An Quang faction staged a hunger strike May 31–June 2 at the An Quang pagoda. About 2,000 Buddhist monks and laymen conducted a similar fast in other parts of the country.

Several thousand students carried out an anti-government protest May 29 at the state funeral of former Chief of State Phan Khac Suu [see p. 412G3]. The police used tear gas to disperse students who marched toward the presidential palace after the funeral. Six students were arrested when they threw rocks at police.

A Buddhist nun burned herself to death June 4 in protest against the war and the government. The incident occurred at Phanrang, about 165 miles northeast of Saigon. A Buddhist monk immolated himself by fire for the same reason in Saigon June 11. At the monk's funeral June 14, about 100 Buddhist women and youths carried signs reading "Americans go home."

Students demonstrated briefly June 13 near the U.S. embassy and in front of the U.S. Armed Forces' television station.

Student protest action in Saigon June 15 took on a strong anti-American tone during a demonstration denouncing the Thieu government. A U.S. military police jeep was set afire with gasoline, and its occupant, an American sergeant, was beaten as he fled the burning vehicle. About 300 high school and university students clashed with police as more than 60 of the city's 124 unions began a 24-hour strike. The walkout was in support of 283 government employes dismissed for lack of work.

Saigon police July 11 used tear gas to break up a peace march of about 1,000 South Vietnamese college and high school students and a small group of visiting American pacifists.

The Vietnamese demonstrators were marching to the National Palace to deliver a statement demanding an end to the war and the Americans were enroute to the U.S. embassy to submit a similar petition. Both groups joined for part of the way and police disrupted the procession. About 30 students and three American correspondents, wearing black peace armbands, were arrested. All were later released. The newsmen included John Steinbeck IV, son of the late author and part-time correspondent for CBS and the Dispatch News Agency.

The American peace delegation, organized by an American Quaker group, the Fellowship of Reconciliation, had come to Saigon to meet with Vietnamese opposition leaders.

President Nguyen Van Thieu warned July 15 that he would "beat to death" any South Vietnamese who called for "immediate peace, in surrendering to the Communists." Denouncing peace demonstrations and other recent anti-government manifestations, Thieu said: "We cannot have peace . . . at any price. There must be peace with conditions and that peace will come with the strength of our army."

Saigon University students July 17 held a conference demanding an end to the school's military training program. Police broke into a university building and seized three organizers of the protest conference. The students fought police with sticks, stones and gasoline bombs and recaptured their three leaders.

Con Son prison scandal. An American who inspected a South Vietnamese prison July 2 with two U.S. congressmen charged that civilians imprisoned there were subjected to inhuman conditions and brutality.

The accusation was made July 6 by David Luce of the Division of Interchurch Aid of the World Council of Churches following a tour of the Con Son Correction Center, on Con Son Island, 60 miles off the South Vietnamese coast and 140 miles south of Saigon. Luce's findings were confirmed by Rep. Augustus F. Hawkins (D, Calif.) and Rep. William R. Anderson (D, Tenn.), members of a House panel on Southeast Asia.

Luce said 500 of the 9,000 prisoners at Con Son were confined in small stone compartments, known to the Vietnamese as "tiger cages," and that many of them were unable to stand. The cages measured 5 feet by 9 feet and had bars on the top. The prisoners were suffering from malnutrition, physical abuse and filthy conditions, Luce said.

A spokesman for the U.S. embassy in Saigon July 7 denied American responsibility for conditions at the prison. Roy W. Johnson said the U.S. mission was "aware of the shortcomings of the corrections program in Vietnam. Our advisory efforts and assistance are designed to help the Vietnamese government . . . to improve their system," but the South Vietnamese Interior Ministry was solely responsible for the matter.

The South Vietnamese Information Ministry July 9 confirmed the existence of the cages, but defended their use. The ministry said that 400 inmates were confined to them temporarily as a disciplinary measure for rebelling against prison rules. The ministry statement said they were "neither political prisoners nor prisoners of war but Communist criminals."

The Saigon government began an inquiry of conditions at the prison July 10. Premier Tran Thien Khiem said, "If as a result of the investigation, reports are accurate of the mistreatment of prisoners, then the government will take steps to redress the situation and order abolition of the tiger cages."

The government disclosed July 14 that more than 500 prisoners had been flown from Con Son to Saigon and were awaiting release. Government sources said their return was not related to the controversy over conditions at the prison. The prisoners were flown out in American planes. U.S. officials said South Vietnamese authorities had requested the American airlift July 7 to remove the 500 prisoners who were said to have completed their jail terms. American assistance was asked because South Vietnamese ships were unavailable due to Cambodian operations, Saigon officials said.

Red Cross observers had made two visits to the Con Son prison (the latest in February), but an official of the organization said in Geneva July 14 that, in accordance with its standard practice, the findings would not be made public. However, sources in Geneva disclosed July 14 that the Red Cross inspectors had found that conditions at Con Son were "not too bad" and that most of the inmates were listed as common criminals. Of the 9,000 prisoners, 50 were classified as prisoners of war, the sources said.

The treatment of prisoners at Con Son was reported and condemned in Washington July 7 by Reps. Hawkins and Anderson. They had toured Con Son July 2 as members of a 12-man special panel on a fact-finding tour of the war area for the House. The committee, headed by Rep. G. V. Montgomery (D, Miss.), had arrived in Saigon June 21, had split into groups to visit Cambodia, Laos and South Vietnam, and returned to Washington July 4.

Montgomery filed with the House July 6 a "consensus" report that supported the U.S. military intervention in Cambodia as a success, recommended that the U.S. troop withdrawal from Vietnam should be continued "at least as fast as now scheduled" or at a faster rate, and cited the South Vietnamese economy as the country's major problem. The report contained only a brief paragraph on the Con Son prison stating that "some conditions which required remedial" action had been observed and assurances of an investigation had been obtained.

Hawkins and Anderson gave Washington reporters details July 6 of their visit to Con Son. Anderson called use of the "tiger cages" an "atrocious way to treat human beings" and Hawkins said Con Son had "the worst" prison conditions he had ever seen. They reported that some of the caged prisoners had lost the use of their legs.

A staff member of the special House panel, Thomas R. Harkin, 30, who accompanied the two representatives to Con Son, charged July 7 that the "consensus" report was a "whitewash" and that exclusion of a detailed report on Con Son constituted "an attempt by the majority of the committee to suppress the most significant finding of the entire trip."

State Department spokesman Carl E. Bartch expressed July 8 the concern of the U.S. government about the Con Son situation and said the Saigon government was investigating it.

Hawkins and Anderson offered July 13 a resolution calling on Congress to "condemn the cruel and inhumane treatment" of political prisoners in South Vietnam and urged President Nixon to insist upon remedial action. The House Foreign Operations and Government Information Subcommittee, headed by Rep. John E. Moss (D, Calif.), called July 13 for a U.S. investigation of conditions at Con Son and other POW and military prisons in South Vietnam. Moss urged "that we become deeply and promptly involved" in the situation. The Hawkins-Anderson resolution was introduced in the Senate July 14 by Sen. Edmund S. Muskie (D, Me.) and nine other co-sponsors. The Moss panel also announced plans July 14 for hearings on the subject.

Brutal treatment of civilian prisoners at another South Vietnamese jail was alleged at a Congressional hearing in Washington July 17. Dr. Marjorie Nelson told a subcommittee of the House Committee on Government Operations of prisoners being beaten and tortured at the Province Interrogation Center in Quangngai. The center had shifted from American to South Vietnamese control. It was not clear whether Americans were in charge when the alleged torture occurred, but Dr. Nelson said she was certain Americans were aware of what was going on.

Dr. Nelson had treated prisoners at the center from September 1968 to October 1969 while serving with the American Friends Service Committee. She said the structure was built to house 500 prisoners but contained up to 1,300 when she was there. Dr. Nelson said South Vietnamese authorities had informed her that more than 80% of the inmates were political prisoners. After speaking with the prisoners, she concluded that their 'political crimes' often consisted of having "improper or incomplete papers" and other relatively minor infractions.

Con Son prison reform. The South Vietnamese government announced July 21 that it had suspended the use of the controversial "tiger cages" at its prison on Con Son island.

A communiqué based on a government inspection of the jail the previous week said the quarters would be "immediately overhauled to provide adequate hygienic facilities." About 500 prisoners in the tiger cages had been removed to regular cells July 21 while repairs were being made, a government spokesman said.

The communiqué reiterated Saigon's contention that the separate cells had been used "for temporary incarceration of undisciplined and obstinate prisoners who had created disturbances." The statement noted that "prison camps in advanced countries also are provided with such special disciplinary quarters."

International Red Cross representatives charged in a report made public July 24 that seven of 24 North Vietnamese soldiers imprisoned at Con Son had been mistreated in violation of the Geneva Convention on treatment of prisoners of war. The North Vietnamese, originally in prisoner-of-war camps, had been transferred to Con Son after being found guilty of committing murder after their capture. The Red Cross officials, who had visited the prison Feb. 10–12, said the seven Communist captives were confined to their cells all day, kept in chains for 13 hours a day and were not given enough fresh food or drinking water.

A copy of the Red Cross report was given to the U.S. government.

Senate elections held. Candidates of the anti-government An Quang Buddhist faction won 10 of the 30 contested seats in South Vietnam's 60-seat Senate in elections held Aug. 30. It was the first time the militant An Quang had filed a slate of explicitly Buddhist candidates.

According to final results announced Sept. 14, the Buddhists' Lotus Flower slate received 1,149,597 votes. The remaining 20 seats were evenly divided between the two Roman Catholic slates— the pro-government Sun, which polled 1,106,288 votes, and the independent Lily, which received 882,274 votes.

Piaster devalued. A devaluation of the South Vietnamese piaster was announced by the Saigon government Oct. 3. The new exchange rate of the piaster was cut from the current 118 to the dollar to 275 for foreign individuals. Governments, including the U.S., would still be required to exchange piasters at the less favorable 118 rate. South Vietnamese officials said the new rate was aimed at encouraging foreign investment and exports and curbing the black markets.

The devaluation, long urged by Washington, had been approved by the South Vietnamese Senate Sept. 18 by a 41–1 vote. The Senate, however, rejected a request by President Nguyen Van Thieu for emergency economic powers, including the right to impose tariffs by executive decree. Emergency powers had been approved by the House of Representatives June 23 by 67–25 vote but the Senate's action reversed its decision.

Ky visits U.S. South Vietnamese President Nguyen Cao Ky paid an unofficial 2½-week visit to the U.S. in November and December. Ky originally had been scheduled to visit the U.S. in October to address a right-wing rally in Washington. But he postponed the trip on the advice of Washington officials who feared that his appearance in the U.S. before the American elections would embarrass the Nixon Administration.

Ky arrived in New York Nov. 15. His first stop was at the Military Academy at West Point, N.Y. Nov. 16. Speaking to 1,000 senior cadets and officers, Ky warned that Cambodia would fall to the Communists "within 24 hours" if South Vietnamese forces operating in that country withdrew. He said the U.S. and South Vietnamese military intervention in Cambodia in May was "the turning point of the war," forcing the Communists to resort to low-level guerrilla tactics in South Vietnam." "I don't want to claim victory while the fighting is still under way, but I think I can say the central effort of the enemy has been defeated," Ky said.

Ky spoke with President Nixon at the White House Nov. 24. After the meeting, Ky said he had told the President of the seriousness of the economic problems facing South Vietnam as a result of the reduction of the American military force there and of the rising cost of equipping and maintaining South Vietnam's million-man army.

Addressing a gathering at the National Press Club in Washington later Nov. 24, Ky described himself as a misunderstood moderate, "an ex-hawk turned dove," whose principal purpose was to end the fighting in his country. Ky denied U.S. press descriptions of him as a "militarist, a rightist, an American puppet and the spearhead of American imperialism."

Among the other highlights of Ky's visit:

Ky Nov. 25 attended a closed reception given him by the Senate Foreign Relations Committee, whose members were often critical of his views. Committee Chairman J. W. Fulbright (D, Ark.) said Ky had agreed with his view that all foreigners should withdraw from Vietnam and the rest of Asia at the earliest possible date. Another committee member, Sen. George Aiken (R, Vt.) said after meeting Ky: "We developed quite a lot of mutual understanding. We are not as far apart as some would have it."

Ky flew to Texas Nov. 28 and met with former President Lyndon B. Johnson at the LBJ Ranch.

Ky addressed the Commonwealth Club in San Francisco Dec. 1 while 2,700 anti-war demonstrators gathered to protest his presence. Part of the crowd broke off and clashed with police. The demonstrators, hurling stones and fruit, were dispersed by police tear gas. Ten were arrested.

In his speech to the Commonwealth Club, Ky appealed to Americans to "understand" that "aggression cannot succeed." Ky said he did not come to the U.S. "to convince the United States to maintain troops in Vietnam" but to support "the aspirations of the 17 million people of Vietnam."

A Saigon newspaper, the English language Vietnam Guardian, asserted that the main purpose of Ky's visit to the U.S. was to build himself up as a challenger to President Nguyen Van Thieu in the 1971 presidential elections. The Guardian was a supporter of Duong Van Minh, an opponent of Thieu and a possible candidate in the elections.

A pro-Ky newspaper, Lap Truong, said Ky had been praised by the doves of the U.S. Senate Foreign Relations Committee because he convinced them that he was "determined to fight the Communist aggressors, but is also determined in his search for peace."

Viet refugee data criticized. A U.S. General Accounting Office report Dec. 5 disputed official statistics on the war refugee relief program in South Vietnam. The report, prepared for the Senate Subcommittee on Refugees and Escapees, headed by Sen. Edward M. Kennedy (D, Mass.), labeled as "misleading" official data issued in 1969 by the Nixon Administration and the Saigon government that there had been a "dramatic" reduction in the number of refugees—a decrease from 1.4 million in February 1969 to 268,000 by December 1969.

In addition to the official refugee number, the GAO said, there were 572,000 orphans, war widows and disabled persons "in need of assistance."

The GAO's assessment of the 1970 refugee relief and social relief programs in Vietnam was that "they have not indicated encouraging results with respect to war victims and community developments." The programs, currently dealing with some 600,000 persons, handled feeding, resettlement, payment of allowances and construction of schools.

In releasing the report, Kennedy said the conclusions reflected a "warped sense of reality and progress which pervades so much of our country's activities throughout Indochina."

Kennedy released a GAO report to his panel Dec. 12 citing shortages of skilled medical help, deficient facilities and a lack of reliable statistics concerning the South Vietnamese civilian health and war-related casualty programs. It said official figures on civilian casualties, a total of 245,700 since 1967, reflected only admissions to South Vietnamese Health Ministry and U.S. military hospitals and omitted any helped elsewhere or dead of wounds before treatment. The subcommittee estimated the total of civilian casualties since 1965 at more than a million, including at least 300,000 dead.

Kennedy said the data made "a mockery of our government's claim about conditions among Vietnamese civilians, and about the progress of the Saigon government" in dealing with the problem.

Index

Note: This index follows the Western usage in regard to most Vietnamese names. A Vietnamese individual, therefore, would be listed not under his family name but under the last section of his full name. *E.g.*, Mrs. Nguyen Thi Binh would be indexed thus: BINH, Mrs. Nguyen Thi (not NGUYEN Thi Binh, Mrs.). Exceptions are usually the cases of monks or others (*e.g.*, Ho Chi Minh) who use adopted names; such persons are generally listed under the first sections of their names (HO Chi Minh, not MINH, Ho Chi).

A

ABRAM, Morris B.—145
ABRAMS, Gen. Creighton W.—64, 73, 93, 113
ACADEMIC & Professional Alliance for a Responsible Congress—139–40, 146
ADDERLEY, Sgt. 1. C. Tyrone J.—102
AERIAL Warfare: Defoliation—90. Helicopter use—15–8, 36, 38, 48, 53, 93–5. Reconnaissance flights—20, 99, 103–6. South Vietnamese bombing raids: Cambodia—36, 51, 112, 118. U.S. bombing raids—19, 20–2, 87, 92; U.S. bombing raids: Cambodia & border—2, 17, 19, 33, 35–6, 45, 48, 67, 80–1, 93, 112–3, 115, 118; Ho Chi Minh Trail—99; Laos & border—17, 19, 21–2, 29, 88–91, 93, 97; North Vietnam—20, 88, 99–100, 103–5
AGENCE France-Presse—100
AGENCY for International Development (AID)—28, 89
AGNEW, Judge E. Harry—160
AGNEW, Spiro T.—105. Antiwar protesters—7, 136, 142–3, 154. Asian tour—114–5. Cambodia—62, 114–5. Laos—24, 27. South Vietnam tour—6. War critics—149–52
AICHI, Kiichi—50
AIKEN, Sen. George D. (R., Vt.)—40, 47, 49–50, 77, 100–1, 184
AIR Force, U.S.—22, 34, 90–1, 93, 99. Casualties—88, 103
AIR-America (Thailand-based airline)—29
AIRBASES—See names
ALABAMA, University of
ALAMEDA (Calif.) Naval Air Station—160
ALBANIA—65
ALLEN, Sen. James B. (R., Ala.)—77
ALLEN Jr., Dr. James E.—146–7
ALLOTT, Sen. Gordon (R., Colo.)—77, 155

AMALGAMATED Clothing Workers of America (AFL-CIO)—147
AMALGAMATED Meat Cutters & Butcher Workmen (AFL-CIO)—148
AMBORT, 1st Lt. Louis R.—174
AMERICAN Civil Liberties Union (ACLU)—148, 160
AMERICAN Federation of Labor & Congress of Industrial Organizations (AFL-CIO)—59. See also MEANY, George; also affiliated unions
AMERICAN Federation of State, County & Municipal Employes (AFL-CIO)—143
AMERICAN Friends (Quakers) Service Committee—163, 182
AMERICAN Legion—144
AMERICAN Nazi Party—58
AMERICAN Newspaper Guild—149
AMERICAN Society of International Law—13
AMERICAN University, Wash.—156
AMHERST College, Mass.—139
AM Leang, Cambodia—78
AM Rong, Maj.—69–70, 81, 113
ANDERSON, Sen. Clinton P. (D., N.M.)—77
ANDERSON, Rep. William R. (D., Tenn.)—181–2
ANGKOR Wat, Cambodia—111, 115
ANGTASSOM, Cambodia—43
ANHOA, South Vietnam: U.S. airbase—93
ANKGEN, Cambodia: Government post—37
ANNAMESE (ethnic group)—42–3
ANPHU, South Vietnam—35
AN Quang (Buddhist group)—168, 180, 183
ANTHANH, South Vietnam—19
AQUINO Jr., Sen. Benigno—47
AREY Ksach, Cambodia—114
ARKANSAS—149

ARMED Forces Vietnam Network (AFVN) (radio & TV network)—161
ARMY, U.S.: Cambodia—52-3, 63, 67-8, 72, 77-80, 83. Casualties—1, 15-20, 25-6, 29, 48, 52-3, 63, 68, 78, 80, 82, 87, 90-1, 93-7, 108, 163. Draft resistance—See under DISSENT. U.S. War crimes trials—168-75. Withdrawals & strength—63, 68, 80, 82, 94 First Cavalry Division (Airmobile)—53, 82, 91. 3d Infantry—168. 6th Battalion—170. 7th Regiment—15. 9th Infantry Division—174. 11th Armored Cavalry Regiment—52. 11th Infantry Brigade—169-71. 20th Infantry Division—168. 25th Infantry Division—53. 52d Military Intelligence Detachment—170. 101st Airborne Division—91, 108. 123d Aviation Battalion—170. 173d Airborne Brigade—16. 196th Infantry Brigade—18. Special Forces—18-9, 67, 90, 168-70
ASHAU Valley, South Vietnam—16
ASSOCIATED Press—42
ASSOCIATION of Southeast Asian Nations (ASEAN)—13
ATTOPEU, Laos—88, 92
AUSTRALIA—6, 9, 19, 52, 69, 84

B

BACHUC, South Vietnam—93
BAKER Jr., Sen. Howard H. (R., Tenn.)—77, 101
BAKER, Scott—172
BALL, George W.—63
BAN Hatsaikhoune, Laos—90
BANKARAI Pass, North Vietnam—100
BARBER, James D.—149
BARKER Jr., Lt. Col. Frank A.—170
BARTCH, Carl E.—67, 182
BATANGAN Peninsula, South Vietnam: Refugee village—15-6
BATOR, Francis—54
BAYH, Sen. Birch (D., Ind.)—77, 126
BEGIN, Rev. Robert—157
BELL, Steve—41
BELLMON, Sen. Henry (R., Okla.)—77
BENJOYA, Mitchell—158
BENNETT, Rev. Dr. John C.—54
BENNETT, Sen. Wallace F. (R., Utah)—77
BERNSTEIN, Lester—64
BERRIGAN, Rev. Daniel—156
BERRIGAN, Rev. Philip—156
BEXLEY Hall Theological Seminary, N.Y.—146
BIBLE, Sen. Alan (D., Nev.)—77, 126
BINDINH Province, South Vietnam—16, 94
BINH, Mrs. Nguyen Thi—12, 14, 175. Peace efforts & conditions—124, 131
BINHLONG Province, South Vietnam—48
BLACK, Justice Hugo L.—157
BLACK Panthers—137
BLATCHFORD, Joseph H.—147
BOATMAN, Capt. Kenneth W.—170
BOGGS, Sen. F. Caleb (R., Del.)—77
BO Keo, Cambodia—64, 80-1

BOLAND, Rep. Edward P. (D., Mass.)—55
BOLOVENS Plateau, Laos—89
BOND, Gen. William R.—18
BOYD, Pfc. Thomas R.—173-4
BRANDEIS University, Mass.—137-8, 140, 144
BRAY, Rep. William G. (R., Ind.)—73
BRENNAN Jr., Justice William J.—157
BREVET, Cambodia—39
BREWSTER Jr., Kingman—137, 140
BRICKNER, Rabbi Balfour—54
BROOKE, Sen. Edward W. (R., Mass.)—8-9, 49, 58, 77
BROWN Jr., Rep. George E. (D., Calif.)—145
BROWN, Ossie B.—171
BROWN, Sam—54
BRUCE, David K. E.—104, 130. Paris talks—125, 127-8, 132-3. POWs—166
BUDDHISTS—168, 179-80, 183
BUILDING & Construction Trades Council of Greater New York—143
BUNDY, McGeorge—63
BUNKER, Ellsworth—6, 63, 66, 73, 178
BURDICK, Sen. Quentin N. (D., N.D.)—77
BURGER, Chief Justice Warren E.—147, 157
BUSH Jr., Capt. Joseph K.—26
BYRD, Sen. Robert C. (D., W. Va.)—74-5, 77

C

CALHOUN, Maj. Charles C.—170
CALIFORNIA—138-9, 144, 158
CALIFORNIA, University of—138-41, 148, 153
CALLEY Jr., 1st Lt. William L.—2, 169, 171-3
CAMBODIA: Arrests—38. Allied military activity—31, 35-6, 38-9, 41, 45-8, 51-3, 64, 66-8, 78-80, 82; border clashes—2, 18-9, 33; U.S. troop withdrawals—2, 63, 68, 80, 82-3. Civilian casualties—44, 67, 79; evacuation—39. Communist activity—14, 35-9, 41, 43-4, 53, 64, 67-8, 78-80, 111-2, 114-8. Coup d'etat—33. Demonstrations—35, 37-8. Government forces: casualties—33, 38-9, 80, 117; military activity—38-9, 41, 43-4, 48, 52, 64, 67-8, 78-81, 111-2, 114-8. Foreign relations & aid—40, 67, 69-71, 81; U.S.—38, 40-1, 71, 81, 84, 113-4, 119-20. Naval blockade—51-3. Republic formed—116. Sihanouk—See under 'S.' UN appeals—37-8, 40. Vietnamese civilians: casualties—41-3; evacuation—43, 70, 81
CAMBODIAN People's Movement of United Resistance—65
CANADA—52
CANNON, Sen. Howard W. (D., Nev.)—73, 77
CANTERBURY, Brig. Gen. Robert—136
CANTHO, South Vietnam—179
CAPRON, William—54
CARADON, Lord—51
CARNEGIE Commission on Higher Education—155
CASE, Sen. Clifford P. (R., N.J.)—77

CASEY, Maj. Gen. George W.—91
CASUALTIES—See under specific country or branch of service
CATHOLICS, Roman—156-8, 160-1, 183
CEASEFIRES—See under PEACE Efforts
CENTRAL Intelligence Agency (CIA), U.S.—24, 28-9, 89, 178
CENTRAL Office for South Vietnam (COSVN) (Communist mobile base)—48, 53, 63-4, 68
CERF, Christopher—149
CEYLON—13
CHAMBAK, Cambodia—118
CHAMBERLAIN, Owen—148
CHARLOTTESVILLE Pledge (draft resistance statement)—156
CHAT, Lt. Col. Truong Dinh—36
CHAU, Tran Ngoc—177-9
CHAUDOC Province, South Vietnam—35-6, 54, 68, 93
CHAUTHUAN, South Vietnam—15-6
CHEEK, Dr. James E.—150-1
CHENG Heng—31-3, 112, 114
CHHUON, Lt. Col. Koh—118
CHICAGO, University of—141
CHINA (Nationalist), Republic of—50
CHINA (Communist), People's Republic of—44, 84, 122. Cambodia—50, 64-5
CHIPHOU, Cambodia—39
CHOU En-lai—44
CHULAI, South Vietnam—96
CHUP, Cambodia—38, 67-8
CHURCH, Sen. Frank (D., Ida.)—40, 61, 74, 77, 113, 129
CHURCH of the Brethren—158
CLARK, Ramsey—145
CLIFFORD, Clark M.—62, 107-8, 146, 149
COAST Guard, U.S.—94
COLGATE University—140
COLLEGE Press Service—137
COLUMBIA, District of—See DISTRICT of Columbia
COLUMBIA Broadcasting System (CBS)—181
COLUMBIA Eagle (U.S. freighter)—34
COLUMBIA University—137, 139
COMMUNIST Party of the U.S.A.—153
CONCERNED Officers Movement—160
CONGRESS, U.S.—See under UNITED States
CONGTHANH, South Vietnam—96
CONNOR, John T.—54-5
CON Son Correction Center, South Vietnam—181-3
CONTI, Dennis I.—171-3
COOK, Sen. Marlow W. (R., Ky.)—49, 77
COOPER, Sen. John Sherman (R., Ky.)—23-4, 40, 49, 61, 77, 101, 129, 152
COOPER-Church Amendment—61-2, 74-7, 113, 119
CORNELL University—137-8
CORRIGAN, Mrs. (no first name given)—146
CORRIGAN, Right Rev. Daniel—146
CORSO, Sylvester T. Del—135, 137
COTTON, Sen. Norris (R., N.H.)—49, 75, 77

CRANSTON, Sen. Alan (D., Calif.)—25, 77
CRANSTON, William W.—153
CROWTHER, Right Rev. Edward—146
CUBA—65
CULLEN, Michael D.—156
CURTIS, Sen. Carl T. (R., Neb.)—77
CUSHING, Richard Cardinal—160-1
CZAPLYSKI Jr., Pvt. Lawrence Joseph—159

D

DAKRONG Valley, South Vietnam—87
DAKSEANG, South Vietnam: Special Forces Camp—18-9
DAN, Nguyen Trieu—14
DAN, Pham Quang—70
DANANG, South Vietnam—173-4
DANH, Col. Lo Cong—88
DANIEL 3d, Capt. Aubrey M.—171-2
DARST, David—156
DAVISON, Lt. Gen. Michael S.—64
DEFENSE, Department of (U.S.)—See under UNITED States
DEFOLIATION—90, 152-3
De HAAN, Dale S.—175
Del CORSO, Sylvester T.—135, 137
DELLINGER, David—164
DEMOCRATIC Party, U.S.—3-4, 59. Policy Council—3, 5
DENVER, University of—144
DEUANE, Col.—22
DEVERS, Capt. David R.—163
DIEM, Ngo Dinh—179
DILLARD, Maj. Gen. John A. B.—87
DISSENT, U.S.
    Arrests & convictions—54, 58, 138-9, 145-6, 156-7, 159
    Campus unrest & developments—138-9, 143-5; Administration's reaction—136-7, 140-2, 150-1; investigations—136-7, 153-5; Kent State incident—135-7; lobbying efforts—139-40; university strikes—137-9, 144-5
    Congress—23-5, 40, 48-50, 55, 61-3, 148; bombing resumption—100-2; Cambodia—112-3; Cooper-Church amendment—61-2, 74-7; Tonkin resolution—55, 75-7
    Demonstrations: antiwar—55, 137-8, 155, 160, 184 (see also specific cities); war supporters—143-4, 149; worldwide protests—50-1
    Desertions—159; draft resistance (conscientious objector)—155-8, 160-1; prosecutions—158-9
    Government protesters—57, 146-7
    Labor unions—147-8
    Lobby & political action—139-40, 145-6, 149
    Military—159-60; censorship—161
    Nobel laureates—148
    Religious groups—146, 156-8, 183
DISTRICT of Columbia (Washington)—139, 160. Demonstrations—54, 58-9, 143-4, 146, 150

DISPATCH News Agency—181
DO Cao Tri, Lt. Gen.—116
DOCKING, Gov. Robert—144
DOHERTY, Spec. 4 William F.—169
DOLE, Sen. Robert J. (R., Kan.)—74-5, 77, 126
DOMINICK, Sen. Peter H. (R., Colo.)—49, 77, 101
DON, Tran Van—168
DONG, Pham Van—44, 65, 164, 167, 180
DONOHUE, Thomas—178
DONPHUC, South Vietnam—112
DOUGHERTY, Michael—157
DOUGLAS, John W.—146
DOUGLAS, Justice William O.—157
DOW Chemical Co.—156
DUAN, Le—17
DUCLAP, South Vietnam—67
DUDMAN, Richard—79
DUFFY, 1st Lt. James Brian—174
Du PONT de Nemours & Co., E. I.—148-9
DURSI, Pfc. James—172
DYKE, William—138
DZU, Maj. Gen. Ngo—177

E

EAGLETON, Sen. Thomas F. (D., Mo.)—77
EASTLAND, Sen. James O. (D., Miss.)—77
EBERHARDT, David—156
EHRLICHMAN, John D.—141
ELLENDER, Sen. Allen J. (D., La.)—77
ELLISON, Col. Richard W.—81
EPISCOPAL Peace Fellowship—146
ERVIN Jr., Sen. Sam J. (D., N.C.)—77
ESSLEY, Steve—160

F

FACE the Nation (CBS-TV program)—40, 62, 73, 102, 123, 150, 155
FANNIN, Sen. Paul F. (R., Ariz.)—77
FARRAR, Gov. Frank (R., S.D.)—154
FEDERAL Bureau of Investigation (FBI)—136, 153, 156, 159
FELLOWSHIP of Reconciliation (American Quaker group)—54, 181
FERNANDEZ, Rev. Richard—54
FERNANDEZ, Sosthene—42
FINCH, Robert H.—58, 62, 142, 146
FINDLEY, Rep. Paul (R., Ill.)—55
FIRE Base Barnett—92, 94
FIRE Base O'Reilly—92, 945
FIRE Base Ripcord—91-2
FIRE Base Tun Tavern—88
FISHER, Sen. O. C. (D., Tex.)—73
FISHOOK (Cambodia)—52-3, 115-6, 118. Fishook Operation—45-8
FLORIDA—139
FLORIDA, University of—139
FLORIDA Memorial College—145
FLYNN, Errol—39
FLYNN, Sean—39
FOARD, John—160
FOISIE, Jack—28

FONDA, Jane—160
FONG, Sen. Hiram L. (R., Hawaii)—77
FONT, Lt. Louis Hall—160
FORD Foundation—63
FORREST, 1st Lt. John J.—158
FRANCE—50-2, 165. Peace proposal—11-2, 14
FRANCE Soir (newspaper)—51
FRIDAY, William C.—141
FRIEDHEIM, Jerry—68, 80, 100, 112
FROSCH, Frank—116
FROST, David—142
FULBRIGHT, Sen. J. William (D., Ark.)—98, 149, 151, 166, 178, 184. Cambodia—48-50, 55, 61-3, 71, 75-7. U.S. bombing—101-2, 106

G

GALLAGHER, Raymond—60
GALLUP Poll—59
GANDHI, Indira—51
GAVIN, Lt. Col. David C.—170
GAVIN, Lt. Gen. James M.—63
GEORGE Washington University (Washington, D.C.)—58-9, 139
GEORGIA—149, 159
GEORGIA, University of—139
GERMANY, West—52
GIAP, Vo Nguyen—65, 107
GLASSER, Lt. Gen. Otto J.—90
GLATKOWSKI, Alvin—34
GODLEY, George—23
GOLDBERG, Arthur J.—145
GOLDWATER, Sen. Barry (R., Ariz.)—77, 126, 144
GOODELL, Sen. Charles E. (R., N.Y.)—40, 55, 58, 77
GORE, Sen. Albert (D., Tenn.)—23-4, 49, 63, 119, 148
GORMAN, Patrick E.—148
GOTBAUM, Victor—143
GORTON, John—9, 52
GRAVEL, Sen. Mike (D., Alaska)—77
GREAT Britain—51-2, 84
GREEN, Pfc. Samuel G.—173
GRIFFIN, Sen. Robert P. (R., Mich.)—8, 40, 49, 61, 74, 77
GROMYKO, Andrei A.—122
GUINN Jr., Lt. Col. William D.—170
GULF of Siam—34
GULF of Tonkin Resolution—55, 75-7, 119
GURNEY, Sen. Edward J(ohn) (R., Fla.)—77

H

HABIB, Philip—13-4, 20, 121-2, 125
HAEBERLE, Ronald L.—172
HAIPHONG, North Vietnam—100
HALPERIN, Morton H.—147
HANCOCK (U.S. aircraft carrier)—160
HANGEN, Welles—78
HANH, Col. Vo Huu—177
HANNAH, Dr. John A.—89
HANSON, Sen. Clifford P. (R., Wyo.)—77
HARGIS, Rev. Billy James—155

HARKIN, Thomas R.—182
HARLAN, Justice John M.—157
HARLOW, Bryce N.—61, 73
HARRIMAN, W. Averell—3–6, 59, 66, 129, 149
HARRINGTON, Fred H.—141
HARRIS, Sen. Fred R. (D., Okla.)—11, 49, 77
HART, Gary—145
HART, Mrs. Jane—146
HART, Sen. Philip A. (D., Mich.)—77, 146
HARTKE, Sen. Vance (D., Ind.)—77
HARTMANN, Capt. Vincent M.—174–5
HARVARD University—54, 141
HATAY Province, North Vietnam—100, 104
HATFIELD, Sen. Mark O. (R., Ore.)—34, 55, 77, 101, 129, 151
HATFIELD-McGovern Amendment—151–2
HATINH Province, North Vietnam—20, 100
HAUNGHIA Province, South Vietnam—109
HAVERFORD College, Pa.—139
HAWK, David—54
HAWKINS, Rep. Augustus F. (D., Calif.)—181–2
HEARD, Dr. Alexander—57, 141, 150–1
HELICOPTER Use—15–8, 36, 38, 48, 53, 93–5
HELLER, Walter W.—150
HELMS, Richard—24, 28, 106
HENDERSON, Col. Oran K.—170
HENG, Cheng—31–3, 112, 114
HENKIN, Daniel Z.—47, 102, 105
HERROD, Lance Cpl. Randell D.—173–4
HERSHEY, Lewis B.—157
HESTER, Dr. James M.—137
HICKEL, Walter J.—56, 140
HIEN, Tran Ngoc—178
HIEPDUC, South Vietnam—87
HIN Nil—38
HIRSCHKOP, Philip J.—157
HITCH, Charles J.—141
HO, Hoang—178
HOABINH, North Vietnam—100
HOANG, Brig. Gen. Nguyen Thanh—177
HOC, Tran Khoa—155
HO Chi Minh—87
HO Chi Minh Trail—16, 21–2, 89, 99
HODGES, S. Sgt. Kenneth L.—169, 171
HOGAN, John—156
HOIAN, South Vietnam—87
HOLLAND, Sen. Spessard L. (D., Fla.)—77
HOLLINGS, Sen. Ernest F. (D., S.C.)—77
HOLY Cross Cathedral, Mass.—161
HOLYOAKE, Keith—6
HOOVER, J. Edgar—135–6
HORNER, Pfc. Charles R.—159
HOWARD University—150
HRUSKA, Sen. Roman L. (R., Neb.)—77
HSINHUA (Chinese Communist news agency)—44, 65, 116
HUBBARD, Al—161
HUE, South Vietnam—179
HUE, Col. Tran Van—35
HUGHES, Sen. Harold E. (D., Ia.)—55, 77, 129
HUMAN Sciences Research, Inc.—175

HUNGARY—165
HUNTER, Rev. David R.—54
HUTSON, Pvt. Max D.—169
HUTTO, Sgt. Charles E.—168
HYLAND, Adm. John—34

I

ILLINGWORTH (U.S. Artillery Base)—18
ILLINOIS—139
ILLINOIS State University—144
INDIA—13, 51–2
INDONESIA—40, 50, 69, 89, 122
INOUYE, Sen. Daniel K. (D., Hawaii)—77
INTERNATIONAL Business Machines Corp. (IBM)—148
INTERNATIONAL Control Commission (ICC)—15, 28, 69, 123
INTERNATIONAL Red Cross—165, 181–3
IOWA—139
IOWA, University of—139
ISSUES and Answers (NBC-TV program)—40, 62, 65, 150, 175
IZVESTIA (Soviet government journal)—13

J

JACKSON, Sen. Henry M. (D., Wash.)—77, 101, 108, 126
JACKSON (Miss.) State College—155
JAPAN—13, 50, 52, 69, 77, 122
JAVITS, Sen. Jacob K. (R., N.Y.)—49, 58, 101, 126
JENCKS Act—172
JENMIN Jih Pao (Chinese Communist Party newspaper)—84
JEVNE, Capt. Franz—173
JOHNSON, Capt. Dennis H.—170
JOHNSON, Lyndon B.—59, 184
JOHNSON, Roy W.—181
JOHNSON, Pfc. Timothy P.—159
JORDAN, Sen. B. Everett (D., N.C.)—74, 77

K

KAMPOT, Cambodia—41
KAMPOT Province, Cambodia—37
KANDAL, Cambodia—41
KANE, Ronald—136–7
KANSAS—144
KAUFMAN, Judge Frank A.—158
KAUL, T. N.—123
KEMPER, Ronnie—141
KENNEDY, Sen. Edward M(oore) (Ted) (D., Mass.)—9, 28–9, 149, 166, 184
KENNEDY, Lt. Col. Reid—172–3
KENT State University, Ohio—54, 56, 58–9, 135–7, 154–5
KENTUCKY—139, 160
KENTUCKY, University of—139
KEP, Cambodia—44
KERR, Dr. Clark—155
KERR, Lt. Gordon—160
KHAMDUC, South Vietnam—91–3
KHANG, Tran Chau—178
KHESANH, South Vietnam—91

KHIEM, Tran Thien—84, 131, 181
KHMER Krom (ethnic Cambodian Special Forces)—67, 81, 111–2
KHMER Rouge (Cambodian Communist guerrilla group)—67–8
KHMERS (Cambodians)—42–3
KHMER Serai (Cambodian rightist movement)—81
KHOMAN, Thanat—84, 115
KHOUNANG Sounthavong, Lt. Col.—27
KIMSEA, Maj. Soeung—79
KING, John F.—98
KING, Stanley—146
KINTUONG Province, South Vietnam—36
KIRIROM, Cambodia—111–2
KIRK, Norman—6
KISSINGER, Henry A.—49, 60, 141
KISTIAKOWSKY, George—54
KITTIKACHORN, Thanom—98, 115
KLINE, Pfc. Terrance A.—159
KNOKSY, Col. Thong Phanh—88
KNOWLES, Gov. Warren—138
KOKITHOM, Cambodia—53
KOMPONG Cham, Cambodia—37–8, 41, 63–4, 80, 117–8
KOMPONG Som, Cambodia (formerly Sihanoukville)—37, 51
KOMPONG Speu, Cambodia—79
KOMPONG Thom, Cambodia—70, 78, 80, 115
KONTUM Province, South Vietnam—19
KOREA, People's Republic of (North)—65
KOREA, Republic of (South)—50, 67, 69, 84, 98, 114, 175
KOREAN Marine Behavior Toward Vietnamese Civilians in Phuyen Province (1967 report)—175
KOSTER, Maj. Gen. Samuel W.—169–70
KOSYGIN, Aleksei N.—6, 27, 44, 50, 64, 122
KOTOUC, Capt. Eugene M.—169
KOUN Wick—84
KOUROUDETH, Lt. Col. Kim Eng—42
KRATIE, Cambodia—53, 81
KRATIE Province, Cambodia—37–8
KRAUSE, Allison—135
KREK, Cambodia—39, 118
KRICHTEN, Lance Cpl. Michael S.—173–4
KY, Nguyen Cao—7, 12, 23, 51, 112, 124, 131, 155, 183–4. Cambodia—66, 70–1. U.S. visit—183–4

L

LABOR-Student Coalition for Peace—143
LADD, Jonathan F.—81
LAIRD, Melvin R.—7, 175. Cambodia—57, 60–1, 66–7, 81, 119. Laos—23–4, 89. POWs—102, 105, 166–7. Reconnaissance flights—99, 106. U.S. bombing—99, 102, 105–6, 112–3
LAM, Tran Van—12, 42–3, 54, 66, 71, 84, 89, 167
LAMDONG Province, South Vietnam—91
LAMONT, Nicholas—145
LAN, Lt. Gen. Lu—177

LANASA, Sgt. John R.—174
LANE, Mark—160
LAOS—29, 69, 117. Civilian casualties—21, 89; evacuation—22, 88. Communist activity—2, 21–2, 29, 32, 88–90, 92. Government (Royal Laotian) forces: casualties—21–2, 88–9; military activity—25, 27, 32, 88–90. U.S. role—25–6; bombing raids—16, 97
LAP Truon (South Vietnamese newspaper)—143
LATIMER, George W.—172
LAU, Ha Van—13
LAWRENCE, Spc. 5 Robert E.—161
LAWYERS Against the War (LAW)—146
LE, Nguyen Thanh—99, 103–4, 123. Peace talks—121, 125, 130–1.
LE, Quang Hiep—14
LEARY, Howard R.—143
LEBANSIEK, Cambodia—80–1
LEDOGAR, Stephen—14, 122
LEE Jr., 1st Lt. Robert G.—174–5
LEKHI, Ramnik—79
LEONARD, Jerris—136
LEVI, Edward H.—141
LEVY, Howard B.—160
LEWIS, Rhomas P.—156
LICHT, Gov. Frank (D., R.I.)—142
LIFE (magazine)—62
LILY (South Vietnamese political party)—183
LINDSAY, John V.—143, 145, 150, 161
LIVINGSTON, Brian W.—173
LONG, Sen. Russell B. (D., La.)—77
LONGBINH, South Vietnam—174
LONG Cheng, Laos—22
LONG Tien, South Vietnam—88
LONG Tieng, Laos—29
LONGVEK, Cambodia—81, 111
LON Nol, Lt. Gen.—34, 39, 65, 69, 73, 82, 114. Cambodian take-over—31–2. Communists—35, 37. Military aid—71. South Vietnam—66, 112; Vietnamese massacre—43. U.S.—37, 40, 47
LORD, Bishop John Wesley—54
Los ANGELES Times (newspaper)—22, 26, 28
LOTUS Flower (South Vietnamese Buddhist political party)—183
LOVE, Gov. John A. (R., Colo.)—73
LOWENSTEIN, James G.—166
LUANG Prabang, Laos—88
LUCE, David—181
LUPER, Col. Robert B.—170

M

MACLEAR, Michael—167
MADDOX, Gov. Lester—144
MAGNUSON, Sen. Warren G. (D., Wash.)—77, 126
MALAYSIA—69, 122
MALIK, Adam—13, 50, 69, 122
MALIK, Yakov A.—8, 12–3
MALONE, Joann—157
MALONEY, Rev. Dennis—157
MAM, Huynh Tan—179
MAN, Do Van—174

MANDEL, Gov. Marvin—138
MANLY, Maj. Gen. D. E.—136
MANOR, Brig. Gen. Leroy J.—102-3
MANSFIELD, Sen. Mike (D., Mont.)—8, 12, 27, 49, 126, 129, 155. Cambodia—61-2, 65, 77, 119. Laos—21, 23-5. U.S. bombing—101, 113
MANUFACTURING Chemists Association —149
MAP—46
MAPLES, Robert Ean—173
MARINE CORPS, U.S.—91, 95. Casualties—15, 17-8. 1st Marine Division—173-4. War crimes—173-4
MARSHALL, Justice Thurgood—157
MARYLAND—138, 149, 156, 160
MARYLAND, University of—138, 144
MATAK, Prince Sisowath Sirik (Cambodia)— 31-3, 44, 65, 112
MATHIAS Jr., Sen. Charles McC. (R., Md.)—23-4, 77,·148
MAY, Ernest—54
McCARTHY, Sen. Eugene J. (D., Minn.)—6, 77, 145, 147
McCLELLAN, Sen. John L. (D., Ark.)—77
McCOY, Charles B.—149
McGEE, Sen. Gale W. (D., Wyo.)—77
McGOVERN, Sen. George S. (D., S.D.)—25, 55, 77, 101, 129, 149-52, 154
McINTIRE, Rev. Carl—143-4, 149, 155
McINTYRE, Sen. Thomas J. (D., N.H.)—73-4, 77, 126
McKAY Jr., Clyde W.—34
McKINLEY, Robert—168-9
McKNIGHT, Maj. Robert W.—170-1
McNAIR, Gov. Robert E. (D., S.C.)—73, 139, 144
MEACHAM, Stewart—58
MEADLO, Paul D.—171, 173
MEANY, George—59, 147-8
MEDINA, Capt. Ernest L.—169-70, 172-3
MEET the Press (NBC-TV program)—108
MELLON (U.S. Coast Guard cutter)—34
MELVILLE, Arthur—157
MELVILLE, Mrs. Catherine—156-7
MELVILLE, Mrs. Marjorie—156
MELVILLE, Thomas—156
MEMOT, Cambodia—48
METCALF, Sen. Lee (D., Mont.)—49, 77
METHODIST Church—54
METHUNE, Stuart—178
MEYER, Rev. Bernard E.—157
MICHIGAN University—144
MILLER, Gerald—78-9
MILLER, Sen. Jack (R., Ia.)—77
MILLER, Jeffrey Glenn—135
MILLIKEN, Gov. William—144
MINNESOTA, University of—140-1
MINUTEMEN—144
MISCHE, George I.—156
MISSOURI—149
MITCHELL, S. Sgt. David—168-9, 171-3
MITCHELL, John N.—59
MIXNER, David—54

MONDALE, Sen. Walter F. (D., Minn.)—6, 77
MONDULKIRI Province, Cambodia—41, 81
MONTGOMERY, Rep. G. V. (D., Miss.)—182
MONTOYA, Sen. Joseph M. (D., N.M.)—77
MOOS, Malcolm—141
MORGAN, Sgt. Hugh—161
MORGAN, Rep. Thomas E. (D., Pa.)—50
MORROW, Michael D.—79
MOSS, Sen. Frank E. (D., Utah)—77
MOSS, Rep. John E. (D., Calif.)—182
MOSS, Rev. Robert V.—54
MOULAPAMOK, Laos—90
MOVEMENT for a New Congress—140, 145
MOYLAN, Mary—156
MUGIA Pass (North Vietnam-Laos border)— 100
MULLOY, Joseph T.—158
MUONG Soui, Laos—22
MURPHY, Sen. George (R., Calif.)—73, 77
MURPHY Jr., William H.—158
MUSKIE, Sen. Edmund S. (D., Me.)—6, 40, 49, 77, 101, 129, 182
MUSLIMS—158
MYKHE, South Vietnam—168, 171
MYLAI Massacre—168-73

N

NAM, Col. Nguyen Khoa—177
NATIONAL Advisory Commission on Civil Disorders—154
NATIONAL Broadcasting Co.—168
NATIONAL Catholic Conference—146
NATIONAL Committee of Salvation—69
NATIONAL Council of Churches—54
NATIONAL Guard, U.S.—54, 56, 58-9, 135-9, 144, 154-5
NATIONAL States' Rights Party—144
NATIONAL Strike Information Center—137
NATIONAL Student Association (NSA)—138
NATIONAL United Front of Kampuchea (Cambodian political group)—65
NATIONAL Youth Alliance—144
NAVILLE, Marcel—165
NAVY, U.S.—33, 51-3, 93-4, 160, 165
NEAK Leung, Cambodia—41, 112
NEARIREATH, Queen Kossamak (Laos)—32
NELSON, Sen. Gaylord (D., Wis.)—77
NELSON, Dr. Marjorie—182
NEUSTADT, Richard—54
NEW Jersey—138, 144, 160-1
NEW Mexico—139
NEW Mexico, University of—139
NEWSWEEK (magazine)—63
NEW York—139, 183. Demonstrations—143-4, 161
NEW York City Bar Association—145
NEW York Times (newspaper)—34, 57, 77-8, 80, 156, 160, 170
NEW York University—137, 139
NEW Zealand—6, 13, 52, 69, 84

NHAN Dan (North Vietnamese Communist Party newspaper)—17, 50, 104, 107, 123, 219
NHIEK Tioulong, Gen.—31
NIXON, Richard M(ilhous): Cambodia—45-7, 50, 56, 71-3, 82-3; aid—106, 119-20. Dissention—56-8, 136-7, 140-2, 150-1; campus—140-2, 153-4; Congress—119-20; war supporters—149. Foreign policy—4-5. Ky visit—183-4. Laos—21, 25. Peace negotiations—24-5, 27, 127-8. POW rescue—102. U.S. bombing—105-6. Vietnamization—3, 5, 7-8, 56, 72, 82-3, 128; aid—5; free elections—123-5
NOLAN, John E.—166
NOOTER, Robert H.—28
NORDSTROM, Gary Owen—174
NORTH Carolina, University of—141
NORTHERN Illinois University—144-5
NORTHWESTERN University, Ill.—144
NOTRE Dame University—137
NOUTH, Penn—65
NUNN, Gov. Louie B.—139

O

O'BRIEN, Lawrence F.—59, 147, 149
OGILVY, Gov. Richard (R., Ill.)—139
OHIO University—144
OLSEN, Gregory—171
O'NEILL, Sgt. John H.—163
OPERATION Fishook (Cambodia)—45-8
OPERATION Parrot's Beak (Cambodia)—46-8
OPERATION Plain of Reeds—36
OR Kosalak—37
O'ROURKE, Joseph—157
OTTINGER, Rep. Richard L. (D., N.Y.)—146
OUDONE Maniboth, Col.—27

P

PACKARD, David—62, 130, 159
PACKWOOD, Sen. Robert W. (R., Ore.)—77
PAHURA, Lt. James—160
PAKISTAN—13, 84
PAKSANE, Laos—22
PAKSE, Laos—21, 88
PAKTHA, Laos—89
PALME, Olof—167
PAO, Maj. Gen. Vang—21-2
PARIS Conference—2, 43. Cambodia—50. Communists—99, 103, 121-2, 132-3. POW exchange—165-6. Stalemate-13-4. U.S. peace plan—128-9, 131. U.S. bombing—20, 99, 104
PARROT'S Beak, Cambodia—39, 46-8, 53, 63, 111, 116
PARSON, Col. Nels A.—170-1
PASTORE, Sen. John O. (D., R.I.)—77
PATHET Lao (Patriotic Front of Laos, pro-Communist Laotian forces)—23, 26-8, 65. Military activities—21-2, 29, 89-90, 92; casualties—21-2. Neo Lao Hak Xat—26
PATRICK, J. Milton—60
PAUL, John—173

PEACE Commencement Fund—145
PEACE Corps, U.S.—147
PEACE Efforts: Ceasefires & violations—15, 17, 87, 108-9, 126-8. Proposals—11-2, 26-8, 37, 126-7. See also PARIS Conference
PEAM Chikang, Cambodia—118
PEARSON, Sen. James B. (R., Kan.)—11, 77
PEERS, Lt. Gen. William R.—169-70
PELL, Sen. Claiborne (D., R.I.)—101
PELLETIER, Joan—141
PEMBERTON, John DeJ.—148
PENN Nouth—31
PENNSYLVANIA—145, 161
PENNSYLVANIA, University of—137-9, 144
PERCY, Sen. Charles H. (R., Ill.)—77, 126, 129
PEROT, H. Ross—164
PHANRANG, South Vietnam—180
PHILIPPINES—52, 67, 69, 84, 98
PHIMPACHMAN, Phau—26
PHOUCUM, Laos—89
PHOU Pa Sai, Laos—32
PHOU Saphong, Laos—88
PHU, Brig. Gen. Pham Van—177
PHUM Kampo, Cambodia—38
PHUYEN Province, South Vietnam—175
PIERCE, Nathaniel W.—146
PIKE, Rev. Thomas—146
PLAIN of Reeds—36
PLAINE des Jarres, North Vietnam—2, 21, 27, 89
PLEIKRONG, South Vietnam—95
PLIMPTON, Francis T. P.—145
PNOMPENH, Cambodia—31, 35, 53, 69, 79
POLLARD, Dr. Thomas—147
POMME Peang—31
POND, Elizabeth—79
POTOFSKY, Jacob S.—147-8
PRASOT, Cambodia—41-2
PRATT, Judge John H.—157
PRAVDA (Soviet Communist Party newspaper)—13, 33, 129
PREAH Vihear, Cambodia—81
PREK Khdam, Cambodia—117-8
PRESBYTERIAN Church—54
PRESIDENT's Commission on Campus Unrest—153-4
PREYVENG Province, Cambodia—37, 41, 80
PRICE, Rep. Melvin (D., Ill.)—73
PRINCETON University—137-40, 155
PRISONERS of War—132. Camp raids—101-5, 165. Deaths—163, 165-6. Lists—163-4, 166-7. POW families—163-4. Prisoner interview—167-8. Releases—33, 122, 164-5, 167. Treatment—165, 167-8, 181-3
PROTESTANTS—54, 161
PROUTY, Sen. Winston L. (R., Vt.)—77, 126
PROXMIRE, Sen. William (D., Wis.)—77
PUK Rusey, Cambodia—114
PUOK, Cambodia—118
PUSEY, Nathan—141

Q

QUAKERS: American Friends Service Committee—163, 182. Fellowship of Reconciliation—54, 181
QUAN Doi Nhan Dan (North Vietnamese army newspaper)—106-7
QUANGBINH Province, North Vietnam—20, 100, 104
QUANGNAM Province, South Vietnam—16, 87, 95, 175
QUANGNGAI Province, South Vietnam—19, 90, 95, 170
QUANGTIN Province, South Vietnam—90
QUESON Valley, South Vietnam—17-8
QUIGLEY, Thomas—146

R

RADCLIFFE College (Cambridge, Mass.)—137
RAHMAN, Tunku Abdul—6
RAMBO, A. Terry—175
RAND Corp.—175
RANDOLPH, Sen. Jennings (D., W. Va.)—77
RARICK, Rep. John R. (D., La.)—144, 155
RATANAKIRI Province, Cambodia—41, 52, 81, 117
RAZAK, Tun Abdul (Malaysia)—6
REAGAN, Gov. Ronald (R., Calif.)—138-9, 142
REECE, Norval D.—145
REFUGEE Situation in Phuyen Province (1967 report)—175
REID, Rep. Ogden R. (R., N.Y.)—55
RENMIN Ribao (Chinese Communist Party newspaper)—See JENMIN Jih Pao
REISCHAUER, Edwin O.—54
RESERVE Officers Training Corps (ROTC)—135, 138-9
RIBICOFF, Sen. Abraham (D., Conn.)—77
RICHARDSON, Elliot L.—28, 60, 65-6, 163
RIVERS, Rep. L. Mendel (D., S.C.)—33, 40, 47, 129
ROCHESTER, University of—141
ROCKEFELLER, Gov. Nelson A. (R., N.Y.)—62
ROGERS, William P.—13, 39-40, 84-5, 108, 123-4, 129, 142, 167. Cambodia—49, 56-7, 60, 67, 73, 80-1, 84; aid—119. Laos—24-5, 28. Peace efforts—11, 27, 51, 130. U.S. bombing—80-1, 105, 107
ROMNEY, George—58
ROSENBLUM, Frank—148
RUMANIA—65

S

SAANG, Cambodia—41-3, 111
SAIGON, South Vietnam—16, 91, 95, 95. Riots & demonstrations—180-1
SAIGON University—179, 181
SAMBAUR, Yem—43
SAM Thong, Laos—29, 32, 88
SANGKUM (political movement) (Laos)—33

SARAVANE, Laos—88-9, 92
SARTRE, Jean-Paul—159
SAU, Ly Van—122
SAWADA, Kyoichi—116
SAXBE, Sen. William B. (R., O.)—77
SAYAVONG, Maj. Gen. Tiao—22
SCHELLING, Thomas—54
SCHEUER, Sandra Lee—135
SCHIEL, Cpl. Kenneth—169, 171
SCHROEDER, William K.—135
SCHUMANN, Maurice—11, 51
SCHWARZ, Pvt. Michael A.—173
SCHWEIKER, Sen. Richard S. (R., Pa.)—77
SCHWEITZER, Cmdr. Robert J.—167
SCOTT, Sen. Hugh (R., Pa.)—49, 60-1, 74, 77, 126
SEAMANS Jr., Robert C.—99
SE Bang Valley, Cambodia—80
SELECTIVE Service System—155-9; see also 'Draft resistance' under DISSENT, U.S.
SENATE, U.S.—See 'Congress' under UNITED States
SENOMOROM, Cambodia—53
SET Bo, Cambodia—68
SEVAREID, Eric—161
SHAFER, Gov. Raymond P. (R., Pa.)—142
SHEPPARD, Gary—39
SHIPPING—34, 37
SHULTZ, George P.—142
SIAM, Gulf of—34
SIEMREAP, Cambodia—78, 116
SIEVERTS, Frank A.—163
SIHANOUK, Prince Norodom (Cambodia)—2, 12, 44, 50-2, 116. Deposed—31-2
SIHANOUKVILLE, Cambodia (later Kompong Som)—37, 51
SIKES, Rep. Robert L. F. (D., Fla.)—129
SIMONS, Col. Arthur D.—102
SINGAPORE—69
SISAKET, Thailand—78
SKOUN, Cambodia—80, 112-3
SLASKI, Michael—157
SLEDGE, Charles—171
SMEDBERG III, W. R.—63
SMITH, Pvt. Gerald Anthony—168
SMITH, Sen. Margaret Chase (R., Me.)—77
SMITH, Sen. Ralph T. (R., Ill.)—77
SNOUL, Cambodia—52, 116
SOARIENG Province, Cambodia—33
SOCIETY of Jesus—156
SOCTRANG, South Vietnam—93
SONGMY (Mylai), South Vietnam—168-70. See also 'Mylai massacre' under WAR Crimes & Atrocities
SONTAY, North Vietnam—102-5
SONTHANG Village, South Vietnam—173-4
SOUTH Carolina—139, 159
SOUTH East Asia Treaty Organization (SEATO)—84
SOUPHANOUVONG, Prince (Laos)—27, 44, 92
SOUTH Carolina, University of—139, 144, 160
SOUTHERN Illinois University—139

SOUVANNA Phouma, Prince (Laos)—23, 51, 89, 92. Peace efforts—22, 26–8
SPARKMAN, Sen. John (D., Miss.)—77, 101
SPOCK, Dr. Benjamin—54
SPONG Jr., Sen. William B. (D., Va.)—77
SREY Saman, Brig. Gen.—44
STANFORD University, Calif.—137–8, 141
STANTON, Rep. J. William (R., O.)—140
STEINBECK IV, John—181
STENNIS, Sen. John (D., Miss.)—49, 61, 77, 98
STEVENS, Sen. Ted (R., Alaska)—77, 126
STEWART, Justice Potter—157
STONE, Dana—39
STUDENTS for a Democratic Society (SDS)—34
STUNG Chral, Cambodia—117
STUNG Treng, Cambodia—81
SUBIC Bay, Philippines—34
SUGARMAN, Capt. J. L.—174
SULLIVAN, William C.—153
SUN (South Vietnamese Roman Catholic political party)—183
SUPREME Court, U.S.—157–8
SURAMARIT, King Norodom (Laos)—31
SURIN, Thailand—78
SUU, Phan Khac—180
SVAHNSTROEM, Bertil—163
SVAYRIENG Province, Cambodia—35, 39
SWAN, Capt. Michael K.—171
SWANN, Capt. Donald A.—34
SWEDEN—159, 163–4
SWEDISH Vietnam Committee—163
SYMINGTON, Sen. Stuart (D., Mo.)—23–5, 50, 77, 89, 98, 106, 119
SYRACUSE University—141
SYRIA—65
SYVERTSEN, George—78

T

TAFT, Rep. Robert (R., O.)—136
TAIWAN—114
TAKEO Province, Cambodia—37, 41–3, 51, 64
TALMADGE, Sen. Herman E. (D., Ga.)—77
TAM, In—33
TAMKY, South Vietnam—87
TANCHAU, South Vietnam—54
TANG Krasang, Cambodia—68
TANG Nay, Laos—88
TARR, Curtis W.—158
TASS (Soviet news agency)—12, 23, 27, 83, 107, 122–3, 127
TATUM, Edward L.—148
TAYNINH Province, South Vietnam—17
TELLER, Edward—153
TERRELL Jr., Col. Ernest—36
TEXAS—144
THAILAND—22, 29, 69, 78, 84, 94, 97–8, 114–5. Cambodia—50, 67, 71
THANAT Khoman—84, 115
THANG, Ton Duc—65, 166
THANGBINH, South Vietnam—175
THANH, Maj. Gen. Nguyen Viet—35

THANHMY (Baren), South Vietnam—90
THANOM Kittikachorn—98, 115
THANT, U—35, 165. Peace efforts—35, 37, 51, 123
THAO, Duong Dinh—130
THAUTHIEN Province, South Vietnam—92
THBENG Menachey, Cambodia—81
THIEU, Nguyen Van—6–7, 130–1. Cambodia—57, 66, 81–2, 112. Economy—183. Mylai massacre—168. Political developments—177–8; censorship—179; demonstrations—180–1; free elections & coalition government—123–4, 131. Land reform—179
THO, Le Duc—14
THO, Nguyen Huu—44
THOMAS, Randall B.—160
THOMPSON, William P.—54
THUATHIEN Province, South Vietnam—163
THUDUC Officers Training School (South Vietnam)—16
THUONGDUC, South Vietnam—95
THURMOND, Sen. Strom (R., S.C.)—77, 144
THUY, Xuan—52, 104. Peace negotiations & developments—13–4, 103, 125–6, 128, 130–3, 212
TIEN, Vu—163–4
TIMES (London newspaper)—34
TIN Sang (Morning News) (South Vietnamese newspaper)—179
TOA, Col. Dang Ngoc—16
TOAI, Doan Van—179
TODAY (NBC-TV program)—27–8
TOLSON, Lt. Gen. John J.—159
TONKIN Resolution—(1964) 28, 55, 75–7, 119
TONLE Bet, Cambodia—64, 68, 80
TORRES, Sgt. Esequiel—169
TOTUNG, Prey—118
TOWER, Sen. John G. (R., Tex.)—49, 73, 77
TOWNES, Charles H.—148
TRAM Khnar, Cambodia—118
TRI, Lt. Gen. Do Cao—67, 70
TRINH Heanh—42
TRUONG, Maj. Gen. Ngo Quang—177
T'SOUVAS, Spc. 4 Robert W.—169
TUONG, Cao Van—178
TURNER, George—144
TURNER, Thomas—173
24th EVACUATION Hospital (Longbinh, South Vietnam)—6
TY, Pham Huy—43, 70
TYDINGS, Sen. Joseph D. (D., Md.)—77, 161
TYRELL, Col. Robert L. F.—27

U

UDON, Thailand—97
U MINH Forest, South Vietnam—96–7
UNION for National Draft Opposition (UNDO)—155–6
UNION of Soviet Socialist Republics (USSR)—5, 12–3, 22–3, 33, 50, 107, 122, 129–30

UNION Theological Seminary—54
UNITED Church of Christ—54, 149
UNITED Methodist Church—54
UNITED Nations (UN)—37–8, 51, 165
UNITED Presbyterian Church—54
UNITED Press International—116
UNITED States:
　　　　Aerial Warfare, Air Force, Army—See under 'A.' Agency for International Development—21
　　　　Cambodia—2, 17, 19, 33, 35–6, 38, 45–8, 52–3, 71–2, 77–8, 80–2, 112–4; invasion—50–1. Civilian casualties—26, 78–9. Coast Guard—34. Congress—6, 24–5, 40, 48–50, 60–1, 63, 66, 100, 102, 105–6, 119, 182, 184; dissent & controversy—3–6, 23–5, 48–50, 55, 97–8, 100–2, 105–6, 119–20, 181–2; Cooper-Church amendment—61–3, 74–7; defoliation issue—152–3; Hatfield-McGovern amendment—152–3; peace efforts—126, 129; resolutions—11, 40, 61–3
　　　　Defense Department—20, 34, 53, 68, 89, 90, 97, 104–5, 160–1; Allied troop allowances—97–9;. POWs—164–6; war crimes investigations—169–70, 175; see also AIR Force and ARMY under 'A,' NATIONAL Guard and NAVY under 'N,' 'Troop withdrawals' below. Dissent—See under 'D.'
　　　　Laos—16, 21, 25–6, 89–90, 92, 97
　　　　Peace efforts—See PARIS Conference and PEACE Efforts under 'P.' Prisoners—See under 'P'
　　　　Selective Service System—155–9; see also 'Draft resistance' under DISSENT, U.S. South Vietnam—See under VIETNAM, South. State Department—3, 12, 22, 22, 24–6, 33–4, 44, 58, 60–1, 66–7, 71, 89, 97–8, 108, 113, 147, 163, 166. Supreme Court—157–8
　　　　Thailand—97–8. Troop withdrawals—2, 63, 68, 80, 82–3, 93–4; strength—1, 93 War crimes—See WAR Crimes & Atrocities under 'W'
UNIVERSITIES—See specific name(s)
UNIVERSITIES Antiwar Fund—149
UNIVERSITY of Alabama—145
UNIVERSITY of California—138–41, 148, 153
UNIVERSITY of Chicago—141
UNIVERSITY of Denver—144
UNIVERSITY of Florida—139
UNIVERSITY of Georgia—139
UNIVERSITY of Iowa—139
UNIVERSITY of Kentucky—139
UNIVERSITY of Maryland—138, 144
UNIVERSITY of Minnesota—140–1
UNIVERSITY of New Mexico—139
UNIVERSITY of North Carolina—141
UNIVERSITY of Pennsylvania—144
UNIVERSITY of Rochester—141
UNIVERSITY of South Carolina—139, 144, 160
UNIVERSITY of Virginia—139–40
UNIVERSITY of Wisconsin—138–9

V

VANCE, Cyrus R.—129, 149
Van DEERLIN, Rep. Lionel (D., Calif.)—174
VANDERBILT University—150
VANHANH, South Vietnam—179
VANN, John—178
VENEZUELA—52
VETERANS of Foreign Wars—144
VIET Cong—44. Cambodia—37–8, 65; see also under 'Military activity' below. Ceasefires—See under PEACE Efforts.
　　　　Military activity: Cambodia—33, 35–9, 41, 44, 53, 64, 67–8, 78–81, 111–2, 114–8; casualties—15–6, 18–9, 39, 41, 43–4, 48, 52–3, 59, 63, 67–8, 78–9, 82–3, 88, 90; Laos—88–90; prisoners—39–40, 163. South Vietnam—15–9, 48, 53, 63–4, 68, 87–8, 90–5, 109; strength—77; Thailand—78
　　　　Peace talks—103, 121–2, 126–7
VIETNAM Clergy & Laymen Concerned About—54, 146
VIETNAM, Committee of Liaison with Families of Servicemen Detained in North—163–6
VIETNAM, New Mobilization to End the War in (New Mobe)—54, 58
VIETNAM (North), People's Republic of: Civilian casualties—100, 105. Foreign relations & aid—33, 35, 44, 122
　　　　Military forces & activities: casualties—15–9, 21–2, 32, 36, 38–9, 41, 44, 48, 52–3, 59, 63–4, 67, 78–9, 82–3, 87–8, 91–3, 96, 108, 111–2, 114, 116–8; Cambodia—14, 35–9, 41, 43–4, 53, 64, 67–8, 78–81; 111–2, 114–8; Laos—21–2, 29, 32, 88–90, 92; South Vietnam—18, 48, 87–8, 91–5, 109; strength—3, 21–2, 77; Thailand—78. 2d Army Division—16; 66th Regiment—91; 304th Division—91
　　　　Peace negotiations—13, 103, 121–2, 129–33; see also PARIS Conference and PEACE Efforts. POWs—163–7
　　　　U.S.—83, 106–7; bombing raids—99–100, 103–5
VIETNAM (South), Republic of: Cambodia—33, 41–3, 68; civilian evacuation—70, 81. Civilian casualties—15–6, 18, 87, 90, 93–7; atrocities—41–3, 163–75; see also WAR Crimes & Atrocities. Coalition government & free elections—123–4. Defoliation—90. Economy—183.
　　　　Military forces & actions: casualties—1, 15–6, 18–9, 21, 36, 39, 44, 48, 52–3, 63, 67–8, 78, 82, 87–8, 91–6, 108–9; 111, 117; Cambodia—35, 38–9, 41, 44–8, 52–3, 63–4, 66–7, 78–80, 82, 111–2, 114–8; POWs—122, 164–5, 167, 181–3. 1st Infantry Division—92, 177; 21st Infantry Division—177; 22d Infantry Battalion—79; 52d Task Force—118. Marine forces—78, 80, 116. Naval forces—51–3
　　　　Peace efforts—See PARIS Conference and PEACE Efforts. Political & domestic developments: elections—183; government

suppression—177–81; Indochina conference—69; land reform—179; strikes & demonstrations—177, 179–81 Refugees—51, 53–4, 184. Terrorism—15–6, 18, 48, 87–8, 90–6. Thai forces—97–8 U.S. aid—179; troop withdrawals—2, 63, 93–4
VIETNAMESE Workers (Communist Party)—17
VIETNAM Guardian (Saigon newspaper)—184
VIETNAM Veterans Against the War—161
VINHBINH Province, South Vietnam—18
VIRGINIA—139
VIRGINIA, University of—139–40
VY, Nguyen Minh—14

W

WALLACE, Gov. George—144
WALLIS, W. Allen—141
WALSTAD, Spc. 4 David G.—174
WAR Crimes & Atrocities: Army trials & convictions (U.S.)—168–75. Cambodia—41–3, 69–70. Korean controversy—175. Mylai massacre—168–73
WARNKE, Paul C.—59, 148
WARREN, Chief Justice Earl—145
WASHINGTON, D.C.—See DISTRICT of Columbia
WASHINGTON Post (newspaper)—80, 92, 127, 164
WASHINGTON Star (newspaper)—141
WATKE, Maj. Frederic—170
WATSON Jr., Thomas J.—148
WEDEL, Cynthia—54
WEISS, Mrs. Cora—165–6
WELSH 2d, Elliott A.—157
WENDT, Rev. William A.—146
WEST, Charles A.—172
WEST, Francis—175
WEST Germany—52

WEST Point (U.S. Military Academy)—160, 169
WHEELER, Gen. Earle G.—7
WHITE, Justice Byron R.—157
WHITE, Robert I.—136
WHITEHURST, Sen. G. William (R., Ind.)—73
WHOLESALE, Retail & Office Workers Union—58
WILBER, Cmdr. Walter E.—167
WILLIAMS Jr., Sen. Harrison A., (D., N.J.)—77, 148
WILLIAMS, Sen. John J. (R., Del.)—77
WILLINGHAM, Capt Thomas K.—170–1
WILSON, Harold—51
WINNE Jr., George M.—139
WISCONSIN—138–9
WISCONSIN, University of—138–9
WOOLWARD, Paul—149
WRIGHT, T. Sgt. Leroy M.—102

X

XIENGKHOUANG, Laos—22

Y

YALE University—137, 140, 145
YARBOROUGH, Sen. Ralph (D., Tex.)—77
YARMOLINSKY, Adam—54
YEM, Sambaur—67, 69, 71
YOST, Charles W.—13, 51
YOUNG, Rev. Andrew—145
YOUNG Jr., Brig. Gen. George H.—170–1
YOUNG, Sen. Milton R. (D., N.D.)—77, 126
YOUNG, Sen. Stephen M. (D., O.)—28
YUGOSLAVIA—65

Z

ZIEGLER, Ronald L.—29, 67, 74, 124, 126, 136, 142, 147, 167. Cambodia—36–7, 55